Tools & Techniques of PRACTICE MANAGEMENT

1st
ION

BRUCKENSTEIN
DRUCKER

Edited by
STEPHAN R. LEIMBERG

The National Underwriter Company
A Unit of Highline Media LLC

5081 Olympic Boulevard • Erlanger, KY 41018 • www.NUCO.com

Acquisition/In-house Editor: Sonya E. King, J.D., LL.M.

ISBN: 0-87218-653-9
Library of Congress Control Number: 2004113630

This publication is designed to provide accurate and authoritative information in regard to the subject matter covered. It is sold with the understanding that the publisher is not engaged in rendering legal, accounting or other professional service. If legal advice or other expert assistance is required, the services of a competent professional person-should be sought. - From a Declaration of Principles jointly adapted by a Committee of The American Bar Association and a Committee of Publishers and Associations.

published by

THE NATIONAL UNDERWRITER COMPANY

The National Underwriter Company
P.O. Box 14367
Cincinnati, Ohio 45250-0367

First Edition

Printed in the United States of America

DEDICATIONS

Joel P. Bruckenstein

To my wife Viviana and to our children Kevin, Alan, and Eric.
I couldn't have written this without your
love, support and understanding.

David J. Drucker

"To my loving family —
my mother, my wife Susan, my daughter Gracey —
and to all the canines that have ever enriched my life."

PREFACE

Practice management, alas, is but a withering tree along financial planning's educational avenues. Financial planning curricula, such as those of the College for Financial Planning and the almost 200 universities nationwide offering a CFP® preparation major, all but ignore the topic of practice management. Only in recent years have the national and regional conferences of financial planning and the professional associations seen fit to include a practice management track; yet attendance at practice management sessions does not earn continuing education credit.

This is part of the problem ... the study of practice management is neither rewarded nor regarded as highly as the study of technical topics like investment portfolio design, tax avoidance strategies, or risk management. Earning one's CFP® designation gives one the right to strap on a very sophisticated tool belt, but it confers no knowledge of business management. That's as it should be, many educators and Certified Financial Planner Board bureaucrats would say. "We can't teach CFP® candidates how to be effective businesspersons; that's not our job." "Practice management is too broad a subject. It is the responsibility of each practitioner to garner the required skills through additional studies and field experience."

Is practice management really so expansive a subject that students can't get some benefit from just one, intensive course? Frankly, we don't think so. The book you are about to read is one in a series dubbed *"The Tools & Techniques,"* which, until now, has covered only technical subjects. Since almost everything you need to know to run a financial planning practice fits nicely into one *Tools & Techniques* volume, maybe practice management *isn't* so broad a subject after all? Sure, there's always more one can learn about any subject, but that doesn't excuse one from at least taking a surface look – and *The Tools & Techniques of Practice Management* goes well beneath the surface.

What is practice management anyway? It's the difference between a good technician making a so-so living while spending too many hours each day doing something he once loved, and a small business owner who's still passionate about his work, which provides him more than enough income and leisure time to meet all of his personal needs. To invoke an old cliché, "it's working smarter, not harder." It's what transforms the planner's tool belt full of tools into something much more: an organization, a living entity with a mission to assist others in a critical aspect of their lives. Understanding the importance and vastness of practice management will lead you—as it has us—to vigorously challenge its absence from financial planning's training grounds.

We'll go so far as to declare that the person with only average technical skills but a keen sense of (1) how to market, (2) how to convert prospective clients into clients, and (3) how to manage a growing business will be far more successful as a financial advisor than a good technician who possesses only rudimentary versions of these skills. This, in fact, is the essence of the argument for honing your practice management skills.

The Certified Financial Planner Board of Standards, and some educators, would argue that practice management is not critical because it does not serve the public interest and it does not help you serve your clients. In other words, they are saying that it is you who benefits from practice management skills, not the public, so it is beyond the scope of the CFP® educational program and continuing education requirements. We could not disagree more strongly with this argument.

There are currently about 43,000 CFP® certificants in the United States. That is not nearly enough to satisfy the demand for competent financial planning expertise. If today's financial planners are only working at a fraction of their true potential, some consumers in need of help are going unserved.

Ideally, of course, one should want to have it all—technical skill *and* practice management aptitude. The combination of the two is what produces truly great financial planning organizations, whether 20-person firms or sole practitioner shops.

So, don't be misled by the light emphasis the planning profession places on practice management. If you want to know its real priority in the minds of veteran planners, cruise the hallways of professional conference venues in between sessions and eavesdrop on planners' conversations. I guarantee you the vast majority of those conversations will have something to do with running a practice—not whether separately managed accounts are better than mutual funds, or the correct methodology for doing a Monte Carlo simulation.

The topic of practice management fits well into The National Underwriter's *Tools & Techniques* series because there are practice management strategies, or techniques, and practice management technologies, or tools. Dave Drucker is primarily responsible for the techniques chapters in this book; Joel Bruckenstein is primarily responsible for the tools portion. That being said, we are constantly cross-pollinating each other's ideas as we work on our monthly newsletter *Virtual Office News* (www.virtualofficenews.com), a practice management and technology periodical for financial professionals.

In the course of our work, we are constantly interacting with other experienced advisors, and some of the ideas presented in this book are the fruits of those conversations. While we can't thank each of you individually, you know who you are, and we thank you for sharing your ideas with us and, through this book, with a much wider audience.

It is the sincere wish of your authors that this volume can provide you with the answers that you have not been able to find elsewhere and, in so doing, will allow you and your clients to achieve your personal and professional goals.

Joel P. Bruckenstein
David J. Drucker

FOREWORD

The practice of financial planning is advancing rapidly, but perhaps not at the pace needed for the advancement of practice management. *The Tools & Techniques of Practice Management* is for experienced practitioners as well as new practitioners needing guidance in developing their businesses. Essentially, it is for planners who want to have very well run practices.

When I first heard that Joel and David had written a practice management book I was immediately excited, thinking "How can I get a copy of it quickly?" Their work has always been timely, incisive, practical, and at the forefront of the profession. This book is an extension of their prior work–comprehensive and instantaneously useful. This is not a theoretical book, but a practical guide to organizing and running a practice today. In fact, I have immediately begun to apply it to my practice.

This book is an extraordinarily valuable work not only because it contains Joel's and David's years of experience and uncommon wisdom, but also because it includes some of the best thinking from dozens of leading practitioners.

What I like best about the work is how "in context" it is. As financial planning practitioners, we are pulled by many forces and significantly challenged to be both grounded and focused. By beginning the book with Balancing Personal and Work Lives (Chapter 1), and then focusing on other foundational, organizational issues in Chapters 2 through 5, the book is as relevant and timely as an engagement with a practice management consultant. The authors, both having built successful practices, remade themselves to reclaim their lives by doing something very different from the practices that had driven them. Their approach is: begin with the end in mind, and then be very practical in using systems and tools that allow you to maximize what is most important to you in living the life you want to lead by building (and maybe continually remaking) a practice that supports your values and goals. Does that sound familiar to you? As financial planners, we take our clients through a similarly rigorous process. Now, we also need that same rigor in managing our practices!

But be forewarned, this is a serious work with many biting observations. In simple, direct ways the authors ask us as practitioners to make difficult decisions and to be accountable to our values. The marketplace is demanding that we run better practices and it appears that this trend will accelerate. Too many financial planning practices exist to satisfy the whims and quirks of the unique personalities of independent stubborn pioneers (did I really say that?).

As Mark Tibergien has said, the practice of financial planning is at an entrepreneurial crossroads, consumed by the daily grind of meeting client needs. Will we manage our practices, or continually be caught in dysfunctions – being driven by factors we cannot control, and being unwilling to deal proactively with things we can control by good leadership and management? Here in these pages is the wisdom of practitioners who have dealt with many of the same challenges that we face:

In Chapters 7 and 10, the authors cover marketing and client service. An ounce of the ample clarity here reaps huge rewards for each of us.

Even Chapter 14 (Ethics) is intensely practical and useful in practice.

Client communication tools and techniques are included in Chapters 15, 26, 27, 31, and in several other chapters on technology, including Chapter 39 (Collaboration Tools).

You will find wisdom in areas of outsourcing (Chapter 16), taking on a partner (Chapter 17), compliance (Chapter 18), managing growth (Chapter 19), coaching (Chapter 20), buying and/or selling a practice (Chapters 21 and 22), and many other important topics.

About two-thirds of the way through, you will find Chapter 24 (What's the Next Step?), which helps you integrate and put together all the previous material.

For those familiar with the technology writing of Joel and David (see *Virtual-Office Tools for a High-Margin Practice* (Bloomberg Press, 2002), you will love the last third of the book on technology tools. All of us know that we must continue to integrate better and more successfully the best technology tools available. If you are thinking of making a change in technology tools, these chapters are a must read!

Long before I got to the end of the book in my first read, I felt like I was having a private consulting arrangement with the authors worth thousands of dollars. Every page is packed with indispensable alternatives and understanding.

There is a significant need in the profession for better management of practices. We are finding the practice of financial planning more demanding all the time. There is more knowledge and there are more tools available, but that can complicate things. Financial planning is becoming a developed profession. The operating systems and controls for the delivery of our services allow for sustained profitability as greater competition continues to build.

As you start to read, I challenge you to begin to ponder ways that you can create a plan to put its wisdom into use with feedback and accountability. You may want to use the Table of Contents for a long-term systematic review of areas of your practice, perhaps a week at a time. Create a step-by-step process for reworking the way you run things by working with a consultant, coach, or study group.

Lastly, I hope the authors will keep this work current by conducting workshops and collaborating with coaches and consultants, study groups and professional associations. This book needs to be updated continuously in electronic form. It is too important, relevant and timely of a work to let it get stale.

J. Jeffrey Lambert, CFP®
Co-Managing Partner
Lighthouse Financial Planning, LLC

Program Director
Personal Financial Planning Certificate Program
University of California, Davis Extension

CONTENTS

Appendices

Chapter 1

BALANCING PERSONAL AND WORK LIVES

The Techniques chapters of this book are placed in what we think of as a chronology of decisions one must make in managing his or her financial planning practice. You will notice that the first several chapters deal with organizational issues like selecting a business model and naming your practice.

Before work, though, comes life. So from an organizational standpoint, we believe you need to address the issue of how your business will fit into your life. What you want out of life, and the people in your life who depend upon you, are factors that must influence the many structural decisions you will make about your business.

There are two extremes. On the one hand, there are many business owners in our profession who do whatever they feel they must to grow their business and attend to their clients, while letting the rest of their lives simply take up whatever excess time is left over. This form of balancing might be called the "default method" because, in the absence of planning, the practitioner defaults to whatever minimal personal life he has time for after attending to his practice. His life, in total, is usually characterized by long workdays, an inability to spend his waking hours thinking about much more than his business and, often, discord or a lack of communication between himself and family members.

At the other extreme is the planner who has made a conscious choice in the way he has structured his business to have plenty of time for everything important to him ... not just his business, but also his spouse, his children, his faith, and his community. His ability to spend time in all of the important areas of his life makes him an interesting, well-rounded individual. Success in his personal endeavors makes him more creative as a businessperson, and success in his business frees him up to indulge in those other areas of life so critical to his overall well-being.

The extremes, or anything in between, are your choice. It's not unusual to begin planning one's advisory firm venture with a quantitative business plan. Your plan probably anticipates the necessary amount of financing, sets quantitative goals (e.g., growth rates and owner's compensation), and speculates about the types of clients and compensation structures that will help you reach these ends.

However, a more enlightened business planning approach would be to step back and conceive your business plan within the broader context of your life plan. What do you want your life to look like now and in the future? Do you have or do you want a family, and how large might it be? Where do you ultimately want to live? Are there volunteer activities or community projects you would like to have time for if possible? Are certain hobbies or exercise routines important enough to demand a slice of your day? If you dive into a quantitative business plan without considering the bigger picture, your life will look like your business plan instead of the life plan you really wanted – but failed to consider.

As we said, your own life goals are your choice; we can't tell you what they should be. However, we can illustrate for you the kinds of balanced plans other successful practitioners have created for themselves. Consider Michael Joyce, for example. As this is being written, Joyce is the Chairman of the National Association of Personal Financial Advisors (NAPFA). He is owner of the firm Michael Joyce & Associates, P.C., with offices in Richmond, Virginia and Bethlehem, Pennsylvania.

By his own description, Joyce's typical day goes something like this: "I will usually get up before the rest of my family – around 5:30 a.m. – and either go to the pool to swim or do a workout conducted by an ex-Navy Seal. I get back home at about 7:00 a.m., ready to take our 2nd- and 4th-graders to school at 7:45 a.m. while Cindy, my wife, takes care of our 5-month-old. (Cindy's a 'balancer' too; she's running a half marathon in a few weeks, is CFO of a small biotech company, and is Board Chair for Stop Child Abuse Now). After dropping the kids at school, I then go into the office for meetings or to work on client projects and go home for lunch and run four to five miles. My office is only about 1.5 miles from my home. Back to the office for the afternoon and home between 5:30 p.m. and 6:00 p.m. with a briefcase full of reading and client files. After eating dinner and spending some quality time with my sons, bedtime for the boys is 7:30 p.m. – we read to them until about 8:15 p.m. – I then go into our home office and I will do an hour or so more of work."

Joyce also incorporates into his work life the ability to "... bolt out to attend a school function or pick my sons up at car pool." He says "training for triathlons is equally as important to my job and has actually made me more productive at work." As if that weren't enough, Joyce still finds the time to volunteer for Meals on Wheels once a month and coach his older boys in flag football, baseball, and lacrosse.

Joyce exemplifies a level of balance perhaps more appropriately dubbed "blending" whereby his every day is a mix of personal and work activities. Other advisors who have successfully met this challenge balance the different areas of their lives in larger segments. Kathleen Cotton of Cotton Financial Advisors, Inc., in Lynnwood, Washington does this by working from her remote office three to four months a year (November, December, February and May) in Puerto Vallarta and usually takes another two to three weeks vacation a year in a different location. "I stay connected to the office via a virtual private network (VPN) and e-mail." Cotton doesn't worry about replicating all her software on a laptop for her travels. She just "plugs" into the server in her office with her laptop and has access to all programs and data. She says, "My office staff sends me alerts when something special is occurring that requires my attention immediately." Cotton is beginning to blend by letting go of her total immersion in office affairs in exchange for extended time in places she'd rather be, although the two are purposely intertwined.

The point is ... achieving balance can take many forms. For some, like Michael Joyce, it's a blending of daily personal and work activities. This is also true for Bill Bengen of El Cajon, California, who breaks up each day to make room for a variety of personal matters. Bengen artfully describes this "blending" phenomenon as: "I take frequent breaks during the workday for exercise, meeting with friends, conversing with my wife, reading, napping, playing with the dogs, examining my bubble gum card collection, or puttering about the place. Or is it more accurate to say that I occasionally work during my breaks from playing? I really can't tell anymore. Life is more like a rainbow, with the edges of the colors blurring into one another, than an artist's palette, where the hues are distinct and separate. I like it that way. The pot of gold is not at the end of the rainbow, but in the rainbow itself."

In other cases, like that of Kathleen Cotton, achieving balance may mean long stretches of vacation time followed by long periods of work. The topic is presented here as one planners should consider as they construct a business plan. But how about planners already practicing for a number of years that want to reclaim their lives?

It can be done, as Brian Sutliff figured out. The owner of Sutliff Financial Planning, Inc. in Columbus, Ohio, Sutliff left a large, nearby firm that offered him great career advancement opportunities, as he says, "to claim my life back." Sutliff lives 40 minutes outside of Columbus, and decided to open a small office there where he works several days a week when he's not in his main Columbus office. To keep the lifestyle he created, Sutliff knows he must limit his growth. He presently has 50 high-net-worth clients and $55 million of client assets under management at Charles Schwab & Company. With the above move, and by hiring a part-time professional to replace a departing paraplanner, Sutliff made the time to get his Masters Degree from the College for Financial Planning. Whatever financial success he will have achieved at this level of operation, Sutliff derives invaluable compensation in the form of being able to take his kids – ages 7, 5, and 3-year old twins – to dance and other activities. "I am involved in so much more of their lives now," he says.

Blending can also be achieved by the young planner starting out as demonstrated by 29-year-old Marnie Aznar, owner of Aznar Financial Advisors in Morris Plains, New Jersey, and married mother of a two-year-old daughter. Not only does Aznar juggle a practice and a family, she works alone. Aznar maximizes her technology options and stretches out her workday to keep intact this lifestyle where she can work or spend time with her daughter, as she wishes. With a functional website, a paperless office, and a competent CRM, Aznar finds she can manage her clients' affairs, be there for her family, and still have time to teach finance courses at Fairleigh Dickinson University where she earned her MBA. It helps that she's flexible with her time – working during the early and late ends of the day while being with Chloe, her daughter, and husband in between.

Your co-authors rebalanced their own lives by moving to different geographical locations than the ones in which they originally set up shop. Dave Drucker split up a partnership to move his family from the Washington, D.C. suburbs to Albuquerque, New Mexico, while Joel Bruckenstein made a similar move from the suburbs of New York City to Miramar, Florida. Drastic moves like these are not uncommon when veteran practitioners wake up one day to discover they've built successful practices at the expense of many other life goals. Tenure in the business, age, and, oftentimes, unanticipated life events may conspire to change your priorities when you least expect it.

And if common sense or a sudden change in priorities doesn't motivate you to develop a coordinated business and life plan, perhaps your own service mix will. The phenomenon known as "Life Planning" has become – and we predict, will continue to become – an increasingly central focus of many planning engagements. This means that planners will be redirecting their goal-setting efforts with clients to include in-depth assessments of clients' values, feelings around money, and true goals – not the usual "send-the-children-to-college" and retire comfortably goals – but goals more aligned with the clients' lifelong wishes and dreams.

As you work more in this vein with clients, you may find it necessary to serve as a role model, which means you should have your own work and personal life in balance to show clients that they, too, can achieve the balance they crave.

HOW TO DO IT

- Working at home will enable you to stay with young children.
- Get outside help if needed; a mid-day nanny can help the younger planner stay on track or get a much-needed rest.
- Break out of the 9-to-5 rut; a flexible time schedule can free you up to work or play at unusual hours.
- Find out how maximizing the efficiencies inherent in new technology applications can give you more hours in the day.
- Dust off your business plan; maybe the ambitious growth targets behind your workaholism are robbing you of the time you need with your family or non-work pursuits that can add depth and meaning to your life.

WHERE CAN I FIND OUT MORE?

1. George Kinder, *Seven Stages of Money Maturity: Understanding the Spirit and Value of Money in Your Life* (New York, NY: Dell Books, 2000).
2. Jacob Needleman, *Money and the Meaning of Life* (New York, NY: Doubleday Books, 1994).
3. Karen Ramsey, *Everything You Know About Money Is Wrong: Overcome the Financial Myths Keeping You from the Life You Want* (New York, NY: ReganBooks, 2001).

Chapter 2

SELECTING A BUSINESS MODEL

As Figure 2.1 (below) shows, there are many different ways to slice and dice your business model decision.

To some people, deciding upon a business model implies selecting a tax structure. Should I operate as a sole proprietor, a pass-through entity (e.g., a partnership, LLC, or S corporation), or a taxable entity (i.e., a C corporation)?

But tax status is just one piece of the decision. Other "screens" we can use to set parameters for our business model decision are regulatory structure, firm size, client economics, office type, and compensation structure. Obviously, many of these screens overlap. For example, many planners who target the middle-income market charge hourly fees. Licensed advisors generally earn some of their income in the form of commissions. And large firms tend *not* to operate out of home offices.

To get further into this subject, we'll address each of these business model categories and tie them together as we go along.

REGULATORY STRUCTURE

Few advisors would actually say to themselves, "by whom do I wish to be regulated?" Regulatory structure

Figure 2.1

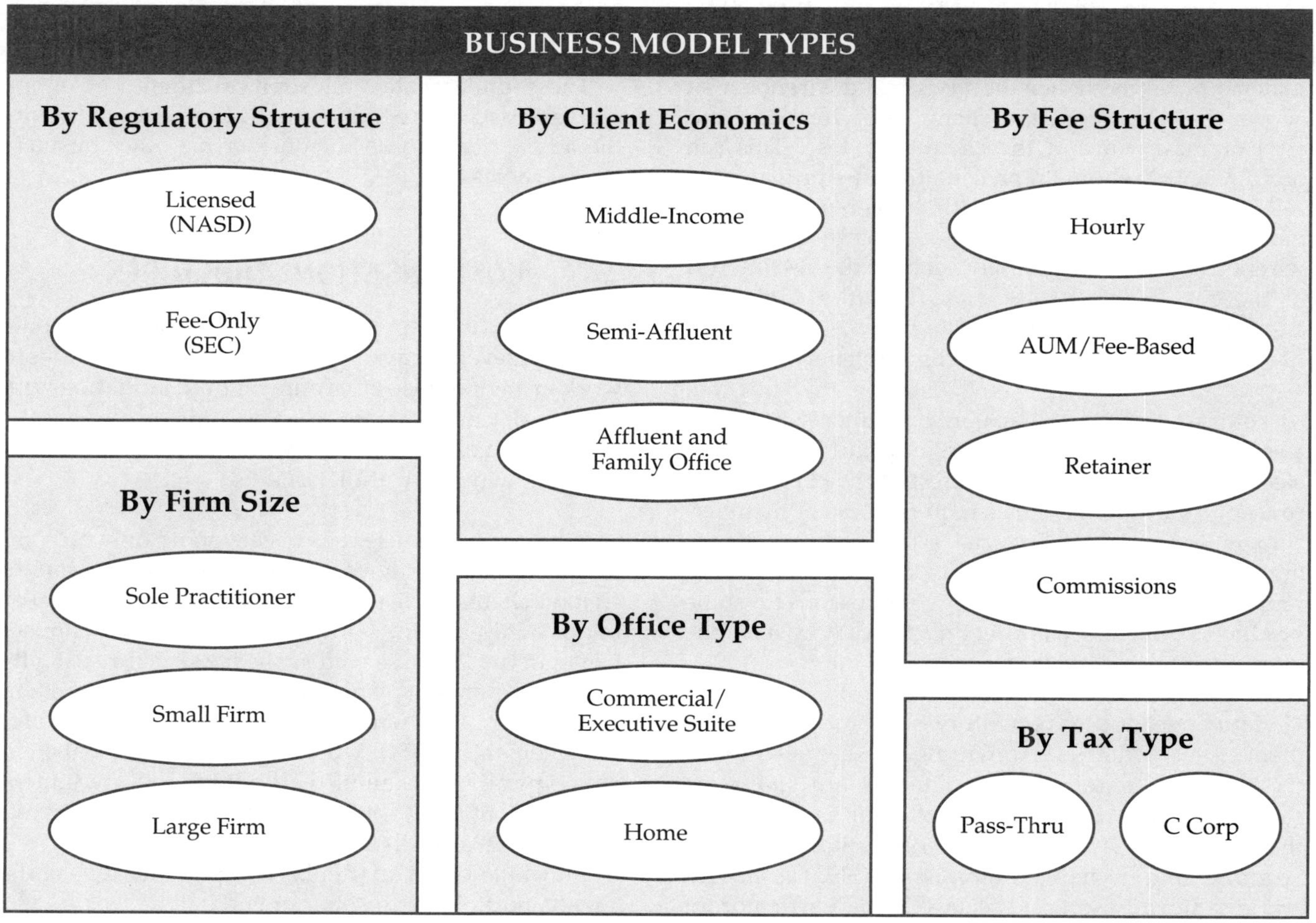

is more something that's backed into after thinking through the type of organization in which one wants to work, and what one's philosophy is to be towards clients.

Licensed advisors typically sell products to their clients. They may work in a "wirehouse" environment (e.g., Merrill Lynch, Smith Barney), or they may set up their own offices while affiliating with an independent broker-dealer, or BD (e.g., Linsco Private Ledger, Raymond James). These advisors' business philosophies sometimes differ from those of non-licensed, or fee-only planners, because their philosophies could be dictated by their compensation.

In a wirehouse, there may be pressure to "produce" (i.e., sell). This pressure should make clear to the wirehouse advisor that he works not only for his client, but also for his employer. Although this planner may view these different entities as collaborating at a round table, one could argue that the table is actually rectangular. What we mean is ... if the advisor, his client, and the wirehouse could all take their places at a round table, that would imply a planning situation that is balanced for all parties – in other words, a win-win-win situation. Unfortunately, what may happen is that when the advisor and wirehouse sit across the table from the client, the wirehouse and advisor may win and the client may lose. This can occur when wirehouse representatives are pressured to sell proprietary products with higher-than-average management fees or securities inventories by the wirehouse, which may or may not be in the best interest of the client. This reality may force the advisor to adopt the philosophy that he can balance the needs of his client with the demands of his employer.

Contrast this with a fee-only planner who earns fees instead of commissions. He may find it somewhat easier to truly put the best interest of the client first (a concept central to the ethics requirements of membership in every major financial planning professional organization). In the middle sits the independent BD representative, who may charge commissions for some products while also working on a fee-only basis in the offering of other services.

Having made the regulatory structure choice, the planner – wittingly or unwittingly – has also made the choice of regulator. All planners are subject to regulation. The independent planner is subject to the Investment Advisor Act of 1940 enforced by the Securities and Exchange Commission (SEC) at the federal level (for advisors overseeing $25 million or more of client assets under what the SEC defines as "continuous and regular supervisory or management services"), or by the states (if advisors fail to meet the SEC's requirement, or manage less than $25 million). The wirehouse and independent broker-dealer rep is subject to oversight by the National Association of Securities Dealers (NASD). Both regulatory bodies have precise requirements for operating procedures that have multiplied and grown more stringent in the new millennium. The difference is in the advisors' resources for ensuring compliance with these regulations. Wirehouses and independent broker-dealers generally have compliance departments – legal teams – that monitor representatives' activities. While this creates a more restrictive environment in which to work, it protects the advisor and his broker-dealer from potential liabilities associated with non-compliance.

The independent RIA must meet the SEC's or states' regulatory requirements through his own devices. That is, he must be his own compliance officer and, while encouraged to hire independent legal assistance in doing so, such assistance represents an added financial burden many advisors forego in favor of a do-it-yourself approach that is, at the least, time-consuming.

These fundamental philosophical differences among regulatory structures must usually be confronted before the advisor can go on to consider his other business model choices.

COMPENSATION STRUCTURES

Compensation structure constitutes a business model choice in several ways. First, an advisor who decides to work in a wirehouse environment or in affiliation with a BD, as discussed above, must be comfortable with the commission or fee-based compensation structures that go along with these affiliations.

Whereas wirehouse reps once worked only on commission, many wirehouses now encourage their reps to sign up clients for fee-based services. These are similar to the "wrap-account" arrangements some wirehouses began in the 1980s, as well as the fee structure used by many independent planners in which they bill the client a fee that is a percentage of the client's assets under management (AUM). Under these arrangements, clients typically have all of their advice and investment management (and, sometimes commissions on investment trades, as well) included in the one fee. The fee is usually billed each quarter based upon the value of the client's portfolio at the quarter end date.

The second way in which compensation structure may constitute a business model choice is in the type of client implied by the compensation. Wirehouse reps who are compensated by commissions often (though not exclusively) work with middle-income clients who prefer to have a portion of their compensation come "off the top" or the back end of their investment in the form of a commission rather than writing a separate check to the broker. And, as mentioned earlier, many fee-only advisors now service middle-income clients by charging hourly rates for the time they spend in a meeting with the client, as well as the few hours they may also spend in preparation for the meeting, or doing follow-up work requested by the client.

The other compensation structure to consider in designing a business model is retainer fees. Advisors working with clients on an ongoing basis often prefer retainer fees to assets-under-management fees. The retainer is a fixed annual fee billed periodically throughout the year, which can be changed at the mutual consent of the advisor and client if the client's situation or the advisor's overhead warrants an upward or downward adjustment. This fee also has implications for client type, usually being used for more affluent clients who may or may not require asset management but definitely want the ongoing involvement of an advisor to keep an eye on their financial affairs. As opposed to an individual, the client may even be an entire family being served under what is now popularly called the "family office" model wherein several generations of clients' planning needs are served in a coordinated manner.

CLIENT ECONOMICS

Client economics become a business model choice because they go hand in hand with compensation structure, as discussed above, or they may also be a starting point for many advisors in their choice of a business model.

Frequently, advisors begin constructing their business model by thinking about the types of clients they wish to work with and, particularly, those clients' socioeconomic characteristics. In many cases, they will work with clients whose economic profiles match those of their own, or of their parents. Can a twenty-something planner work with retirees? Can an advisor of modest background work with the highly affluent? The answer to both is yes, though it may not come naturally at first. Regardless of the type of client we ultimately target as one function of our business model, we usually start out with the familiar and comfortable. And some never progress beyond that group, which is fine if it is the advisor's conscious decision to do so and it generates sufficient income to meet the advisor's lifestyle.

Client economics also become a business model choice because they affect practice economics. Two very different business models are needed, for example, to service middle-income clients and affluent clients. The first tends to be a high-volume business, and the second a practice with a more concentrated client base. It is not unusual for a broker serving the middle market to have a base of clients he's worked with in the past or present numbering between 500 and 1,000. A successful practitioner serving the very affluent, on the other hand, might have between five and 50 clients, and have an equally or far more lucrative practice as the broker with ten or twenty times that number.

TAX TYPE

The taxable nature of your business will probably not be your first consideration, and it's not the main focus of most advisors' business models, but it's indeed an important consideration. Because you can find discussions of the different types of taxable or pass-through entities in any number of books written for entrepreneurs, we won't go into detail here.

Suffice it to say that entities are either "pass-through" (i.e., income, deductions, and credits are passed through and reported on the owners' personal returns) or taxable. Another way of saying this is that they are sole proprietorships, S corporations, partnerships, limited liability companies (LLCs) or similar entities, on the one hand, or C corporations, on the other. Why would anyone want to adopt a business entity with a separate taxable status that could subject him to double taxation (i.e., a C corporation)? Because (1) the advisor might get a few more choices when it comes to selecting benefit plans (e.g., medical reimbursement plans must be implemented through a C corporation if it is to benefit the owner), and (2) often it isn't difficult to create a zero or negative taxable income in the corporation, hence eliminating the double-tax threat.

FIRM SIZE AND OFFICE TYPE

These two decision points usually go together since a large firm with many employees doesn't generally fit in a home office (without remodeling, that is).

But a bigger issue than sheer size and numbers is the philosophical difference between the two. To illustrate this, let's consider two extremes: a 20-person advisory firm, and a sole practitioner. Holding other variables constant, let's further assume that each firm strives to provide the same service – a comprehensive, wealth management service including financial and estate planning, investment management, and certain "concierge"-type services.

Large firms sometimes get that way through deliberate action, and sometimes by default. A successful advisor will often start out as a sole practitioner, add clients easily, and accumulate employees to serve his growing client base. One day he wakes up and finds himself at the helm of a large firm. He may or may not want the people-and-project-management job he's thus created for himself, but that's what he's created. He must either accept his management role, or tailor his organization in such a way as to allow him to go back to doing the tasks he truly enjoys – which may not be managing people, but working with clients.

In other cases, the large firm becomes such because it's owner deliberately grew it. Much theory and commonly-accepted wisdom says that a large advisory firm is more beneficial than a small one because it can:

- Institutionalize itself, that is, divorce its identity from that of its owner and thus become more valuable to a buyer;
- Provide better client service; and
- Provide the one-stop shopping experience that many clients want.

However, large companies have well-documented effects on their owners, including unbalanced lives due to overworking, stress, poor health, and so on. The owner and manager of a large firm must take precautions not to let his business consume his life.

A small firm is generally believed to provide a more balanced lifestyle for its owner. This is not necessarily true. The owners of both large *and* small firms must be careful not to lose their identities to excessive work. The difference for a sole practitioner is that he does not need to be in an office Monday through Friday from 9:00 a.m. to 5:00 p.m. to interact with his onsite employees. Either he will have *no* employees, or he will work with remote employees or "virtual work partners" – that is, independent contractors or separate businesses that perform for him the functions, which the large firm owner has hired employees to perform. By dealing with remote workers, often in different time zones, the sole practitioner is freed up to live the different aspects of his life (work, play, etc.) when he desires.

Large firms must generally commit to commercial office space, which means they are subject to the vagaries of rental space price fluctuations, and the difficulty of forecasting space requirements for a growing firm. Small firms or solo practitioners can work from a home office if amenable to their clients, which gives them added efficiency (no commute) and, often, greater comfort with less stress.

Both size firms can meet in the middle by renting office space in an executive office suite center. In fact, this can be more cost-effective than standard commercial space, particularly if employees do not need to work in the same physical space at all times and/or face-to-face client meetings are infrequent.

Is there a difference in the perception clients will have of you if you choose a large firm over a small firm, or vice versa? Yes, and the perceptions can work for or against you. A large firm with swank offices may put off middle-income or particularly cost-conscious clients, such as depression-era retirees. Conversely, corporate executives may not feel they are getting the expertise and professionalism they seek if they visit a home office. All advisors make first impressions, and those impressions must be reasonably within the clients' tolerance limits given who they are and what they expect from a professional service.

PUTTING IT ALL TOGETHER

After blending all of the above criteria, a number of distinct business models have emerged in the financial services industry. This is not to say that you must adopt one of these. You're free to mix and match the above business model choices any way you wish. But these will at least give you an idea of what's out there in the way of competition.

YOUR BUSINESS MODEL

This chapter should give you the high points to consider in designing your own business model. As you can see, there are a number of variables to take into account, and they fit together in ways that are limited only by your imagination. Your business must suit your personal and lifestyle needs, as well as your income needs

BUSINESS MODEL 1: INDEPENDENT BD REPRESENTATIVES

Adam Bennett and Charles Davidson, independent BD reps, share space in an executive office suite complex and are both supported by one service assistant, Ellen Foster. This three-employee advisory firm might be set up as a Limited Liability Company (LLC). It serves semi-affluent clients with a combination of compensation structures – a fee-based structure for planning and asset management, and a commission structure for products sold in implementing the plan (or subsequent plan updates). As licensed planners, Adam and Charles are subject to regulation by the NASD, and if they've set up their own RIA, then the SEC also regulates them.

BUSINESS MODEL 2: SOLE PRACTITIONER

George Harrison works from home as an independent RIA. He has no employees, instead using virtual work partners. George maintains a C corporation with generous benefit plans so he can provide for his family's medical care, future schooling, and retirement. He serves middle-income clients using an hourly fee structure. For a different set of clients, he also manages $15 million with an AUM fee structure and is state regulated in these activities.

BUSINESS MODEL 3: LIMITED LIABILITY COMPANY

John Kincaid, a successful advisor with many years in the business, operates an LLC serving very affluent individual and family office clients. With the assistance of 20 employees, he provides a one-stop shopping experience for his clients, including performing many concierge services, such as purchasing new cars, setting up vacations, etc. John specializes in alternative investing as well as the use of more traditional portfolio components. Managing $350 million, his firm is a federally covered advisor regulated by the SEC. John charges his clients retainer fees ranging from $5,000 to $25,000 a year. The firm operates from 8,000 square feet of prime, commercial office space.

and your clients' needs. It is up to you to design it to keep everyone concerned both happy and profitable.

WHERE CAN I FIND OUT MORE ABOUT IT?

The Garrett Planning Network, Inc., (GPN) is a nationwide network of professional, Fee-Only™ financial advisors. GPN members are dedicated to providing financial advice to people from all walks of life, on an hourly as-needed basis. See www.garrettplanning network.com. See also *Garrett's Guide to Financial Planning: How to Capture the Middle Market and Increase Your Profits* (Cincinnati, OH: The National Underwriter Company, 2002).

Chapter 3

NAMING YOUR PRACTICE

Your practice needs a name, and that need puts you squarely in the middle of an unresolved controversy – should you use your own name, a generic name, or a descriptive name? Like so many decisions in the practice management area, there is no right or wrong choice, but there are important considerations you should be aware of. Let's examine some other advisors' thinking on the subject to learn what those choices are.

Many new entrants to the planning field use their own names in the name of their firm. This personalizes the business and lends an air of prestige to the owner and primary advisor (often the start-up firm's only employee). However, some advisors believe their long-term interests will be better served with a more "corporate-sounding" name. "When I am ready to retire, I want this business to have an identity of its own. I believe this will give the business more market value," says David Lewis of Resource Advisory Services, Inc., in Knoxville, Tennessee.

Additionally, Lewis puts a strong emphasis on his use of the word "Resource" in dealing with clients. "We talk about allocation of all client resources, including human capital. We work with clients to better understand all their available resources and the variety of things that can be accomplished with them. We talk about using the resources of Resource Advisory Services, Inc. to solve problems for clients, and generally make their lifestyles better. The ways this word can be used to strengthen the understanding of a relationship to us seems unlimited," says Lewis.

The opposing viewpoint is expressed well by Harris Creech, CPA, CFP®, owner of Harris S. Creech Fee-Only Financial Planning, LLC, of Solon, Ohio, for the following reason: "It is highly unlikely anyone else around would use it. The name says what I do – I am a CPA and CFP who provides fee-only financial planning," says Creech. Creech alludes to the television commercials of the financial services firm ING in which the actors all know the company's purpose as soon as they hear the name. Says Creech, "I have no idea what ING does, and I doubt prospective clients know, or care."

Does the choice therefore come down to creating value versus clearly stating your firm's purpose? Not necessarily. Doug Macdonald of Macdonald Shymko & Company, Ltd., in Vancouver, British Columbia, has used his and another principal's name in the name of his firm for 30 years now. Macdonald says, "Over time, the name of the firm becomes institutionalized." In other words, "Macdonald Shymko & Company Ltd." has been around so long that Macdonald believes it now represents the company and not any particular individuals *within* the company.

And Bruce Berno of Berno Financial Management, Inc., in Cincinnati, Ohio, adds "many brokerage firms like Lehman Brothers or Charles Schwab were named after individuals, so even individual names can become brand names."

However, if one wants to convey a firm's function in its name, it can usually do so more easily with a corporate name than with one's own name. Consider "Commission-Free Financial Planning Solutions, Inc.," the Cedar Falls, Iowa, firm owned by Jon Ford, or Casey Rea's "Sound Futures, Inc." of Columbus, Ohio, or Sherry Hazan-Cohen's "Dream Achieve" in Plano, Texas.

Of course, some names neither clearly state the firm's purpose nor create that institutional aura. David Diesslin's decision to name his Fort Worth, Texas firm simply "Diesslin & Associates, Inc." follows from the advice he received after hiring a public relations firm. His consultant advised that he position his firm squarely among other professional businesses in his area – like law and accounting firms that often take the names of their founders.

Using one's own name can have other drawbacks that few stop to realize. David Lewis kept his firm's name somewhat generic, he says, because "if I used my name, there might be an implication that other people should aspire to having their names added to the business name, like a law firm. Lewis doesn't want his veteran employees to think the opportunity for partnership status exists just because the firm uses the owner's name for its own. Lewis adds, "Using my name might also lead to a situation where clients wonder why their primary contact in the firm doesn't have his or her name in the title." Lewis sees using a corporate name as a way to avoid these dilemmas.

Some advisors go through several iterations before arriving at a name that works. Before he named his company "Commission-Free Financial Planning Solutions, Inc.," Jon Ford called it "Ford Financial Solutions, Inc." Unbelievably, Ford Motor Company brought a trademark infringement case against Ford, who says, "In January 2000, we received a two-inch thick packet, which we mistook for a belated holiday gift. Instead it was a packet of legal documents." Ford learned that six months earlier, the motor company had applied for the exclusive right to use "Ford Financial Solutions" for its finance division and then discovered this "little guy" in Iowa already had it. Ford succumbed to the pressure and changed his name.

Richard May's early business school training guided him in his name selection. "I learned that any corporate name should be short *and* it should definitely tell what the company does." Apparently, these guidelines proved easier in theory than in execution. May (of West Chester, Pennsylvania) first named his firm "Chester County Tax and Investment Advisory Company, Inc.," and later settled on "RKM Advisors, Inc."

Another naming strategy is to hint at the function of the firm as well as include another name that may be impersonal, but strategically motivated. Maura Murphy chose the name "Ashland Financial Solutions" for her Ashland, Oregon firm so she would be one of the first ads appearing in the Yellow Pages under "Financial Planners." And Paul Baumbach chose the name "Mallard Asset Management" for his Newark, Delaware firm, he says, "to personalize the company and to provide an easy source for an ice-breaking discussion during an initial meeting with a prospective client." It seems that, as a kid, Baumbach and his family raised mallard ducks.

Sometimes the advisor chooses a name other than his own because his name is simply too difficult to pronounce or remember. Carl F. von dem Bussche named his Palm Harbor, Florida firm "Financial Guidance Group, Inc." because, he says, "with a name like 'von dem Bussche,' what choice did I have?" And Naomi Scrivener opted for "Back Office Solutions" for her Georgetown, Texas company because she felt her own name would have been a stumbling block in marketing. (She also wanted prospective advisor-clients to have a visual image of a firm doing the "back office" aspects of financial planning.)

Coupling one's own name with a slogan can be an effective approach to establishing an identity. Chip Addis' reasoning in naming his Wayne, Pennsylvania firm – "Addis & Hill, Inc., Where Money Meets Life" – after himself and his partner was as follows: "We feel that people seek out fee-only firms because they want objectivity. It is pretty evident that clients tend not to trust big institutional firms. So, why would we want to look the same as the big players?"

As Addis has proven, if one chooses a name that doesn't denote the function of the firm, it can always be expanded with a follow-on slogan, something that's become increasingly popular in recent years. Doug Heimforth's Los Altos, California firm is named "Heimforth Wealth Management," which is already descriptive, but Heimforth adds to it the slogan "Coaching for Financial and Life Success" since a large part of his services is using coaching skills he's acquired to help clients reach their stated goals.

Another valid naming strategy is striking just the right symbolism. Sheryl Clark named her Tucson, Arizona firm "Sunrise Financial" because she wanted something positive and uplifting. Says Clark, "I see Sunrise as giving the feeling of new beginnings with a long day in the sun. Most of my clients tend to be younger rather than older and I felt that this suited them and me."

We give credit to the above named advisors for thinking long and hard about their name choices. Of course, sometimes the reason for a particular name is much simpler. Says Joel Ticknor of his Reston, Virginia firm, Ticknor Financial, Inc., "I chose my eponymous firm name so I wouldn't forget it."

Your author, David Drucker, has had two tries at the name game. In my earlier firm, my partner, Mary Malgoire, and I used our names to create "Malgoire Drucker Inc." No one could ever pronounce or spell my partner's name correctly, but people *did* find it distinctive. On the second try, with my own firm *sans* partner, the name became "Sunset Financial Management, Inc." However, one must be careful of the symbolism, as I subsequently learned. As a retirement planner, I wanted a name that gently implied that I worked with retirement-age clients. But one client in particular said he flinched every time he heard the new name because he took it to be a constant reminder of his eventual demise.

Seriously, we've tried to demonstrate that there are many ramifications to a particular choice of name. Try to get it right the first time. You'll save yourself a lot of money by not having to reprint stationary and re-program your website.

Practical Pointers

DOMAIN NAME ISSUES

You will want your business name to translate into a domain name for your website. So don't forger to consider:

- Whether your business name is available? (You can check at websites like (http://www.register.com/)
- Whether an individual's name is more likely to be unique and, therefore, available than a generic business name
- If the domain name you want isn't available, a little tweaking may make it so by:
  - Adding "Inc." or "LLC" onto the domain name if you have a corporation (e.g., "SunsetFinancialInc.com").
  - Adding a hyphen between the two words in a business name (e.g., "Sunset-Financial.com").
  - Abbreviating a portion of the business name (e.g., "SunsetFin.com").

TRADEMARK ISSUES

If you want your business to qualify for trademark protection, remember:

- Trademarks allow companies exclusive use of the names they've chosen, helping consumers identify and distinguish their services in the marketplace.
- A distinctive name will be easier for customers to remember and make it receive greater trademark protection.
- To search for existing trademarks, go to http://www.uspto.gov/main/trademarks.htm.
- In addition to trademarking, you may need to register your business name with your state or county clerk's office.

Chapter 4

LOCATING YOUR OFFICE

You have essentially four choices for locating your office: your home; commercial office space; rented space; or the client's office (or some combination of the four). There are pros and cons to every office configuration. Let's explore them.

HOME OFFICE

The home office has many advantages, particularly if one wants to be near his or her family. In other words, a home office is conducive to a practice in which one is attempting to balance his life with his work. A planner can be home at those rewarding moments when other parents are stuck in an office – when his kids leave for or return home from school, when a spouse has free time for lunch, or the family dog offers a welcome mid-day break in the form of a walk around the neighborhood.

Other advantages include a very short commute, the cost savings, and the ability to take some hefty tax deductions by writing off a portion of one's utilities, cleaning, landscaping, property taxes, and even paying oneself rent, and/or depreciating a portion of the home's value.

Some clients may feel more at ease in a home office, leading to a more rapid building of rapport with you. Your author worked primarily with retired couples, widows and widowers, folks who are sometimes intimidated by a fancy commercial office, or don't like the long drive and parking responsibilities that a commercial office often requires.

But there are disadvantages, too. Not all clients will accept a home office. Some may not appreciate a home office and see it as a sign of inexperience. It's difficult to generalize here, but corporate executives and wealthier (i.e., multi-million dollar) clients, in this author's experience, sometimes view the home office negatively.

If the home office is an adjunct to commercial space – a place where the advisor works one or two days a week – that can pose problems, as well. Melissa Hammel of Brentwood, Tennessee works at home occasionally as a respite from Hammel Financial Advisory Group's commercial offices. She shares several problems that are common for many at-home workers depending upon their geographical positioning. "Where we live, we do not have cable [for Internet access] so we tried the satellite route. The way I work is to log onto my computer at work and operate that way. Well, it was rather frustrating. The system was quite delayed, along with locking up our server at work periodically. I would spend half an hour doing something that would have taken only a few minutes in the regular office," says Hammel. As broadband Internet access has gone from nice to necessary, some at-home workers may be disadvantaged.

Hammel experienced press-related problems too. "I was contacted by a local newspaper to comment on recent tax law changes after our office sent out a press release to that effect. Well, sure enough, the reporter called while I was working at home and I did not have any of my tax law notes. I was so nervous that she would ask me a question and I would give her the wrong information." Of course, this problem is exacerbated by Hammel's first problem – lack of easy access to the critical data maintained in her regular office.

Mary Gibson, a San Juan Bautista, California advisor, cites some of the problems home office workers typically have when clients must enter the "family" part of the home to get to the "professional" part of the home. Says Gibson, "my office is our spare bedroom and clients have to go through the house to get to it. So the number one issue is having to live in 'House Beautiful' all the time. My husband is a saint and helps. We are the envy of our friends who marvel that we don't ever seem to have anything out of place." This problem is remedied by having a separate entrance to your home office, but most home office advisors buy their homes before they decide to establish a home office, so the configuration of the home isn't always ideal. In addition to a separate entrance, the ideal home office has a separate suite of rooms (e.g., conference room, working area, and file room) so clients don't have to experience your personal life before they're ready to do so.

Gibson also talks about another common gripe most home office workers have: the lack of separation between "Gibson the Friend," and "Gibson the Advisor." "Even though I have been home-based for a while, things changed when family and friends knew that I was home all the time. It became just fine for them to drop in or call whenever they wanted to. Before, I might be gone; now they know I am at home. So, I now screen calls, and I have posted office hours on my front and back doors. My signs read, 'Mary L. Gibson, CFP, Office Hours M-F 8 to 5. By Appointment Only. If you do not have an appointment, please call before knocking.' This has significantly stopped family and friends from just coming by," says Gibson.

Bonnie Hughes in Rome, Georgia confesses that the technological sophistication required by a home office sometimes eludes her. "I remain somewhat technically paralyzed in that I know exactly what I need to know technology-wise to get work done, but there is a need to get better at technological solutions and I do not have the time to devote to it. I think if I were in a corporate structure, I'd have the training planned into my time or the solutions provided by the structure. I have no idea how to fix this because every time I have hired help in this area, they have only lightened my wallet, not my headaches." Alas, hiring a qualified computer consultant seems to be *at least* as hard as hiring a competent financial advisor.

And, as mentioned earlier, some clients may balk at the very notion of a home office. Says Brian Wruk in Gilbert, Arizona, "one prospect called me from his cell phone in his car when he first came to visit me. He wanted to verify that he was in the right place. I said 'come on in ... I have a home office.'" Wruk's client was OK with his home office, just a little hesitant at first. Of course, a home office can strike exactly the right chord with a family-oriented client, says Wruk: "Other people come, see my kids' toys and, if they're big on family, they think it's great. So [there are] both sides to it."

Working at home also poses technological challenges and decisions. For example, if you're a telephone power-user, you may need two lines – one for outgoing calls, and the other for outgoing/incoming faxes or outgoing/incoming modem transmissions. This means a two-line phone, two lines from the local phone company and maybe a two-line answering machine. On the other hand, if you're technologically adept, you may be able to get by with *no* phone lines. Your author has a cable modem for Internet access, handles all of his incoming and outgoing faxes from his computer, and uses a cell phone for all phone calls. You, too, can duplicate this setup.

COMMERCIAL OFFICE SPACE

Turn the advantages and disadvantages of the home office on their head, and you've got the commercial office. The advisor who makes a long commute to his commercial office often loses touch with his family. When all of one's work must be done outside the home, overwork means long hours away from the family. If you work long hours, you can't take a break to walk the dog, eat lunch with your wife, or tuck in your kids at night. And commercial office space is expensive; it adds a large cost element to your overhead.

Nevertheless, many clients like and expect to see you in a commercial office. You can command respect with commercial office space from clients who like to think their advisor is competent and successful, traits that a commercial office confirms for them.

OFFICE SPACE RENTALS

Isn't this the same as commercial office space? No. Here we're talking about what are usually called "executive office suites." This is ready-made office space complete with office equipment, telephones, Internet access and secretarial support. These offices can be rented by the hour, by the day, or by the month.

While some advisors may rent this type of space day in and day out because they find it convenient and don't want to have to purchase the equipment or labor that is available with this setup, others use executive suites as an adjunct to the home office. For example, you might work in your home office three or four days a week, and group client meetings into one or two days a week, holding them in your rented office suite. This can be the best of both worlds as you have fancy (enough) office space to please most clients, and you can keep your home and home office as messy as you desire.

THE CLIENT'S OFFICE

All of the office configurations discussed thus far present the location decision: where are your clients located *vis-à-vis* your chosen office space? Where do they live and work? Is your office convenient to them? If not, you may need to keep evening or weekend hours to accommodate them, a further drain on the time you'd rather be spending with your family.

Meeting clients in their own space is an option that is used in conjunction with a home office. However, this setup has two distinct disadvantages. First, clients don't see you in your own space. Some clients need to see your "home base" to develop the faith that you're the "real deal." Also, always meeting clients in their space gives them a psychological advantage that may allow some clients to control the meeting, which you should be in control of.

The second disadvantage is the cost. True, meeting the client on his turf allows you to avoid the direct costs of a "real" office, but those costs are replaced with the cost of your commuting time. You will be in the car more than you will care to be, and time spent in traffic is time not spent working. Sure, you can listen to cassette tapes and pick up some continuing education credits, and maybe return a few phone calls. But you can't program a spreadsheet or fit in as many client meetings as you could if you were stationary and had your clients coming to you. And don't forget the direct transportation costs (and traffic delays) you'll incur, as well.

A variation on meeting in the client's office is meeting clients over a meal. This usually isn't advisable with a new client, but clients with whom you've worked for a while will often like this type of get-together. Meeting over lunch lends an informality that is conducive to relationship building. And it puts you and the client on neutral ground, which reduces the advantage the client has when you meet in his territory.

SUMMARY

In summary, remember there are pros and cons to every business decision. For the office decision, you must balance, at a minimum, considerations of cost, tax benefits (or lack thereof), client psychology, location, and technology. If you're starting out and cost is an overriding factor, consider one of the "hybrid" solutions – the executive office suite or client's office, coupled with a home office. Otherwise, consider all the factors carefully and choose the most balanced solution for you.

Chapter 5

SETTING A COMPENSATION STRUCTURE

This topic – setting a compensation structure – is very broad, and goes hand-in-hand with designing a business model and identifying a target market.

A planner's choice of compensation structure implies the type and net-worth-size of clients he wishes to work with, what the emphasis of his work will be, and which other types of professionals he may be similar to. For example, if a planner charges fees based on the percentage of assets-under-management (AUM), he may give the impression that investments are his primary focus even though he may also offer financial planning services. If a planner charges by the hour, the client may expect a limited engagement (as he would have with his attorney or accountant) rather than a long-term relationship. And, if a planner charges minimum fees, his minimum indicates whether the planner deems his prospects' affairs too minor to warrant his attention.

The two primary means of compensation in the financial services industry are fees and commissions. The following are the most common structures:

- Fees and commissions:
  - "Fee-offset" fee structure
  - "Fee-based" fee structure
- "Fee-only" structures:
  - AUM fees
  - Retainer fees
  - Hourly fees

FEES AND COMMISSIONS

A significant number of planners use some combination of fees and commissions. Many offer life insurance or annuity products or work in large wirehouse environments. In either case, separate billing for financial planning services independent of product sales might have been discouraged or unavailable. In either case, many have made transitions to independent broker-dealer (BD) settings that allowed them more freedom to offer the services and compensation arrangements needed for their practice.

These advisors may still earn the majority of their income from commissions (unless they are deliberately transitioning to fee-only status), but charge a separate fee for financial planning. The fee may be a negligible "loss-leader" fee, or a higher fee designed to actually compensate them for time spent developing a financial plan.

The "Fee-Offset" Fee Structure

Licensed planners who want to simulate a fee-only arrangement but don't want to give up their licenses often use this fee structure. They charge fees to their clients and also earn commissions from product sales. However, the fees they charge are meant to fully compensate them for the planning work they do. Therefore, they offset the fee by the amount of commissions received so that the total payment from the client – through direct fees and indirect commissions – is fixed at the total fee level the client initially agreed to.

The "Fee-Based" Fee Structure

The fee-based fee structure is popular with planners who want their fee structure to signal a transition away from commissions towards a type of planner-client relationship. In some cases "fee-based" is really just another name for "AUM fees" (see below) because these representatives have left behind an old-style brokerage relationship (i.e., presiding over accounts in which stocks, bonds and proprietary mutual funds are bought and sold) and moved to a role of "gathering" assets, which they place under management with third-party separate account managers. The client is charged a fee based upon the amount of assets involved, and that fee generally covers the manager's fee, the client's trading costs, any financial planning the representative may be doing, and other services the representative provides.

Assets-Under-Management (AUM) Fees

As discussed above, assets-under-management fees are assessed as a percentage of the assets being managed by the advisor. This fee structure is called "fee-based" when used by a BD representative, or "AUM fees" when used by an independent Registered Investment Adviser (RIA) (i.e., an advisor registered with the Securities Exchange Commission (SEC) and/or a state regulatory body but not affiliated with a BD nor regulated by the NASD, historically known as the National Association of Securities Dealers).

Advisors charging AUM fees usually do financial planning as well and the fee for that planning may be included in their AUM fee, or may be charged separately.

Retainer Fees

This type of fee is generally used by independent RIAs. A retainer fee is a flat, annual fee, usually billed quarterly, which represents the advisor's total charges for all services performed for the client. These fees are determined in many different ways, but generally reflect the client's entire financial picture as well as the time the advisor expects to spend with the client and the value he hopes to add to the relationship.

Some advisors "build" these fees by: (1) approximating the time they expect to spend with the client over the 12 months subsequent to the setting of the fee; (2) applying an hourly rate; and (3) adding to that an appropriate charge for the assets they will manage. Of course, retainer fees can be charged in the absence of asset management services too, as in the case of an advisor who consults with small business clients but doesn't manage their personal investment assets. Some advisors also determine retainer fees by using a formula that reflects the client's total net worth and/or earned income.

Hourly Fees

Some advisors charge clients in much the same way some attorneys and Certified Public Accountants (CPAs) do – by tracking all of the time they spend working for the client and applying an hourly charge. In recent years, the hourly fee structure has been used successfully by independent RIAs wishing to serve a primarily middle-income clientele, who typically want to pay by the hour rather than entering into a long-term advisory relationship via a retainer or other fee structure.

CHOOSING A COMPENSATION STRUCTURE

"Fee-Only" isn't a fee structure, per se, but a philosophy of billing. It means that the advisor's only income is paid directly by the client – never through commissions. Thus, retainer fees or AUM fees or hourly fees, for which the client writes a check to the advisor (or authorizes the advisor to deduct from his investment account), are all fee-only methods of charging clients. Planners who use one of these fee structures and advertise their fee-only status feel that it suggests to the client that they are more objective in their advice because their recommendations will not be affected by the potential for commission income.

We said earlier that our choice of compensation structure implies the type and net-worth-size of clients we wish to work with, what the emphasis of our work will be, and what other types of professionals we may be similar to. How is this so? We can draw some general conclusions, though none represent hard and fast rules. For example, we mentioned above that the hourly fee structure is desirable to less affluent clients. To a lesser extent, it is also desired by high net worth clients who may just want a second opinion to confirm the direction they've taken by way of their own counsel, or perhaps the counsel of another full-time advisor.

If you are considering hourly fees, though, recognize that it's not a value-added fee structure. You simply invoice the client for the amount of time you spend – no more, no less. (Well, in some professions it may be "more," but that's not something you want to be in the position of having to explain to your clients). The point is that your income is capped by the time you spend working. To get more income, you must either work more hours or continuously raise fees.

The other drawback to hourly fees is that clients know they will be charged when they contact you. Therefore, this fee structure is not effective if you are trying to build long-term client relationships. By having frequent contact with clients, a planner can successfully build a clientele and solidify client relationships. However, if the client controls this process because he's fee-sensitive, the relationship will not progress, and you may find yourself having difficulty in getting clients to pay invoices unless the client has pre-approved the hours you intend to spend on his work.

Like hourly fees, the commission-only compensation structure is also one that generally appeals to less wealthy clients who would rather their advisor take a piece of the action than present them with a bill requiring them to cut a check.

The AUM and retainer fee structures generally attract wealthier clients. First, they imply no product sales, although that, too, isn't a hard and fast rule. Retainer fees in particular are often the way that experienced attorneys and CPAs charge their clients; thus, these fees can convey an aura of greater professionalism. They also imply that the advisor will take a more holistic approach towards his client rather than seeing his job as simply selling a product or creating a financial plan. Advisors on retainer often provide "concierge" services to clients, which means simply that they go above and beyond the client's financial plan to help the client – and often his extended family – coordinate all of their affairs. In this regard, retainer fees are sometimes representative of a "family office" practice.

The "fee-based" fee structure implies a specific business model since wirehouse and independent broker-dealer representatives primarily use this structure. Some would say that the similarity between "fee-based" and "fee-only" is intentional (i.e., that wirehouse marketing departments came up with a phrase that would confuse the general public into thinking their representatives do the same thing that fee-only planners do). Although many fee-only independent RIAs use the AUM fee structure, which is essentially the same as a fee-based fee structure, their services usually differ greatly from those of wirehouse planners.

So, in short, the sophisticated client may form judgments about you, your intentions, your expertise, and your professionalism by the way you are compensated. It is up to you to recognize the importance of adopting a compensation structure that is strategically coordinated with your choice of business model and target market.

Whatever you do, the client must be convinced that you and he are on the same team. This concept of aligning interests comes up repeatedly among AUM-fee proponents. "For years, I have told clients that I am in the same boat with them, to the extent our fees are based on the size of their portfolios. I have benefited from that arrangement greatly," says David Lewis of Resource Advisory Services, Inc., in Knoxville, Tennessee.

Other advisors argue that, to the contrary, AUM fees inappropriately focus the client on the asset management service to the exclusion of all the other services the advisor performs. They believe that retainer fees do a better job of instilling in the client an appreciation for everything that you, as his advisor, do for him.

There are other reasons to question AUM fees – namely, the unpredictability of the income stream they generate, and the greater probability of conflicts of interest to which they subject the advisor. AUM fees fluctuate with the investment markets. Advisors using this fee structure must compute a different fee every quarter after having calculated the market value of each client's portfolio. In prolonged periods of poor market performance (e.g., calendar years 2000 through 2002), advisory firm revenues will suffer dramatically unless new clients are aggressively sought to add new assets to the advisor's total revenue base.

Conflicts may also develop that can usually be avoided with other fee structures. Few clients consider their investment accounts untouchable. If they're moving up to a new home and need a down payment in excess of the proceeds from the sale of their old home, they'll tap their investment account for this money. A planner compensated by AUM fees will, therefore, lose revenues. Suppose the client first asks the advisor's opinion about his housing transition? Can the advisor advise against the purchase and still be objective? A multitude of other conflicts can develop just like this one. Clients whose trust you've earned may have no doubts that your advice is truly objective, regardless of your means of compensation. But some may always wonder.

On the other hand, retainer fees aren't perfect either. Unlike AUM fees, they do not automatically adjust upward when you increase the value of your clients' wealth (either through savvy planning or because the market simply ticks upward). The client's approval must be obtained before retainer fees can be raised.

For advisors charging flat fees, it is critical that clients understand that flat fees will be raised periodically for inflation, increasing complexity in the client's financial affairs, or other valid reasons. When your author switched his clients to a flat-fee structure in the late 1980s, he told them he wasn't going to raise those fees every year, but that he'd review them bi-annually (assuming that nothing changed dramatically in their lives). This process highlights a delicate tradeoff: does one raise fees every year or every *other* year so the increase feels manageable to the client, but comes far sooner than he really expected? Or, does one raise them every three or four years, which is less obnoxious to the client, until they see the magnitude of the increase? (Even if only raising fees for 3% annual inflation, four years' worth can be off-putting to many clients.)

When it *is* time to raise fees, you need to make your case. One way to do this is to demonstrate the results of your work and appeal to your clients' sense of fairness. You can also create "comparables" – that is, show them what other advisors are charging and how reasonable your fees are, even with an increase.

Whatever compensation structure you ultimately select, make sure you understand its ramifications for revenue predictability and growth, marketing effectiveness, firm image, and client relations.

WHERE CAN I FIND OUT MORE ABOUT IT?

1. Sheryl Garrett, *Garrett's Guide to Financial Planning: How to Capture the Middle Market and Increase Your Profits* (Cincinnati, OH: The National Underwriter Company, 2002).

2. Jeffrey H. Rattiner, *Getting Started as a Financial Planner* (Princeton, NJ: Bloomberg Press, 2000).

3. John E. Sestina, *J.K. Lasser Pro Fee-Only Financial Planning* (New York, NY: Wiley, 2001).

Chapter 6

PERSONAL TIME MANAGEMENT

Are you controlling your time, or is it controlling you? No matter how efficient your internal business systems are, and regardless of the quality of the people you hire or outsource to, if you can't manage your time, then you can't be an effective businessperson.

Modern time management is a blend of commonsense techniques we've all heard before and the computer technology available today in the form of contact managers (see the Sidebar, below), schedulers, and workflow systems. First, let's discuss the fundamentals and how to carry them out. (Parenthetically, you'll notice a similarity between these steps and what you ask your clients to do to bring their expenses under control. Time is money, right? Then start enhancing the money value of your own time!)

TIME MANAGEMENT FUNDAMENTALS

#1: Keeping a Diary

Step one is keeping a diary. For at least three representative workdays (or a full week if possible) keep a log of where all of your business – and personal – time goes. At the end of the week, add up how many minutes you spent on these and other tasks:

- Talking on the telephone;
- Meeting with prospective clients and "gatekeepers";
- Meeting with clients;
- Number crunching and plan writing;
- Portfolio management;
- Administrative chores;
- Marketing activities;
- Professional growth and improvement;
- Personal needs and obligations;
- Personal relationships; and
- Personal hobbies.

How do you *want* to spend your time? If you base your revenues on billable hours spent generating plans, you'll probably want to maximize time spent in this area. If you are the chief rainmaker in your firm (or the only person in your firm), you'll probably want to spend a large portion of your time marketing. If you are a veteran advisor with a large staff, you'll want to spend your time on business strategizing, which is always the principal's job, and all other activities that still give you enjoyment and enrich your life.

Complete your diary, total your time, and find out where your time went versus where you want it to go. Do a pie chart. Like the client who uses his checkbook to tally inflows and expenses and is shocked to learn how much his/her family spends eating out, you'll probably be surprised to find out how much time you spend on tasks that are not the "highest and best use" of your time and that you should be delegating, that don't add value to your client services, or that you simply detest.

#2: Analyzing How You Spend Your Time

Step two is taking a hard look at why you're spending time on activities to which you've assigned a low priority. Be honest with yourself. Many people do administrative chores when they know they should be planning or talking to clients because those administrative tasks give them the satisfaction of a job completed quickly (unlike a financial plan, for instance). Others do administrative work simply as an escape from more demanding or "painful" work.

Another game we play is to take every call that comes in, no matter how much it interrupts our priority work. Most of us are outgoing by nature. We want that social contact, either by phone or in person. Well, everything in moderation, as they say. If you rationalize overly long conversations with the thought that clients and their advisors need to be schmoozed at every opportunity, you just may be creating excuses to avoid priority work. What clients and others usually need to develop trust in you isn't lengthy phone calls, but brief, timely responses – by phone or email – to their questions. Immediate responsiveness, not time-wasting communications, is the key.

Often, the high priority work that contributes directly to our success is work that requires blocks of time. We all know what it's like to land a new client, receive his or her data, analyze it before formulating recommendations, and then get sidetracked by another project. If we don't get back to that work for a couple of days, we will probably have replaced all the information that was firmly lodged in our short-term memory with different data. That means we'll waste time reviewing data we already analyzed once.

One of the most critical time management techniques you can employ is that of creating blocks of time in every chaotic day when you can minimize interruptions and maximize your attention to high-priority activities. Make an honest assessment of just how important each of those competing tasks are that keep you from stringing together 180 or 240 consecutive minutes to accomplish something really important. It might be examining a new client's documentation, preparing a speech, or writing an article for publication in a professional journal.

If those other little tasks are nagging at you as you try to confine yourself to one long task, get over it. Most entrepreneurs are guilty of underestimating the difficulty or length of time it will take to complete a project, failing to take into account the daily unanticipated emergency, or simply scheduling more than they have time to accomplish in a day. You're not going to get to everything on your schedule no matter how you structure your time. Despite your greatest fears, these tasks won't get lost completely, anyway, thanks to digital calendars and schedulers. Any good "to-do list" product will enable you to put all of your to-do lists in one place (another essential time management lesson) and assign a priority to every task. Having done this, you will change priorities and shuffle tasks around as necessary until everything gets done in its proper time.

Another key to time management – one that may be familiar to you even if you don't practice it – is to review your calendar first thing each morning before doing any work. Realistically prioritize everything on your list, with special attention to those tasks that add the most value to client services and/or give you the greatest enjoyment (assuming the "real work" is getting done by somebody else in your firm).

Having established your priorities, decide when you want to do the high-priority work. If you're a "morning person," for example, then schedule your three- to four-hour time block in the morning. Don't make the mistake of scheduling your critical time to coincide with that period of the day when your energy is low. (For many, that time is immediately following lunch.)

If you are a sole practitioner, the more you try to wear all of the necessary "hats," the more critical this chapter will be for you because of the sheer multitude and variety of tasks you're responsible for, including but not limited to:

- Servicing broken computers;
- Approving payables;
- Trying out new software;
- Conducting meetings; and
- Taking phone calls from clients, associates, wannabe financial planners, would-be clients, friends, family members, doctors' offices, vendors, charitable organizations, brokers, wrong numbers, and (in spite of the perfect firewall and junk mail filter) deleting spam and checking to see if anything important ended up being blocked and shunted to your spam filter file.

Undoubtedly everything on the above list must eventually be attended to. And, at first, most of these tasks will seem urgent, maybe reaching crisis proportions on occasion. But practice putting them aside. Reflect on each new day in which you've managed to insert a block of productive time. By the end of the day, did you really regret having put off until tomorrow a lower-priority task? Hopefully you'll feel more satisfied because you accomplished more of the things you consider truly important. Wake up each day and immediately write down the three most important things you must accomplish.

TIME WASTERS

Now that we've looked at the things you *should* be doing, let's focus on ways in which you may be wasting your time – just in case you're not clear on the concept. The importance of technology to time management efficiency was mentioned early in this chapter. Many of the following items allude to technology you should be using if you want to maximize your time management effectiveness:

#1 : Going to the "File Cabinet"

Ideally, you won't have any file cabinets other than the 12" x 21" file drawer that comes with your desk. Do your filing on electronic media. Scan (better yet, have a secretary or an associate scan) all of the paper that enters your office, whether it be client tax returns, estate planning documents, SEC records, trade orders ... everything. However, choose carefully the software you use to archive the graphic files that result from these scans because a poor choice can make these files as hard to find as if they were on paper. (See Chapter 33 for recommendations.)

By creating a relatively paperless office, you'll save time three different ways. First, you will eliminate the time it takes to walk to the file cabinet and/or figure out on which employee's desk the file you want is sitting. Second, you will be able to find random information quickly with digital searches rather than the manual searching that goes on within an open file cabinet drawer. And, perhaps most important, you will be able to respond to client questions without having to call the client back since the information you need will be at your fingertips.

#2: Using the Wrong Client Contact Management System

Why do you choose a particular contact management system? You need a database to store client contact information, as well as letters, notes and other text-based communications that flow into and out of your office each day. Therefore, most people focus on the "architecture" of a contact manager when choosing a database ... that is, how well will it organize all of my important data? If it has a built-in word processor, how will the documents it creates co-exist with documents I've already created with my existing word processing software? Will the workflow systems hard-coded into the database approximate the systems I've already created, or will they require me to make a major effort adapting my pre-existing systems to the new software?

These considerations are definitely important, but think about this for a minute – systematizing is easy. You could create a simple, effective system of storing client information and tracking work with a spreadsheet if you had to. *Finding and retrieving stuff* is the hard part. You handle thousands of details for hundreds of clients. Having a systematic way of getting it into a contact manager or client relationship management (CRM) system is worthless if you can't get it out quickly, easily, and in a readily usable form.

#3: Keeping More Than One "To-Do" List

Multiple "to do" lists are a cardinal sin, as noted for years by time-management experts. Everything that you need to spend your time on in a typical day should filter into one list. The reason is simple. The one activity you must keep coming back to all during the day is prioritizing. All of the many tasks you're responsible for will bombard you with demands on your time. As every new demand arrives, you need a way to weigh it against all outstanding demands.

Do you have emails from important clients getting stuck for days in an email inbox separate from your to-do list? Are those clients getting angry and demanding more attention or faster response times? If a client's work is that important, you need to have a way to move it to its proper priority the minute it arrives – whether by letter, phone call, or email. In order to do this, you must maintain only one, comprehensive list.

#4: Failing to Edit your Emails

Many readers will have a difficult time understanding how they're supposed to *save* time by going back over what they write and re-reading it. Most people think email is just something for scribbling out short messages they can shoot off without a second thought. Well, think about the last time your sloppy writing caused a miscommunication, and the extra time you wasted straightening it out. Think also about the way you look to clients and others when you send out something unedited, full of typos and poor grammar. Is that really the way you want to represent yourself to the world?

#5: Preparing and Sending Out Marketing Materials (or Having Your Staff Do It)

Use your website for marketing – that's why you installed it. Make it the central repository of all your marketing material. Refer people to your website. Informing new prospective clients is just that simple.

If your prospective client is "Internet-challenged," you'll need to make some exceptions and probably resort to mailing a paper presentation. But most potential clients are coming in the door Internet-ready. Unless you only work with the upper decile of computer phobic individuals, you're probably now seeing this trend.

#6: Failing to Delegate Outside the Confines of Your Office

You let an employee fix the computers that break down in your office because he knows more about technology than anyone else on your staff. Yet, you can't figure out why your network keeps crashing. Hire an expert. Or perhaps you've got a secretary who does her job well but can't fix the printer when it breaks and has to bother somebody whose time shouldn't be spent on these kinds of things. Hire a virtual assistant with his or her own printer. Become aware of the many virtual opportunities that exist to serve you.

If you're guilty of three or more of these time-wasters, you need to take a hard look at your personal productivity. Time management is a lot like financial planning. You have to start out with a close look at where your time goes. Then think about what's best for you ... how you should be spending your time to achieve the success you want. Finally, develop a plan to get from here to there by creating blocks of time, while identifying and controlling time-wasters.

WHERE CAN I FIND OUT MORE ABOUT IT?

1. Peter Drucker, *The Effective Executive Revised* (New York, NY: HarperBusiness, 2002).

2. Julie Morgenstern, *Time Management from the Inside Out: The Foolproof System for Taking Control of Your Schedule – and Your Life*, 2nd ed. (New York, NY: Henry Holt/Owl Books, 2004).

3. Alan Lakein, *How to Get Control of Your Time and Your Life*, reissue ed. (New York, NY: Signet Books, 1996).

4. Daniel Evans, *How to Build and Manage an Estates Practice* (Chicago, IL: American Bar Association, 1999).

CONTACT MANAGERS, ALSO KNOWN AS CLIENT RELATIONSHIP MANAGEMENT (CRM) SOFTWARE

One of the greatest challenges advisors face is selecting an appropriate CRM package. Features vary widely from program to program, as do prices. General purpose products that may suit your needs are available, as are specialized programs designed solely for the financial planning professional. A CRM package selected wisely and used religiously will have a positive effect on your personal time management.

In Chapter 31, we will look at a number of specific products that advisors have used successfully to transform their practices, and we'll tell you how to select the right CRM software for you.

Chapter 7

MARKETING

In Chapter 8, we will talk about developing a target market. But first, you need an overview of marketing strategies.

What is marketing? At its essence, it's getting your name out there and letting people know who you are, what you do, and how good you are. Ultimately, it's telling your story to your target market.

But let's start at the beginning. How do you get your name out there? The uninitiated usually think first of advertising as the best way to do this, and perhaps this method works well if you're selling cars. But remember, yours is a personal service business. It's not doing nails, or walking dogs – its handling people's money. Think about it ...your form of marketing must begin the process of instilling familiarity and trust in your prospective clients because what you want to do for them taps into the most personal of services – discussing with them the plans and dreams they have for their money and wealth.

The ways in which you get your name out to your target market will depend on your business model and whether yours will be a high volume or low volume business. Although it's not really a black and white issue, we'll treat it that way to make a point. A typical high volume business would be that of a wirehouse representative or an independent broker/dealer representative, both of whom primarily earn commissions, but neither of whom do a lot of sophisticated financial planning. The target market for these advisors (or "financial consultants" as they're sometimes called) is very broad. Therefore, a shotgun approach generally works well for these folks.

DIRECT MAIL AND SEMINARS

The most popular high volume marketing strategies are direct mail and seminars. Direct mail is essentially a numbers game. You buy a mailing list, usually arranged by zip code, which allows you to target geographic areas by socioeconomic characteristics. Then you mail your marketing materials "to whom it may concern." This might be the method by which you advertise and get prospective clients to attend your seminar. Or these materials may promote products you want to sell because their financial rewards suit you.

The seminar is a lower-numbers, but higher-touch process. Conducting a seminar on planning strategies such as 529 college savings plans or 401(k) retirement plans, which emphasize the use of products you sell, gives you the opportunity to show your face to a crowd. If you have or can learn good speaking skills and develop rapport with your audience quickly, a seminar will put you in front of people who may call you afterward for an appointment and, eventually, open an account with you.

Another way to do this with less product emphasis and somewhat more credibility is to teach adult education or (open) university classes on financial planning. There's less opportunity to sell products, but more opportunity to show your prospective clients (students) how astute and professional you are. This is part of trust building, although a smaller part than most people think. The bigger part of trust building, however, is listening, so if you structure your class or your seminar for lots of interaction, you can demonstrate your listening skills as well as your ability to truly help people.

Will direct mail and seminars work for attracting high net worth clients—the ones usually sought by those with low volume business models and a handful of experienced, fee-based broker/dealer reps? In this author's opinion, no. Putting myself in the prospective client's shoes, if I'm earning a six-figure income and I have $1,000,000 of investable assets, it's not likely I'm going to open your direct mail piece. Instead, it's going to land in the trash faster than week-old leftovers.

Seminars can work if you already have high net worth clients and can entice them to bring their friends to your seminar. Many experienced advisors have used this strategy with success. The venue doesn't have to be a seminar, though; it could also be a party or a dinner.

THIRD PARTY ENDORSEMENTS

But if high net worth clients are what you're primarily after, other marketing approaches will work better than direct mail and seminars. The key to handling wealth is that it involves not only trust, but also risk. Prospective clients have read about smart, successful people who have lost their money to unscrupulous brokers or peddlers of alternative investment products that usually sound too good to be true. They want to be able to immediately trust you at a very high level, one where the risk that you'll betray that trust is all but totally avoided. And the best way to overcome the perception of risk is to have a third-party endorsement from a reputable source. With direct mail, seminars, and advertisements, the advisor toots his own horn. And while he may be very good at doing it, and very convincing, too, it's still not the same as having a third-party endorsement.

Once you understand this, you'll probably gravitate to a different channel for new clients. You'll look for third-party endorsements from existing clients and other professionals with whom you do not compete. You won't get large numbers of clients from these sources, but you don't *want* large numbers. You're like the United States Marines ... you're just "looking for a few good men [and women]." If you can get a valued client to say good things about you to his high net worth friends, the recommendation will carry weight. These prospective clients are "pre-qualified" – in other words, they've been told from someone who has experienced your advisory service what you can do for them and that you're trustworthy. You don't need to spend as much time with these individuals explaining your service; they often come in wanting it. They may ask "when can we get started" before you've had a chance to give them your usual introductory talk.

Referrals from Existing Clients

Yet, asking for referrals from existing clients is a bit trickier when they're high net worth clients. You can't offer these clients a free dinner at Outback Steak House for every new client they send you. They are breaching their own confidentiality and taking a risk by recommending you. Many clients don't want even their closest friends to know they work with a financial advisor. This is particularly true of the "Millionaire Next Door" client – that is, the one who still occupies his very modest starter home and drives a Chevrolet, but has several million dollars in the bank.[1] These folks tend to be very secretive about their money and still believe it's in poor taste or not prudent to discuss such matters with friends and, for that matter, relatives.

Experienced advisors have their favorite methods for approaching these clients to ask for referrals, but suffice it to say that your approach should be low-key. When meeting in person with these clients – and only after you've been together for a year or more, and have no doubt you've earned their trust – you might discreetly say at the end of a meeting something to the effect of "we are taking new clients if you know of someone who you believe would benefit from our services," and leave it at that. Some advisors do the same thing in their client newsletter so that all clients receive this friendly, low-key reminder each month or each quarter.

Referrals from Other Professionals

Getting referrals from other professionals isn't quite as sensitive a process as soliciting referrals from high net worth clients. That's because it's a *quid pro quo*. If you're both true professionals serving a similar market, you'll welcome the opportunity to refer clients to each other for two reasons. First, you'll become a valued resource for the other professional (e.g., an attorney or accountant). If you've won this person's trust, you can make him look good, and vice versa. Second, the "cross-marketing" that can occur between the two of you will ultimately earn both of you new income.

So how do you approach these professionals? Most advisors will look for places where such professionals congregate. A good example is your local estate planning council (assuming you live in a city large enough to have such a group). An estate planning council will typically have estate planning attorneys, CPAs, trust officers, life insurance agents, and financial planners as members. They usually meet once a month over dinner, perhaps listen to a speaker, and spend lots of time networking.

Joining such organizations and attending their meetings can be an effective marketing strategy, but advisors often overlook an even easier one: networking with your clients' own professionals. Many clients already have trusted attorneys, accountants or other professionals when they become your client. Since a comprehensive planning service requires that you coordinate planning with these folks anyway, it's the perfect opportunity to network with them.

It usually goes something like this: new clients Mr. and Mrs. Johnson give you their financial information, divulging the identities of the other professionals with whom they work, and their permission to contact those persons. You call the Johnson's CPA, Arthur Young, introduce yourself, and explain how you see your work coordinating with his. It's a good idea to assuage any fears he might have about your invading his "turf" by letting him know that what you do will complement his role in helping the Johnsons. As you work through the planning process, you have one or more opportunities to contact Mr. Young. At some point in the process, you suggest that the two of you get together for lunch. At that luncheon, it will be assumed that its purpose is to allow each of you to tell the other about what you do, in general, for all of your clients. A successful cross-referral relationship will often develop from such a process. And because you've worked together and demonstrated your process to each other, referrals will be at least partially pre-qualified.

There are two possible problems with this system. While it worked well during the 1980s and even during the 1990s, more than a few professionals today are in MDPs (multi-disciplinary practices) and, therefore, want to compete, rather than collaborate, with financial advisors. And others want referral fees, whereas a decade ago, they would have settled for a non-financial, cross-referral relationship. So know whom you're dealing with. It will be difficult to hold yourself out as a true professional if you pay for referrals, something that *must* be disclosed to those prospects.

Referrals Resulting from Media Contacts

The third source of new clients that come with a third-party endorsement is clients who contact you after having read about you, or having read something you wrote in the press. Keep in mind, though, that working with the media takes time. Media contacts must be cultivated and sustained.

You probably know other advisors who are sought out by the media (i.e., the financial planning press or consumer financial publications) for comments on stories being written. Tell those advisors what your specialties are and how you would like to contribute to media stories. If they are called for input to a story in one of your areas of expertise, request that they direct the press person your way, too, so you can get some exposure.

You can also cultivate media relationships by regularly supplying them with story ideas. Two ways to do this are through your newsletter and by direct contact. In addition to client and professional lists of persons to whom you should send your monthly (or quarterly) newsletter, make up a press list as well. Include people whose columns you read in financial periodicals and newspapers. Have them receive your newsletter, which may give them story ideas as well as information on reaching you for comment. However, a word of caution ... if you used a "canned" newsletter (i.e., one produced by a newsletter service), the stories will tend to be generic and probably not of interest to the media because the topics will be commonplace and probably have already been covered. If you write your own newsletter – the best kind of newsletter – you can create original story ideas that will be of greater appeal to the media.

Not a writer, you say? No problem. You can find writers who will write the newsletter for you. You just need to come up with the concepts and details of your stories. Or perhaps you write a first draft and hire an editor or local reporter or English teacher to polish it up. Either way, don't forgo a newsletter simply because you don't fancy yourself a writer; an original newsletter can be a powerful marketing device.

The other way to get in front of the press is to feed specific story ideas to specific writers. Get the email address of several of the writers who write on subjects of interest to you. Hopefully, you will recognize new angles to those subjects that no one is writing about. Email those ideas to the writers on your list. This can be of great help to them and increases the likelihood they will call you to do a story and seek your input.

Once you are "published" – either an article you authored yourself for a financial planning periodical or an article in which you were quoted – buy reprints or make clean copies and hand these out to prospective clients. Also, upload them to your website as PDF files that can be downloaded and read by individuals fishing around on your site for information. This is the third-party credibility we've been talking about. If a potential client is looking at you and a local competitor and you're pretty equal in all respects except that you've got a third-party endorsement, you should be the one they choose.

Dos and Don'ts of Working with the Media

Having said all of this, there are dos and don'ts when it comes to working with the press. Some of these are this author's opinions and not necessarily the common perceptions of all advisors in the field. I've been on both sides of the table as a writer and as an advisor, and it's that experience from which my comments originate.

When I was new to the financial planning profession, I quickly discovered the power of media exposure. I also discovered that journalists fall into one of two camps. There are those who decide upon a story that will sell (often one that explodes into provocative words in some

140-point font on the front page of a glossy monthly), and they craft all the inputs to the story to meet their premise. Then, there are those who start out with the seed of a story, do their research, conduct their interviews and craft the story based upon what they find out along the way. They aren't particularly interested in which way the story goes, which is to say they have few preconceived notions. They can make the story interesting and valuable regardless of how the facts play out.

You will know you're dealing with the first type when they "guide" you to say the precise words they need to make their conclusion work. It feels a little bit like being a plaintiff whose attorney is guiding him through his testimony in court. Your conversation with the second type of journalist, however, will feel like a friendly discussion, with you responding to lots of open-ended questions. You will feel more relaxed and therefore more quotable.

My advice to you is to figure out whom you're dealing with and how you want to respond. The second type of journalist isn't a problem, but you will someday participate in an interview with the first type in which the premise of his story doesn't agree with your experience. In fact, it might even seem dishonest and irresponsible to you to let yourself be guided in the conversational direction he wants you to go. So don't. Speak your mind. What you say will probably get axed, but you will retain your integrity. If it gets printed and you aren't misquoted, then you will have performed a service to the readership and perhaps have caused the reporter to back off from a sensational story with little basis in reality. If what you say is used and you are misquoted, demand a retraction or at least fire off a letter to the editor. Follow up to make sure it's acknowledged.

Which is to say, don't take for granted what I was told about working with the press when I started out as a financial advisor. The "experts" on such things said:

> "The press rules."
>
> "The press can make you or break you."
>
> "Be in awe of the press."
>
> "Give it what it wants, even if its demands seem excessive at times."

This mandate led me into numerous interactions that frequently left me feeling disappointed. The one that changed my attitude forever involved *Money* magazine. During President Clinton's administration, a *Money* reporter called to say the magazine wanted to do a major piece on the finances of key Congressmen using information collected under the Freedom of Information Act. If we accepted the assignment, I (my former partner and most of our staff) would be called upon to devote considerable time to dissecting tax returns and inferring from them the financial management mistakes the victims of this exercise had made.

Including staff time, our office devoted about 40 hours to this project. It never appeared in *Money*. In my naiveté, I had assumed the magazine's representative with whom I was dealing was high enough up in the *Money* pecking order to guarantee us exposure for the work we had performed. Instead, our work product may never have made it even as far as the cutting room floor.

Which leads me to my theory of dealing with the press: be generous, but be careful. It's a good idea to spend a bit of time here and there with journalists, whether or not you are quoted or credited in their articles, to establish your media base. Be helpful to them with story ideas, or just chatting to help them feel sure about an angle they're taking in a story or to get a second opinion (yours) on a story line they may be thinking about.

However, when it comes to big, time-demanding projects, it should be a *quid pro quo*, much like your cross-referral relationship with other professionals. Sure, the reporter you deal with can't give you an ironclad guarantee that your words will appear in print, but I believe he or she should make a good-faith effort, if he uses your time, to find a way to keep you in his story. If he doesn't, I recommend you not waste your time with that person again. If he's representative of his fellow reporters from the same publication, then you're dealing with an entire corporate culture that you might want to avoid in the future. *Money* magazine is on my personal to-be-avoided list.

You'll know when to give a media person another chance and when not to. If you've not worked together before, then consider it a trial run. The reporter doesn't know your exact area of expertise, and you don't know his style, either. It's a prospect meeting of sorts. But, if you worked with this person once before and responded impressively to 60 minutes of questions only to find a one sentence reference to you in his article, *don't* accept it unquestioningly. If you paid good money to a public relations expert to get you in print and that was the best he could do, you wouldn't use his services again, would you? Well, time is money. Dealing with the press is a business transaction and you have a right to a fair deal.

Another service the press may call upon you for is to produce clients. The press likes to use real people in its financial planning stories and will ask to interview your clients. Should you suggest to your clients they be guinea pigs for the press? My opinion is no. Most of the time, there is more to lose than to gain. Clients, particularly wealthier ones, want to preserve the confidentiality of their situations, which they won't be doing if they talk to the press. They may, at best, look at participation in a story as a favor to you and, at worst, frown upon your very request that they participate. Sometimes, clients will be interviewed and then not used in a story, which leads to anger and frustration for both you and the client. All in all, I disagree with this practice and avoid it.

Internet

In addition to all of the above, don't forget the Internet as a marketing tool. As we've said throughout this book, having a website is essential. It gives prospective clients a convenient place to go to find out more about you without any pressure or risk, and it's a much more cost-effective means of getting the word out than having printed up hundreds of expensive, glossy brochures whose contents change from one month to the next.

MARKETING PROFILE: LOU STANASOLOVICH

Most of these lessons are reflected in the marketing program of the most effective marketer I know in the financial planning industry – Lou Stanasolovich, owner of Legend Financial Advisors, Inc. in Pittsburgh, Pennsylvania. Whereas many advisors slow down or stop their marketing efforts once their practice reaches critical mass, Stanasolovich and his team keep up the marketing effort with a system they've refined over the years that I would venture to say is the best in the business.

Unlike most planners who find one or two successful marketing strategies and focus on them exclusively, Stanasolovich markets on multiple fronts, which include:

- Maintaining a voluminous media database;
- Sending out regular press releases;
- Making regular appeals for client referrals;
- Volunteering to provide information and quotes to journalists on assignment;
- Distributing his *Financial Advisory Briefs;*
- Sending mailings to prospects;
- Optimizing search engines for his website;
- Conducting "viral" marketing;
- Advertising;
- Sending out email newsletters;
- Following-up with leads from professional associations; and
- Sponsoring events where his staff is speaking.

To make his ambitious marketing machine work smoothly, Stanasolovich has 11 full-time and six part-time employees plus his eight interns (whom he gets from Duquesne and Robert Morris Universities) attuned to the mechanics of the firm's marketing program. At any given time, he appoints two or three "marketing" interns to learn from himself or Christopher Kail, Legend's Director of Marketing (and a former intern), the specific duties associated with all of the firm's marketing efforts.

Stanasolovich's databases are at the core of the entire strategy. Legend maintains three distinct databases for specific types of mailings. First is an ACT database containing the email addresses of over 2,700 editors, reporters, writers, and other media contacts. Second is the 17,000-name prospect database Legend maintains using CoolerEmail (http://www.cooleremail.com/index.ice) to email a newsletter prospective clients have elected to receive. CoolerEmail tracks recipient activities, telling Legend how many emails were sent, read, bounced, and the number of recipients who may have unsubscribed.

The firm periodically sends to national media personalities their *Financial Advisory Brief*, a printed publication in which the staff can pitch its expertise on current issues. According to Stanasolovich, "the briefs are a great resource for the media which often uses them for future stories in which they may call us for interviews." Legend's third database, which they maintain using Mailloop (http://www.mailloop.com/), is the one used for this purpose.

These three databases are so critical to Legend's various marketing initiatives, that "... our marketing interns spend approximately 1,000 hours per year researching financial print publications and their editorial staff to keep our contacts up-to-date," explains Stanasolovich.

For example, Legend uses its databases to select the names of local media persons to whom it sends news of business expansion plans, grand openings, personnel changes, new service announcements, public appearances, or selection of a staff member for inclusion by a publication on a prestigious list. But press releases aren't "blasted." "We attempt to send them to writers with columns that fit the subject of our press release," says Stanasolovich. He also puts his press releases on his website and in newsletters so they receive maximum exposure.

"Not only do we respond to press requests by writers on assignment," says Stanasolovich, "we also track upcoming stories publications are expected to be working on, something made possible by our knowledge of their editorial calendars." (I can attest that I have been contacted by Legend almost every time I've asked for help on a story through NAPFA or the CFP Board's media relations departments, and I occasionally receive from them article ideas, something that is very helpful to writers.)

Most planners keep their eyes open for special interest articles that match certain clients' unique circumstances. Sending such an article to a client is an effective way of letting your client know that you're always thinking about her individual needs. But how many advisors do this with prospective clients? "I determine what kind of articles would be generally newsworthy to, say, possible clients we've seen in the last six months, and we mail them out," says Stanasolovich. For example, his prospects recently received an article on interest rate trends by Bill Gross (Chief Investment Officer of PIMCO) that was applicable to the vast majority of them.

Legend also gets more out of its website than the average advisory firm. First, they mine it for as much information as it can yield. "We purchased "Weblog Analyzer" (Webtrend.com), which tells us how many first-time visitors have come to our website, the total number of visitors, the number of hits per particular page, multiple visits, etc. We're finding we get between 1,200 and 2,000 visitors per month," says Stanasolovich. And it's this traffic flow as much or more than anything else that accounts for Legend's Web-based marketing success. Last year, $102,000 in new revenues could be traced to new client activity originating from Legend's website. So far this year, $61,000 in new revenues has come from the website.

Of course, the trick is search engine placement. Do you keep deleting all of the spam you get from outfits wanting to improve your search engine results (in other words, how close your website is to the top of the Google list when someone searches on "financial advisor")? Maybe you'll think twice knowing that this tool is largely responsible for Legend's superior website traffic and consequent new client sign-ups. Legend continuously tracks its keyword rankings on search engines, i.e., Yahoo, Google, MSN, AOL, Lycos, AskJeeves, and Altavista.

Has Stanasolovich tried more traditional marketing strategies, like advertising? "We did," he replies. "It was a complete failure. We spent many thousands of dollars advertising on the fourth largest radio station in Pittsburgh, which is geared specifically to our target market. We announced that we were on the *Worth* list, *Mutual Fund* magazine's Top 100 Advisors list, and that we're fee-only. We received two calls in one year from the ads."

So what is the sum total of all of Stanasolovich's marketing efforts? In 2002, Legend achieved 231 interviews by print and online media sources along with eight radio and 13 television appearances by Stanasolovich or his staff. These led to 83 appointments and 40 new clients. In 2003, the firm was on track to show similar numbers and revenues, revenues already being up 30% over last year (Legend charges retainer fees so this increase represents revenues from new business).

It could be said that it takes a larger firm like Legend to employ enough people to carry out all of these marketing strategies and handle all of the subsequent new client traffic. But, whatever size your firm is, you can probably find or borrow a few ideas from Stanasolovich and his team that you can scale to your own business.

WHERE CAN I FIND OUT MORE ABOUT IT?

1. Martin Baird, *The Seven Deadly Sins of Advisor Marketing* (MartinBaird.com).

2. Harry Beckwith, *Selling the Invisible: A Field Guide to Modern Marketing* (New York, NY: Warner Books, 2004).

3. Harry Beckwith, *The Invisible Touch* (New York, NY: Warner Books, 2000).

4. Jeffrey Fox, *How to Become a Rainmaker: The Rules for Getting and Keeping Customers and Clients* (New York, NY: Hyperion, 2000).

5. Michael E. Gerber, *The E-Myth Revisited: Why Most Small Businesses Don't Work and What to Do About It* (New York, NY: HarperBusiness, 1995).

6. Oren Hariri, *Leapfrogging the Competition: Five Giant Steps to Becoming a Market Leader* (Rocklin, CA: Prima Lifestyles, 1999).

7. Daniel Kennedy, *The Ultimate Marketing Plan: Find Your Most Promotable Competitive Edge, Turn It into a Powerful Marketing Message, and Deliver It to the Right Prospects* (Holbrook, MA: Adams Media Corporation, 2000).

8. Philip Kotler, *Kotler on Marketing* (New York, NY: Free Press, 1999).

9. Stephan R. Leimberg, *The 6 Magic Steps of Power Marketing* (Cassette tape and outline) (www.Leimberg.com; 610-924-0515).

10. Michael Lovas, Beyond *Wave Marketing: How to Add Credibility to Your Relationship Marketing Program* (Credibility Marketing Press, 1998).

11. Peter Montoya and Tim Vandehey, *The Brand Called You: The Ultimate Brand-Building and Business Development Handbook to Transform Anyone into an Indispensable Personal Brand* (Peter Montoya, 2003).

12. Al Ries and Laura Ries, *The 22 Immutable Laws of Branding: How to Build a Product or Service into a World-Class Brand* (New York, NY: HarperCollins Publishers, 1999).

CHAPTER ENDNOTES

1. Thomas Stanley, Ph.D. and William D. Danko, *The Millionaire Next Door: Surprising Secrets of America's Wealthy* (New York, NY: Simon & Schuster, 1996).

Chapter 8

DEVELOPING A TARGET MARKET

When we say "target market," we mean a clientele or client type. In other words, developing a target market means having a plan to deliberately target or attract the clientele you want to work with. Such a plan will lead you quickly down the path of building an efficient practice, while working with clients who are more likely to bring you satisfaction rather than headaches.

What does "efficiency" have to do with target marketing? That's simple. To the extent that you can serve a niche, you can focus your internal office systems, planning software, continuing education, and other aspects of operating your practice and updating your skills on one market. All financial advisors are generalists in that they must know a lot about the six core areas of financial planning. But the general can still be narrowed down considerably by serving a target market.

Establishing a target market will come naturally to some, and only through repetitive trial and error for others. Some new advisors transition into the advisory profession from the ranks of the clients they will target (e.g., airline pilots, engineers, or teachers). Others may no longer care to work with clients that remind them of their former bosses or co-workers. Perhaps you've had about as much of the executive suite as you can stand; now you'd rather work with small businesspersons or Gen-Xers.

Sometimes occupational groups start out as the focus of our marketing efforts, but we later shift that emphasis to specific personality types. We find out it's not engineers we're attracted to *per se*, but that we enjoy working with clients who are very precise in their thinking, and who can look at a table of figures as an aid, rather than a hindrance, to understanding. Or, perhaps it's not teachers that are attractive as clients, but young, single women because the planner, herself, is young and single.

However, some of us didn't formerly work with *any* particular type of person that we would care to serve in a client capacity. In other words, some of you starting out in the financial advisory world won't have the slightest idea whom you want to work with. Even if you do have a clue, you probably won't turn away those persons falling outside your target market because you'll need the income. Perhaps only after you've worked with a hundred or so different clients (i.e., the trial and error approach) will you have a good feel for the type of client you want to target.

CRITERIA FOR DEVELOPING A TARGET MARKET

Can we be more scientific about target marketing? Let's explore the steps involved in developing our preferred market. First, recognize target marketing as the process of defining one or more types of persons you want to work with and developing effective ways to seek out and convert those persons into clients. When we think about our "best" or "ideal" clients, we can generally distinguish them from other clients on the basis of five criteria:

1. Age/Life Cycle;
2. Occupation/Employer;
3. Personality;
4. Value; and
5. Wealth.

Age is an indicator of life cycle. Many planners feel most comfortable working with clients their own age – persons making life transitions similar to themselves. Many of us have the capacity to work with older clients, though, because we have parents and we understand their needs. In fact, if you're a member of the "sandwich generation" (i.e., your parents are living and you have pre-college-age kids of your own), you can probably relate well to clients of almost any age. Just ask yourself what ages or points on the life cycle you enjoy the most.

Personality is important to most of us in distinguishing the types of clients we care to work with. For those who come from sales backgrounds, all personalities may represent a challenge. For most of us, though, we know immediately if we are compatible with a prospect on the basis of personality. There are personality traits we specifically like and dislike. Perhaps the traits we least like are those we sometimes find in ourselves and can't accept. Nonetheless, while we can't expect to enjoy every facet of our clients' personalities, we can eventually learn to identify in the prospect meeting those with whom we are clearly incompatible and to refer them on to someone else if we can afford to. Or we can transition them to a staff planner or another principal within our own firm.

Occupation, or in some cases, one's employer, will be a distinguishing factor for some advisors. As mentioned earlier, it may be more of a personality trait that attracts us to a particular clientele than an occupation even though the two appear to overlap at times. When occupation or employer *does* play a role, though, it can be a commanding one. For example, Washington, D.C.-area planners often work with federal government employees. By concentrating on this group, they can "economize" by learning one set of benefit plans rather than different plans for each and every client they accept.

Values are possibly the most critical item on the list. If your client's values substantially contradict your own, then you will either not be able to work with that person, or will have to charge a high enough fee to make it all worthwhile. For example, if you're someone who is satisfied with a modest home and who doesn't like to get rid of a car if it's still running, you might have a lot of trouble working with someone your age who buys palatial homes and luxury cars they will trade in within two years. In these kinds of situations, an advisor may find it easier to work with someone of a different generation than himself. For example, clients who grew up during the Depression usually have very different – and often refreshingly sober – attitudes towards money and spending.

Wealth, the final criterion, can be very useful in targeting clients. Clients of different economic statuses tend to have financial issues that readily correlate with their level of wealth. For example, the federal estate tax laws, with ever-changing unified credit amounts and on-again/off-again estate tax repeals, demand the use of specialized trusts with clients of higher wealth, but simpler treatments for less wealthy clients. The same applies for the Internal Revenue Code and its application to clients of varying income levels. By targeting clients of a specific wealth/income level, you can pinpoint those planning areas and related tax regulations on which you will need to focus.

Of course, you might also select clients based upon your own wealth orientation. Advisors with middle-class upbringings often prefer to work with less wealthy clients, while advisors accustomed to wealth better understand more affluent clients' attitudes towards wealth and feel more comfortable with their associated lifestyles.

SIZING UP PROSPECTIVE CLIENTS

Let's combine all five criteria and profile several clients to see if they fit the target market you're contemplating serving. First, let's say you practice what you preach to your clients. That is, you save diligently for your own future financial independence and your kids' educations. You live comfortably but not lavishly.

A high-income prospect your own age approaches you for help. Actually, he doesn't call you – his wife does. She takes care of the kids in their $400,000 / $600,000 / $1,000,000 (pick one) home while he does doctor / lawyer / executive-type things twelve or more hours a day. She has this sense that while they live very well, they're not really planning for their future. They pay for their children's private school costs out of the husband's current income. When it gets right down to it, though, the only investments they have are his pension plan and their vacation home.

He agrees they should be doing more than they're currently doing. In fact, when he comes in for your initial interview, you find out he's full of investment ideas. He lets you know that growth stocks are the place to be, but that internationals are out. He also spends a half hour talking about his corporate conquests since you (so astutely, you thought) asked him and his wife some open-ended questions to find out more about their planning objectives.

Contrast this client with the 60-year old who is at the end of his or her career. This prospect may have had many business conquests, or he may have paid the price of mediocrity to reap the reward of security. But that doesn't matter, because now this couple has a retirement bundle, grandchildren they love, reasonably good health, and whatever dreams they haven't yet pursued. They know what they don't know about investing, no matter how much or how little of it they've done on their own. They live in a modest home and have simple tastes. And they're pleasant to talk with, the kind of people with whom you will begin to chat about personal topics early on in your relationship.

These are extreme examples of prospective clients who you will need to size up *vis-à-vis* the market you want to serve. You will be able to characterize some prospective clients in your initial meeting as falling directly or partially inside your target market. Below that is the "gray area" where you will have to make your best guess and either accept or pass on the prospect.

PLANNER PROFILES

What do some of our industry's more highly publicized advisors say or demonstrate about the target markets they've chosen? Sheryl Garrett, an advisor since 1987 and presently the founder and owner of the Garrett Planning Network in Shawnee Mission, Kansas, will work with nearly anyone. That's not because she hasn't defined her target market, but because she's defined it seemingly outside the limits of our five criteria.

Garrett designed a business model that permits an advisor to consult with clients by charging an hourly fee. While working as a staff planner at a local firm serving high net worth clients, she discovered that she would rather handle simpler planning issues for clients who don't need asset management. While mostly middle-income clients gravitate to Garrett's hourly fee structure, she occasionally does planning for high net worth clients as well – those not looking for a permanent advisor but, rather, a second opinion. So, while Garrett's target market appears at first to be different than others because of her hourly fees, it's more a case of her wanting to serve less wealthy clients and having developed a business model that permits her to do that while still earning a suitable living.

Bob Keats, a principal in Keats, Connelly and Associates, Inc. in Phoenix, Arizona, works primarily with Canadian clients. This is a natural for Keats since he's a dual citizen of Canada and the United States. As such, he holds both the CERTIFIED FINANCIAL PLANNER™ (Canada) and CERTIFIED FINANCIAL PLANNER™ (United States) professional designations.

As we've discussed, not all planners are as deliberate as Keats in their choice of a target clientele. Bob Willard, owner of Willard & Co. in Colorado Springs, Colorado, works with ophthalmologists. With a military background and a Midwest upbringing, Willard had no particular attraction to eye doctors, but his first major client was one. Fashioning himself as a "financial bodyguard" – a planner who played a role in all of his ophthalmologist's business deals – Willard became known for his proactive advisory style and was subsequently hired by other ophthalmologists. Now, it's his practice specialty.

HOW TO TARGET CLIENTS AND PROFESSIONALS

Okay, so now that you've figured out what types of clients you want to target, how do you do the targeting part? Actually, it's really just highly focused and applied common sense. Figure out where these prospective clients hang out, what they read, and to whom they already go to for help. For example, if you're targeting a profession, there's probably a professional association they belong to. Find out what that association is and what opportunities might exist for speaking to its members at regular gatherings or periodic conferences.

If there are one or more trade publications that appeal to your target clients, write an article for publication or at least get quoted by one of the publication's staff writers or regular freelance writers. Sending story ideas to a writer will usually get his or her attention. Or just try sending an email introducing yourself and your expertise so that that writer might call on you the next time he needs a source for an article.

There are probably other professionals (CPAs, attorneys, etc.) your target clients go to for help, aside from the kind of help you want to give them. Find out who those people are and introduce yourself to them. Other professionals can be an excellent referral source if they think you can make them look good in front of their clients. Let them know you can provide complementary expertise that will allow you both to do a better job for those clients you hope to work with together (either the other professional's existing clients or clients you expect to meet down the road).

As the advisors in our earlier examples have done, try thinking about those clients you like best and what they have in common in terms of age, occupation, personality, value systems, and wealth. Finding a common thread and following it to a target clientele will enable you to focus your work energy and enjoy more satisfying client relationships.

WHERE CAN I FIND OUT MORE ABOUT IT?

1. Thomas Stanley, *Marketing to the Affluent* (New York, NY: McGraw-Hill Trade, 1997).

2. Steve Moeller, *Effort-Less Marketing for Financial Advisors* (Tustin, CA: American Business Visions, 1999).

Chapter 9

QUALIFYING A PROSPECTIVE CLIENT / CONDUCTING A CLIENT-MAKING MEETING

QUALIFYING THE PROSPECTIVE CLIENT

To those new in business, qualifying the prospective client may be a foreign concept. Perhaps, desperate to pay this month's mortgage and other bills, you're in the "I'll take as a client anyone who fogs a mirror" phase of your practice development. This phase, and your attitude towards prospective clients, may be one of the great Catch-22s of the advisory profession. It really comes down to receiving "bad" revenues now or "good" revenues later.

How could income be "bad" or "good"? Here's the deal: taking every prospective client that comes along will bring in revenue, which most practitioners sorely need in their startup phase. However, that also means you're probably not fine-tuning your target market to the extent that you should be (see Chapter 8, Developing a Target Market). Basically, you're fishing with a mile-long net rather than with a line and a hook. This is not ideal because you'll end up with a hodgepodge of clients – a client base you will need to "prune" several years down the road if you're to re-establish efficiency. How did efficiency enter the discussion so soon? Because serving lots of different types of clients is inefficient – or more accurately, serving both clients with simple *and* complex needs is inefficient.

And this is what tends to happen in a new practice. The new planner is often young (with little or no gray hair) and he often works with clients like himself. After he's been in business a few years, he gains confidence and starts working with clients who have more complicated needs (and he's *definitely* got some gray hair by then). The first tier of clients he takes probably won't meet his minimum fee several years down the road (unless the planner is targeting the middle market; see Chapter 8).[1] But the advisor will keep them on as clients anyway because they trusted him and agreed to work with him when he was new in the business. This type of client loyalty and sentiment is laudable, but not particularly profitable.

We're not advocating you fire these clients. Instead, we're recommending you not take them in the first place. The earlier you figure out exactly what your target market will be, and gear all of your efforts to picking up clients representative of that particular market, the more efficient you'll be because you'll be designing your internal systems to meet a narrower purpose. Hence, your systems can be kept simpler and, therefore, more cost-effective.

So, "bad" revenues are the fees you earn early on by taking all comers, some of whom you may come to resent some day. "Good" revenues are the revenues that come later in the game from your targeted clients. They take longer to attract, but they're clients you'll want to keep for as long as they'll have you as their advisor.

With these lessons in mind, let's talk about the process of actually qualifying the prospective client. One thing you'll learn quickly is that your best chance of landing your new client happens when you're sitting face to face with him or her. You may or may not sell financial products, but you definitely must sell yourself, and you're well aware of this truth. When you get in front of a prospective client, you're typically at your best – your demeanor is engaging, you're actively listening and occasionally demonstrating your expertise, and, most important, you're building the rapport that is the beginning of the trust necessary to win and retain this client for a very long time.

Therefore, your tendency will be to meet as many prospective clients as you can so as to boost the probability of "closing" them. This is another example of those seemingly innocuous mistakes advisors often make early in their careers because those advisors don't have that much to do and they believe their time isn't nearly as valuable as it will be later in their career. So you schedule meetings with lots of warm bodies and do your qualifying right there in the meeting. Perhaps you spend an hour or an hour and a half talking to each prospective client, only to find out that about half of them (or far fewer if you're targeting properly) qualify for your services.

Why wouldn't they qualify? Well, they're either too big, too small, too complicated, not complicated enough, too demanding, too dependent, or you simply don't think you can get along with them over the long run. The point is that you should invest valuable time finding this out. You may think you have a lot of time on your hands, but you really don't. You should be spending the time you're not using to work on client plans early in your career on marketing, creating the best possible internal operating systems, and other "foundational" activities.

So what's the answer? The answer is to become an expert conversationalist – by phone, that is. When the prospective client calls for the first time, be glad to give them five, ten, or fifteen minutes being as helpful as you can be. As soon as you determine they are right for your practice, proceed directly to the only goal that makes sense – getting them in the door. Once you know they fit your "ideal client" profile, schedule that appointment.

At this stage, some planners take additional steps that are (and probably always will be) the subject of great debate. In an effort to qualify the prospective client (we use the term "prospective client" rather than "prospect" deliberately; prospective client humanizes and gives dignity and individuality to the person we want as our client, whereas "prospect" is all too often the object at the other end of a dart) even further, they require him to take some kind of additional step before the meeting, such as completing some type of paperwork (e.g., the planner's client questionnaire form). A thorough client questionnaire form may be many pages long and require the prospective client to dedicate two or three hours to complete it properly. According to the proponents of this strategy, this lengthy exercise tests the prospective client's resolve. If he can't make time to meet this requirement as a prospective client, then he probably won't do it as a client either. In other words, it's a way of discovering whether the person is one of those hard-to-deal-with clients (see Chapter 11) who think you're going to do everything for them – the type of client who doesn't understand that financial planning is a team effort and that his participation isn't optional.

The other school of thought is that you should not put any roadblocks in the prospective client's way. Instead, you should get him in the door, have him sign your contract, and *then* make life difficult for him. In fact, the planners who prefer this strategy say that the prospective client isn't likely to make a real commitment to the planning process until he's gotten this far, so the "test" the other planners force him to take doesn't yield any useful information anyway. Either way, you should learn to identify the desirable prospective client quickly by phone.

What kinds of questions should you ask the prospective client? In early meetings, it works well to ask a lot of open-ended questions, ones that let the prospective client talk freely, hopefully open up to you, and begin to build rapport.

However, on the telephone, you want to be more focused in your questioning. Otherwise, your prospective client will take as much of your time by phone as she would have done in person. You're going to ask questions like:

> *"Are you looking for a one-time financial plan or an ongoing advisory relationship?"*
>
> *"Why do you feel you need a financial advisor?"*
>
> *"After we've worked together, what outcome would tell you it's been a successful engagement?"*

The first question (and others like it) is one that must be asked to properly qualify the prospective client. If the potential client wants a plan, but you want a long-term relationship, then you have a disconnect. If the prospective client wants hourly advice, and you only take clients needing investment management, you're not going to have a match anyway.

In summary, you should make up a list of questions that *must* be answered in that initial call in order to give you the information you need to reject the person as your client (perhaps suggesting that he or she consult with a fellow professional who may be more appropriate), or alternatively, to invite him or her to your office.

How about the non-ideal prospective client? You'll usually be able to weed that person out in the first few minutes of your phone conversation. He may weed himself out by asking a question right up front such as "what are your fees?" If you're serving the middle market with an hourly rate, as many planners do these days, this won't be a particularly bothersome question, and one you can easily answer. But if you work solely with high net worth clients, this question will tip you off to the great likelihood that this individual may be of modest means and may not have worked with a planner before. Your answer, of course, will be something to the effect of "our fees vary by client depending upon his or her degree of financial complexity." A high net worth client will usually understand and accept that answer, while a middle-income client may feel you're being evasive and end the call soon thereafter.

Fees may not be the deal killer, though. Perhaps the prospective client has $2,000,000 of incentive stock options. Meanwhile, you don't know the difference between an option and deferred compensation plan, much less having helped a high-powered executive develop a plan for *exercising* stock options. You would be right to turn down this type of engagement unless you think you can serve this client by partnering with another planner or professional who has the requisite expertise. On the other hand, if you believe you can handle this assignment, let the prospective client know. It may be that you already have a client who works for the same company as the prospective client, meaning you're already familiar with the employer's benefit plans, including its stock option plan. This can carry great weight in convincing the person you're the best planner for him.

Whatever the outcome, if you must decline a planning engagement don't leave the individual empty-handed. Go out of your way to know other professionals who work in your field. Most likely you will have local planners who work with even more sophisticated clients than your clientele, and others who work solely with lower-income or middle-market clients. You can do a good deed, and establish goodwill, by referring the individual to another advisor who can help. You may also open up a new referral source by doing so. If you take the time to understand what others in your field are doing, they'll usually return the favor, and someday you'll have a new client on your doorstep who comes pre-qualified (that is, if you make very clear to your referral sources exactly what kinds of clients you truly want).

The bottom line is that you should let the telephone become your first line of differentiation and selection. Some may fit your client profile; many won't. And be very careful if you delegate the phone duties to an assistant because the screening function is a critical one. Your assistant must understand as thoroughly as you do the type of client you want and how to take that client from a prospective client call to an in-person meeting with you.

CONDUCTING A CLIENT-MAKING MEETING

Now, you have qualified a prospective client and invited him/her/them to come into your office for a meeting. So what should you do next? As you will see, there is a right way and a wrong way to conduct a client-making meeting. To illustrate how a successful meeting might go, let's dissect one of the author's successful initial sessions from the past.

A prospective client, with whom I ultimately formed a long-term relationship with, first came to me as a referral from a very good client I'd already been working with for approximately eight years. This is significant because there are many types of referral sources, and some are better than others. Ideally, you want a "pre-qualified" prospective client, and this is what you usually get when someone who knows your process very well refers the potential client to you.

Consider the difference between a prospective client who finds you through the Yellow Pages and one who comes referred from a professional with whom you've worked before – or better yet, from an existing client. For example, an estate planning attorney with whom you've collaborated in the past knows a part of your process, such as the way in which you help your clients with their estate planning by taking a team approach. Let's say that when you get to the part of the client's plan requiring estate planning, you first make broad recommendations, and then help the client find an appropriate attorney. You might tell the client he or she needs a bypass trust, a family limited partnership, an advanced medical directive, or some combination of the above. The attorney, someone you've worked with on a number of mutual clients in the past, understands you've made a series of recommendations. So when you and your client enter the attorney's office, that client is pre-qualified *vis-à-vis* that attorney's services. You introduce your client to the attorney, and you all sit down together to plan the client's estate.

When the situation is reversed, and the client has contacted the attorney first, the attorney subsequently refers the client to you by telling him why he needs your financial planning services (to the extent the attorney understands your services). The attorney knows your role as a member of the client's estate planning team best, but he may not be as familiar with your role as the client's trusted – and hopefully most central – advisor. Nevertheless, that is a good start.

An even better start takes place when the referring person knows the entire scope of your services as well as an existing client does. By contrast, a prospective client that comes to you from the Yellow Pages knows only what he's read in the phone book. If your ad is fairly descriptive, the individual might know how you charge for your services, whether you represent a broker/dealer or whether you are an independent planner, and where you are located. Other than those things, though, you must spend much more time acquainting that person with your services than you would if he'd been referred by another professional or by a client.

In my case, the prospect was "prepped" by my client of eight years, so she had at least a passing acquaintance with my methods and, more important, with the nature of my services. She wasn't coming in for a financial plan, *per se*, but for a relationship. And that's a very important understanding for the prospective client to have, whether he or she gains that understanding from your referral source, or from the explanation she received from you in a phone call prior to your meeting.

On this occasion, I walked into my conference room to find a mid-seventies-aged woman, slightly nervous, but pleasant in demeanor – in other words, just like most of my existing (targeted) client base at that time which was made up of approximately 50% widows.

It soon became apparent that she had a mental checklist of a dozen or more items that she needed immediate answers to. Forget the private rehearsal you may walk through mentally before meeting a new prospective client. If it includes (1) meet and greet the client, (2) remember to smile, (3) invite him or her to have a seat, (4) offer the client something to drink, and (5) tell him or her about your services – well, you can forget this last item.

In public speaking classes, speakers are taught to find out if the audience is uncomfortable in any way before proceeding to speak. If someone is cold or hungry or has a headache, they're not going to be able to hear you. You must take care of their problem first. This is a bit difficult to do in a room of 100 people. But I've done it in classrooms of 15. Invariably, if I ask whether anyone needs anything before we begin, someone will say, "could we close that window a little bit?"

And so it is with your prospective client. Not only are you *not* going to have the opportunity to do the talking in the beginning of the meeting, it is not wise to do so anyway. The reasons for this are twofold. First, the potential client needs to take the strain off his or her brain. Those dozen or so questions are creating quite a pressure that needs to be relieved immediately. The prospective client is going to blurt them out faster than you can give answers anyway, so you'd better listen well, and plan to do your talking later. You have to successfully pass this initial test or you will lose this person from the start.

In the case of my prospective client, the questions were not only easy to answer, but welcome, because they gave me a chance to demonstrate expertise, authority, and calmness. They were, primarily, questions about her money – where it was, why it was only paying such and such, how was she supposed to carry out this and that, and so on. Although these are easy questions for you or me, they are world-shaking questions for the unindoctrinated. As I calmly demonstrated that I understood each "problem" and its solution, she gradually relaxed. She started listening better, her speech became less rapid, and other clear body language signaled it was safe to proceed to the next step.

I asked her a series of open-ended questions about her situation:

> *"When had she been widowed?"*
>
> *"What had it been like managing money in her household before her husband's death?"*
>
> *"What was it like now that she was alone?"* (Note that this last question is open-ended enough to elicit a finance-related or non-finance-related response. If she's in anguish over her husband's death, she may need to grieve for a few minutes in your presence before continuing.)

Other questions I felt were important to ask were things such as:

> *"Did she feel she had enough to live on?* (At this point, I'd already looked at the papers she'd brought in and could see she had a total of $1,500,000 spread all over town. But, I wanted to know if *she* knew she had that much money.)
>
> *"What would allow her to relax and enjoy life?"*
>
> *"Who was giving her advice now?"*

This last question elicited a very revealing piece of information. Until this point, my judgment was that this nervous woman was quite intelligent and capable despite her discomfort. She answered the last question by saying all of her relatives were giving her advice (cousins; nephews, etc.). She went on to say she liked taking advice from several of her female cousins, but disliked taking advice from her male cousins. ***"Tell me more,"*** I said. She responded, "My male cousins tell me *'do this ... don't do that.'*" In other words, they were condescending and simplistic in their advice to her.

> *"What was it like handling money with your husband?"*

Much the same, it turned out. Her husband would sit her down every three months or so and force her to look at investment statements and other financial documents. *"When I'm gone, you've got to know this stuff!"* he would say. If she tried to take notes, he would say, *"don't take notes, you'll learn it better if you're forced to remember it!"*

Needless to say, reviewing financial matters just once a quarter (not to mention her husband's attitude) wasn't conducive to any retention at all.

If you're a male, you may have one of two reactions to these stories. Either you're going to feel annoyed with your widow-client and think something along the lines of "well why couldn't you understand this stuff?" or you're going to feel annoyed with these men (possibly of a different generation than yourself) who don't know how to educate another person with a respectful attitude.

If it's the latter feeling you get, then you're in the right place. All you have to do is go with your feelings and you've passed the second test. Your prospective client wants an advisor who can create just the right blend of competence, caring, authority, deference and respect. You probably qualify if you've gotten this far in the meeting.

> *"You mentioned your nephew. How's he involved in things?"*

It turned out her husband, sitting on $1,500,000 and ingrained with a Depression-influenced spending pattern (e.g., reusing plastic twist ties from the produce section of the grocery at least ten times before throwing them out), felt they needed long-term care insurance. The nephew, an insurance agent, played no small part in furthering this belief, but refrained from being the one to actually sell them the insurance. Instead, he referred several of his associates to them.

Next, her husband died. Yet, the insurance agents were still calling the widow. She didn't know long-term care insurance from excess liability coverage, but figured if hubby started it, she'd better not drop the ball. All she needed by the time she came in to see me was someone she could trust to say, *"Let's stop and re-examine this decision. Maybe you don't need to deal with these folks after all"* (the latter being a reference to the agents who were still clamoring for her business even though one-half of the original premium was irretrievably lost upon her husband's death).

At this point in the conversation, the prospective client was so relaxed that she was breathing regularly and encouraging me to talk more. We talked a bit about her money – specifically, where and how it was invested, and which important decisions were imminent. Her money, invested exclusively in CDs, was scattered all over town and she was unaware that because much of it was qualified money, she had important decisions to make, such as: changing account titles and beneficiary designations; accelerating or deferring excise taxes (this was before the tax law change that eliminated excise taxes on qualified money); and so on. However, I didn't need to make all of these decisions for her in our first meeting ... I just needed to make her aware of them, and show her that I could and would help her with these decisions when the time came.

The last test to be passed was to calm her fears about investment risk. Her cousins were not only filling her head with unwanted advice, but also conflicting advice, too. One had said, *"stick with the bank CD's."* The other cousin had taken a flyer in the Twentieth Century Ultra fund with his own money, hadn't bailed out during one of its many severe dips (probably due to mental paralysis), and had hung on to earn an impressive return. Consequently, he was adamant that she should invest the same way he had.

Once the widow was allowed to speak freely, I learned that she didn't want to take any unnecessary risk. But she also didn't want CDs of over $100,000 each at nine different banks in town. Simply reassuring her that she didn't need to take a lot of risk and that we could easily consolidate her funds for simpler management met the requirements of this last test.

Let's say you're the advisor in this situation. You've now successfully convinced your prospective widow-client that you're not like every other man in her life spoon-feeding her advice. Not only are you calm, but you have a calming effect on her as well. You exude quiet authority, are respectful, and can be trusted. If you've gotten this far, you very likely have yourself a new client.

But suppose your prospective client isn't an older widow, but someone much younger than yourself. Or, suppose you're a female planner in your late-20s and your potential client is a male corporate executive in his mid-50s. Or, perhaps your prospective clients are an older couple with a net worth that belies their modest appearance. Regardless of age, gender, income, or other differences between you and your prospective client, many of the same lessons apply. You always want to listen to what's on the potential client's mind before telling your side of the story. Remember that you're selling a financial advisory relationship, and that a relationship means give and take – except your client is paying *you* to be in the relationship, so that entitles him or her to go first. In most cases, if you begin the relationship properly, you won't need to get through a canned sales spiel to secure the planning engagement. Once your prospective client sees that you have the social skills requisite to a planner-client relationship, that you're sensitive to his or her pressing concerns, and that you have a modicum of financial expertise, you'll have an excellent chance of getting the job.

Nonetheless, learn to read between the lines of certain prospective clients. Younger persons (e.g., a single adult with his or her first job out of college, or a young couple having their first child) often feel intimidated. They may know little about personal finance and are worried you will talk down to them or expect them to know more than they know. Being sensitive to this can help you put them at ease quickly and increase the odds in your favor that they will want to work with you.

Male corporate executives often work long hours in a highly competitive environment. If the executive is close to retirement, he may be aware that he's been playing a corporate "game" much of his life and he'll be ready to start planning his departure to a more civilized existence. The younger male corporate executive is more likely to be caught up in the "game" and excited to tell you about his corporate conquests. Professionals (e.g., doctors, lawyers) may behave similarly. If you like and want to work with these kinds of clients, acknowledge their chest-thumping, but let them know who's boss, too. They've come to *you* because (1) they've had to admit they can't be good at everything and want you to manage their financial affairs while they go off and do the hunter-gatherer thing, or (2) they want to control their investments, yet they need your assurance that they are doing it right. The latter type of client can be trouble, so realize the meeting isn't just a way for you to begin a new relationship. It's also a way for you to anticipate a relationship that might ultimately fail, and to decline involvement before it even starts.

Another type of prospective client (and my personal favorite) is the retired couple that exemplifies all the traits of *The Millionaire Next Door*, as described by authors Thomas J. Stanley and William D. Danko in their 1996 book of the same name.[2] These folks typically display modest tastes and tend to keep money issues close to the vest. They will appreciate a quiet, discreet and professional manner on your part. Try any flamboyant sales tactics with them and you likely will never hear from them again.

Realize that I've given you only stereotypes in the last few paragraphs. Suffice it say that the more client-making meetings you sit in, the better you will get at sizing up potential clients quickly and knowing how to guide and/or react to them in your meeting. Just remember the "Golden Rule of Listening" if you remember nothing else, and you can't go too far wrong.

CHAPTER ENDNOTES

1. For successful strategies for targeting the middle market, see Sheryl Garrett, *Garrett's Guide to Financial Planning: How to Capture the Middle Market and Increase Your Profits* (Cincinnati, OH: The National Underwriter Company, 2001). To order by phone, call 1-800-543-0874. Online orders can be placed at: http://www.nationalunderwriter.com/nucatalog/.
2. Thomas J. Stanley, Ph.D. and William D. Danko, Ph.D., *The Millionaire Next Door* (New York, NY: Simon & Schuster, October 1996).

Chapter 10

CLIENT SERVICE

Servicing clients is a big topic, so let's subdivide it a bit. First, there is client service. Next, there are client services. Do they seem redundant?

Client service pertains to the infrastructure of your firm and the mindset of your service team. Do you have the forms, checklists, systems, and people in place to respond to your clients with a cost-efficient, high tech, high-touch service? And, perhaps even more important, do you and all of your team members have the mindset that says, "Responsiveness to clients is our most important priority?"

Client services are the various things you do for clients. At one extreme, you might simply provide hourly advice on an appointment basis–that being your only client contact. It's a fairly regimented service–you talk to your clients at pre-scheduled times, and verbal advice is generally the only "deliverable" you offer. At the other extreme, clients can reach you or your team day or night and request anything from a financial plan update to a replacement copy of their misplaced IRS Form 1099, or even help in scheduling their summer vacation.

Do you have to offer a broad array of client services? That's an important question for you to ponder as you establish your business model, because having the expertise and the attendant fee structure to offer many different services is a very fundamental business decision. Must you offer good client service? Absolutely, there's no question about this! Regardless of business model choice, good client service is fundamental to your image, your competitiveness and, ultimately, your survival. And great client service is the key to increasing your market share, moving to the next level of financial success, and achieving your dreams.

INFRASTRUCTURE

Personnel

Good client service is a function of infrastructure and mindset, or attitude. Let's talk about infrastructure first, which we can further break down into personnel and systems. Is good client service synonymous with having lots of personnel? Does it take a receptionist, a back-office support person, or any other specific employee function to guarantee good client service? Well, it takes the function, but not necessarily the employee.

To illustrate, consider the simple act of an established client (we'll call her Sandy Smith) making contact with her advisor within a firm. The firm may be a 30-employee organization with 15 financial planners and other assorted support personnel, or a sole practitioner sitting alone in a home office. In either case, there must be a procedure by which a valued client such as Sandy gets what she needs when she calls a contact number or reaches you by email, perhaps through your website. In the larger firm, it could be a receptionist with whom she makes initial contact. Or, it might be a person designated as the "relationship manager" who functions within a team that is a subset of the entire employee roster and serves a defined portion of the firm's clients. In the case of a sole practitioner, he *is* the relationship manager (as well as the receptionist, the back-office support person, the planner, and so on).

In other words, it doesn't matter who's responsible for ensuring that Sandy makes contact with her advisor. What matters is that she gets satisfaction when she calls. Ideally, Sandy should get to speak to the person she ultimately wants to reach. If that is not possible, then she should get to speak to another person on her planning team. (Of course, this won't happen in a sole practitioner firm.) If that is not possible, then Sandy should have her message taken by a real person and her call returned promptly by her advisor. If that is not possible, then she should be able to leave her message on her advisor's voicemail system and have her call returned within some reasonable period of time. Note that as we move along the spectrum of possibilities, the quality of service to Sandy declines. Are we making too much of a simple phone call? Perhaps, but this illustrates service differences and how they're not always a function of having more people.

The fact that Sandy, our hypothetical client, is calling instead of emailing indicates a measure of urgency. These days, clients who have the option of either calling or emailing typically use email when they don't need an immediate response. An email may mean "get back to me within 24 hours," whereas a phone call might mean "I need to hear from you before the end of the day, if not sooner." Is this true for all clients? No, the meaning behind different forms of contact will differ by client. It's your job to know each client well enough to understand how quick a response they expect to each form of inquiry.

It may sound like the sole practitioner is at a disadvantage, but that doesn't have to be the case. The sole practitioner firm is a perfect example of where infrastructure, or systems, can play an essential role. If he's not in his office, the sole practitioner could let his client find him by using a telephone forwarding service (see Chapter 29, General Office Hardware). Such a service provides the advisor with one phone number which, when called by a client, tries to find the advisor, in a sequential fashion, at every phone number the advisor entered into the system when he first enabled it. Perhaps his phone system rings him first at his commercial office, then at his home office, then on his cell phone, and then on his home phone. If it finds him nowhere, it offers the caller the opportunity to leave a message in the advisor's voicemail system.

Another system a sole practitioner might employ is hiring a virtual assistant, to whose phone number the advisor's calls are forwarded if he doesn't answer his office phone. Alternatively, you could combine the two systems and make the virtual assistant one of the "nodes" on the calling sequence of the forwarding service. The point is ... firms of all types can provide good client service using the right combination of personnel and technology as long as the focus is kept on the client and the client's needs. We've used the example of an incoming client call, but this philosophy applies to all services. Having said that, we think you will find that of all the services you perform for clients, the most important one is being available to answer questions and give advice. That is what the seasoned client most depends upon you for. Therefore, the phone call example is one of the best we could use in this instance.

Systems

What other systems, or aspects of one's infrastructure, are important – if not essential – to providing good client service? At the top of your list should be a full-featured Client Relationship Management (CRM) software system on which you run your business (see Chapter 31 for specific recommendations). Once called contact management software, CRM software has evolved far beyond its earlier status as an "electronic Rolodex."

CRM software is, or should be, the gateway to your most critical client information. It should store and make readily available all client communications, whether incoming or outgoing, or whether by written correspondence, email, fax, or notes taken after phone calls and in-person client meetings. It should be able to receive scanned images of important client documents (e.g., wills, tax returns) and append them to your clients' records. And it should be the "traffic cop" for the client work that flows among your employees or virtual work partners. While you will likely still need to use separate software for specific client services like financial planning and investment management, your CRM software should be able to connect to the output of those programs to further consolidate in one central place all essential client information.

Here's another way to understand the utility of a full-function CRM package. It's the one program that all employees and virtual work partners use all day long to manage client interactions. For example, if an employee (Andrew) takes a call from a client (James Jones), he should be able to upload Mr. Jones' entire record from within your CRM software with a single click of the mouse and see what interactions other employees have had with that client for any historic period, whether those interactions occurred the same morning, or 10 years ago. If a document underlies an action that was taken for Mr. Jones, the employee should be able to call up an image of that document to assist him in answering Mr. Jones' follow-up question. Andrew should notate the client's phone call in his record so that another employee can reference those notations the next time Mr. Jones calls. These types of systems are commonplace in most large institutions, but not in most small-and-mid-sized planning firms.

Assiduous note taking by all employees is a habit that is critical to an effective CRM system. This serves not only a client service function, but a liability management function, too. You may wonder, "If this important task cannot be avoided, can it be simplified?" The answer is "yes." Email serves this purpose beautifully and should become your primary means of communicating with clients when the client isn't demanding an immediate, "live" phone response. Email is effective because it provides the written record you need for all client communications. Clients will email you when they wouldn't dream of picking up the phone and "bothering" you. And by encouraging interactions that might not otherwise take place, email can strengthen a client relationship. Clients will value a quick email response (even though they don't usually expect one) as much or more than a quick response to a phone voicemail.

Website

Another critical infrastructure system all advisors need today is a website. A website is essential to maintaining the impression that you value each client's patronage and even develops a sense of community with clients. All clients should know that they can go to your website when they need to revisit that suggestion you made for college funding in your last client newsletter, initiate an email to your new portfolio manager, or find a link to that credit bureau you recently recommended. Updating your website frequently will give the impression that your company is a living entity, always changing, growing, and improving. A dynamic website will help reinforce the client's belief that he's chosen the right advisor, one who is constantly looking for ways to help his clients interpret the changing economy and financial system in which they live.

CULTIVATING THE RIGHT ATTITUDE

Finally, once your infrastructure is in place, good client service will depend on all employees having the right mindset, or attitude. We won't get into how you go about incentivizing employees to treat clients the way you want them treated; that's a topic for a separate book. Suffice it to say, there is a mindset that causes clients to feel extremely well cared for. If you and your employees can project that mindset consistently, you will have taken a major step towards elongating client relationships and reducing potential liability claims, not to mention the high costs of client turnover.

To better understand this mindset, think about the best service you ever received from a personal service firm. What comes to mind for me is my virtual assistant, Sherry Carnahan of Total Office, Inc. in Akron, Ohio. Sherry does for me what an on-site receptionist would do for most other planners – tasks such as: printing and mailing written correspondence; mail-merging client newsletters with the client listings in my CRM to get these bulk mailings out the door; or scheduling consecutive meetings for me with large numbers of clients when I travel out of town to cities where I have large client concentrations.

What makes Sherry's service so good is her anticipation of my needs and her ability to help in areas in which I might not have even realized she had an expertise. I may get an email from her reminding me that a client hasn't responded to a request for information and offering to follow-up for me. Or, when I encounter a problem with my website, she may make a suggestion to solve the problem based upon something she learned by working on the website of one of her other small business clients. And all of our contacts are cordial. Sherry's cheerfulness always makes her a pleasure to work with.

Are Sherry's own needs being met by providing this kind of service? Well of course. Sherry's paid by the hour, so the more work she can drum up from me and other clients, the more money she makes. Yet, Sherry is so incredibly helpful and caring in her attitude towards me, and my business, that I always welcome her contacts. Over the years, we have come to know each other personally, as you will your best clients, and that has added even more depth to our relationship. I wouldn't think of trading Sherry for another virtual assistant, and that's how you always want your clients to think of you. Give them consistently good service, and they always will.

Chapter 11

PROBLEM CLIENTS

You might be surprised to see a chapter on the subject of "problem clients," but every practice has them. The longer you're in business, the better you'll get at spotting them, but even veteran advisors will tell you they have a few. Some clients you took on because you didn't or couldn't (perhaps due to inexperience) detect the tell-tale signs. Some you may have accepted as clients because you needed to pay the rent, or your staff's salary, or the bill from your children's camp or college and weren't wise enough to "just say NO." And some are just impossible to see coming – they seem ideal during your first meeting, but show their true colors later on. Dealing with problem clients effectively is as much a practice management skill as finding clients in the first place.

What's wrong with a problem client is that – by definition – the odds are high that this type of person will end up driving you and/or your staff crazy, cost more in time and expense than he or she will bring in, and be much more likely to sue you. (Steve Leimberg says that, "It's not whether you win or lose in court that counts…it's how much it costs to play that game!")

There are probably more types of problem clients than we have the space or the time to document, so we'll highlight a few of these personalities and how to deal with them. Before we do that, though, let's define the term "problem client." The problem client *isn't* a client who fails to meet your circumstantial definition of an "ideal client." In other words, a client you take on in year one with $200,000 in assets and a modest income doesn't become a problem client five years later simply because your definition of an "ideal client" has changed to someone with at least $1,000,000 in assets and a $200,000 or greater annual income.

A "problem client" is what he is because of his personality. Dealing with a problem client is therefore a matter of (1) understanding his personality and either coaxing him to play by your rules, or (2) firing him – and doing so as quickly as possible. Here are descriptions of a few problem clients you may encounter.

THE "I'M-TOO-BUSY-WHICH-IS-WHY-I'M-PAYING-YOU-TO-HANDLE-IT" CLIENT

This problem client doesn't understand that financial planning is a two-way, interactive process. He or she dumps some information in your lap and expects you to carry on without him. Here are a few of the tell-tale signs by which you'll get to know this client:

- He'll insist on meetings during the evenings or weekends when you would rather be tending to personal matters.
- He'll spend your time telling you all about his corporate conquests, his investment home runs, his new luxury car, or his latest home remodeling job, rather than taking seriously and concentrating on the planning process he's engaged you to accomplish.
- He'll procrastinate indefinitely when it comes to getting you the documentation you need to do his planning.
- He doesn't return your phone calls.
- He'll reschedule many or most of your meetings.
- He won't keep track of his living expenses, so creating an accurate cash flow statement is out of the question.
- He may even disappear in the middle of the planning process.

Yes, this last characteristic is said partly in jest, but at one time or another, all of these characteristics have presented themselves in my own client base, if not within the same person.

THE OBSESSED-WITH-INVESTMENT-PERFORMANCE CLIENT

As most of us tell clients, we're not in the performance game, so temporary market declines shouldn't matter that much. But it's interesting how quickly clients forget they're investing for the long term when their portfolios are going off in a direction opposite of that we'd hoped for.

Some clients become obsessed with investment performance. Their portfolio, as a whole, may be performing competitively but, as is bound to happen, some individual investments within the portfolio will be losing money. Try as you might, you can't get this client to focus on the portfolio's overall performance. Instead, he keeps coming back to those handful of losers and wondering out loud why you didn't pick something with a higher Morningstar rating (which is, in itself, probably a gross oversimplification of your investment selection process).

THE COUNTER-VALUE CLIENT

A client is a problem if your values and his/her values differ significantly.

Here's a personal example. Your author grew up as the Baby Boomer child of Depression-era parents. Unlike many others of my generation, I grew up with my parents' values towards money (e.g., don't go heavily into debt, spend wisely, don't buy extravagant homes or cars … you get the picture).

Most prospective clients my own age have very different values. One of my earliest clients was a couple whose most important goal was coming up with $25,000 (in 1984 dollars) to give their daughter a proper bat mitzvah. Even as a fellow Jew, I couldn't relate. Others from my generation can be found driving Beemers (i.e., BMWs) and living in heavily-mortgaged homes costing $500,000 and up, while in their 50s their retirement savings amount to just a few dollars accumulated in their latest employer's 401(k) plan.

But that's just me. You'll have your own "counter-value" client. Essentially he's anyone whose values are radically different from yours, so much so that you are repeatedly forced to bite your tongue when in his/her presence.

THE TWO-MINDED CLIENT

This problem client can't make up his or her mind about anything. You listen intently to the client's ideas, create an investment strategy and financial plan that reflects what you believe you heard, and communicate it and obtain agreement from the client. The next thing you know, the phone is ringing and the client is questioning you about why you did such-and-such, and whether you shouldn't instead consider this-and-that.

This client needs to see or experience what you're doing for them in a way that's difficult to anticipate. It's not just a matter of figuring out their preferred learning style or checking their body language for personality clues. They simply don't know what they want, though they might know it if they see it.

To complicate matters, this client may know a little bit about investing. I sometimes rue the day *Morningstar Mutual Fund Values* found its way into the public library. I'm convinced it's not a tool for public use, contrary to what Morningstar's own marketing strategists may believe. It's hard enough getting professional advisors to understand star ratings, much less convincing my clients that sometimes contrary investing means buying one- and two-star funds. (This might also be called the "second-guessing client.")

So how do we deal with this type of client? By the time you identify him or her for what he or she really is, it may be after you've already made a major time commitment. Ask this client to stick with a strategy, get it in writing, or gently find him or her another advisor to work with. How far you bend over backwards, as always, is a function of where the hunger curve, the self-esteem curve, the altruism curve and the profit motive curve all intersect.

In this person's favor, it can be said that this client usually knows the torment he or she is unintentionally putting you through and will be loyal if you choose to work through all the analytical iterations this type of client seems to require.

THE SOMETIMES-COMPETENT CLIENT

On a more serious note, some clients will literally go in and out of consciousness on you. They're just naturally absent-minded or attention-deficit, they're taking medication, or they're simply getting old. They don't remember much of what you say. And they're often quite happy to delegate *all* of the decisions to you.

It might seem like the thing to do here is give them what they need, but protect yourself by having them sign statements detailing what they've agreed to. This certainly can't hurt from a liability standpoint. Or, better yet, have them bring a mentally alert friend with them to your meetings – a kind of proxy for their memory. This is usually a close friend or son or daughter who will often become instrumental in their care should they travel down the road to dementia, or worse, so you'll end up dealing with the friend or relative in the client's behalf.

THE NUMBERS GEEK

We've all got an engineer or two in our client base, or we've heard the stories about them. This is the client who loves the pages and pages of numbers you produce – the more the better. The problem is the more you produce, the more he wants: What if this? What if that? What if we raise this guy's fee a bit to account for the extra labor involved?

One of the Numbers Geeks I once worked with was not only enamored with numbers, but with the planning process as well. Apparently, he had taken some adult education classes somewhere along the way. When I asked him for the usual data, he gave me a financial plan for himself – complete with his own prescription for his asset allocation mix. I had half a mind to give it back to him in a fancy cover and charge him the agreed-upon fee.

HANDHOLDING CLIENTS

This is my ideal client. He or she is more coherent than the "Sometimes-Competent Client," and much less of a know-it-all than the "Numbers Geek." This client really appreciates what you do for him or her. This client's only problematic tendency is to give away too much responsibility for decisions.

It takes some extra effort to find ways to involve this client in the work. Having the client bring someone along to meetings – as with the "Sometimes-Competent Client" – isn't a bad idea. Finding ways to explain things simply and communicate more effectively is good, too. Sometimes you must subtly say or do things to help this client increase her own confidence in her ability to take more responsibility. This client's tendency will be to lean heavily on you and, frankly, this often makes for a very long-term relationship, the kind we all like. Just don't wake up one day in a courtroom full of this client's children making allegations about you that appear all too true because your client remained aloof from the planning process.

THE DISAPPEARING CLIENT

I have one client I simply can't find. She dropped off the face of the earth with no forwarding address. She occasionally takes a little money from her account for her living expenses, wherever she is. I want to advise her, to catch up on things, to do my job. I am still managing her financial assets, of course. And the fee's being paid from her custodial account. I figure when she's ready, she'll either resurface or move the money elsewhere. Short of skywriting, I don't know how to contact or deal with this client.

HANDLING THE PROBLEM CLIENT

Life's too short to work with problem clients. As mentioned earlier, you can try to change the client or you can fire him. How do you change a problem client? You refer him back to the contract he's signed. Your contract should include paragraphs to the general effect of:

> *Disclosure – Client agrees to fully disclose all matters pertinent to Client's financial affairs, including but not limited to, information regarding Client's financial objectives, expenses, assets, liabilities, investments, insurance, taxes, and estate planning programs, retirement plans, and any personal matters which may have a bearing on Client's current or prospective financial status, as well as subsequent changes to any of the above. It is not Advisor's responsibility to discover facts which are not made readily available to Advisor; and*
>
> *Termination of Agreement – This Advisory Agreement may be terminated by either Client or Advisor, without penalty, upon written notice. Advisor agrees to furnish Client all written work and recommendations to the date of written notice of termination. Client agrees to pay for work completed and unbilled as of the date of receipt of written notice by Advisor.*

You can gently remind the client that he's in violation of your contract when he doesn't provide you with timely data. If he still doesn't comply, then you can invoke the second paragraph and fire him.

Firing a client is an art. If the client is relatively new – that is, you're still engaged in his initial planning and there's little invested emotion on either side, you can refer him to the above contract clauses in the letter you sent him and explain that, in retrospect, you believe your working arrangement was ill-conceived and that you are exercising your privilege to terminate it.

If the individual has been a client for a while, then firing him may be more difficult. One method employed by some planners is to "graduate" undesirable clients. They tell the client that he's grown in his understanding of personal finance and there's nothing the planner can any longer do for him that the client can't do for himself. The client leaves with a good feeling and everyone's happy.

In other cases, the planner, being somewhat more honest, tells his client that the client no longer fits the planner's business model and that the planner is in the process of paring back his client base. In this instance it is desirable to help the client find a new home. There's usually another planner who would appreciate the referral and who would find the client desirable because he would be a good match for his ideal client profile.

In any event, you need to develop the practice management skill of recognizing a desirable – and undesirable – client when you meet him. It's far easier in the long run to make a tough decision up front than to wait until a serious series of problems arise.

If you can't spot the undesirable ones during the stage at which a mutual decision to work together is made, then you need to learn to deal with them once they show their true colors. We'll say it one more time: life's too short to work with problem clients.

Chapter 12

DEALING WITH THE CLIENT'S OTHER PROFESSIONALS

If you position yourself as your client's most trusted advisor, then other professionals and outside experts – even those with whom the client was working before he met you – will be, or perhaps feel, subordinated to you. You will need to know how to make them part of the team that serves the client while coordinating and controlling their input. The three aspects of working with other professionals, then, will be finding them, coordinating their efforts for the benefit of the client, and dealing with the occasional interpersonal relationship problems that may arise.

CRITERIA FOR SELECTING PROFESSIONALS

Let's start with the client who needs a particular professional on his team and doesn't already have that "slot" filled when he comes to you. It's important to remember that the professional you help your client find (e.g., the attorney, CPA, trust officer, valuation expert, or other individual) becomes as much a reflection of your own professionalism as an employee or virtual assistant you might hire. If the name of your company includes "& Associates," this professional will be, in a broad sense, one of the valued "Associates" referred to in your company's name.

How do you select the best professional for your client to work with? The selection criteria must go beyond simply choosing someone whom you believe will generate a return referral to you; that must be – at best – a secondary consideration, competence being the first. But even competence is only one criterion. As is true in so many other aspects of financial planning, client psychology is a major component of the decision about whom to bring in to work with you and your client on a piece of his or her financial plan.

Early in my planning career, I referred a client to an accountant for tax return preparation. The same accountant had worked with my partner and me as our firm's bookkeeper, but had not yet prepared a tax return for us. In her capacity as our bookkeeper, I knew her to be careful and conscientious in the production of our numbers. It didn't occur to me that this personality trait might be just what my client wanted to avoid.

Risk is as much of an issue in tax planning as it is in investing. Some clients will tell you they want to avoid an IRS audit at all costs. They would rather pay too much than too little in taxes if doing so will ensure their avoidance of an audit (something many clients perceive to be the case, even though the "system" doesn't always work that way). However, my clients, whom I naively assumed were risk avoiders (weren't most clients?), were quite the opposite; they actually preferred to take calculated risks. On the other hand, the accountant preferred to risk nothing, and enforced her viewpoint on my clients with little flexibility.

At the end of the tax season, my clients made it quite clear to me that they didn't want to use this person next year. They were equally clear that my decision to refer them to her led them to question my own sensitivity to their needs and desires. As a result of that experience, I now look for a more flexible personality in the CPAs I choose to send my clients to – professionals who can give the clients anything they want – within reason and within ethical bounds.

Another intangible your clients may be particular about is the outside professional's ability to meet a deadline. Some of our retired clients lead very laid back, comfortable lives and, unless they're embarking on lengthy travels, really don't care if an attorney completes their estate planning next week or next month. But beware of the corporate executive that is used to riding herd on his underlings and enforcing deadlines. That person probably won't be happy with the attorney you use who doesn't produce some documents quickly, even if the attorney's competence is beyond reproach and his fee is reasonable. The client will only see that the attorney's unable to deliver on time, and will lose faith in the attorney, and in you.

METHODS OF FINDING PROFESSIONALS

These are just a few examples of issues that can arise between you and clients in the context of finding suitable professionals for them – issues that don't relate directly to competency. Let's take a step back, though.

Suppose you have no professional contacts to refer a particular client to and need some fast. How do you go about finding them? Start the same way your clients are probably finding you – referrals. Ask other members of your professional associations or attorneys and accountants with whom you already work for referrals to qualified experts. The attorney, to whom you send many clients needing estate planning, may not have any associates practicing family law, but he probably knows some in other firms who do.

A method that some planners use to select good estate planning attorneys in a community to which they are newcomers or when they're new to the profession is to seek referrals from bank trust officers. Here's how this method works: Call the trust departments of several reputable banks and ask a trust officer "which local attorneys do you refer clients to?". Ask enough trust officers the same question until you find several attorneys whose names begin to come up more than once. Then you have your "short list" to recommend to clients.

Perhaps the best way to find competent practitioners is to join a local estate planning council. Merely by joining, you'll obtain a directory of members that will list individuals by profession. By attending meetings, you'll get to know many of them personally. Note who in your community are officers, committee members, or speakers – or who has written articles for the estate planning council's newsletter. Read estate and financial planning magazines such as *Estate Planning* (published by Research Institute of America) or *Trusts & Estates* (published by Primedia) and see if a local attorney or CPA has written an impressive planning article.

The due diligence part of this exercise is no different than if you had picked attorneys' names out of the Yellow Pages. You still need to spend some time with them to check them out, be it a meal or a brief meeting in their office. Call them up and let them know very briefly who you and your clients are, and that you need some good professionals to work with your clients. Ask whether you could visit them for half an hour in their office and have them tell you about themselves and their practices, or perhaps take them to lunch and do some cross-marketing.

Few professionals will turn you down unless they are overwhelmed with work or sense that your clients don't fit on their own "ideal client" list. Perform your due diligence as you would with a prospective client. Listen; don't talk ... other than to ask some open-ended questions. You might ask an attorney what kinds of estate planning issues and/or clients he spends most of his time working with. Does he or she also design pension plans, or handle particularly tax-intensive work such as charitable trusts?

Pay as much attention to the professional's manner of speech, body language, personal appearance, and other non-technical characteristics as you do to the technical ones. Pretend that you are your client sitting in front of this person and saying to yourself, cynically, "what kind of so-called 'expert' did my financial advisor send me to? Does this guy know what he's talking about?" Is he or she polite and cordial, or condescending and curt? Again, resist the temptation to expound about your own services. There will be plenty of time to market to that person later on.

Attorneys have sometimes been my single largest source of new clients. Perhaps the reason is that estate planning, like nothing else, gives you the opportunity to show off what you know if you take that opportunity. I find that opportunity presents itself when doing estate planning with one's client, as follows: I begin by addressing the client's estate planning requirements as part of his financial planning. By the time I'm finished with the client, she's been exposed to the basic concepts of estate planning, including not only tax avoidance, but the mechanisms of asset transfer as well as lifetime protections afforded by vehicles such as trusts and medical directives. I run the numbers to illustrate to my client the financial consequences of the concepts I've explained. I make it clear, however, that the attorney has the final say, and that all of this is preparatory to our work with him.

I give my client the names of three attorneys and a brief description of each one's practice, background, fee structure, and personality. I encourage the client to interview each one by phone until they find one they feel they can work with. We then schedule a meeting, either at my office or the attorney's office. We meet, kick around ideas, the attorney goes through his usual explanation of unified credits and durable powers, and the client begins to get the gist of the exercise. So by the end of the meeting a framework has been established for the client's estate plan. The client has the job of thinking about appointments of guardians, trustees, and executors. The attorney will prepare some draft documents and I will receive a copy as well as my clients. I review the drafts and write a brief letter of comments or questions to the attorney, with a copy to my clients.

What do I do in our meeting? I deferentially ask questions and put forth ideas on my client's behalf. It is done with respect for the attorney's knowledge, which is greater than mine. (The only time that hasn't been the case has been when the client chose his own attorney rather than one I referred him to – often a bad idea since the client often doesn't understand that the attorney who handled his last mortgage closing isn't necessarily well versed in tax law). Almost invariably, I am able to clarify concepts the client didn't understand, but was embarrassed to ask the attorney to explain again. I sometimes think of things the attorney might otherwise miss. I have demonstrated my knowledge to the attorney; not to mention, I have brought him one of my valued clients.

If you deal with other professionals this way, you will serve your clients well, build a list of experts, get referrals because you've spent time with that expert demonstrating your ability, and – perhaps most important – you will further your education in that other person's area of expertise.

POTENTIAL PROBLEMS

So, these are powerful methods of finding and establishing your role with other professionals with whom your clients can work. Ideally, you want to be the proverbial "hub," standing right next to your client, with his other professionals radiating out from you as the "spokes." Problems can arise, however, whenever you have more than one advisor serving the same client. No matter how hard you work to clearly agree on who will do what and to whom the client belongs, be aware of the following potential problems.

Sometimes you will find yourself competing for the hub position, particularly if your client has been working with another professional longer than he's worked with you. For example, a CPA who's been preparing the client's tax returns for 10 years may see himself as occupying the hub position just because he's known the client longer and because he deals in financial matters. He may perceive himself as more qualified than you are, even if he has not had your training. Other professionals frequently misunderstand the strength of a good financial planner's generalist abilities or the breadth of his training and knowledge. But, most important, if you are doing your job, then you are in constant communication with your client while his other advisors may consult with him once a year, at best. That gives you the stronger relationship with the client.

I have found an exception to this – the small business owner client. This client, typically having more complex tax planning needs than most individual or family clients, may have a very close relationship with his CPA and/or attorney that you will not (and should not attempt to) change. You probably don't have equal qualifications to the specialist this client depends upon; thus, you should find a way to coordinate your activities with his. You will still have the opportunity to take the hub position, depending upon how your role shapes up and the degree of personal interaction you have with your client.

And then there's the other professional who has been satisfied to take an ancillary role for many years, but decides to broaden his services so that they overlap, or even duplicate, yours. If you were "on the scene" first, and the other professional is a true professional, there should be no problem separating out your roles so that the other advisor continues to provide the limited services to which your client has been accustomed while you continue as his trusted generalist.

For example, a CPA who once prepared tax returns and assisted in tax planning for a dozen of my clients hired a new employee who was Series 7-licensed. The CPA began approaching some of my other clients about setting up 401(k) plans and selling them investments for these plans. Fortunately, we had no trouble coming to the understanding that my clients would never be approached with this service as I would continue to be the sole arbiter of whether or not they needed such vehicles and, if so, how they would be implemented for the client.

The last situation to be aware of is the "other professional" who doesn't act like one. This is usually the other advisor (lawyer, CPA, whomever) who was on the scene first and sees you as a threat. He will try to undercut your advice by sniping at you behind your back. It usually takes the form of getting your client in a meeting or on the phone to tell the client you've made a mistake of some sort. Or you made a recommendation he disagrees with. It's the old game of trying to inflate one's sense of importance by deflating yours.

A true professional never acts in this manner. He cooperates congenially with the client's other advisors. If he finds a recommendation has been made with which he disagrees, he calls the other advisor – not the client – and deferentially discusses the recommendation with that advisor. There will often be a justification that you will not at first have understood. However, if that is not the case and you have "caught" the other advisor in a recommendation that is harmful to, or not ideal for, the client, give him the benefit of the doubt ... at the very least, the first or second time. If, over time, you judge his competency to be lacking, then tactfully advise your client as such and help the client find a replacement.

Acting with professionalism, even as others fail to do so, will keep you in good stead with your client and his other, more reputable, advisors.

Chapter 13

SURVEYING CLIENTS

Have you ever wondered what would happen if you asked your clients how you were doing as their financial advisor?

While a co-principal in the financial advisory firm of Malgoire Drucker Inc., Bethesda, Maryland (1984 - 1997), my partner and I conducted a client survey after the end of the first year, when we felt secure in the belief that our clients – even if dissatisfied with some aspects of our service – weren't going to stage a wholesale walkout.

Our survey (which allowed one-half page for each response) posed only two questions:

"What are we doing well?"

"What could we be doing better?"

We received 12 responses – a 17% response rate – which was probably good by some people's standards, but made me wonder what the other 83% of our clients were thinking. Presumably, their unresponsiveness didn't mean they were unhappy with our services or they would have quit. Maybe they were just too busy to respond, a fact of life we're all familiar with. Or perhaps they were unhappy with our services and just too busy to quit!

Five of the 12 respondents answered only the first half of the survey. In other words, they took the time to tell us what they liked about our services, but voiced no complaints of any kind. Of the remaining seven respondents, only one wrote at length about what we could be doing better. Most clients were probably reluctant to say anything negative, even though criticism was invited and anonymous responses were permitted (in fact, all of our respondents except for one signed their survey forms). Nonetheless, we had 12 responses we could learn from. Clients responded that we were doing well at the following activities:

- Financial planning and management;
- Mailings and reporting;
- Responding promptly to client questions and generally being available;
- Explaining difficult concepts;
- Finding new investment products; and
- Occasionally providing advice that clients had not specifically contracted for.

It was pleasing – although not entirely unexpected – to hear that our clients thought we were pretty good financial planners and investment managers. More important to me, though, was their perception that our quarterly investment reports and annual performance and tax reports were indeed beneficial because we spent a lot of effort creating and publishing those materials.

As for our availability, I believe that when clients call and don't reach their advisor the first time, they should hear from him the same day or – at the very least – within 24 hours. That type of responsiveness immediately sets the advisor apart from most other professionals the client deals with and is another way the advisor has of letting his clients know that they are valued. The respondents indicated they had noticed our responsiveness, and appreciated it.

A few respondents mentioned that we explained things well. They thought we went to extra lengths to make things clear. A few clients thought we did a good job of keeping up with investments and introducing them to new products and services they wouldn't have discovered on their own. One respondent even mentioned he appreciated when we took the time to render advice outside the scope of our contract with him at no charge. This type of comment is helpful because it confirms that features of our service, which we as advisors believe are valuable, are in fact recognized by our clients as having value, too. We certainly don't want to waste our time making extra efforts to do things that go unnoticed or unappreciated by our clients.

Nevertheless, the survey's second-half comments were of even greater value since they exposed weaknesses in our systems. Clients said they thought we could do better at:

- Attending to administrative details;

- Sending out educational mailings or providing seminars;
- Staying in contact;
- Sending out quarterly statements sooner after the end of the quarter;
- Explaining changes in investment accounts; and
- Providing higher returns on investment (this item being mentioned by only one respondent).

These responses show that no matter how good a job we do at the "core" tasks (i.e., planning and investment management), failing to facilitate changes smoothly and professionally can undermine your credibility and professional image. We can be courteous and conciliatory when we forget to attend to necessary details, but every client has a breaking point at which he or she will throw up his hands and say, "that's all I can take." We need feedback – and we need constant feedback! The point is we wouldn't have known this was an issue for our clients if we hadn't surveyed them.

Returning to our survey results, we found that some responses canceled out other responses. One client thought we did a great job of explaining things, while another wanted more explanation. One liked our mailings and educational pieces; another thought we didn't communicate enough. These are not examples of faulty surveying as much as they are an indication that you simply will not be able to please all of your clients all of the time. Some clients have special needs that don't fit neatly into an administrative system that equates standardization with efficiency. If we decide we're going to cater to those needs, then we must have systems to handle the extraordinary as well as the standard. And we need foolproof ways of remembering to do those things that make clients feel special.

The importance of client surveys is that we get "full disclosure" from our clients as to what they do, or don't, value. This feedback is critical to our efficiency as small businesspersons. Spending time and money on internal functions the client doesn't value not only wastes resources, but also leaves resources unavailable for a different set of services the client might value more.

For example, through the use of comprehensive wealth managers, some advisors have successfully impressed upon clients the proper role of investing in their financial planning and their drive towards critical goals. Clients of such an advisor may no longer place a high value on having portfolio statements mailed to their homes each quarter, preferring instead to look at their portfolios at their convenience on-line. So if the advisor continues to mail out statements, he is wasting valuable resources that could be employed elsewhere. A client survey may be necessary to enlighten him to his clients' change of mind.

PLANNER PROFILES

Let's take a look at a few survey forms designed by planners in the field to see what kinds of information they deem necessary to refine their service offerings and business procedures.

Tom Grzymala, owner of Alexandria Financial Associates, Ltd., in northern Virginia, uses a very simple, typewritten form (see 13.1) that solicits many of the same kinds of responses I did on my earlier survey, but also asks the client whether he feels he's receiving value that is more or less commensurate with the fee he's paying. In addition, it asks clients point blank what they see as Alexandria's most valuable services and whether they would be willing to refer friends and colleagues to the firm. These responses are invaluable to Grzymala when he's contemplating raising fees or reconfiguring his service mix.

Gary Greenbaum and Tom Orecchio, of Greenbaum and Orecchio, Inc., in Old Tappan, New Jersey, use two different questionnaires in desktop-published form (see Figure 13.2). The first is designed for veteran clients, the other for new clients. In addition to the kinds of questions discussed above, older clients of the firm are asked:

> *"How did you first learn about G&O?"*
>
> *"Has G&O coordinated with your other professional advisors?"*

After all, if you're taking the trouble to survey your clients, you can ask anything you want. You're not confined just to service-related questions.

In its survey designed for new clients, Greenbaum and Orecchio change the focus to the firm's intake process: how the client found out about the firm; the nature of the client's first contact with the firm; the effectiveness of the client's first meeting with Greenbaum and Oreccio personnel; and so on. This way, these advisors get helpful feedback on the impression they make on new clients and how they can improve the critical process of getting prospective clients in the door and "closing" them on their services.

Figure 13.1

ALEXANDRIA FINANCIAL ASSOCIATES, LTD.

Client Evaluation

Please rate our service from 1 (Excellent) to 6 (Poor) based on the following criteria:

	Excellent					Poor
Results relative to what you wanted.	1	2	3	4	5	6
Accuracy.	1	2	3	4	5	6
Promptness.	1	2	3	4	5	6
Written recommendations, materials, provided to you	1	2	3	4	5	6
Presentation Meeting.	1	2	3	4	5	6
Ease in understanding the work done.	1	2	3	4	5	6
Your advisor as a communicator.	1	2	3	4	5	6
Office convenience & comfort.	1	2	3	4	5	6

How would you describe our fee structure? (Please check one)

___ Value greatly exceeds cost

___ Value somewhat exceeds cost

___ Value matches cost

___ Cost somewhat exceeds value

___ Cost greatly exceeds value

What is your appraisal of our overall service and product? ____________________

____

____

What do you consider to be the major strengths of Alexandria Financial Associates? ____________

____

____

What do you see as any weaknesses of AFA? ____________________

____

____

Reprinted with permission of Tom Gryzmala, Alexandria Financial Associates, Ltd., Alexandria, VA (http://www.afawealth.com/pages/index.htm).

Figure 13.1 (cont'd)

What services that we provide to you are the most valuable? ______________________

____

____

Do you have any suggestions for improving our services? ______________________

____

____

Is there anything you would like to be done differently? ______________________

____

____

Have you implemented the financial planning recommendations we've provided? If not, why? __________

____

____

Would you refer friends or colleagues to AFA? If not, why? ______________________

____

____

Your comments (what have I forgotten to ask?) ☺

____

____

____

____

Your name (optional) ______________________

Thank you for competing this questionnaire and helping us make AFA a steadily improving company!

Tom

Tom Grzymala, CFP©

Reprinted with permission of Tom Gryzmala, Alexandria Financial Associates, Ltd., Alexandria, VA (http://www.afawealth.com/pages/index.htm).

In a final example, Keats, Connelly and Associates, Inc., of Phoenix, Arizona, hired Advisor Impact, the surveying arm of CPA firm Moss-Adams LLP, of Seattle, Washington, to design and conduct its client survey. Because the survey form is proprietary, it cannot be reproduced in this book, but we can discuss some of the questions asked by the survey.

What is somewhat different about the Keats, Connelly survey is its listing of statements about their relationship with Keats, Connelly that clients are asked to rate on a 5-point scale between "Critical" and "Not at All Important." The statements include potentially informative items, such as:

"Having an advisor with a professional office environment is..."

"The accuracy with which my account is handled is..."

"The speed at which my calls are returned is......"

The first item provides useful information about an overhead item that is significant for most advisors – an area where cost cutting, if possible, can save big dollars. The second statement can tip off the advisor to "perfectionist" clients (i.e., those who will give him mental demerits if details in the handling of their accounts are overlooked). And the third item will, likewise, alert the advisor to clients who most greatly value a rapid response.

The survey goes on to ask clients such questions as:

"How often do you expect to meet with you advisor?"

"How many reviews do you feel should be face-to-face rather than by telephone?"

"How would you prefer to receive written communications from your advisor?"

Harnessing Survey Technology

Technological advances have made it extremely easy for advisors to find out what their clients are thinking. In Chapter 35 (Client Survey Software), we profile a few specific products that are, in our estimation, uniquely suited to the needs of financial advisors. We suggest that you read Chapter 35 upon completion of this chapter.

Numerous other survey software products exist, and some of them may be of interest to you. Online services include: Zoomerang (www.zoomerang.com); Supersurvey (www.supersurvey.com); and Hosted Survey (www.hostedsurvey.com). Desktop packages include: SurveyPro (www.apian.com); Survey Crafter (www.surveycrafter.com); and Survey Gold (www.surveygold.com).

Again, a survey can educate you as to service improvement tips, cost cutting or time saving ideas, and client preferences that can positively reinforce a relationship.

The bottom line: Every client feels valued when certain things happen, but not every client responds equally to the same stimuli. One client feels he's being heard and valued by his advisor when his phone calls are returned promptly. Another one wants regular contact initiated by the advisor, whether that contact is an email, a phone call, or a mailing of written material geared specifically to the client's circumstances. Yet another client may want a bi-monthly lunch meeting with his advisor, and won't feel he's being heard unless he gets it.

The client survey is your window into what your clients are really thinking. Most clients are ready to tell you what they're thinking; they just need to be invited to do so. The client survey is that invitation.

Figure 13.2 – Veteran Clients

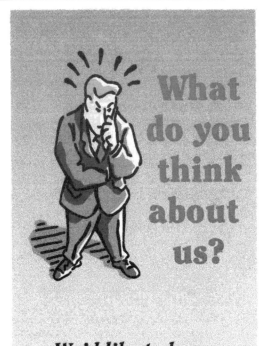

Thank you...

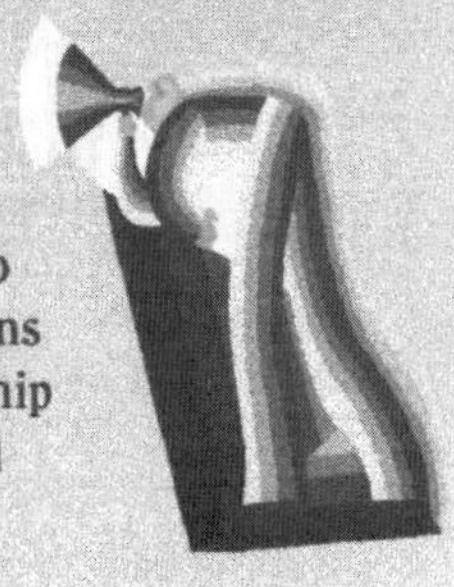

for taking the time to answer a few questions about your relationship with Greenbaum and Orecchio, Inc.

Your observations and perceptions will help us communicate better with our existing and perspective clients.

The first series of questions deals with why you initially selected us as your wealth manager. The balance asks for your evaluation of some of our sales and marketing materials.

Please check off all appropriate responses to each question in the survey, and feel free to make suggestions in the "Comments" section.

We've enclosed a stamped, self-addressed envelope for your convenience.

Thanks for your help.

If you have any questions, please call Dick Deutsch at (201) 768-4600.

Recommend us to a friend, family member, or to a business associate.

As your know, there are a lot of good reasons why you can recommend Greenbaum and Orecchio, Inc. to others who need wealth management services. Our shared rewards program is one.

SHARED REWARDS - For everyone you recommend who becomes a G&O wealth management client, we'll make a one-time contribution of $250 to $1500 to your favorite charity.

Here's some other good reasons to recommend us:

- We can help them achieve their goals
- We are fee only *(we take no commissions)*
- We are a fiduciary *(no conflicts of interest)*
- We can reduce their taxes and expenses
- We are available when they need us
- We are rated one of the top wealth managers in the country by Wealth Manager Magazine
- We have top credentials and expertise
- We offer to work with their accountant/attorney
- We can minimize their financial risk
- We offer unique investment opportunities

Call us with your recommendations.

GREENBAUM AND ORECCHIO, INC.
Wealth Management Services
1 DeWolf Road
Old Tappan, NJ 07675-7015 Fee Only
(201) 768-4600 • Fax (201) 768-1111
Info@InvestmentCounsel.com
www.InvestmentCounsel.com

What do you think about us?

We'd like to know your opinions about our services, communication, and marketing.

GREENBAUM AND ORECCHIO, INC.
Wealth Management Services

Reprinted with permission of Gary Greenbaum and Tom Orecchio, Greenbaum and Orecchio, Inc., Old Tappan, NJ (http://www.investmentcounsel.com/Advisors/investmencounsel/).

Figure 13.2 – Veteran Clients (cont'd)

1. Why did you seek out a new wealth manager?
☐ Unhappy with current financial advisor ☐ Retirement
☐ New wealth *(inheritance, lottery, etc.)* ☐ Sale of business
☐ Death/disability in family ☐ Other ______

2. How did you first learn about Greenbaum and Orecchio, Inc. (G&O)?
☐ Attorney ☐ Accountant ☐ NAPFA ☐ NFLPA ☐ Friend/Family member
☐ Business associate ☐ Marketing materials ☐ Internet directory ☐ Other

3. What were the most important reasons for choosing G&O?

☐ Integration of financial planning and investment counsel
☐ Fee only compensation *(no commissions, hidden costs)*
☐ Cost of services
☐ Wide range of services
☐ The firm acts as a fiduciary *(can only act in client's best interest)*
☐ Size of the firm *(large enough for excellent service, but small enough for personalized attention)*
☐ Professional credentials/affiliations of the staff
☐ Experience of the staff
☐ Recognition of the firm *(by media, outside organizations)*
☐ Independence from financial products/vendors *(no conflicts of interest)*
☐ Investment strategy *(use of Modern Portfolio Theory)*
☐ Investment access *(institutional products, alternative investments, etc.)*
☐ Focus on reducing cost, expenses and portfolio risk
☐ Coordination with client's accountant and/or attorney
☐ Assistance with implementation of financial planning action steps
☐ The firm educates its clients, and communicates with them on a regular basis
☐ Personality/knowledge of staff contact at G&O
☐ Other *(please list)* ______

4. Do you consider G&O's wealth management investment strategy:
☐ Aggressive ☐ Middle of the Road ☐ Conservative

5. Was your first contact with G&O by:
☐ Telephone ☐ Correspondence ☐ Office visit

6. How long after your initial contact before you had a meeting with G&O staff?
☐ 1 week or less ☐ 2-4 weeks ☐ 1 month+ ☐ 6 months+ ☐ 1 year+

7. What occurred at your initial meeting with G&O staff?
☐ Fact gathering about you & your situation ☐ G&O verbal presentation
☐ G&O audio/visual presentation ☐ G&O comparison to competitors
☐ Question and answer session ☐ Other ______

8. What questions did you have about G&O and its services that were not answered at the first meeting?

______

______

9. What follow-up occurred after your initial meeting? Did you receive:
☐ Telephone call ☐ Letter ☐ Brochures ☐ Newsletter ☐ Video
☐ Other ______

10. Did you schedule a follow-up meeting before your start-up? ☐ Yes ☐ No

11. What occurred at the second meeting?
☐ More fact gathering about you ☐ More information about G&O services
☐ Modern Portfolio Theory demo ☐ Design of sample portfolios
☐ Question and answer session ☐ Other ______

12. Having completed your start-up with us, how would you rate G&O in each of the areas below, on a scale of 10 *(best)* to 1 *(worst)*:

Understood your current condition, constraints and financial goals? Rating: ____
Provided you information to help you make informed decisions? Rating: ____
Coordinated with your accountant and/or attorney? Rating: ____
Designed your portfolio using the very best financial products? Rating: ____

13. If you saw them, how would you rate the following G&O marketing materials?

Small Tri-Fold Brochures

Appearance	☐ Excellent	☐ Good	☐ Fair	☐ Poor
Understandable	☐ Excellent	☐ Good	☐ Fair	☐ Poor
Informative	☐ Excellent	☐ Good	☐ Fair	☐ Poor
Overall Impact	☐ Excellent	☐ Good	☐ Fair	☐ Poor

Large Corporate Brochure

Appearance	☐ Excellent	☐ Good	☐ Fair	☐ Poor
Understandable	☐ Excellent	☐ Good	☐ Fair	☐ Poor
Informative	☐ Excellent	☐ Good	☐ Fair	☐ Poor
Overall Impact	☐ Excellent	☐ Good	☐ Fair	☐ Poor

Newsletter

Appearance	☐ Excellent	☐ Good	☐ Fair	☐ Poor
Understandable	☐ Excellent	☐ Good	☐ Fair	☐ Poor
Informative	☐ Excellent	☐ Good	☐ Fair	☐ Poor
Overall Impact	☐ Excellent	☐ Good	☐ Fair	☐ Poor

Video - CD - DVD

Appearance	☐ Excellent	☐ Good	☐ Fair	☐ Poor
Understandable	☐ Excellent	☐ Good	☐ Fair	☐ Poor
Informative	☐ Excellent	☐ Good	☐ Fair	☐ Poor
Overall Impact	☐ Excellent	☐ Good	☐ Fair	☐ Poor

(continued on back page)

Figure 13.2 – New Clients

Thank you

for selecting Greenbaum and Orecchio, Inc. as your wealth manager.

Since you are a new client we are interested in your observations and perceptions about how we contact and communicate with our perspective clients.

We would appreciate it if you would take a few minutes to complete this questionnaire about why you selected our firm, as well as an evaluation of some of our marketing materials. We've included a postage-paid, self-addressed return envelope.

This information will be kept in the strictest confidence.

Please check off all appropriate responses to each question in the survey, and feel free to make comments in the "Other" section. We'll incorporate your suggestions when we upgrade this information for future contact with perspective clients.

If you have any questions, please call Dick Deutsch at (201) 768-4600.

13. What improvements could be made to better communicate our benefits to prospective clients?

____

____

Thank you for taking the time to complete and return this questionnaire. Your comments and suggestions are greatly appreciated.

Your name *(optional)* ________________________

Why not recommend us to a family member, friend, or a business associate?

As your know, there are a lot of good reasons why you can recommend Greenbaum and Orecchio, Inc. to others who need wealth management services.

- We can help them achieve their goals
- We are fee only *(we take no commissions)*
- We are a fiduciary *(no conflicts of interest)*
- We can reduce their taxes and expenses
- We have top credentials and expertise
- We offer to work with their accountant/attorney
- We can minimize their financial risk
- We offer unique investment opportunities
- We are available when they need us

Plus, for everyone you recommend who becomes a G&O wealth management client, we'll make a one-time $500.00 contribution to your favorite charity.

Call us with your recommendations at (201) 768-4600.

GREENBAUM AND ORECCHIO, INC.
Wealth Management Services
1 DeWolf Road
Old Tappan, NJ 07675-7015
Fee Only
(201) 768-4600 • Fax (201) 768-1111
Info@InvestmentCounsel.com
www.InvestmentCounsel.com

What do you think about us?

As a new client, we'd like to know why you selected us as your wealth manager.

GREENBAUM AND ORECCHIO, INC.
Wealth Management Services

Reprinted with permission of Gary Greenbaum and Tom Orecchio, Greenbaum and Orecchio, Inc., Old Tappan, NJ (http://www.investmentcounsel.com/Advisors/investmencounsel/).

Figure 13.2 – New Clients (cont'd)

1. Before you chose Greenbaum and Orecchio, Inc. (G&O) why did you seek out a new wealth manager?

- ❑ Unhappy with current financial advisor
- ❑ New wealth *(inheritance, lottery, etc.)*
- ❑ Death/disability in family
- ❑ Retirement
- ❑ Sale of business
- ❑ Other ____________

2. How did you first learn about G&O?

❑ Attorney ❑ Accountant ❑ NAPFA ❑ NFLPA ❑ Friend/family member
❑ Business associate ❑ Marketing materials ❑ Website ❑ Other____________

3. What were your most important reasons for choosing G&O?

- ❑ Integration of financial planning and investment counsel
- ❑ Fee only compensation *(no commissions, hidden costs)*
- ❑ Cost of services
- ❑ Wide range of services
- ❑ The firm acts as a fiduciary *(can only act in client's best interest)*
- ❑ Size of the firm *(large enough for excellent service, but small enough for personalized attention)*
- ❑ Professional credentials/affiliations of the staff
- ❑ Experience of the staff
- ❑ Recognition of the firm *(by media, outside organizations)*
- ❑ Independence from financial products/vendors *(no conflicts of interest)*
- ❑ Investment strategy *(use of Modern Portfolio Theory)*
- ❑ Investment access *(institutional products, alternative investments, etc.)*
- ❑ Focus on reducing cost, expenses and portfolio risk
- ❑ Coordination with client's accountant and/or attorney
- ❑ Assistance with implementation of financial planning action steps
- ❑ The firm educates its clients, and communicates with them on a regular basis
- ❑ Personality/knowledge of staff contact at G&O
- ❑ Other *(please list)* ____________

4. Have you been satisfied with G&O's wealth management services?

❑ Yes ❑ No Comments ____________

5. Have any questions you've asked been answered to your satisfaction?

❑ Yes ❑ No Comments ____________

6. Have you received reports and correspondence on time?

❑ Yes ❑ No Comments ____________

7. Has G&O coordinated with your other professional advisors?

❑ Yes ❑ No Comments ____________

8. Has G&O provided you education and information to make informed decisions?

❑ Yes ❑ No Comments ____________

9. Has G&O updated your asset allocation to reflect major changes in your lifestyle?

❑ Yes ❑ No Comments ____________

10. Are you satisfied that you are accomplishing your long-term financial goals?

❑ Yes ❑ No Comments ____________

11. If you saw them, how would you rate the following G&O marketing materials?

Small Tri-Fold Brochures

Appearance	❑ Excellent	❑ Good	❑ Fair	❑ Poor
Understandable	❑ Excellent	❑ Good	❑ Fair	❑ Poor
Informative	❑ Excellent	❑ Good	❑ Fair	❑ Poor
Overall Impact	❑ Excellent	❑ Good	❑ Fair	❑ Poor

Large Corporate Brochure

Appearance	❑ Excellent	❑ Good	❑ Fair	❑ Poor
Understandable	❑ Excellent	❑ Good	❑ Fair	❑ Poor
Informative	❑ Excellent	❑ Good	❑ Fair	❑ Poor
Overall Impact	❑ Excellent	❑ Good	❑ Fair	❑ Poor

Newsletter

Appearance	❑ Excellent	❑ Good	❑ Fair	❑ Poor
Understandable	❑ Excellent	❑ Good	❑ Fair	❑ Poor
Informative	❑ Excellent	❑ Good	❑ Fair	❑ Poor
Overall Impact	❑ Excellent	❑ Good	❑ Fair	❑ Poor

Video

Appearance	❑ Excellent	❑ Good	❑ Fair	❑ Poor
Understandable	❑ Excellent	❑ Good	❑ Fair	❑ Poor
Informative	❑ Excellent	❑ Good	❑ Fair	❑ Poor
Overall Impact	❑ Excellent	❑ Good	❑ Fair	❑ Poor

12. How can we provide better service to you?

____

____

13. Comments ____________

____

Name *(optional)* ____________

Chapter 14

ETHICS

A book on practice management would be remiss if it did not include a major chapter on ethics, because our dealings with other persons' money are infused with the possibility of doing wrong over doing right. Ethics come into play in many investment and planning contexts, including the fee structures and business models we adopt, as discussed below.

DEFINING ETHICAL BEHAVIOR

For now, let's address the question of ethics at its most basic level: What, in any context, does ethical behavior look like? As Tim Hayes, a planner with Landmark Financial Advisory Services, LLC in Pittsford, New York, and instructor of the "Morality in Business" course at Rochester, New York's St. John Fisher College says, "Sometimes ethical guidelines are as clear-cut as thinking on the order of 'what would a good Christian Jew [or Moslem or Buddhist] do in such-and-such a situation.' The Bible and the Talmud offer many references and much guidance on ethics and business. The Talmud says the first question that will be asked of a Jew at the heavenly court is whether or not he conducted his business affairs honestly. And the Bible says nothing that prevents us from running a profitable venture."

These may be useful references if you have a strong religious background. But, what if you don't? What if you're a business school graduate with a strong profit motive and a purely secular notion of right and wrong? To address this void, the Certified Financial Planner Board of Standards has decided you must have a certain number of continuing education credits specifically in the area of ethics to maintain your CFP designation and, presumably, guard against wrongdoing. And those credits are typically acquired by taking courses in situational ethics – what would you do in such-and-such a situation involving you and your client?

This method is employed because ethics is often not a clear question of right and wrong, but a nuance somewhere in between the two. Sure, a planner thinking about putting his 85-year-old widow's entire portfolio in a C-rated junk bond fund that will pay him a 5% upfront commission is facing a rather black and white ethical decision. But what if he wants to put 20% of her portfolio in such a fund to boost her much-needed monthly cash flow? Or what if it's 10% in a different junk bond fund sporting a less onerous commission structure? As we move from the absurd to the plausible, where do we draw the ethical line between clearly right and clearly wrong? Obviously, there's often no clear distinction … no easy decision.

And, therefore, most ethics courses are situational, because it's in the midst of planning situations that the more challenging ethical dilemmas usually arise. Someone who has thought long and hard about this is Linda Gadkowski who operates a successful planning firm in Centerville, Massachusetts that bears her name. Like so many planners, Gadkowski had a different life before financial planning. It was a dual life – at least from a career standpoint. She was a teacher and she also owned a Sylvan Learning Center franchise. As her Sylvan Learning Center was to her teaching career, Gadkowski's company – Beacon Hill Financial Educators, LLC – now is to her planning practice.

Beacon Hill (www.bhfe.com) is one of the training companies approved by the CFP Board of Standards to offer qualifying CE credits to planners who need to fulfill their ethics CE requirements. Beacon's courses frequently employ a situational context for teaching ethics.

And what are some of those situational contexts? Serving the older client is one that readily lends itself to abuses, conflicts, and questions of right and wrong. While many clients in their 70s and over are quite lucid in their thinking and legally competent to make planning and investment decisions on their own behalf, others are traveling that gradual path to irrationality our legal system characterizes as mental incompetence. In other words, older clients can pose additional ethical dilemmas – over and above other clients – just by virtue of their age.

David Foster, a fee-only planner and principal of Foster & Motley, Inc. in Cincinnati, Ohio, relates a story that demonstrates just one of many ways ethical issues can arise with older, often incapacitated clients – issues that would seldom be present with younger clients:

"I had this old tax return client – he was never a planning client – and occasionally I'd suggest something for his broker to change in his investment mix. At some point, this client's health failed, and his niece Ruth came into the picture. My client told me Ruth would be helping me with his information. A year or two passed and I never talked to the client, just to Ruth, who moved her uncle to a nursing home. So I'm doing his tax return one year and I see he has no more Proctor & Gamble (P&G) dividends. Ruth tells me her uncle gave her all of the P&G stock, which was worth $700,000. I told her she needed to file a gift tax return, and I explained how she'd missed the opportunity for a step-up in basis. Soon after, my client died. Around the time I'm preparing his final return for tax year 2000, the family's attorney calls to inform me that ten other nieces and nephews are suing Ruth [in connection with the P&G stock transfer]. I was even called in to testify. Ruth had to give back everything and pay attorney's costs. This event clarified for me that we have [a greater responsibility with older clients]. My client never asked me for estate advice, and I never had any reason to question him about his inheritors. This was an eye-opener for me."[1]

While this situation didn't involve an ethical choice on the part of the planner, it demonstrates how planners can find themselves in the midst of planning situations where the ethics of someone related to the client – to whom the planner has a fiduciary responsibility – may come into play and implicate the advisor.

To protect themselves from charges of unethical behavior when working with the elderly, some planners believe it's best to anticipate that something may eventually happen and formalize a coping procedure in advance. Ron Pearson, owner of Beach Financial Advisory Service in Virginia Beach, Virginia, an industry expert in planning for parents of disabled children, uses a form with older clients titled "Anticipating the Potential for Incapacity." See Figure 14.1 for a modified version of this form.

While tough ethical decisions may originate because you work with a certain type of client or employ a certain fee structure, others will originate with *any* client by virtue of the many conflicts planners face in the course of their ordinary, day-to-day work.

CONFLICTS OF INTEREST

What is a conflict of interest? It's a situation in which someone has a personal interest sufficient to significantly influence the objective exercise of his duties. As noted earlier, the job of the typical wirehouse broker clearly illustrates this principle. The conflict is the broker's need to choose between mediocre but high-payout investment products, on the one hand, and lower-cost products possibly more appropriate to the clients' goals, on the other.

The most classic of conflicts likely to be encountered by a planner managing his clients' investment is articulated by Steven Cowen of Cowen & Associates in La Jolla, California. Cowen describes a relatively common situation: "Your client asks your advice as to whether to pay off his mortgage but, to do so, he will have to pull $400,000 out of the account you manage. This has happened to me six times in the last year. In all but one case I told the client to pay off the mortgage and I lost the assets from my management. It hurts but it was best for the clients and [making the right choice] cemented our relationship." For planners with a "fee-based" or "assets-under-management" fee structure by which their income is based directly on the level of client assets he manages, this conflict is common. And it can affect the fee-based broker exactly the same way it affects the independent fee-only planner.

Some advisors practice for years and don't think about these kinds of conflicts until they are in the middle of one for the first time. Says Carl Johnson of Ames Planning Associates, Inc. in Peterborough, New Hampshire, "Maintaining one's integrity is a *daily* decision. Integrity, like life, is not gained or lost in a day. If it is lost, it is most often lost slowly, a piece at a time ... so slowly that we don't realize it. It is this erosion that we must protect against."

To prevent the erosion, we need to see long-accepted business relationships and procedures in a different light. Following are four common situations faced by many advisors that may pose hidden conflicts. Later, we will discuss ways to counter these conflicts.

First, there are our interactions with other professionals on our clients' behalves. A local CPA refers to you a good client in his attempt to get on your radar screen. You meet the CPA over lunch, thank him for the referral, discuss the client he referred, and learn more about the CPA's practice. After performing some additional due diligence, you conclude he's competent, reputable, charges reasonable fees, and so you return the favor and use him for your next trusted client needing tax work. It's clear that this CPA will play tit-for-tat if you refer more clients to him, and you could rationalize it by the good work that he does.

Figure 14.1

ANTICIPATING THE POTENTIAL FOR INCAPACITY

As your advisor, I must anticipate the possibility that my clients may, at some age, undergo behavioral changes harmful to their financial well-being. Because there is often little in the way of objective criteria for assessing the difference between rational decisions that may be out of the ordinary, and those that indicate some deeper difficulties, and because it is not my field nor the nature of my training to make such assessments, I have devised this form to prepare for an eventuality that, hopefully, will never occur. In the event of what a court would deem to be mental "incapacity," please indicate below what your expectations would be of me. Choose as many items as seem appropriate.

_____ I would like to have the subject raised with me first.

_____ If, after such a discussion, the concerns are not resolved, I give permission to you to contact one or more of the people listed below and discuss the issue with him/her/them.

_____ If, after such a discussion, the concerns are not resolved, and if I have not given permission to you to contact one or more of the people listed below, I recognize that you may find it necessary to unilaterally terminate our contractual financial planning/investment management relationship.

_____ I give permission to you to contact one or more of the people listed below and discuss the issue with him/her/them, without necessarily raising the subject with me first, if you deem it appropriate.

_____ I would want you or one of the people listed below to arrange for an evaluation by an appropriate specialist (elder-care professional, etc.) at my expense. (Indicate whom you would be willing to have make such arrangements.)

_____ I have listed below those people I would want you to contact under the circumstances referred to above:

Family Member: Relationship _________ Name _________________________ Phone # ____________

Family Member: Relationship _________ Name _________________________ Phone # ____________

Religious Advisor: Name _________________________ Phone # ____________

Physician: Name _________________________ Phone # ____________

Attorney: Name _________________________ Phone # ____________

Accountant: Name _________________________ Phone # ____________

Friend: Name _________________________ Phone # ____________

Other: Relationship _________ Name _________________________ Phone # ____________

Note: Your providing me with this document and my accepting it is in no way to be construed as a commitment on my part to act as your agent outside the normal financial planning/investment management role I have undertaken and agreed to prior to your completing and presenting me with this form. This is not to be considered a part of the services you have contracted with me to perform and you agree, by signing it, that you and your heirs or assigns will hold me harmless if I either act or fail to act on these stated preferences based on my own best judgment.

I have indicated my preferences above and agree to hold [You or Your Firm's Name] harmless as stated above.

Name: (Printed) _________________________

Signature: _________________________

Date: ______________

Reprinted with permission of Ron Pearson, Beach Financial Advisory Services, Virginia Beach, VA (http://www.beachfas.com/).

Do we have a problem here? That question occurred to David Lewis of Resource Advisory Services, Inc. in Knoxville, Tennessee, many of whose clients work with CPAs in relationships established before they came to Lewis' firm. He believed those clients could probably benefit from the more sophisticated accounting and estate planning work his own, preferred accounting firm could offer but, says Lewis, "How far should we go to move a client relationship to another CPA? No one will ever answer these questions definitively. The most we can do is use our best judgment." [Does the less sophisticated accountant – through years of experience together with the client – know the client, the client's family, and the client's business better than a high-powered firm would for a long time? Would a move actually be detrimental in terms of the attention the client would then receive, moving from a big fish in a small pond to a small fish in a big pond?] Lewis' clients might benefit from being moved, but so would Lewis. Sometimes the perception of conflict that comes from the advisor benefiting alongside his client is just as damaging as a conflict in which the advisor benefits at the client's expense.

A related conflict, notes James Richardson, Ph.D., a financial advisor in Akron, Ohio, is "feeling obligated to refer back to other professionals who have sent me referrals." It's safe to say that referrals should take place because the advisor respects the integrity and competency of the professional to whom he is referring, but is it possible we see these qualities where they don't exist when we fulfill our perceived "obligations?" Maybe cross-referrals, as a common business practice, are inherently conflicted.

A second type of conflict that is common – yet just as elusive in its resolution – is that of standardized business practices. Sure, every client is different, but do we have to perform a different process to plan for each individual? That would be inefficient. Yet do we harm the client by standardizing our procedures? This has occurred to Matthew Reading of MTR Consulting in Austin, Texas, who discusses the pros and cons of standardized systems: "Internal systems give consistent service but, by creating a service 'template,' you may miss things. If you don't go down new roads when interviewing a new client, you could miss important information about them." Yet we know that standardization occurs not only early in the financial planning process, but should exist in every internal office procedure we employ – if we are profit-minded.

A third conflict is faced daily by advisors earning some or all of their income from product commissions. They routinely must choose among competing products for their clients, some of which have more generous payouts to the advisor than others. Says Elisabeth Plax of Plax & Associates Financial Services in Pepper Pike, Ohio, "I have purposely not associated with a single insurance company so that I can shop a number of them for every client. And I refuse to speak to wholesalers when they are pushing a 'bonus' product," referring to extra payouts or other perks designed to entice the planner to favor one product over another." Clearly, the system in which many of us work is flawed. Most of the time the responsibility to avoid temptation and, in turn, conflicts of interest, is solely our own.

Finally, a very common conflict arises from having clients as personal friends. In our business, the name of the game is relationships. Solid business relationships often lead to personal relationships. It's hard to find a good advisor who doesn't socialize outside of the office with one or more of his clients. Yet, notes Eleanor Blayney of Sullivan, Bruyette, Speros & Blayney, Inc. in McLean, Virginia, "our friendship may cause [my clients] to hesitate to fire me."

Isn't it a *good* thing if the client doesn't leave? Yes, but perhaps only from *your* point of view. Says Blayney, "client longevity may be the single greatest determinant of profitability for our firm. Yet, if you don't take care of your client, they may find it so awkward to fire an advisor *and* lose a close personal friend that they take no action – to their detriment." Blayney admits she often finds herself going even further to provide these clients with added value just to avoid this conflict.

Now that you hopefully see some of the conflicts that are always present yet hidden from view, here are some ways to deal with them. Lewis suggests two strategies: "We can align ourselves [to all with whom we do business] so that the interests are as close to each other as possible, as in a business where all parties share the same vision. Or, we can be extremely open, clear, and transparent about our goals and interests, such that every party involved can clearly know the motivations of all other parties to the relationship. Of course, the best situation is to maximize both these methods."

One commonality among the above examples is that the advisor may be perceived as not having worked hard enough for his client. And "full disclosure" up front, as suggested by Lewis, is probably the best antidote for this problem. Adds Herbert Daroff, an attorney and advisor with Baystate Financial Services, LLC in Boston, Massachusetts, "What's wrong with only doing an amount of work based on the amount of compensation received? The whole issue is the foundation of the practice standards. The more specific you are with your engagement letter, the less there will be a conflict of expectations. If a client wants me to evaluate every mutual fund available on the planet, that will cost a great deal of money."

The other aspect of full disclosure is client education. Matthew Weitzman, advertising advisor with AFW Asset Management in Purchase, New York, claims, "If we can make sure that the client understands the inherent risks in [taking an action we have recommended] and perhaps also how this increased risk might impact future planning goals and projections, but they still elect to have us do so anyway, I believe we have not compromised our position at all. We have advised the client well, educated him on the ramifications of the different options, and then listened to his informed decision. I see this as fundamental to the advisory/planning role."

Conflicts and their resolution will be debated endlessly as individuals try to find within themselves or get from their professional associations' codes of conduct the guidelines for ethical behavior. Yet, adds Hayes, "Sometimes [behaving ethically] will mean we don't get fully compensated for our efforts, but we can also anticipate the entire effort needed [to do a thorough job for our client] and charge for it."

So, the bad news is that none of us are conflict-free and, therefore, exempt from ethical decisions. The good news is that by smartly anticipating everything you must do for a client, determining a fee or commission appropriate to that engagement, fully disclosing everything to your client, and applying the Golden Rule in all your business dealings, you can greatly minimize ethical challenges – those you can anticipate, and those you can't.

WHERE CAN I FIND OUT MORE ABOUT IT?

See Appendix B for the Certified Financial Planner Board of Standards, Inc., *Code of Ethics and Professional Responsibility* (http://www.cfp.net/Certificants/conduct.asp).

CHAPTER ENDNOTES

1. Dave Foster is a co-editor of *The Tools & Techniques of Investment Planning*, written by Stephan R. Leimberg, Robert T. LeClair, Robert J. Doyle, Jr., and Thomas R. Robinson (Cincinnati, OH: The National Underwriter Company, 2004).

Commentary

In this author's opinion, financial services in this country began as one huge conflict of interest – and conflicts of interest equate with questionable ethics. Here we speak of the brokerage industry, this country's primary model for the delivery of financial services.

As consumers, or potential financial planning clients, those of us in my generation grew up with a one-dimensional understanding of financial services: You found a broker and opened an investment account. That *was* financial planning, plain and simple, when I was a teenager in the 1960s. Astonishingly, this model persists today for a huge, if uninformed, segment of the U.S. population. They don't know alternatives exist and they persist in taking this conflict-ridden path to hoped-for financial gain.

What happens when one goes to a broker? The institutional framework for the broker-client relationship dooms the client to struggle against sometimes insurmountable odds in his attempt to realize investment gains. The problems with the broker-client model are well known by now:

- The broker's primary allegiance is to his employer – the brokerage firm, or wirehouse – not to his client.
- The broker is an employee of an institution that manufactures investment products for sale to clients.
- The brokerage firm often invests in many of the same securities its brokers seek to put in client accounts.
- The broker derives different levels of compensation from different products; that is, his employer pushes him towards an ethical dilemma every time he recommends a product to a client.

These are just a few of the conflicts brokers deal with and pass on to their clients every day in the form of unsuitable investments, excessive account turnover, and other activity that has the net effect of diminishing client account balances while fattening brokerage firm coffers. Mutual gain is virtually impossible except in a raging bull market.

Is this too harsh an indictment? Perhaps. We know that many large wirehouses now encourage their brokers to adopt a fee-based model that lessens the everyday conflicts they face in working for their clients. Nonetheless, not all brokers will adopt the new model, and those who do will still sell commissioned products.

The point of this history lesson is that this is the thinking and the ethical model from which the financial planning industry sprang in the late 1960s and early 1970s. And change is slow in coming. Brokers working within wirehouses today are still faced with most of the same ethical dilemmas faced by their historical counterparts.

Independent planners, a phenomenon that didn't exist in the mid-1900s, fortunately aren't as hamstrung by the institutional frameworks in which wirehouse brokers have toiled. Within this segment of the industry, a number of fee structures have evolved to move planners more towards their clients' side of the table. Most notable are the fee-only planners who receive no commissions but are, instead, compensated directly by their clients at all times. Does the fact of being fee-only eliminate all conflicts and ethical dilemmas? Some fee-only planners naively think so. But conflicts affect planners of all compensation stripes.

Chapter 15

COMMUNICATING TO MANAGE CLIENT EXPECTATIONS

The phrase "managing expectations" has taken on a relatively narrow meaning for most advisors: educating clients about investing so that when portfolio values inevitably fluctuate, clients will understand and accept the inevitability of those fluctuations. Ideally, they should not be worried about temporary losses in portfolio value or overly exuberant when returns occasionally exceed the averages.

While this is a valid definition of "managing expectations," the concept can be applied, as well, to the advisor's entire service offering, not just investing. You can enhance your client relationships by managing all of their expectations with respect to all aspects of your services.

MODES OF EFFECTIVE COMMUNICATION

First, you need to have a voice with clients. Recognize, however, that you don't get a voice by maximizing assets under management and minimizing client contact. That's a recipe for short-term profits. Instead, you get a voice by increasing client communication. It doesn't matter whether you do this in the form of meetings, phone calls, emails, or newsletters (you should be using all of the above). The point is that you need to get clients hanging onto your next word.

We've all heard about clients who do nothing without calling their advisor first. An advisor once told me a story about a client who hadn't eaten in days. "Why not" asked the advisor? "Because my refrigerator broke and I couldn't reach you to ask about buying a new one," answered the client. It's not necessarily your job to make every client as dependent upon you as this one, but the story is useful in describing a relationship in which the client seeks the counsel of her advisor before anyone else's counsel. Note, however, that this position of authority is not achieved with infrequent client communication.

Most advisors have a primary and secondary means of client communication. Some advisors are more extroverted, thriving on face-to-face contact and, therefore, may like to have quarterly (or even more frequent) in-person meetings as their primary form of client communication. Others may meet less frequently with their clients, preferring to keep up contact with frequent bulletins or newsletters. Clients enjoy receiving my monthly bulletins if they are not "canned," but written in a conversational tone directly to the clients about topics that are interesting to them.

In between the quarterly meeting or the monthly bulletin, clients need to have an open line to your office. They need to be able to have contact with someone in authority in as short a time as possible and, certainly, within 24 hours at a maximum. Check to be sure it is impossible for clients to forget where you are and how to reach you – by phone, fax, email, or snail mail – and be certain that your clients' line of communication to you and your staff are as easy and quick as possible.

USING MARKET FLUCTUATIONS TO MANAGE EXPECTATIONS

Now that you have their attention, you can manage all sorts of client expectations, not the least of which are expectations about the investment markets. For years now, veteran advisors have been saying in the media right after stock market crashes that their phones haven't been ringing off the hook. They almost boastfully recount how they and their clients have remained calm, knowing that the markets would resume their upward march as these advisors have told their clients so many times in the past.

This is perhaps an example of managed expectations, but it's also an example of a missed opportunity. Not all clients can be persuaded to relax when markets crumble. You may think they're relaxed because you don't hear from them. But you have an opportunity to be sensitive to their real, unvoiced concerns by sending them a bulletin with some calming words. It doesn't have to be fancy. You can do it by U.S. mail or simply by email. Let your clients hear you reiterate your usual mantra about how the market will go through down cycles from time to time. Be there for them. Create what Florida advisor Gene Balliett fondly calls "client glue" with your stream of communications.

GIVING ADVANCE NOTICE *BEFORE* CHANGE IS KEY

But don't stop at market upheavals in managing client expectations. You can use the same system for all kinds of things, particularly hard-to-hear information. What kinds of changes might we want to make that would be difficult for clients to hear? Realize, first of all, that change is hard for most people. If you're going to make any kind of change that will affect clients, no matter how small or large, some clients will get anxious. It could be something as small as changing the format of the quarterly investment report you send them (all the more reason to manage their anxiety). Really hard-to-hear changes might include new partners, fee increases, a change in the person who is their primary contact within your firm, or even preparing clients for the fact that you're going to retire.

As someone once said, a good public speaker tells you what he's going to tell you, then tells it to you, and then tells you what he told you. Managing client expectations works the same way. "No surprises" should be your guiding principle. Communicate early and communicate often. The more momentous the occasion, the earlier and more frequent the communication should be.

When my former business partner and I split up our firm and I planned to move my practice and client relationships out West, I started telling clients 18 months in advance. The process started with an explanation in client meetings of what I was thinking of doing. Following those meetings, a letter went out to all the clients explaining, from a very personal standpoint, my reasons for wanting to make the change. The letter also explained how I envisioned continuing to serve them from a far-away location. Following that letter were more meetings. Then I sent out requests for signatures to paperwork changes. At this point, only two out of 50 clients were unwilling to remain with me. One was converted after another meeting. The other I lost. Not a bad track record, all in all, but it never could have been done if I'd surprised these clients with the news shortly in advance of the actual change.

I actually learned this trick from my daughter. Children don't want to go to bed and most will tell you they're not tired even when their eyelids begin to get heavy. If I tell my daughter it's bedtime when it's her actual bedtime, I'll have a fight on my hands. But if I prepare her 15 minutes in advance by saying "it's your bedtime in 15 minutes," the objections are fewer. Giving her "notices" at the 10- and 5-minute intervals follows that initial announcement. Consequently, by her actual bedtime, she's ready to go brush her teeth and get in bed without too much grumbling. Clients aren't that much different from kids. They all want what they want, and they all like a certain amount of routine. You just have to manage their expectations.

A word about how websites fit into this picture: Don't be fooled into thinking that because you maintain a website and post regular client bulletins to it that your clients are actually reading them. Few clients (or anyone, for that matter) will go to a website of their own volition. They need to have information pushed to them. You can email your communication or e-mail a notice to them that the communication is now on your website, and provide a link to that page on your site. Just don't assume that putting a message there in cyberspace, in and of itself, will keep your clients informed. Communicate more with your clients and you will be rewarded with greater loyalty and the ability to make changes in your practice you never thought possible.

MANAGING INVESTMENT RETURN EXPECTATIONS

Having said all of that, let's return to managing expectations around investing. This task can be particularly challenging during a severe upturn or downturn, no matter how much you may have prepared your clients in advance with theoretical information. Why a severe upturn? Upturns can be more damaging to client relationships than downturns because clients may come to believe they no longer need an advisor. In the 1995-1999 market upturn, many advisors experienced net client outflows as clients decided they could make money on their own (after all, everyone was doing it, especially the "day traders") so, with little thought to the valuable, non-investment services their advisors may have been providing, they left to do their own thing.

Downturns are challenging too, though, because most advisors use asset allocation strategies, which, by definition, do not achieve the highs and lows of pure stock market returns. It's ironic, for instance, that many advisors who diversified portfolios in 1997 had a relatively poor year when the S&P 500 was up over 33%.

As most advisors tell clients, we're not in the performance game. But it's interesting how quickly clients forget this when their portfolios are lagging an otherwise bullish market. Different educational approaches work for different clients. For example, during this period, one client brought to my attention that, according to his calculations, he'd earned nothing on his combined accounts for 1997. Understand that clients (even quantitatively-oriented ones) seem to always miscalculate rates of return, which is no surprise since they seldom have the knowledge or the tools to make these calculations correctly. Notice what happens when we take slightly different measurement periods for this client in question before, during, and after the problems I was having in his portfolio due to a small allocation to emerging foreign markets:

3/31/96 - 3/31/97	12.4%
4/30/96 - 4/30/97	10.4%
5/31/96 - 5/31/97	13.6%
6/30/96 - 6/30/97	17.8%
7/31/96 - 7/31/97	24.9%
8/31/96 - 8/31/97	17.3%
9/30/96 - 9/30/97	19.7%
10/31/96 - 10/31/97	12.1%
11/30/96 - 11/30/97	8.3%
12/31/96 - 12/31/97	7.0%
1/31/97 - 1/31/98	3.3%
2/28/97 - 2/28/98	6.6%
3/31/97 - 3/31/98	11.2%

Calendar year 1997 just happened to have a starting point and an ending point that yielded the third lowest return of any 12-month period within the 24 months illustrated above. When the client viewed the entire series of time periods, he could see much more clearly how panic selling in Southeast Asia caused a dip in overall returns not nearly as severe as he'd thought, and how the rebound from oversold levels caused the swift reappearance of more satisfactory returns.

Another client also thought he'd earned nothing in 1997 and, in fact, was certain that several accounts were in the red. Furthermore, he said the only positive returns he had received were in his TIAA-CREF accounts, not in the accounts I was managing.

When he first came on as a client, and periodically thereafter, I would analyze the offerings in his TIAA-CREF and advise him to spread his CREF balance between the standard equity offering and the bond market account. Because this balance was considerable, we didn't need to invest in U.S. large-cap equities in his other accounts. We used his TIAA for fixed income and most of his real estate exposure. Therefore, the accounts I maintained for him were confined to U.S. small-cap and foreign emerging market stocks, plus some more fixed income. Most of the small cap funds I used were down about 5% in the last quarter of 1997, so my accounts held the client's worst performing assets, which were balanced by his other accounts.

This is one of those instances where I'm glad I'm in the financial management business and not in the asset management game. The difference is this: As an asset manager, I probably would have been charging a percentage of assets and focusing my attention strictly on "my" accounts; thus, my performance would have been narrowly judged. And, in fact, this is what the client tried to do. It was up to me to remind him the reason I charge flat fees is because we are watching and making deliberate decisions on everything he owns—all of his accounts. It was me who instructed him on the allocations to maintain in his TIAA-CREF, and that is very much a part of his total portfolio over which I have influence. Therefore, I told him, we did not earn returns of 4.63%, as applied to only his accounts under my direct supervision, but rather returns of 7%, as applied to all of his accounts. (As with the first client, this client's returns were significantly higher in the 12-month time periods adjacent to calendar year 1997.)

What further calmed this client was a breakdown of returns from the various asset categories. His U.S. stocks (large and small together) were up 19.6%, the cash earned 5.17%, his bonds earned 6.16%, the real estate increased 15.03%, and the internationals lost 6.71%. He could see then that the problem was quite isolated.

What both of these clients forgot in all of this is that they had chosen, with my guidance, portfolios designed to earn returns higher than those afforded by T-bills and which, therefore, would bring some volatility. Statements by me to the effect that 1997 was one of those "down" years we knew we would have along the way had fallen on deaf ears. The reason was they kept reading in the paper and seeing on the news how the U.S. market was tripping over itself to rack up yet another outstanding year of performance.

Fortunately, not all of our clients are so "tuned in" to the numbers. I find that most clients take all of this pretty philosophically, as I do. For those clients, I compared returns for calendar year 1997 with year-to-date returns through September 30, 1997, as well as from inception to both September 30, 1997, and December 31, 1997. They could see that Southeast Asia's problems had caused a temporary downturn in what was otherwise a fine track record (as measured by achieving their agreed-upon, target returns, not by "beating the market").

The mandate from those clients upset by 1997's performance, I decided, was that I must be more effective in explaining my brand of investing, and in helping them to anticipate and accept both the downs and the ups.

Although your clients will accept, and even implement, your portfolio recommendations, you don't know (and, often, they don't know either) what their risk tolerance really is until it's tested. The best we can do in the meantime is keep hammering away on the meaning of risk – that is, managing their expectations.

Chapter 16

HIRING EMPLOYEES OR OUTSOURCE PARTNERS

Employees ... can't live with them, can't live without them. Not to denigrate those fine people that help us grow our practices (and may even become our partners), but employees are a mixed blessing. Good ones accelerate your success; bad ones can slow you to a crawl.

But, we may be moving too fast. There are so many possible aspects to a discussion about employees; it's hard to know where to begin. There's hiring and firing, matching them to the job, matching them to the culture of the firm and the personalities of their co-employees (or just you, the owner), promoting their career growth, keeping them happy, and so on. As you may surmise, employees aren't cogs that you pay for a day's work; they're complex important human beings as well as essential tools that can leverage your success – but who require much "care and feeding."

And that's why a new trend has developed toward outsourcing. Advisors have begun outsourcing all manner of jobs to what I like to call "virtual work partners" (VWPs). They outsource administrative tasks, such as mass mailings and new account applications. They even outsource more complicated tasks like data entry for a financial plan, or rebalancing of client portfolios.

Who are these people to whom these tasks are outsourced? Well, not surprising is that most are past employees – of someone. They're people who worked for others as administrative assistants, bookkeepers, investment managers and, yes, financial planners. What they have in common is the fact that they couldn't be fully satisfied depending upon an employer to meet all of their needs. They find they can do this better working for themselves.

To summarize, either employees or VWPs can give you the support system you need. (And don't make the mistake of being a sole practitioner who has *no* support system; that is a sure way to inefficiency and low profitability. Be a "sole principal" instead.) There are many differences between the two, the biggest one being that the VWP is entirely self-run and self-motivated. The "care and feeding" aspect of employees is all but absent with VWPs, and that's one of their main attractions.

VIRTUAL WORK PARTNERS VS. EMPLOYEES

Before we talk further about the advantages of each, let's discuss the ways in which they're similar. Whether you're considering hiring an employee or a VWP, both need to:

- Be competent;
- Agree (we strongly suggest, in writing) to keep client information confidential;
- Have their job communicated clearly; and
- Have functional workflow systems.

Some advisors object to the idea of using a VWP because they believe they can't control their work. Actually, there's little difference between employees and VWPs in this respect. Just because someone sits in a cubicle within the walls of your company doesn't mean you can control them any more than if they sit in a room inside their own home. Most work is accomplished and facilitated these days by computer networks, whether they run throughout adjacent cubicles in the same physical structure, or whether they bounce around cyberspace from one computer node to another – perhaps thousands of miles apart.

Work control isn't really different; collaboration is. It's sometimes easier to collaborate on a financial plan with several employees if you're all within the same walls. But even the process of gathering around the conference room table, coffee cup in hand, is changing. It's just about as easy to share the work product that is the focus of your collaboration over the Internet as each person calls into a "bridge line" to form the discussion group. The only thing lacking is eye contact. This is one of the advantages of having on-site employees.

What are some of the disadvantages? As an employer, you become largely responsible for your employees' career development, which is not the case with the VWP. It used to be you could hire someone for a job, never vary the job, perhaps give them a little more money each year, and expect them to stick around for a decade or more. Those days are long gone. Everyone wants career advancement now, and that's a good thing. It keeps us from burnout, keeps us satisfied with our work and ourselves, and undoubtedly promotes all kinds of other benefits.

But it's a big responsibility for the employer. In most cases nowadays, if you hire someone for a position and don't have a career path in mind the day you hire them, you risk losing them at some point. And losing employees, just like losing clients, is a source of tremendous inefficiency. Any businessperson will tell you it costs much more to suffer the turnaround, rehiring, and retraining of an employee (or a client) than it does to give them what they want in the first place so they stay with you indefinitely.

Some advisors find all of this to be an interesting challenge. They may have gotten into the field because they liked planning and liked counseling clients, but they become intrigued with the aspect of managing a growing firm. If they're naturally "people persons," they may derive great satisfaction from managing the needs of a growing staff. Sure, it happens, but in my experience, it's rare. More often, advisors complain that they spend their days dealing with employee problems and no longer have the time necessary to service their major clients. Employees become a headache unless you're good at managing people, you enjoy managing people, or you've been able to grow your firm large enough to afford a middle management person to do the people management work for you.

Okay, we've explored some of the pros and cons of employees versus VWPs. And I may seem biased against employees, but that's not entirely true. My vision of the efficient firm of the future is one that uses both employees and VWPs. A trend that's now emerging in some very efficient corners of the industry is one where all administrative tasks are outsourced, and all professional positions are kept in-house. So, for example, a firm that might once have been comprised of a principal, several CFPs and/or CFAs, and three or four administrative persons, like a secretary, someone to do portfolio accounting, and a paraplanner for financial plan data entry, now finds it can more efficiently farm out the last three positions to VWPs. A VWP expert at his or her specialty is easier to manage by virtue of her take-charge attitude, so the overall personnel management function is simpler and less time consuming for the principal. And he's kept in-house what he can't very well outsource.

Of course, the above parameters describe a firm that could handle, say, 150 high net worth clients and $300,000,000 under management. Some advisors find they can exist perfectly well with the above-mentioned VWPs and *no* employees, serving fewer employees with fewer assets, but nonetheless providing themselves a very handsome income and benefit stream. In either case, VWPs make this possible. A sole principal with no professional staff can build a network of half a dozen VWPs to cover all of his administrative chores, using just as much time from each as needed. But he could never hire six employees to perform the same jobs. Even if he could get them on a part-time basis, the training, time management, haggling over partial benefits and other details would claim too much of his valuable time.

WHAT TO LOOK FOR WHEN HIRING

So, let's say you've figured out what your firm is going to look like from a people perspective. You will have some employees and maybe some VWPs, as well. How, exactly, do you hire someone? One theory is that you test your applicant, and the number and types of possible tests are unlimited. However, an indicator that many look to for information about a person's personality and probable work habits is the Myers-Briggs Type Indicator (MBTI®) test (http://www.cpp.com/products/mbti/index.asp).

The MBTI® consists of a long series of multiple choice questions designed to find out where an individual sits on four continuums, each of which defines a pair of opposite characteristics. These are "Extraversion-Introversion," "Sensing-Intuition," "Thinking-Feeling," and "Judging-Perceiving."

These pairings are in no way judgmental. An introvert is not less capable or less desirable than an extrovert, as a person. The same applies with the other pairs. However, some combination of these four characteristics describes each of us, and may or may not describe those that we hire. This is not to say that we always want to hire clones. Upon understanding all of the permutations of personalities these characteristics describe, it will become apparent that certain groups of characteristics may well go better with one functional job position, and others another.

For example, we may well want an "ISTJ" (introvert, sensing, thinking and judging) person to do our accounting or portfolio administration. This combination of characteristics often defines a person who is hardworking, pays attention to detail, isn't distracted looking for social interaction, and can think through problems and make decisions about how to handle them. You may or may not, on the other hand, want this person sitting in a meeting with your clients.

So whether you go for a clone, or for someone whose characteristics *complement* your own (or make up for your shortcomings), the Myers-Briggs test might be the way to find him or her.

That's fine, you say, but ... "how can I require a job applicant to take this lengthy test as a prerequisite for hiring? That sounds illegal, at worst, and impractical, at best." You may be right, but perhaps we can draw from the test, itself, in making up the questions we will ask our job applicants in their interviews. Let's start by characterizing the kinds of questions asked in the MBTI®. Myers-Briggs questions typically give the test taker multiple choices, and the choices point (though not always obviously) to tendencies the test taker has towards one or the other end of one of the four Myers-Briggs continuums. For example, a question might posit a social situation and ask which of several behaviors the test taker thinks he would exhibit, with the answer placing him one step closer to one end of the Introvert-Extrovert continuum.

Can you ask these questions in a job interview? Probably not. But they could easily be modified and, when put in the context of a financial advisory firm and its day-to-day activities, be made meaningful and acceptable. For example:

"Mr. or Mrs. Job Applicant, I want to ask you some general kinds of questions to get an idea of your work style. There are no right or wrong answers, so feel free to speak frankly:

1. Do you like to work in an office with lots of social contact, or do you prefer environments where you can work long periods without distraction by others?

2. If you were assisting me with specific clients, do you think you would work better with very imaginative people, or with more down-to-earth, realistic people?

3. It gets pretty busy around here and sometimes you'll be juggling a lot of balls at the same time. To help you in that type of environment, do you find it helpful to make lists, or does the idea of making a list of what you should get done leave you cold?

4. As I said, it gets pretty busy around here. How do you feel about working under pressure? Specifically, do occasional emergencies excite you, or do you try to anticipate things so that you won't have to work under the pressure of an emergency?

5. Sitting in meetings with prospective clients, we meet many different kinds of people. Some planners try to attract certain kinds of people they feel they get along with best, and others work with anyone and everyone because they can talk easily to almost anyone for as long as they have to. Which kind of planner would you be? (Really.)

6. Some of our clients have a very poor grasp of financial concepts and really approach the work we do from a somewhat emotional or sentimental rather than logical standpoint. Do you think you would prefer to deal more with a logical client, or a sentimental client?

7. If I give you a loosely defined task to do, would you be more inclined to find out how it's usually done and do it that way, or to find a new way to do it that you think is better?

8. If you heard that an older client's spouse had just died, would your first reaction be to be concerned about the loss the client had suffered, or to think about the estate planning steps the client should take?"

We've just asked our job applicant eight questions that include four pairs designed to elicit responses that will give us a glimpse into his Myers-Briggs characteristics. Obviously, this does not approach the thoroughness of the full test, but could nonetheless give us new information in a format useful to a real life determination of whether our applicant is the "clone" or the "complement" we're looking for.

Can you guess which questions give us information about which characteristics? Some are quite obvious, while others are not. First, questions about introversion versus extroversion are usually obvious. A simple, Myers-Briggs kind of definition of these traits is that an extrovert gets a charge from being around others, and "loses" charge by being alone. The introvert experiences just the opposite, feeling energized by alone time and reluctantly giving up that energy to a social gathering.

It's easy to see how these personalities could fit into a financial advisory practice, which requires much detail work behind the scenes, as well as much social contact with clients. Questions 1 and 5 are designed to give us information about our applicant's tendency towards introversion or extroversion.

Sensing versus intuition means relying on known data rather than innovative thinking. It also sometimes means paying attention to details versus seeing the big picture. Questions 2 and 7 give us feedback on this pair of traits.

Thinking versus feeling means relying more on thoughts than feelings, being truthful instead of tactful, or treating others fairly (according to a consistent system) rather than treating them based upon their individual needs. Questions 6 and 8 get at these characteristics.

Finally, judging versus perceiving means being able to make judgments or decisions easily, as opposed to perceiving, or taking in more and more data and pushing decisions forward. While judging may sound preferable to perceiving, these are very complementary characteristics, as are all of the above. Those who make decisions easily are in danger of acting on too little information, while those who perseverate indefinitely are in danger of making untimely decisions. Questions 3 and 4 address these traits.

What is your Myers-Briggs type? You should find out what you are before going forward. You can learn more about the MBTI® and other personality tests (http://www.cpp.com/products/mbti/index.asp) and other sites you will find through your own Internet search efforts. But be mindful of the guidelines discussed on the Myers-Briggs site for what constitutes a valid test and a valid use of test results before you put all your faith in an online version of the MBTI®.

If you find this information useful so far, but still aren't sure whether you should hire or outsource, here are some additional thoughts for you to consider. Sometimes, trying to establish a dependable team of employees is like building a pyramid out of marbles. Just when you think it's stable, one slips away and, in the smaller firm, that's all that's necessary to unhinge the whole operation, at least temporarily. In other words, the financial planning field is an entrepreneurial one. I'm not sure why – because many financial advisors are great at serving their clients but only so-so at running their businesses – but so many who enter this field want to be their own bosses. This has important implications for the hiring process.

Why do advisors have so much trouble retaining good employees? First, as I said earlier, this is an entrepreneurial business we're in. We're all individualists and the people we hire often are, too. Once they reach a certain level of competence and confidence, they judge themselves ready to do it their way. They are destined to start their own planning firms whether we like it or not. And this was true from the day we hired them.

Second, it's difficult to retain employees in a popular field such as financial planning. Financial planning and advisory services have been and continue to be a very desirable career path – so desirable, in fact, that labor supply often outweighs the job opportunities, at least among established, independent planning firms. Our employees are often eager to accept a low pay scale – one the labor market has created – initially. But after a couple of years, if they haven't already left and they have a high perception of their value, they often want more money than their positions may be worth in the marketplace.

The popular solution to this problem for some advisors is to give the employee an ownership interest. The problem is … if he doesn't agree with the way you run your business, he doesn't want to own a piece of it. Or, perhaps the opposite is true – she wants a piece of the business before you're ready to give it to her; ultimately, that becomes a reason to leave.

For those readers who remember Business Administration 101, there's an important lesson that many of us forget. Of course, this lesson wasn't framed in the context of a service business because we didn't have a predominantly service economy (at least not when I was first studying business). The lesson was framed in terms of manufacturing, but it's no less valid for firms like ours today. The lesson is ... don't make something yourself if you can buy a better, cheaper version from someone else. Translating that for a financial planning practice ... don't create a staff function in-house that can be accomplished better and less expensively by a VWP.

How can a VWP be both better and cheaper than an employee? Actually, it's not that far-fetched. If I hire a secretary, I must pay his salary and payroll taxes, give him benefits, vacation leave, and other things that cost me time or money. I must provide him with a computer, a high quality printer, and other expensive toys. I have to train him, sometimes not just in my methods, but also in more elementary things such as the Microsoft application software. If he's not right for the job, I risk a lawsuit in dismissing him.

Now, suppose there were a person or company who said to me, "We're expert at what we do, the services we offer include not only secretarial work, but bookkeeping, airline reservations, meeting scheduling and other administrative functions. We don't need to be in your office to do it as long as you're facile with email and the Internet. We have all of our own equipment, software, office space and access to as many of our own employees or independent contractors as we may need. We charge a flat hourly fee for the work we do, so you don't need to be concerned about any of the ancillary costs of an employee. And, if you're not satisfied, there are no strings attached. Since we have competitors, we have to do a good job at a fair price and intend to earn your trust."

This would be quite different from dealing with an employee, wouldn't it? Yes, you say, but don't you still have to hire such a firm, acquaint them with your way of doing things, and supervise them? Yes, this is true, but it's a different experience because the independent provider is entrepreneurially motivated. They are often much quicker than an employee to come to the realization that your client's satisfaction and welfare form the yardstick for measuring the success of what they do.

Hopefully, you are equipped with enough ideas now to make your staffing decisions. And, it may not be a matter of choosing between employees and VWPs. As discussed earlier, many firms will find the greatest efficiency and growth in using some combination of both.

WHERE CAN I FOUND OUT MORE?

1. David J. Drucker and Joel P. Bruckenstein, *Virtual-Office Tools for a High-Margin Practice: How Client-Centered Financial Advisors Can Cut Paperwork, Overhead and Wasted Hours* (Princeton, NJ: Bloomberg Press, 2002).

Chapter 17

TAKING ON A PARTNER

The decision to take on a partner can occur when you're first starting out as an advisor, or after many years in practice. Either way, the decision should not be taken lightly. There are few drains on one's energy and creativity as great as a partnership that's not working.

Although new and experienced planners may both seek partners, their reasons for doing so are usually different. The author was in a fourteen-year partnership that began when he entered the business. My partner and I both had the sense that we didn't know enough as individuals to launch a successful practice. We each had valuable skills and knew they could be combined to form a whole greater than the parts. Fortunately for us, it worked.

Planners who have struggled through the early years alone and are now successful might see a partner as a financial and emotional drain. At that stage in one's development, he's usually making good money and may easily be able to run the whole show with one or more staff persons. Why mess with a good thing by adding a partner? Why split control and have someone else telling you how to run your business?

Advisors who are closer to retirement might look at a partner as a successor to whom the clients can be sold. Henry Wendel, originally of Queens, New York, tried this strategy. He knew he would be moving to the Southwest in a couple of years when he hired a young CPA interested in financial planning. Henry's plan was to share an interest in the business they developed together, and cut a deal on his "original" clients when he moved. The problem, says Henry referring to his ex-partner-to-be, was that "he wanted to become an instant millionaire."

Some of us look for partners and get much more. Russ and Vicki Schultz of Laguna Niguel, California, began as partners and wound up married. Are they still good business partners? Yes, says Vicki, but they must be careful not to talk about business all of the time. She makes it clear that it's important to separate your business and private lives.

Vicki also feels it's an advantage for a man and woman to be partners since one or the other can relate to almost any client. She explains that, in the beginning, she and Russ used to both meet with clients and determine whether the client wanted a male or female advisor. Now they split the clients based upon other considerations but, if the female half of a client couple is not getting Russ' message, Vicki might step in and work with her temporarily.

Perhaps you're an established planner wondering how you can obtain the benefits of a partnership while avoiding the biggest cost: loss of control. Wendel, in his former career life as a CPA, used a partnership arrangement that provided the best of both worlds. He and his CPA associates shared overhead and staff, the business they brought in was their own, they were able to share ideas, and they posed a front as a unified firm. "As far as the clients were concerned, we were a partnership – they didn't know," says Wendel. The informal partnership worked so well, they later made it a legal partnership.

Some planners would probably have partners no matter what stages their practices are at. Pat Kambourian of Tucson, Arizona, says she wouldn't have it any other way. A partner (in her case, Pat Raskob) gives her someone to bounce ideas off of and allows her to be part of a team. The two Pats work on all clients together initially. That way they get to know all the clients and, Pat believes, and that lessens the risk of liability.

What does it take to make a partnership successful? Based on my own experience, I believe there are five core requirements:

1. *Complementary skills* – Two people who have the same talents are just as well off by themselves. My former partner and I were each capable of doing just about everything, but we each had our strengths: hers was networking and marketing, mine was developing internal systems and analytical tools. Together, we were able to build a firm with a wide variety of human resources.

2. *Shared values* – If you both really believe in the type of service you want to provide your clients, you will be able to avoid many of the typical

conflicts that pit many partners against each other after a few years.

3. *Common needs and goals* – If you and your partner don't agree on how much earnings to retain for practice development and how much to pay out in salary and benefits, you've got a problem. My former partner and I didn't always agree early in our partnership, but we were able to successfully negotiate many of these issues. My relatively greater needs for income almost always influenced me.

4. *Similar work ethic* – If you're splitting income 50-50 and one partner's idea of hard work is 10-hour days while the other's idea is being in at 10:00 a.m. and out by 4:00 p.m., you'll have difficulties. This type of situation led to the breakup of his first partnership many years ago, says Dave Diesslin, of Fort Worth, Texas. The partnership was "an experience on balance I would rate as very positive," but Dave and his partner just didn't share the same work ethic.

5. *The ability to talk about feelings* – Your partner's going to do or say something eventually that you resent. It may happen again and again. Don't talk about it. Let the bad feelings accumulate. Ultimately you'll hate each other and your partnership will dissolve. If you can't emote with your partner, get some outside professional help.

Besides being able to talk about feelings that come up between you, partners should be able to talk about feelings in general. Randy Hedlund of Overland Park, Kansas, waited most of the 1980's before taking on a second partner after his first partnership dissolved amicably. Randy likes partnerships. One of the things he likes is that, when he's having a problem with something, he has someone to whom he can go to "unload." Randy says, "After five minutes [of talking to my partner], I'd give myself the answer."

What are the partnership pitfalls to be avoided? Several issues seem to come up over and over again.

Money often gets in the way eventually with most partners. The financial benefits of a partnership can be tremendous. By two people sharing fixed expenses, you can raise profit margins or have many things you couldn't afford on your own. But revenues are much harder to share than expenses are to split because partners often make unequal contributions and have different work styles. A common problem is the perception that the partner who brings in the clients is contributing more to the partnership, even though the other partner may work just as hard at internal, yet critical, functions. A revenue-sharing formula is a must.

The "ego trip" is a common pitfall for many partnerships. When two partners each want all the recognition and all the glory, the relationship will be too competitive with not enough cooperation. Let's face it, part of our compensation is feeling good about the help we've given others and the great ideas we've watched grow into fruitful action. Partners must learn to share these rewards.

The partnership between Dick April and Bob Maloney didn't last, according to Dick, for the very reasons cited above. Dick went on to practice alone, while Bob took another partner – his wife, Joanne. Apparently, Bob has a clearer understanding with his present partner than he had with Dick. Says Bob, "I'm responsible for new business development and anything Joanne tells me to do."

The last pitfall is that of not knowing your partner well enough before entering into the partnership. We've all heard the cliché, "A partnership is like a marriage." That's true in more ways than one. Marriage partners often see what they want to see in each other until the marriage is legal, which is when the real people emerge. This happens in business partnerships, too. We must be careful not to idealize our partner-to-be's qualities just because we're tired of working alone and want the company of another.

CASE STUDY: THE FORMATION PROCESS OF A PARTNERSHIP

Let's take a look at the formation process of a real partnership. I was approached years ago by two advisors I'd known for several years – John LeBlanc and Bob Siefert, both of the Boston area, who were considering merging their practices. Over dinner, we all brainstormed about the kinds of deliberations that should precede such a weighty decision. At first, I had difficulty with the assignment. How I'd made my own partnership work was something I didn't think about too much anymore. I guess my partner and I had refined it more or less to auto pilot status. But when I thought back to all of the tests and trials that had taken place over the years, I realized that we'd dealt with many potential threats to our union along the way.

I asked John and Bob what they were trying to accomplish with a merger? As they hashed this out, I came up with the following points for them to consider in addition to the points listed above:

- *Decision-making styles* – There are four (or more) possibilities here. You can both make decisions easily, or with difficulty, or you can each be of either persuasion. In our practice, my partner and I had opposite decision-making styles, and that actually worked well for us. She verged on infinite deliberation, while I was often impulsive. In other words, if my partner had owned 51% of our stock, we might still be using the Osborne computer we started the practice with. If it were up to me, we might have crashed and burned long ago after letting ourselves be bought out by one of several suitors that approached us as we were building our business. In combination, we each dampened the other's worst tendency and we made rational and timely decisions (most of the time).

  I told John and Bob they might want to take the Myers-Briggs® test. Named after its two creators, Isabel Briggs Myers and her mother, Katharine Cook Briggs, the Myers-Briggs test measures each of us along four continuums of opposing personality characteristics. I have found this test to be useful in alerting me to how others are different, providing valuable information that might take months to discover in the usual course of getting to know someone.

- *Ability to agree* – Subtly different from decision-making style, the ability to agree is crucial. Without it, two people can function like a large committee instead of a lean and mean, small business team. For all of our differences, and deliberative decision-making styles, we must eventually be able to agree, or at least compromise.

- *Marketing talent* – This is a personal variable because one either is or is *not* capable of person-to-person marketing. This ability occurs naturally in a person or, in the case of someone who straddles the Myers Briggs' introvert/extrovert midpoint (as this author does), it can sometimes be learned. If one doesn't have it at *all*, then he or she is disadvantaged in several ways.

  First, as alluded to earlier, the marketplace values these talents highly, and the partner that lacks these skills has to compensate with another talent that isn't shared by the marketer. Second, even if he has another talent his partner perceives as valuable, he's still at a disadvantage because he's dependent upon someone else to find clients for him to work with.

- *Financial requirements* – What are your personal income needs? Are you both married with family-style obligations? Do you both have mortgages of similar size? Does one of you expect (or have they already realized) a large inheritance? Do you or your partner-to-be have supplemental income that the other one doesn't have, such as a military or first-career pension? Great differences in personal financial needs can influence the motivation you bring to the job and the partnership. You may work better together if you're equally "hungry."

- *Capital contributions* – If you've both been in a business awhile, as John and Bob had been, are you capable of making equal capital contributions? If one person has the beginnings of a real client base and the other has only a few clients, you may need to mix and value several types of contributions.

  When my partner and I started our practice, we had many classes of capital that we had to assign a value to create an equal contribution by each of us. We had the present value of a half dozen client-fee income streams, as well as computers, assorted used office furniture, intellectual property (our own software) and last, but not least – cash.

- *Overhead* – If each partner starts with a going practice, then he also brings with him an overhead commitment. This may not be so much of a problem as it relates to non-salary, non-benefit operating costs; the economies that are possible here are one of the reasons *to* merge. However, problems *can* arise if it's a 50-50 partnership and one partner was taking significantly higher benefits for himself than was the other.

- *Revenue* – The same point can be made about revenues. If one's revenues are so far out of line with the other's that they can't be present-valued at something close to the other's capital contribution, then we may be looking at some sort of buy-in or unequal treatment of one partner.

- *Value-added services* – We all know that certain services have higher profit margins than others. What do you do if both partners bring to the table gross revenues of $100,000, but 50% of one partner's revenues are derived from tax preparation? How do you both feel about the high-volume/low-volume tradeoff? Does one of you feel a strong obligation to work with all socio-economic classes of clients with their divergent profit margins, while the other one wants to skim only the best business off the top?

- *Work styles* – One of you likes wearing blue jeans and working at home several days a week; the other feels more comfortable in traditional business wear and wouldn't think of not being in the office by 9:00 a.m. every day. Is this a problem? It may or may not be, but you need to check it out with each other.

- *How big do you want to be when you grow up*? Do you share goals as to firm size? Have you shared your goals, in general, about where you see the firm being in five or 10 years?

The best way to deal with many of these issues is to write a business plan together. That should help you remember to discuss many of the fine points of merging that you might have otherwise overlooked.

Our friends in Boston merged their practices and are still together as Back Bay Financial Group, Inc. If you're trying to decide whether to look for a partner and hoped this chapter would give you the answer, let me leave you with one thought: most advisors I talk with, even those whose early partnerships have dissolved, have had good things to say about partnerships. But you still need to assess all the facts and decide for yourself. Go into the process, as they say, with your eyes wide open.

WHERE CAN I FIND OUT MORE ABOUT IT?

1. *Know Your Type* – Personality testing for groups and individuals (http://www.knowyourtype.com/) helping individuals, businesses, organizations, teams, governments, couples and those in education determine their unique Myers-Briggs® personality type.

Chapter 18

COMPLIANCE

It makes sense that any business that deals with people's money is going to be regulated and that you as a financial advisor will need to comply with these regulations. As an independent Registered Investment Adviser (RIA), you'll come under the scrutiny and compliance requirements of the Securities and Exchange Commission (SEC) and/or your state regulatory agency, depending upon whether you manage client assets, and how much you manage. If you are licensed to sell investment or insurance products, you'll also come under the regulation of the National Association of Securities Dealers (NASD) and/or your state insurance commissioner. In this chapter, we'll primarily discuss compliance with the SEC Investment Advisors Act of 1940 ("the Act").

Regulation means that you must operate your business according to certain prescribed systems and procedures, and be able to demonstrate your compliance with those prescriptions when and if your regulator's inspector comes knocking at your door (sometimes without prior notice). In a routine SEC compliance inspection, the examiner will be looking for any or all of the records and systems you are required to keep or employ under Rule 204-2 of the Act, such as your Form ADV, your compliance procedures, and your file of client complaints and pending or recent litigation.

If you're not in compliance with all of the procedures the SEC or your state agency (agencies often simply adopt and copy SEC regulations) requires, you will be issued something called a "deficiency letter" and given a fixed period of time in which to bring your firm's procedures into compliance. There is no dishonor in receiving a deficiency letter (assuming fraud wasn't involved). The inspector must justify his existence, so he or she will likely find you deficient in some small matter even if you're generally regulation-conscious and compliant. Simply demonstrate compliance subsequent to receipt of the letter, and then go on to conduct business as usual.

Following several SEC inspections over the years, my firms have been "written up" for minor infractions, usually relatively benign things like the format of a trade order form or the absence of a "Pending Litigation" file even though no litigation was pending. You must do more than appease your inspector; you must actually make the required change. However, doing that shouldn't disrupt your operations in any measurable way if your deficiencies have been as minor as mine.

COMPLIANCE MANUAL

As noted above, one of your requirements is to be ready to demonstrate your compliance procedures, and how better to document this than with a compliance manual. Warren Mackensen of Mackensen & Company, Inc. in Hampton, New Hampshire, knows a thing or two about this having constructed a compliance manual for sale through his separate company, ProTracker Software, Inc.

Not only does a compliance manual lay out in an organized fashion the information an inspector is likely to want, it also demonstrates that you are cognizant of your compliance responsibilities. Having gotten this impression, an inspector is more likely to double-check your records in a few key areas rather than dig into every possible file he can ask for. According to Mackensen, a compliance manual should contain the following:

- The most current copy of your Form ADV;
- A current copy of your written brochure (if you use one);
- Your annual "offer letter" to your existing clients to send them your current ADV or brochure;
- Your Confidentiality of Client Information statement;
- Your state registrations;
- Your firm's personnel list;
- Your client list;
- Your list of managed discretionary accounts and any Powers of Attorney you hold over client affairs;

- Your client contracts with signatures;
- Your client files and client communications;
- Your Investment Policy Statements;
- Examples of how you document your investment recommendations to clients;
- Your trading records and transaction reports;
- Examples of your investment performance reporting to clients;
- Your insider trading policy;
- Your list of accounts terminated in the last two years;
- Your list of client accounts over which you have custody, or your policy preventing custody, if applicable:
- Your record of security purchases and sales for your own accounts and the accounts of your employees;
- Your file of client complaints;
- Your file of litigation against your firm;
- Examples of advertisements you run (or have run) in public media;
- Your newsletters sent to clients;
- Documentation of investment performance you publicly claim to have achieved;
- Samples of prospecting letters used by your firm;
- Your policy on gifts and referral fees;
- Your general overview of your accounting procedures, and a current balance sheet and income statement;
- Your recent trial balance;
- The location of your file of bank statements and reconciliations;
- Your accounts payable;
- Your cash receipts, billing and fee computation methods;
- The location where you file your tax returns;
- Contact information for your professional support persons (e.g., attorney, accountant);
- A copy of your office procedures manual; and
- A page indicating you have conducted compliance reviews quarterly (dated and signed).

And when you conduct quarterly compliance reviews, it's a good idea to make sure the procedures and practices as described in the manual are all being followed.

In some cases, you won't have anything to show the inspector, such as litigation against your firm. However, you should still maintain a file or notebook section labeled as such to demonstrate awareness of the requirement and the fact that no such activities exist.

Client Communications

Some of these compliance areas have been the subject of recent SEC rulemaking, or heightened publicity. For example, the title "client communications" hides broad possibilities in this technological day and age. We communicate not only by written letter, telephone and in person (the latter two types of communication needing to be contemporaneously documented in notes), but also by virtue of the Internet (i.e., your website and email communications). Since most advisors offer financial planning or investment services with their websites, and most advisors aren't registered in all the states that require registration in order to serve one or more clients, they must post a website notice that reads more or less as follows:

> *"This web site is for informational purposes only and does not constitute a complete description of our investment services or performance. This web site is in no way a solicitation or offer to sell securities or investment advisory services except, where applicable, in states where we are registered or where an exemption or exclusion from such registration exists."*

Another variation of this theme is:

> *"This company is a registered investment advisor with the U.S. Securities and Exchange Commission (SEC). In addition to SEC registration, the company is registered*

with the states of Texas, Oklahoma and New Mexico for service of process. We are not limited to these states, as we will register with other states when our client count in any particular state meets registration requirements."

But these requirements are relatively easy to meet compared to email. Email is subject to the same record keeping requirements as all other forms of communication and, as such, must be readily retrievable. The irony is that, while information is usually kept in electronic rather than paper form because electronic searching is potentially faster than manual, paper-based searches, not all advisors can easily find the emails that might be requested of them by an inspector.

For example, if an inspector walked in your door and asked you to produce all of the emails (sent and received) pertaining to Client John Doe between March 1998 and May 2003 could you do it, and how long would it take you? Compliance requires the proper use of technology, not just the indiscriminate "dumping" of emails into a common email program like Microsoft Outlook. (See Chapter 26 for more on how to properly file and retrieve client emails.)

PROXY VOTING, BEST EXECUTION, ASSET CUSTODY

Other regulations or policy areas the SEC has recently highlighted include proxy voting, best execution, and client asset custody. Carol Wilson, a fee-only planner in Salt Lake City, Utah, says, "These regulations don't really affect non-discretionary advisers." In other words, you might avoid the burdens these regulations impose if you don't manage money; but, for many advisors, that won't be realistic. In fact, Mackensen recently added to his above list of compliance manual categories "Proxy Voting" and "Best Execution" since these activities started getting more attention.

Best Execution

The *process* of what an advisor needs to do to comply with "best execution" requirements is laid out in Mackensen's Manual as follows:

- *Periodic assessment* – The Investment Committee, which comprises the Registered Investment Advisers of the firm, meets quarterly to assess whether clients are receiving the best execution. The assessment includes an examination of the firm's practices with regard to:
    - Selection of custodians;
    - Best execution reports from these custodians;
    - Selection of trade away firms for bonds and other securities;
    - Best execution reports from these trade away firms;
    - Service quality received from these firms;
    - Trade prices received;
    - Liquidity; and
    - Alternative means of execution.
- *Information evaluation* – Both qualitative and quantitative factors are considered, as well as technological developments. Consideration is given to:
    - Speed of execution;
    - Reliability of execution;
    - Commission or spread; and
    - Experience of the vendor.

Conflicts of interest are explored. Correction of trading errors and paperwork mistakes at custodians are evaluated. Considerations given to selection of custodians are reviewed.

Must you actually *carry out* the procedures defined in this page from Mackensen's Compliance Manual, or is just having the page ready for the auditors enough? Well, if your procedures say you meet quarterly to assess best execution, then you must meet quarterly and you should file your minutes in your compliance manual for auditors to review. Most of the compliance rules have a logical reason and a professional should attempt to meet the spirit as well as the letter of the law.

Proxy Voting

How about compliance with the new proxy voting regulations that went into effect March 10, 2003 (i.e., where the SEC requires advisors to document their fiduciary efforts to vote proxies in the best interests of their clients, and to disclose to clients how they've voted)? Deena Katz of Evensky, Brown & Katz in Coral Gables, Florida, has a well-developed procedure for compliance: "We vote client proxies for those assets we manage, and we put a record of how we voted up on our website, more for the SEC than for clients [who are less interested]." In fact, Katz spells out her firm's proxy voting policy in the firm's compliance manual, saying:

> *"At the client's request, Evensky, Brown & Katz will vote security proxies in managed accounts. Permission may be withdrawn at any time. The firm policy is to vote proxies in favor of shareholder (i.e., our clients') interests. The following is a summary of guidelines used by the firm...."*

The firm's manual goes on to detail what its vote will typically be for routine proposals, non-routine proposals, corporate governance proposals, shareholder proposals, and material conflicts of interest; the manual also states the firm's policy with respect to proxy voting disclosure. Evensky, Brown & Katz goes one step further, though: "We have a compliance officer which a lot of firms don't have," says Katz. "Our officer constantly reviews [regulations] that come out and either incorporates them into our compliance manual, or we meet and discuss them. She also uses a service – it's NRC – to keep updated on compliance issues that must be addressed and/or included in our compliance book."

We might all like to have a compliance officer keeping track of our compliance responsibilities, but what about smaller firms or sole practitioners for whom the cost of a compliance officer might be prohibitive? Jeff Schafer, of Schafer Financial Management, Inc. in Englewood, Colorado, operates alone and handles compliance duties himself. He is a federally covered advisor who's well aware of his regulatory duties. Schafer echoes a concern common among smaller practitioners: "These regulatory trends are unfortunate. It seems to me many regulations are just solutions in search of problems. It's ironic that SEC examiners want to see our advertising file and, meanwhile, mutual funds are raping and pillaging right under the SEC's nose."

To comply with the new proxy voting regulations, Schafer says, "I chose to get one of the templates from one of the compliance consultants, an off-the-shelf product, that I could customize and format for my needs. It represents an additional cost and paperwork burden. I still just vote proxies in clients' best interests, but it seems there's now more emphasis on process than end result. The template enables me to demonstrate that I've got a policy, and that I am sending notifications to clients annually to show them I'm in compliance."

Asset Custody

Although advisors frequently discuss best execution and proxy voting, the regulation that has attracted the most attention of late is the SEC's new ruling on custody of client assets. Effective November 5, 2003, the SEC adopted long-awaited amendments to Rule 206(4)-2 intended to modernize the 1940 Act's custody rule to enhance protections for advisory clients' assets, harmonize the rule with current custodial practices, and clarify when advisers have custody. What many advisors don't realize is that, for most of us, the new rule is a liberalization of the rule previously in effect. Essentially, you probably don't have custody if you:

- Keep your clients' assets at an "approved custodian" (e.g., a bank or broker/dealer) that provides at least quarterly statements to your clients;
- Send the client an invoice showing how his fee was calculated;
- Turn over to custodians any stock certificates clients may give you within three days;
- Don't receive client payments of over $500 more than six months in advance of service; or
- Hold power of attorney to sign checks on a client's behalf.

Essentially, that means you aren't subject to the requirement that you give clients audited financial statements, you don't have to pay for surprise CPA audits, and you won't incur SEC scrutiny for crimes such as embezzlement.

One exception – an exception that applies to many advisors – is that the SEC deems an advisor to have custody if he has the ability to debit his client's account for payment of advisory fees. However, he will *not* be required to undergo an annual surprise CPA examination, nor provide an audited financial statement based upon this one factor.

Bottom line: how does an advisor most easily adopt the correct procedures and comply with regulations? For example, is it enough for a practitioner to follow Schafer's procedure of leaning on templates to communicate his compliance policies? Matt Bienfang, a Senior Analyst in the retail brokerage and investing area of Needham, Massachusetts' TowerGroup, a research and advisory firm to the global financial services industry, isn't so sure: "The SEC is going to frown on the sole practitioner wearing all hats. It's the fox guarding the chicken house thing. I believe they'll look for a third-party relationship with an attorney or consultant specializing in compliance issues." So, if you haven't yet implemented a set of regulatory policies, you might want to study what other advisors in the industry are doing and the kinds of compliance product vendors are offering, but take to heart Bienfang's advice, as well.

WHERE CAN I FIND OUT MORE ABOUT IT?

1. Norman Boone and Linda Lubitz, *Creating and Investment Policy Statement* (FPA Press, 2004).

Chapter 19

MANAGING GROWTH

Growth is wonderful – if you know how to handle it.

A 20-year veteran with a large office, many employees, and good internal systems will incorporate new clients, even in large numbers, quite smoothly. A planner in business for three years working with one assistant who is suddenly featured in the local newspaper and picks up five ideal clients the next day is in trouble.

Why? Because growth that comes before we have the forms, checklists, systems and personnel to handle it can cause, well, growing pains. It forces us to make important decisions about our infrastructure – decisions that would normally be made more deliberately – before we're ready to make them.

So growth is a problem? In a sense, it is. It's a problem of demand for your services outstripping supply, so we might first look to Economics 101 for the possible causes and solutions. Basic microeconomic theory might suggest that five ideal new clients suddenly showing up on your doorstep means you're not charging enough for your services. Theoretically, if you raise your fees high enough, you'll bring supply and demand into equilibrium.

As a practical matter, though, how much do we raise fees, and are there other ways to deal with this new client flow? We don't want to take this lightly because raising fees too much can choke off other new business, and every time we make a change of this nature, we must amend our ADVs, which is cumbersome. If we decide to raise fees, we must decide whether to do so just for new clients, or for existing clients, as well. Depending upon our fee structure, we might also need to differentiate between planning fees and asset management fees. Raising planning fees is an effective way of controlling the number of new clients we take in while leaving our existing clients undisturbed. If we raise our retainer fees, or the percentages we charge on client assets – either of which fee structure we might use for our management services – then we must "sell" this increase to all clients, not just prospective ones.

Another way to slow the flow of new clients is to raise minimums. Some advisors use a minimum net worth or minimum amount of investable assets a client must possess as a criterion to determine clients they'll serve versus those they'll send elsewhere. However, as more and more advisors move towards retainer fees, some are finding it more appropriate to focus on the minimum addition to cash flow that each new client can guarantee. Therefore, they inform prospective clients that they charge a minimum annual *fee* (after completion of initial planning work) of some amount, say \$5,000 or \$10,000, rather than requiring a minimum amount of *assets*. If the client has a portfolio size and/or financial situation that, to the client, warrants your minimum fee, then you should be indifferent as to the exact size of the client's portfolio.

There's just one problem with this line of thinking – higher fees may exclude middle-income clients. You may say, "We like working with these folks and don't want to turn them away." No one says you have to. But, if you're overworked, you have to find a balance, and price is one way to do it.

Alternatively, you can increase your capacity. If you went to business school in pre-service economy times (as this author did), then capacity was defined as either labor or plant. Now it's more like labor and technology. If your inclination is to grow a big firm and have lots of underlings, with you at the top reaping the financial rewards, then the thought of hiring more staff probably doesn't bother you. On the other hand, if you want to stay small and find other ways of accommodating new clients whose numbers and timing you can't control, then you need other kinds of help.

You really need to examine every aspect of your operation and figure out where you can eliminate non-critical services, systematize processes, and automate tasks. We're talking here about preserving your time and labor resources and/or using more fully the technology available to you.

Are you still producing lengthy financial plans full of somebody else's boilerplate text? Then you're including too much garbage in your plans and overcomplicating the planning process. Just stick to the facts. Get rid of the boilerplate – it's often insulting to your clients, anyway. You're trying to build a flesh-and-blood relationship with the client, not go into the publishing business. In my experience, walking into a meeting with a one-page agenda and several pages of analysis (graphs, spreadsheets, etc.) is more than enough for most clients.

Look for other "services" that clients neither need nor appreciate. Many independent RIAs assume their clients want to receive quarterly portfolio statements consolidating all of their holdings – something the client can't easily produce for himself. There's no doubt such statements are critical, but to whom? You need them to carry out family-wide asset allocation strategies, but the client isn't always as eager to look at them as you might assume. If you're one of those advisors who prints, stamps, and mails these statements to clients, you know how much expense and labor is tied up in this activity. Consider posting the statements to a secure website, instead, or simply eliminating them altogether for clients who show no interest.

Just as plans and reports can be excessive, so can meetings. Meeting time is critical for new client relationships. The initial planning process demands that we meet frequently with the client. Often, a plan is complex enough so that it can't be delivered in one or even two sittings. Spreading out the meetings to review different parts of the plan gives you an excuse to see your client face-to-face repeatedly and build trust rapidly.

However, once the relationship is established and you are both comfortable with and trusting of each other, meeting numbers can be reduced. Some advisors meet with clients face-to-face only once a year. This is possible because they stay in contact between meetings in less time-consuming but still high-touch ways (e.g., particularly personalized emails or email responses, and, to a lesser extent, phone calls).

Finally, have you done the "A-B-C" or the "80/20" analysis? Sit down and classify your clients as "A," "B," or "C." The A's take little time, pay you a competitive fee, and refer lots of new clients. The C's pay you very little, but also take lots of your time. If the C's produce 20% of your revenue, but take 80% of your time, start trimming the fat. "Mr. C Client, my practice is changing [read: I'm tired of working for peanuts]. I can raise your fee, or refer you to a good planner across town. Which would you prefer?"

There! The preceding four ideas just freed up at least five or ten work hours per week. That's five or ten hours you have to absorb those new clients who just came through your door in one big pack following that great publicity you landed. The above are examples of practices that may be more efficient than the ones you presently employ. Technology is the other avenue to efficiency, and you will find many technology tips in the "Tools" section of this book.

In the meantime, let's tackle the question of growth from an entirely different angle. In 1999, a mutual fund company called the Undiscovered Managers Funds, led by CEO Mark Hurley, issued its first of several white papers entitled *The Future of the Financial Advisory Business and the Delivery of Advice to the Semi-Affluent Investor.*[1] This cast growth in an entirely different light, concluding that rapidly increasing competition and, hence, falling prices in the financial services industry would force advisors to either grow (in order to add services and reach economies of scale) or starve. (The white paper also raised the option of creating a marketplace niche so specialized that one could serve it with any business model they desired – small or large).

In mid-2001, after the release of this white paper and its 2000 follow-up (*The Future of the Financial Advisory Business Part II: Strategies for Small Businesses*), I interviewed members of the Alpha Group to get their views on this growth controversy.[2] For those not familiar with the Alpha Group, it's a group of approximately 17 well-known financial advisors nationwide, folks such as Harold Evensky (Evensky, Brown & Katz in Coral Gables, Florida), Ross Levin (Accredited Investors, Inc. of Edina, Minnesota), Jim Budros (Budros, Ruhlin & Roe, Inc. in Columbus, Ohio), and Charlie Haines (Charles D. Haines, LLC in Birmingham, Alabama). Like a "Who's Who" of study groups, these planners retreat several times a year to convene with each other and discuss what they believe are the hot topics of our industry.

Representing mostly larger advisory firms, Alpha Group members were generally sympathetic to Hurley's papers (unlike most of the industry's smaller practitioners). For example, Deena Katz, President of Evensky, Brown & Katz, shares the notion that margin compression – predicted by Hurley as a result of growing competition – is beginning to happen. However, she opined that it's not so much a function of price competition as it is infrastructure costs. "Technology and staffing costs will be the big problem," said Katz, adding "tech is going to kill all of us ... the costs are huge and the learning curve to use the new technology is also huge."

The irony, of course, is that technology is also what helps level the playing field between small and large advisory firms. A one-person advisory shop can have an impressive website with almost the same bells and whistles as a Merrill Lynch. But it works the other way, too. Katz recalls hearing about the technological planning tools that the Raymond James company had created for its reps, and she cited the incredible advantage this gave them *vis-à-vis* even a large (independent RIA) firm, like hers, and how financially burdensome it would be for her firm to create the same capability on its own.

She also agreed with Hurley's notion that staff costs will be high due to competition. "We spend all this time training people, getting them CFPs, and Schwab will be hiring these guys away for $100,000 to $120,000. If you look at the latest Moss Adams compensation study [referring to *The 2000 Financial Planning Association Financial Performance & Compensation Study of Financial Planning Practitioners* performed by the Seattle-based CPA firm of Moss-Adams, LLP], that's the principal's compensation in the case of many independent advisory firms."

I asked Eleanor Blayney, a principal in Sullivan, Bruyette, Speros & Blayney, Inc. in McLean, Virginia, if other firms are making offers to the same prospective employees her firm was interviewing. "Not necessarily, but they may have other offers from tech firms or other kinds of firms that appreciate and can use their training." Blayney added that "As a profession, financial planning has only existed at one level in most firms – the practitioner/owner – and new people they hire will have been trained as planners but will not yet have practiced." In other words, new planners will have more education and aptitude than experience. Untrained, they're attractive to other kinds of businesses; trained, they are attractive to direct competitors. It's a case of heads [I win], tails you lose.

The idea was ventured that perhaps advisors at the higher growth plateaus, like Katz and Blayney, have reached "inflection points" where they need to do things that challenge their skills as managers, like seek outside financing or hire CEO's for their firms. Both Katz and Blayney have hired and fired CEOs, and would be the first to admit that financial planning and business management skills are not the same thing. "Ours was an error in judgment," says Katz, adding that the CEO they hired was "someone we'd worked with and thought we knew, but didn't." In addition, she says, the change their CEO tried to bring about – taking them from a practice to a corporate entity – created a real culture shock. Apparently, most of us are comparatively laid-back in the way we run our businesses, which is no doubt one of the reasons we've chosen to work for ourselves.

There are many challenges that come at the so-called inflection point. John Cammack, an executive with T. Rowe Price Associates, Inc. who was invited to the Alpha Group meeting, discussed with the Group the Price Waterhouse Coopers *2000 North American Private Banking / Wealth Management Survey*.[3] This survey made the point that the private banking industry was bumping up against an unmovable ceiling on the number of clients a relationship manager could handle, which for years had been at approximately 150. Will the financial planning profession yield to this limit as the private banking industry seemingly has? Or will it be the first to crack the barrier and achieve a new level of efficiency?

Blayney's firm is exploring one way of possibly dealing with this enigma. "We're trying to segment our clientele a bit more, in a smarter way, because we have many clients who don't want or require the high touch; they actually want to be much more commoditized," she explains. Blayney concluded it may therefore be possible to break the 150-relationship ceiling by developing different service packages, each with its own cost structure, for different client segments.

Cammack and Hurley both made the points that we are going to face new competition from high-end financial institutions swimming downstream from the $5,000,000 client pool to the semi-affluent ($1,000,000 net worth) market many of us thrive in, as well as from our own referral sources – CPAs and attorneys. Katz said they'd experienced some competition from these sources, and they knew more would come. "Our accounting firm bought an insurance entity, and we know securities will be next. It used to be you could send your client out to a tax attorney or CPA and know you'd get them back, but now they might try to sell the client an insurance policy or mutual fund," she said.

Blayney, too, saw the development of this phenomenon. "We're beginning to feel this at the edges," she said. "While our flow of business is as abundant as ever, the average prospect is better educated and much more aware of his options." All honest financial advisors have been strong consumer advocates, but now it may work against them. Blayney says, "Five years ago people came in and, if they liked you, you might be the only person they interviewed ... they didn't know how to shop for a planner or even what we really do." Furthermore, she added, the only time her firm used to do formal proposals was for institutional prospects. Now they're starting to see individuals who are asking for the same thing. "I don't know if this is part of the trend that Hurley talks about, or if it's because our firm is starting to move upstream into the market of $5 million to $10 million clients," Blayney says.

It seems to me that, if an era of mega-competition is truly upon us, it's the mid-sized firms that will have the toughest time surviving. My theory is they lack both the greater resources of a firm like Katz's or Blayney's, as well as the maneuverability and personal touch of the sole practitioner. Katz and Blayney, not surprisingly, agree. Says Katz of mid-sized firms, "they won't be able to keep their people ... the big guys will come in with 401(k)s and a huge future for these people that the mid-sized firms can't afford." Blayney says of my theory "that seems a reasonable assumption, though, if you talk to mid-sized planners, they probably wouldn't agree." But one thing we *can* agree on is that some of the changes Hurley predicted and that market observers like Cammack now see are beginning to take place, if only subtly. The question is ... how will *you* deal with the question of growth if these are, in fact, the new game rules?

WHERE CAN I FIND OUT MORE ABOUT IT?

1. The Undiscovered Managers Funds' White Papers at: http://www.undiscoveredmanagers.com/research.htm.

2. PriceWaterhouseCoopers North American Private Banking/Wealth Management Survey (October 2000) at: http://www.bnet.com/abstract.aspx?scid=1500&x=80&docid=52983.

3. The Moss-Adams Compensation and Staffing Studies done for the Financial Planning Association at: http://www.fpanet.org/products/index.cfm?do=prodlist&id=13.

CHAPTER ENDNOTES

1. Hurley, et al., *The Future of the Financial Advisory Business and the Delivery of Advice to the Semi-Affluent Investor* (Undiscovered Managers, September 1999), at: http://www.undiscoveredmanagers.com/research.htm.

2. Slowik, et al., *The Future of the Financial Advisory Business Part II: Strategies for Small Businesses* (Undiscovered Managers, September 2000), at: http://www.undiscoveredmanagers.com/research.htm.

3. Price Waterhouse Coopers *North American Private Banking/Wealth Management Survey* (October 2000) at: http://www.bnet.com/abstract.aspx?scid=1500&x=80&docid=52983.

Chapter 20

COACHING: GETTING IT AND GIVING IT

What is the best way to describe the coaching experience? Is it like "leasing" a mentor? To some extent, yes. The dictionary defines a mentor as someone who "serves as a trusted counselor or teacher, especially in occupational settings." A coach is certainly someone we trust, and someone who teaches us, though more about ourselves probably than about our occupational pursuits. In fact, some coaches may know a lot about our occupations, while others know very little and are still quite effective.

How can that be? Because a coach's role goes beyond that of a mentor. A coach is someone who pushes you to be the best you can be. We can all use help remembering or discovering for the first time who we are, what we're good at doing and, even more important, what we're good at doing that brings us enjoyment. (Some might amend that even further to read "enjoyment and income").

But self-discovery isn't enough. Many of us figure out on our own what we like to do, yet still don't spend enough time doing it. It is also the coach's role to push us and hold us accountable. Undisciplined as we are, we often don't hold ourselves accountable for results. It's a bit like that exercise equipment sitting in the den. We bought it. We look at it every day. Sometimes we even use it. But when we use it, we don't always get a good enough workout. A good coach makes sure we get on the treadmill and stay on until we get results.

What does this have to do with financial planning? Both new planners and veterans sometimes hit the proverbial "wall." Sometimes it takes a third party to pull them away and brush off the dust so they can see clearly again. New planners quickly get sidetracked from planning and get discouraged when they discover they must wear all the hats initially (i.e., the marketing, administrative, and planning hats). More veteran planners also get sidetracked from the tasks they really enjoy when they build a practice and find they're managing people more than they're dealing with clients.

In either case, it's very easy to lose your original focus (or never effectively refine it). A coach can be instrumental in helping you get that focus back into view, or helping you narrow or broaden it, so that you quickly and easily get to where you really want to go. Coaches don't all do the same thing, though, and not in the same way. Over the years, planners have told me they've hired coaches to help them grow their firms faster, to get a grip on their priorities, to figure out how to free up more leisure time – whatever they needed at that point in their lives and career development.

Submitting to coaching means opening yourself up to the impressions and guidance of an outsider. You must find someone who understands you and what you're trying to do, and then you have to be willing to bare your finances, business systems, mission statement, soul, and just about everything else that's intimate to you.

I went through this process for one year to help me transition from financial planning to financial writing. Looking for someone who was part psychologist, part writer, and part businessman, I was lucky enough to find exactly those credentials in one person (Geoffrey Michaelson, Ph.D., of McLean, Virginia). With his knowledge of writer's markets, Michaelson was able to feed me a regular diet of marketing ideas and advice on dealing with editors, contracts and, occasionally, rejection. With his 17-year background as a psychologist working with individual clients, he was able to tend to the feelings I had about making a major career change. And, of course, he did what all coaches must do: he held me accountable for achieving my goals.

From this experience and the interviews I've conducted with planners who've been coached, I've concluded that a good coach is just like a good financial advisor. If he or she comes in with a pre-packaged set of routines that ignore who you are as an individual, then the process cannot be completely successful. However, if the coach takes the time and has the background to understand you as a person, you may have a life-altering experience – which is, after all, what you're looking for when you hire a coach.

J. David Lewis of Resource Advisory Services, Inc. in Knoxville, Tennessee worked with Coaching Works, a husband and wife psychologist team, Sharon and John Hoover (also of Knoxville). "They attended a retreat I held for me and my staff, and asked all of us to throw out words and phrases that we thought described Resource's mission." Lewis realized his three staffers had functioned less and less like a team as time had passed, which was one of the reasons he'd scheduled the retreat. "That first retreat ended with me scared to death because there was a vast array of directions in which the staff wanted to go with the firm."

Lewis says, "I next received an email summary from the coach of what had transpired at our retreat, and I started writing a mission statement. It was probably the same statement that would have applied my first day in business, but I hadn't communicated it well to the staff. It ended up being one long sentence. I would wake up in the middle of night, change two words, and go back to sleep. After two weeks, I made one more change, and said 'that's it.' I brought it into the office, printed it out, posted it, and said this is what we're all about."

What was the point of spending so much time on such seemingly insignificant items? "Producing a mission statement made an unbelievable change in our business for everyone. It took six months for the staff to come to grips with the firm's mission, but we went on from there, and our staff meetings have been great," says Lewis. Continuing to work with his coach, he developed an employee handbook, a policy and procedures manual and, after 21 months and more than a few dollars, he was finished.

Summing up the total experience, Lewis says, "They didn't tell me anything I didn't already know. My own MBA work was in strategic planning, but it was incredibly different to have weekly coaching sessions because my coaches held me accountable." Best of all, Lewis now realizes he would have gotten extremely bored with his business if he hadn't gone down the team-building path. "The process also made me more effective with clients once I saw the kinds of questions the coaches asked and how they handled us."

Scott Dauenhauer, president of Meridian Wealth Management in Irvine, California, says his business had been unfocused before he started working with a coach. "I knew what I wanted to do but hadn't been able to put together the tools to do it." Further, Dauenhauer admits to being a bit of a control freak. "I wanted to do everything myself because I liked to control everything. Part of the coaching process is learning to delegate and outsource and focus on what I do best – meeting with clients and solving problems."

How did it all come about? "I wasn't looking for a coach. I'm part of a business owner's group that has regular meetings, and a coach, John Davidson, who joined the group about three months earlier, said something I connected with, so I called him," says Dauenhauer. Using the "TAIS," or The Attentional and Interpersonal Style Inventory, Davidson went through exercises to benchmark Dauenhauer's attitude and work style, and compare him to other people and occupational groups. This turned out to be a remarkably effective tool for producing the coaching results Dauenhauer desired.

A name from the coaching community many readers will recognize even if they haven't received coaching is Dan Sullivan. Bert Whitehead of Cambridge Connection, Inc. in Franklin, Michigan says, "I have been in Dan Sullivan's Strategic Coach program to assist me with strategic planning for seven years now. This coaching enabled me to finally complete my book [*Facing Financial Dysfunction*] and organize Cambridge Advisors (www.cambridgeadvisors.com). I am a true believer."[1]

Melissa Hammel of Hammel Financial Advisory Group, LLC in Brentwood, Tennessee, worked with Sullivan and has this to say: "Dad [partner Richard Hammel] and I took part in Sullivan's Strategic Coaching course, and the most important things we got from the course were to plan days of high productivity, buffer days just to do administrative work, and time off [that will be] totally free of business-related activities. This was so important for both of us that it was worth all the money we paid for the course."

Iris Dayoub of Alpha Financial Management, Inc. in Savannah, Georgia, used a business coach who incorporated life planning, making sure that she kept her physical, social, business, mental, spiritual, and relationship sides in balance. "We used the E-Myth philosophy [referring to Michael Gerber's book *The E-Myth*] to get me working more *on* my business than *in* my business. She has coached me on management skills and led some teambuilding meetings with our staff, and it has been a positive experience."[2]

How does coaching work in a really large firm? Dan Roe, a principal in Budros, Ruhlin & Roe, Inc. of Columbus, Ohio, with three principals and 25 total employees, found out when he hired Leigh Bailey of Minneapolis, Minnesota's The Bailey Consulting Group. "In late 1999, we tried to work on a five-year business plan. We weren't sure if we wanted to adopt a deliberate growth model or just continue to allow growth to happen to us."

Bailey gave the popular Myers-Briggs® personality test to the entire staff (See Chapter 16, "Hiring Employees or Outsource Partners"). The principals tested as extroverts, while the staff revealed themselves to be primarily introverts. "That explained why we weren't communicating effectively during meetings and wouldn't typically arrive at a complete decision," says Roe. His employees were reluctant to contribute in meetings, and the principals realized they were doing a poor job of effectively communicating how the firm's progress would impact each individual's career.

"Now, each of our planning teams is linked to one of the principals and the individual team members meet with that person quarterly to discuss his or her career. As a result, we principals are better able to match staff interests with the need to assign individual responsibilities," adds Roe. As he and his partners work out their growth plan, Bailey's methods will help them share their evolving vision with their employees.

Finding the coach that is right for you may be the hardest part of the coaching experience. One difficulty will be distinguishing coaches from what I call "marketing consultants." Imagine a continuum that begins at one end with very inward-focused processes (i.e., self-examination) with some recognition of one's business context, to the other end where one's business operations are paramount, and recognition of individual abilities is minimal. This is what I call the Coaching Continuum, and the latter end is where the Marketing Consultant Continuum begins. That is to say, you need to know what you need, and you need to know what each coach is able to deliver, before you make a selection.

Perhaps the most inwardly focused coach I know of is Tracy Beckes (http://www.tracybeckes.com/), whose catch phrase is "Helping professionals create effortless, outrageous results." Many newer coaches have gotten their training at Coach U (http://www.coachinc.com/CoachU/) or The Coaches Training Institute (http://www.thecoaches.com/), but not Beckes. These entities appeared around the time Beckes was getting into the field. "I started so early in coaching's evolution that I thought I'd invented it," says Beckes. Unaware of these other coach-training systems, Beckes trained with psychologists Gay and Kathlyn Hendricks at The Hendricks Institute (http://www.hendricks.com) who teach action-based, forward-looking coaching. "They have a coaching model that focuses on high-performing individuals like their own clients – entertainers Kenny Loggins and Bonnie Raitt, and entrepreneur Michael Dell," says Beckes.

Who is Beckes' typical client? "Most of my clients are between 40 and 75, they've been in the business over 10 years, and they're inquisitive and very intelligent. What gets in their way is something inside ... an inner block. That's where I can be most useful, and that's what makes me unique. There are relatively few business coaches who have the ability to look at life and business challenges from that perspective." But Beckes, whose home is Stanwood, Washington, isn't purely about psychology. She also has undergraduate degrees in marketing and finance, as well as an MBA.

Whereas advisors go to Dan Sullivan for a relatively concentrated set of reasons, Beckes' clients are "all over the board. Sometimes they have very traumatic early events in their personal histories that regular coaches won't even pick up on." Due to the intensive nature of her work, Beckes requires a 2-year commitment, more than that demanded by most other coaches.

While Beckes was hesitant to name names due to the highly personal nature of her work, she made it clear that her clients' success isn't necessarily measured in dollars and cents: "Because my clients tend to be high-achieving people in the first place, they're more likely to be looking for personal freedom. My longer-term clients who've worked with me seven or eight years have issues like improving self-esteem as well as increasing income. I have one of the highest-achieving advisors in the country who hired me just to figure out how to experience more joy in her life." Her clients *do* improve their financial circumstances, though. "After just two sessions, a client who hired me last year switched one little thing in his business that added $40,000 to his income."

Does Beckes view Dan Sullivan as a competitor? "I see Dan's style as complementary to mine. In fact, some of my clients work with both of us simultaneously, and I've referred clients to him," says Beckes.

At the other end of the continuum – so far as to almost be pure marketing consultants – are folks like Tom Gau and Ken Unger, who are partners in what they call their Million Dollar Producer coaching program. Gau wants you to know his advantage over other coaches who work with financial advisors: "Most coaches can't know how it feels to deal with clients after three years of a down market unless they've been an advisor." Gau was and still is a producer. (If you're new to the business, or so sheltered on the fee-only end of it that you've never heard the term "producer" before, it generally refers to a financial services person whose success is generally measured by how many dollars worth of fees and commissions he generates; product sales are usually involved. Wirehouse reps and most independent broker-dealer reps are "producers.")

Gau started his own planning firm in southern California in 1987 with much success and, when other advisors saw what he had accomplished, Gau says they began beating down his door to find out his secrets. So he presented his first "Boot Camp" in 1993, a two-day intensive seminar to show people his operation. Advisors who've been through Boot Camp often advance to take Gau's Million Dollar Producer Exclusive Coaching Program.

Gordon Wollman of Cornerstone Financial Solutions in Huron, South Dakota, has been a client of Gau's for about eight years now and says Gau is all he promotes himself to be. "I first heard Tom speak at one of my broker-dealer conferences. I attended his two-day Boot Camp, which helped me get in the seminar business and get my office organized. Tom shares his own office organization systems, and I was impressed ... they worked for me," says Wollman.

Wollman went on to do more work with Gau, and also with Bill Good, a noted marketing consultant to the financial planning community, both of whom he says have been his mentors. But how do we translate his statement that Gau's systems "worked" for him into a concrete measure of success? Wollman shared some of his firm's specs: "I've followed Tom's advice to run my practice like a doctor's office. I now see just prospective clients and delegate everything else. My typical day is 10 to 12 appointments ... sometimes as many as 14. My staff has grown from just a few people to seven full-time and one part-time staff persons. And since I began working with Tom, my revenue has gone up from $350,000 to $1,200,000."

Pretty impressive stuff, but note that there is little, if any, mention of Gau's having helped Wollman gear his work towards what Dan Sullivan calls a person's "Unique Ability." Rather, Wollman followed Gau's advice so as to run his office with peak efficiency. Hopefully, Wollman enjoys and is good at the 10 to 12 prospect appointments he has each day, because that's how he's going to be spending his time now that he's been through Gau's program.

The neat thing about coaching is not only that it can take us to new heights, but also that it comprises a set of skills which, if learned by you, can be used to take your *clients* to new heights. I personally know at least a dozen advisors who, having been successfully coached, are now effective coaches for their own clients. One such group of advisors calls itself MastermindYourIdeal, and is made up of Ted Roman, CFP (Roman Financial Advisors, San Diego, California), W. Tedd Oyler, J.D. (Saugatuck, Michigan) and Robert Walsh, CPA, PFS, CFP (Lighthouse Financial Advisors, Inc., Jersey City, New Jersey).

MastermindYourIdeal (www.mastermindyourideal.com) is a group coaching service for advisors, but it grew out of each of these planners' own coaching and experience. Ted Roman started getting individual coaching in 1997-98, a process that enabled him to transform his advisory business into a high-paying, part-time affair allowing him to use the coaching skills he acquired, and giving him plenty of free time to spend with his wife and his border collies, something he didn't have as an advisor before being coached.

Oyler was a client of Bert Whitehead's (all three are members of the planner network Cambridge Advisors LLC run by Bert) in 1989 and, at Bert's urging, had become a Cambridge advisor by 2000. "Bert put together a special group for entrepreneurial clients which entailed some coaching. I realized coaching was what I'd tried to do as a lawyer but couldn't do effectively with an hourly fee structure. I eventually became one of the coaches for Bert's clients," says Oyler, who also used the coaching he was *receiving* to create his own advisory practice.

Walsh also joined Cambridge in 2000, and Ted Roman was his first coach. "As a financial planner, I've asked myself how we can do better in this business ... what's the next thing. And my answer has been coaching," says Walsh.

All of these men have coached and been coached, the latest instance being their own Mastermind group. They describe it as an 80%-20% process, though not in the way we usually think of the "80%-20%" exercise we sometimes employ to distinguish profitable from unprofitable clients. In the Mastermind scheme of things, each of these guys felt they had 80% of what they needed to make it in their chosen profession. Says Roman, "Ted is really good at verbal skills and communications; Robert is a great technician; and I come from the creative side." The other 20% each wanted was something the others were able to offer through the Mastermind association.

"The big thing for me," says Walsh, "was that I had all this technical knowledge, but it took these two guys to give me confidence to put it into practice. I might say to them: 'I have this client and I'm thinking of doing XYZ ... what do you think of my approach?' There are many pure technicians in our industry, those who just want to crunch the numbers. My 20% was trying to look at things differently and question everything I was doing."

"I had always questioned my value ... how good I was," says Roman. "I didn't charge what I was worth. By teaming up with these two guys, I learned that I was really good at what I do. I don't question it anymore, and I get constant reinforcement that I'm adding value for my clients."

Oyler claims his 20% was really 50%, offering an example of what he's gotten from the Mastermind: A client of mine wanted to buy a bed and breakfast business. I didn't know how to charge this client, and wasn't even sure I wanted to work with him. Ted and Robert threw out some numbers, and I ended up charging the client $8,500. My fee would have probably been $2,000 if I were still an attorney but, with Robert and Ted's assistance, I turned a classic legal assignment into a coaching assignment." Oyler found a way, in what might otherwise have been a very cut and dried process, to introduce coaching services into this particular client engagement.

In summary, Roman, Walsh and Oyler had all achieved a measure of notoriety within Cambridge, if not the wider planning community, as being very capable coaches who had their acts together. "Yet, when the three of us talked on the phone, we'd be kicking ourselves and whining about our perceived weaknesses." After a while, their whining turned into laughter as they realized they had all the brainpower they needed to cause vast improvements in their collective businesses.

So, not only do these three advisors create Mastermind groups, but they serve as each other's Mastermind group on the premise that three coaches examining each other's practices and personal goals together has to yield some powerful results. Roman, who used to give prospective clients lots of leeway in the decision to hire him will now say very directly to a prospective client he knows he can help: "I think the best thing you can do right now is hire me." And they do. Perhaps coaching can make a difference in your career development?

WHERE CAN I FIND OUT MORE ABOUT IT?

1. Tracy Beckes - http://www.tracybeckes.com/
2. Dan Sullivan - http://www.strategiccoach.com/
3. Tom Gau - http://www.mdproducer.com/
4. Ted Roman/Robert Walsh/Tedd Oyler - http://www.mastermindyourideal.com/
5. Bill Good Marketing - http://www.billgood.com/
6. Bill Bachrach - http://www.bachrachvbs.com/

CHAPTER ENDNOTES

1. Bert Whitehead, *Facing Financial Dysfunction* (West Conshohocken, PA: Infinity Publishing, 2002).
2. Michael Gerber, *The E-Myth Revisited* (New York, NY: HarperBusiness; 1995).

Chapter 21

SELLING YOUR PRACTICE

"Succession Planning" is a hot topic among financial advisors these days because a large wave of advisors entered the industry in the early 1980s when they were 30-somethings. Now, in the first decade of the new millennium, they are closing in on retirement and, in some cases, poor health as an expected side effect of aging – and perhaps the stress of their business lives and complex environment. Therefore, they are pondering their succession plans.

There are two types of succession plans: proactive and reactive. A reactive succession plan is used by the advisor who enjoys what he does, doesn't really have a retirement date in mind, and believes he'll remain in practice until forced out by death or disability. It is, therefore, a plan to turn the business over to someone else, perhaps during some type of emergency scenario.

A proactive plan is one to sell the business before such event occurs, and only in recent years has selling a financial planning or wealth management practice become a reality one could count on. With the advent of online markets for financial planning practices, perhaps best exemplified by those of Business Transitions, LLC, a Portland, Oregon firm, advisors can now systematically find buyers for their practices and exact prices ranging from one to two times gross revenues, depending upon the business model they've adopted.

The common wisdom in our industry is that some businesses sell for more than others because:

- They have enough employees so that the business doesn't depend upon the owner;
- They create a steady cash flow stream;
- They're in a growth mode;
- They may have a competitive niche in the industry; and
- They're run like true businesses and not just a source of compensation for the owner.

In other words, the thinking goes, if you want to be a one-principal firm, either working alone or with a small support staff, you've not got much to sell. It is relatively impossible to reduce dependency on yourself since there's no one else in your firm whom the clients can trust. Sure, the clients may let your administrative assistant fill out a form to open a new account with the firm's custodian, but they're not likely to trust that person's advice when it comes to designing a stock option exit strategy.

But, in fact, it's been shown that there are markets for all types of practices. Either small, owner-dependent practices or large, fully staffed practices are desirable and salable to someone. It's a question of preparing the practice for sale and understanding the typical terms that will be applied to the sale.

In a recent report, *Business Transitions* states:

> "One of the most interesting facts gleaned from our experiences with sellers is that regardless of size, some buyer does exist. It doesn't matter if your practice produces $75,000 in revenue or $2,000,000 in revenue. The new emerging trend is that all financial practice owners can grow through individual acquisition regardless of size. The key is how you market your practice to find the right buyer."

The report went on to find that:

1. Over two-thirds of all buyers were looking for firms with gross revenues in the $100,000 to $500,000 range. The advantage of firms in that revenue range is that their purchase is easier to finance and their more modest client list is easier for the buyer to absorb.
2. Asset classes typically wanted by buyers are equity funds and individual stocks rather than hard assets or limited partnerships. These desirable asset classes are often the province of smaller, fee-based or fee-only firms.
3. Assets under management (AUM) wanted by 70% of all buyers were in the $10,000,000 to $50,000,000 range, for reasons similar to those expressed in (1).
4. Practice revenue as a percentage of AUM (i.e., average total fee) desired by 65% of all buyers

> was less than or equal to 1.0%, an area more typically occupied by serious fee-based or fee-only advisors, as opposed to the higher percentages usually produced by planners supplementing fee income with commissions[1].

To cap things off, fee-only firms command the highest premiums of any type of firm listing with Business Transitions. Average multiples of sale prices to gross revenues were 1.1 times for "commission only" firms, 1.7 times for "fee-based" firms and 2.1 times for "fee-only" firms.

Now, here's why it all works, and why you *can* sell your firm, regardless of size or business model. Just keep in mind, there's still a difference in the way small firms and big firms are sold. The tendency of smaller firms to fail at reducing dependency on the owner of the firm doesn't mean the firm isn't desirable, or even that it can't command a "two-times" multiple. It simply means that it must be done on an "earn-out" basis. (For the uninitiated, "earn-out" generally means that some portion of the purchase price – the remainder after the down payment – will be paid over time as a percentage of actual, ongoing gross revenues earned from the clients that were formerly part of the seller's practice.)

There are pros and cons to this earn-out arrangement. The pros are that the buyer can feel protected enough with this structure to accept and manage the likelihood that some client attrition will take place over time. Both buyer and seller must do their best to make the transition work so that the buyer retains clients and the seller's receipts are maximized. The cons are that the selling advisor must stay very involved for some period of time and carefully transition all of his client relationships as well as his internal planning systems.

And, we would add, the resulting terms with which you must be concerned are:

1. Sales price, or multiple of revenues;
2. Down payment, as percentage of total sales price;
3. Earn-out period; and
4. Percentage of revenues the buyer is to pay during earn-out.

While the multiple you get may seem to be the most important factor, that's not always the case. Remember that your true sales price is a present value of all the payments you receive over the course of the buyout. Securing a high multiple isn't that impressive if you receive a small (e.g., 20% or less) down payment, and the buyer's other payments to you span over ten years and your clients aren't likely to stay with your buyer that long.

So the seller will want to maximize the multiple he gets, but also maximize the down payment and minimize the earn-out period. There are also some "intangibles" the seller must remember. Generally, as a seller, you will not be paid separately for the time you contribute following the sale to make sure your systems and clients are successfully transferred to the buyer. To the extent you feel you should be compensated for the time you will spend doing these things, that compensation is folded into the purchase price.

That means your selection of a buyer must depend not only on the terms of the deal he'll accept, but upon him or her ... how successfully and quickly will the buyer achieve a rapport with your clients, take over the role as their primary advisor, and get you out of the picture. The sooner those things happen, the more value you realize from your sale.

Other ingredients of a successful sale relate to your internal systems. The buyer is often purchasing your systems in addition to your clients. Since he must absorb all of the data you have on clients, he may adopt the same client databases and other software you use to run your business.

To the extent you have essential internal processes automated, your business will be more valuable to your buyer. Most advisors collect client information on paper in expandable files kept in large file cabinets. If you're the buyer, the process of getting to know these new clients must include going through these mounds of paper to learn important facts about the clients – that is inevitable. But think about how much easier it will be for your buyer if he doesn't have to deal with paper at all. Suppose you run a paperless office, and your buyer can learn who your clients are by reading through their pertinent information online via the critical client documents you've scanned on your hard drive over the years. That will add tremendous value to your practice.

And perhaps that's the best advice ... put yourself in the buyer's shoes. What would you want to see if you were buying a practice? What would make the transition easier and the practice more valuable to you? Do those things before you market your practice and you will increase its attractiveness, not to mention its ultimate value.

WHERE CAN I FIND OUT MORE ABOUT IT?

1. Visit (www.fptransitions.com – one of several sites maintained by Business Transitions, Inc.) and read the company's latest "Practice Value and Data Survey" which it updates each year, providing detailed information on actual business sales and terms, as well as trends in the industry in sales price multiples and other factors of interest to potential buyers and sellers.

CHAPTER ENDNOTES

1. *RIA Transistions: 2004 Transitions Report* (Portland, OR: Business Transistions Publishing, Inc., 2004) at: http://www.riatransistions.com/index.cfm?fuseaction=press.riaptr.

Chapter 22

BUYING A PRACTICE

Growth is your goal now. You're not planning to retire anytime soon, and you're not so far along in the development of your practice that you've closed your door to new clients. You want more clients and you want them ASAP.

What are your options? Your first option is the traditional one of acquiring one client at a time. The more you invest in seminars, direct mail, and referral programs, the more clients you bring in. But traditional marketing methods yield fairly linear growth accompanied by pitfalls that veteran advisors well understand. Getting results is a time-consuming, expensive, trial and error process, leading many advisors to discontinue their marketing campaigns before they completely pay off. If you *are* successful in getting prospective clients' attention, you must qualify them. Do they meet your age, occupational or gender criteria? Can they benefit from your unique expertise? Do they have the right financial characteristics and will they pay your fee? Remember, nothing is guaranteed.

Your second option is to expand your business exponentially by acquiring an existing client base from someone who has already invested many years and resources into building a practice the hard way. By acquiring his or her practice, you pick up where the seller left off with no interruption in revenues. Instead of marketing, you spend your time servicing your newly acquired clients (in addition to your existing clients). That is, you engage in a service process rather than a sales cycle.

I learned this lesson myself in 2001 as the seller of a small advisory practice I'd been building since 1981. The smart buyer of my client base believed it would be more efficient to pursue the practice acquisition method of growth and began to research the business transitions market. He acquired my practice in May of that year and went on to buy yet another practice the following year.

He is convinced there's no better way to build a practice than through strategic acquisitions. However, he's learned the challenge in the practice acquisition marketplace is catching the seller's attention and enticing the seller to enter into an introductory discussion. In today's market, sellers (depending upon the type of practice) may entertain 30 to 40 offers. In other words, it's very much a "seller's market." Of necessity, they must find one or two bits of information about their would-be buyers so as to eliminate most of them from consideration, simply because they must get down to a manageable number from which to choose.

Therefore, understanding a seller's motivation is key to preparing one's bid for a practice, and ultimately getting a seller's attention. Always remember the seller's top priority: He wants a buyer his clients will stay with, feel confident in, and be comfortable with. They will stay with a buyer if they are being well served, and the seller will therefore get paid.

To appreciate this is to appreciate the mechanics of the typical, small-firm deal. There are four components:

1. The multiple of revenues;
2. The down payment;
3. The earn-out; and
4. The payment period.

The purchase price is first established as some multiple of the seller's revenues. For example, it's not unusual for a fee-only practice, like the one I transitioned, to sell for two times the previous twelve months' fees, or gross revenues, from those clients being sold. The down payment the buyer will pay to the seller at closing is some percentage of this total purchase price. The remainder of the purchase price is usually paid monthly or quarterly as a percentage of realized revenues for an agreed-upon payment period.

Consider this example. Let's say the seller wants to transfer 40 client relationships that earned him gross revenues in the previous twelve months of $200,000. He and the buyer agree upon a 2.0 multiple and a 25% down payment, meaning the buyer pays the seller $100,000 at closing. They then agree upon a payment period of three years for the remaining $300,000 to be paid. Therefore, the buyer will pay $100,000 a year, or 50% of the revenues from the clients, in each of the three years after closing. (If the seller is smart enough to demand a 2.0-

multiple purchase price on a present value basis, then the payments will somewhat exceed $100,000 a year, depending upon the agreed-to discount rate.)

Ah, but there are nuances. First, the subsequent payments can be guaranteed or not. If the buyer signs a promissory note, while not the norm, he is guaranteeing the future payments whether or not he retains the clients. More typically, the buyer and the seller share the risk of client retention by agreeing that the seller will receive his 50% of revenues for all clients who remain with the buyer. If a client quits, both the buyer and seller are out some future income.

The interplay of these components explains why deal terms are what they are. A high down payment shifts more risk to the buyer; a lower one shifts more risk to the seller. A longer payment period shifts risk to the seller; a shorter one to the buyer. If the buyer strongly desires a longer payment period, everything else being equal, the seller might demand a higher multiple to rebalance the risk. And so on.

THINGS TO DO WHEN BUYING A PRACTICE

With this background, we're going to see how my buyer did all the right things to rise to the top of my own 40 would-be-buyers list. First, let's look at what he did right before I even put my practice on the market.

Have the Right Credentials and Experience

If the seller's primary concerns are ensuring a high quality of continued service to his clients and getting paid for the income annuity he has transferred to the buyer, will he value an experienced, credentialed buyer more highly than an inexperienced, uncredentialed one? You bet. Anything that contributes to the likelihood that the seller is going to maximize future revenue during the buy-out, revenue sharing period is going to inure to the buyer's advantage.

Can you buy a practice without credentials and experience? In some cases, yes. Most commonly, such a buyer will have worked in an advisory firm for some period of time and will negotiate to buy some of the clients he's served as he prepares to leave his employer and establish his own practice. However, a buyer in the open market who has a CFP and no experience will be at a distinct disadvantage, forcing a seller to seek terms that compensate for the high level of client retention risk the buyer's inexperience poses. A would-be buyer with neither a CFP nor any real experience is not a realistic candidate to attract the attention of an open-market seller.

My buyer was a CFP with five years' experience... not an industry veteran, but experienced enough to have amassed his own client base and have established a certain level of success as both an advisor and an entrepreneur.

Achieve Proficiency with Technology

A major component of every business transition that both parties often overlook is technology. A financial advisory firm runs on some combination of technology, and that combination is different for every firm. As a buyer, should you limit your bidding only to those firms that use exactly the same kind of computer network, accounting software, portfolio reporting system, financial planning program, and client relationship management (CRM) software that you do?

That would be unrealistic, of course. After all, if there are, say, three possibilities for each of these components, then there would be 243 possible technology combinations. That would make a buyer's market impossibly small. It's much better to be able to demonstrate proficiency with technology that convinces a seller that you can absorb his client data, regardless of the systems he uses, and be up and running quickly.

Arrange Financing in Advance

Sure, the seller is probably going to finance the majority of the deal, but not the whole thing. As a buyer, you need a down payment and you need to be able to cover your portion of the closing costs. If you go through a marketplace like that provided by Business Transitions, LLC of Portland, Oregon, you're going to have some commissions to pay, too. All tolled, you could be looking at $100,000 or more for a small practice. And a smart seller, just like a first-mortgage lender, wants to know you didn't borrow the down payment from an entity that will have any claim to the client revenues needed to meet the seller's earn-out requirements.

My buyer secured lending from family and friends that was subordinated to my claims.

To summarize, my buyer was prepared to step into the marketplace. He gathered or cultivated the resources he needed to meet most sellers' minimum requirements. Armed with these tools, he could look seriously for a seller to court. His next job would be to learn the tricks of the marketplace: how to get a seller's attention, how to make a favorable impression, and how to coax the result he wanted.

But how did my buyer rise to the top of my own 40-would-be-buyers list? Clue: It wasn't just the money. Sure, his bid was attractive but that, alone, wasn't enough to earn him the top spot. There are too many problems with too many buyers that can make a bid with surface appeal worth less than it actually appears.

Here's what he did right:

Pursue a Practice That Resembles Your Own in Key Ways

First, we had similar fee structures; we both ran fee-only practices. Second, we had similar clients; we both targeted semi-affluent retirees and pre-retirees. Is it absolutely necessary that both buyer and seller share these characteristics? No, but it helps considerably. Says David Grau, President of Business Transitions of Portland, Oregon, the online marketplace for buying and selling advisory practices, "sellers of fee-only or other specialized practices almost always pick buyers with similar firms."

As we said earlier, a smart seller has two goals that transcend all others. First, he wants to do what's right for his clients and, second, he wants his clients to stay with their buyer – that's how he gets paid. If the buyer transfers the seller's clients to his firm and then hits them with a different fee structure – particularly if he makes a radical change from, say, fees to commissions – most of the clients will bolt. After all, they have been counseled for years that fee-only is best, and that's one of the reasons they chose their original advisor in the first place.

If the fee structure is the same but the buyer has little experience working with the type of client being sold, that will also hurt the ultimate client retention rate. This was a major hurdle my own buyer had to vault. While his clients were very similar to mine, he was 28 years old to my 53. Did he *really* know how to relate to and develop trust with moneyed clients several generations his senior? Yes, but he had to prove this to me.

Provide Similar Client Services

If the buyer is primarily an asset-gatherer doing superficial, if any, financial planning and bids on a practice that combines full-scale financial planning with investment management, the smart seller will see the buyer needs to master a new skill set. What's wrong with this picture is that the seller is going to be the teacher – perhaps for a very long time. Sure, the seller has a vested interest in client retention and expects to be involved in the transfer of his clients' loyalty to a new advisor, but he doesn't want the process to drag on indefinitely. The longer the seller must remain involved, the lower his return on investment.

It was clear to me that my buyer already knew how to provide the services my clients were receiving because he was already providing them to his own clients.

Ask the Seller for the Right Information

My buyer asked far more initially about my client base than most other bidders, giving me the impression that client retention was just as important to him as it would be to me. With enough information, he was able to confirm our client bases were compatible and develop a detailed timetable for the transition of the client relationships. He convinced me that he had a solid plan to earn my clients' trust and move me out of the picture as quickly as possible. (Some sellers might have mixed feelings about this, but the smart ones know their investment is rewarded more highly the sooner they leave).

Other would-be buyers, ironically some more seasoned than mine, were very eager and financially prepared, yet didn't inspire confidence. By asking questions, the buyer doesn't demonstrate ignorance; he demonstrates sincerity and the understanding that one must dig below the surface for critical information to make the acquisition a success.

Do Your Homework

Our transaction took place within the aforementioned online marketplace – FP Transitions (the Business Transitions, LLC, site dedicated to independent registered representatives). Says Grau, "We think we do a very good job of not only helping to close deals but assisting both buyers and sellers in finding the right match."

My buyer took advantage of FP Transitions as a resource in a way not too many buyers do – he called their staff and asked for help in finding out more about me as a seller. He wanted to know whatever was needed to attract my attention, and he wasn't afraid to go as far behind the scenes as FP Transitions would ethically and professionally allow in order to get some tips on how to approach me.

Grau suggested to my buyer, because I was an advisor seeking a career change from financial planning to writing, that he familiarize himself with my published articles. My buyer did so and gained a small advantage. Don't be afraid to find out who your seller is, particularly if he has achieved some public notoriety. Anything you learn about him personally or professionally that other would-be buyers haven't taken the trouble to ferret out can give you a leg up on the competition.

Carefully Construct Your Buyer's Listing

At FP Transitions, each prospective buyer can list a handful of key features of his firm, and add some brief, general comments. In other words, he's got a very limited opportunity to say just the right things to gain a seller's attention.

Selecting a random buyer's listing from the FP Transitions site, we find the following (paraphrased) general comment: "We are a fast-growing financial planning firm with multiple locations nationwide and are interested in acquiring several small firms. Let us introduce our successful business model to your existing client base." This sounds promising until you read through the rest of the listing. This would-be buyer provides no answer to the question "Designations/Degrees" nor to "Highest Level of Education," which suggests he lacks the minimum desired personal qualifications. For "Operating System Software" he answers "Other" which raises questions about his technology platform. But he really sours things when he indicates he has one year in the business and his total annual gross revenues fall between "$0 and $100,000."

He says he's looking to acquire one or more businesses in the $0 to $900,000 price range, yet his "particulars" suggest he's incapable of doing so. Could he buy anything? Yes, he might be able to purchase a business segment another advisor is attempting to sell, such as the low-fee, less-complex planning segment of that advisor's practice – perhaps clients the advisor picked up earlier in his career and no longer finds appropriate to his business model. In short, when this prospective buyer shares his information with a seller of, say, a $500,000 practice, that seller – if he's smart – will discard that bid instantly.

My buyer's listing, unlike the example above, was internally consistent, as well as congruent with my own listing. That is, it suggested compatibility between the buyer's status and the type of practice he was seeking for purchase.

Demonstrate the Capacity to Serve More Clients

Compatibility between buyer and seller is just part of the equation, though; the rest is capacity. Can the would-be buyer absorb into his practice the clients you are selling? Does he have the idle capacity to do so?

My buyer had a fairly typical five-year-old practice. He could demonstrate that he'd successfully marketed, acquired, advised, and retained high net worth clients to the tune of $15,000,000 under management. Yet, like most solo practitioners with good internal systems, he was nowhere near capacity. It was clear to me that he could take on my 45 high net worth clients ($65,000,000 under management) which required 30 hours per week of my time to advise, and provide them the high level of service to which they were accustomed.

Supposed he'd been at capacity? Would he be out of the game? Not at all, but he'd have had to present me with a game plan for increasing his capacity. If mine was a company with several employees, he might agree to retain them. Doing so would provide a source of continuity for my clients to help them feel more comfortable with the change of management and make me feel more comfortable about the economic security of the staff that had so ably served me.

Or, if there were no seller employees to retain, he might have presented me with the resumes of several associates he intended to hire. In fact, we might have made this a condition of sale. Perhaps a move to new office space would be necessary and also made a condition of sale.

The key to getting your seller's attention and convincing him to choose you to buy his practice isn't slick marketing that covers up inexperience or lack of capacity. Unless the seller is totally naive or ill-advised, he's not going to select you just because you talk a good game ... especially if your vital stats contradict everything you say about your ability to successful consummate the transaction. That is, you must be qualified. Conversely, though, the best buyer may be overlooked *because* he doesn't know how to compellingly present his case and stand out from the crowd.

MAKING THE TRANSITION

Okay, let's say you've won the bid for the practice you wanted ... *now* what do you do? How do you successfully transition client relationships to maintain the maximum possible client retention rate? As we've done all along, let's see what *my* buyer did to retain the vast majority of *my* clients.

Before we address that question, though, let's understand why we're focusing primarily on client relationships ... because they're the most valuable piece of the business. Some buyers *just* buy the client relationships; others buy equipment and leases, and continue to employ seller staff persons. But the greatest value comes from the clients. The present value of their expected fee income, which hopefully will continue well into the future, is far greater than the market value of any other company asset the buyer has purchased.

So the first thing the buyer must do is familiarize himself with his new clients. Sure, he's studied the overviews given to him by the seller during their negotiations. But, now that he actually owns the clients, there are many details about their relationship with the seller that need to be absorbed, depending upon how long they were clients of the seller prior to their purchase, of course.

Ideally, this information exists not in multiple paper files but in computer records. The modern advisor collects critical client information in a client relationship management (CRM) program like Junxure-I or ProTracker, including scanned images of client documents (e.g., tax returns, estate plans), client correspondence and email back and forth between the client and advisor. This level of organization and ease of retrieval makes your job, as the buyer, far easier than plowing through volumes of paper that may be improperly filed, missing or illegible, in the case of handwritten notes.

In fact, the form in which client records were kept by the seller and will be transferred to the buyer is a major negotiating point often overlooked by buyers. Do not fail to estimate the additional work involved in dealing with paper versus digital records and the cost thereof when bidding on a practice. Also, carefully assess the amount of detail the seller has available. When we buy a used car, we want a copy of every maintenance receipt so we know not only what specific repairs were made but also, more generally, how the car was cared for. It's the same process with clients: records are ideally detailed enough to give us a feel for the personal nature of the relationship, not just what transactions the seller executed for the client.

By digesting this information, you'll know more about your new clients than just their net worth as you meet them for the first time. You should have a broad knowledge of them: how long they worked with the seller; what have been his major accomplishments for them; what have they valued most about the relationship; what is their family makeup, and how far down and across the family tree has the seller's influence spread; what are their current issues and goals; and so on.

The familiarity you'll gain by reading your clients' files will be your foundation for establishing your own relationship with them, a process that must occur as a series of in-person meetings. If you have clients who trust you and value your advice enough to pay you a fee each quarter to be their financial advisor, you know what it took to develop each of those client relationships. For most of us, the average developmental stage is about one year. Through meetings, particularly the more intensive and frequent planning sessions most of us engage in with a new client, everyone usually feels pretty comfortable with each other after about 12 months, on average.

Human nature being what it is, a buyer will find it difficult to accelerate this process much, except for one factor – he's been heavily endorsed by the seller. The seller has said to his clients, in so many words, I think so highly of this individual (i.e., the buyer) that I want to be his partner. "What," you say, "the seller's going to be my partner? I thought I was buying his clients!" You are, but you're going to be partners during the transition process. Ideally, you are going to work closely together for at least a year, maybe two, as you meet these new clients together, as some of their trust for the seller rubs off on you, and as they eventually get the same warm feeling about you they already have for the seller.

"Can't we just tell these clients I'm buying this guy's practice and that they're now going to work with me instead of him," you ask further? Not if you want to keep the vast majority of them for the long haul which, according to Grau, is at least 90%. If you think or your seller believes the hard work is done once you close your transaction, you're being naive. Client retention will depend almost entirely on what happens one year out from that date.

So plan to get in front of these clients frequently. If the seller has a meeting schedule with his clients that is any less frequent than once per quarter, find reasons to meet more frequently with the clients during this critical phase. Every in-person meeting is a chance to advance the bonding process between client and buyer.

As time goes on during that first year, use every opportunity to have the buyer insert himself in the process. When you, the buyer, the clients and your seller join together in meetings, both seller and buyer should be sharing the meeting, that is, leading the discussion and answering questions. Later in the first year, the buyer should be playing an even more prominent role, with the seller sitting by quietly and speaking up merely to clarify points or assist occasionally with an answer that the buyer may be struggling with. You are a team. The clients see you as such and are developing ever-greater confidence in the buyer. And they like him personally, too, because after several meetings they've learned things about his family, or his hobbies – things not directly related to his competency as an advisor.

The counterpart to frequent meetings during the relationship-building phase of the transition is a rapid response system. If the buyer doesn't already have such a system, he should implement one that allows all of his clients to find him easily. Nothing builds relationships faster than frequent contact, and ease of access is a prerequisite. Therefore, the buyer should consider having a toll-free phone number, and easy-to-remember email address, and a "find me" phone service. The latter is a service, such as Freedom Voice Systems (www.freedomvoice.com) or EasyTel (www.easytel.net). These essentially follow you wherever you go, trying your office phone, cell phone, home phone sequentially, with total flexibility as to how you program the system. You can also preview callers to determine whether calls are clients or solicitors.

Other kinds of "virtual" systems can improve your accessibility and response time, as well, which becomes particularly important if the client base you are buying is geographically widespread. In the case of my own practice sale, my clients were located in the Washington, D.C., metropolitan area and in New Mexico, and a handful had scattered themselves about the country (e.g., California, Pennsylvania, etc.) as long-term clients often do, moving to the sites of new jobs or to retirement communities. It's necessary to meet and stay in touch with these clients as well, even though a lack of geographic concentration makes it more difficult.

Although it's advisable to make the investment in traveling to meet these clients in person once or twice early on in the transition (as my buyer and I did), staying in touch thereafter will depend more upon email and phone contact than it will with other clients. If these widespread clients, and other new clients as well, are computer literate, the buyer can increase their feeling of connectedness by setting up a client-access website in which clients can find continuously-changing communications from the buyer-seller team, communications that – like in-person meetings – eventually shift to being signed by the buyer alone.

In my own transition, my buyer bought 90% of my clients and transferred them to his Massachusetts firm. I remain listed on his site as an officer of his company, but ex-clients now understand I'm doing behind-the-scenes marketing for the firm via my writing. They've all formed close relationships, first with my buyer, and later with the employees he retained from his second advisory firm purchase, so that my old clients seldom ask for me anymore. If they do, I will occasionally call one to say hello. Does the seller really want to be involved, even peripherally, three years after the sale? If he has financial incentives, he does ... but that's a whole 'nother chapter.

The last piece of the relationship-building puzzle to consider if you have far-flung clients, as my buyer did, is to set up a local presence, or office, where those clients are concentrated. My buyer maintained a Washington, D.C., office in an executive office suite center for one to two years following our transaction, so clients could take comfort from the commitment made to an office right in their midst, in spite of his company being headquartered in another state.

Remember, close personal contact as much as competent advice is what binds all clients to us, so you can't go wrong in following this same formula for newly acquired clients. The only difference is that you're trying to accelerate the bonding process to coincide with the date when the seller is contractually allowed to disassociate from the buyer's firm completely. All of the above strategies will help you accomplish that.

Chapter 23

ERRORS & OMISSIONS (E & O) INSURANCE

There is a continuous stream of articles in financial planning journals and periodicals about the need for Errors & Omissions (E&O) insurance from people like Katherine Vessenes, J.D., CFP (Vestment Consulting, Minneapolis, Minnesota), Bayard Bigelow III, MBA, CPA (The Cambridge Alliance, LLC, Burlington, Vermont) and others. All seem to agree on one thing: all financial planners should be carrying E&O coverage – *even* fee-only planners who don't sell products and tend to think they're immune to the perils that commonly beset licensed planners.

In her article entitled "Your Last Line of Defense: Errors and Omission Coverage" in the January/February 1998 issue of *Financial Advisory Practice*, Vessenes notes there are myths that have been used to resist the need to buy E&O insurance. In Ms. Vessenes' opinion, the number one myth is "I am a fee-only planner. I am above such lawsuits." Ms. Vessenes says this is wrong: "Even though it is true that fee-only planners are less likely to be sued, in a significant market correction, a client's main concern will be reimbursement for losses, not how you were compensated."

When most advisors think of lawsuits, they think of causes common to brokers, such as churning and unsuitable investments. The sales culture in which wirehouse planners operate, directed primarily at maximizing commissions, is more likely to push them into behaviors adverse to their clients. The professional, client-centered advisor reasons that he/she would never do these things and, hence, has little liability exposure.

In fact, Ms. Vessenes suggests that lawsuits are highly correlated to, more than any other factor, the stock market. The desire to recoup losses about which clients were not adequately educated, or which they can't ignore in spite of education, will be the common denominator that drags all planners, not just the fee-only variety, in front of arbitration panels and judges.

Sure, clients will always bring lawsuits against stockbrokers for actions detrimental to the clients' financial well being. And fee-only advisors may even find that premiums for specific limits of liability will be less for them than for licensed planners. Yet no one is immune. If you invest money for your client, or even advise on client-directed accounts, you are at risk. Think about it: why should the provider of financial advice be any less subject to being sued than an attorney or accountant who provides legal or accounting advice.

These points are well taken. However, throughout all of this fine guidance on the subject of managing our liability, none of these authors spends much time on what may be an even more pervasive threat in coming years: the lawsuit that comes not from the client, but from the client's offspring.

Perhaps it takes someone whose primary job is estate planning to really appreciate this risk. As writes Howard Zaritsky, a noted estate planning guru (and co-author of *Tax Planning With Life Insurance*) in his article entitled "Avoiding Malpractice Suits: The View from an Aisle Seat" which appeared in the March/April 1998 issue of *Estate Planning* magazine, "I have spent a significant portion of the last year serving as an expert witness in estate planning malpractice cases, and it seems to me that the odds of being sued are almost wholly unrelated to the quality of the advice given and the services provided." [1]

In other words, avoiding unscrupulous behaviors and even protecting clients' principal in a bear market isn't enough. We best be aware of the five principles Zaritsky expounds in order to avoid lawsuits.

The first principle, while one most advisors probably intuit, is also responsible for their smugness: "People don't sue their friends." If you respect your client by returning calls promptly, attending to the details that are important to him, and showing a genuine, personal interest in his problems – so the thinking goes – he's not likely to sue you. It may be that having done all those things, a client is less likely to sue.

However, the problem, says Zaritsky, comes when the client's dead and gone and his kids meet you for the first time. They have no idea what kind of relationship you had with their mother or father. Aside from their grief, their only concern is whether the estate's value has been maximized for their benefit. And they assume that's what you were doing all those years you worked with their parents. They may not be interested in the fact that mom wanted to sleep at night investing in municipal bonds instead of quadrupling her estate for the benefit of her children.

Although Zaritsky doesn't actually come out a say it, it would seem prudent for those of us who work with older clients to meet – and if the client will permit it – involve his children as early on as possible in the client relationship and as much as possible in the investment and planning decisions you make with the client while the client is alive. This is often difficult when grown children live far from their parents, but sometimes we can do a weekend meeting when the children are in town for a visit so they can know us as people and not as defendants.

Zaritsky's second principle is that truth is not a defense. Just because mom said she wanted nothing but municipal bonds, that doesn't mean the kids won't bring a suit anyway on the grounds that mom didn't understand what she was doing. Rather, they will argue, she did what her advisor told her to do. Worst case, says Zaritsky, the children will bring a suit while your client is still living and your client will deny that he or she authorized you to structure the portfolio as you did! That prevents the client from having to admit to her children that her investment strategy was geared towards her own welfare at the expense of their inheritances.

That's where the third principle comes into play. "An ounce of good notes is worth a ton of explanation." Hear this: "Most of the malpractice cases that I have observed could have been avoided if the estate planner had kept better records, especially regarding the issues that he or she discussed with the client, the decisions that the client made, and the client's reasons for those decisions," says Zaritsky.

For those of us who aren't fond of documenting every step of the client relationship, we should at least document those decisions that have the greatest potential for misunderstandings down the road, says Zaritsky. An obvious, but still overlooked, example Zaritsky provides is that of a client's decision to favor one child over another. Post-death, it must be clear this was the client's decision with no coercion or recommendation by the advisor.

Of course, the system of documentation is important too, since these documents could become court evidence. The most convincing documentation will be that which was made contemporaneously with the event in question. With the commonplace use of email for client communications, these notes are more automatic; as long as we have an effective system of filing and retrieving emails in which potentially litigable decisions were made, we have documentation that should stand up in court. For those decisions that could come back to haunt, Zaritsky also recommends we write a letter to our client documenting how the decision was arrived at, particularly if the client acted contrary to our advice in situations that could ultimately upset one or more beneficiaries.

Zaritsky's fourth principle concerns the conflict between the client's monetary and non-monetary goals. In our world of financial planning, an example might be the client's strong desire to purchase expensive long-term care insurance for peace of mind when she's already sitting on a $3,000,000 estate and has a very modest cost of living. Ten years later, she dies and her son realizes that if he had the accumulated value of the premiums she paid up until her death he'd be $100,000 richer. It's times like these when the fee-only planner will benefit by not having sold his client the insurance in question. Yet, in her son's eyes, we let her – or advised her – to purchase it, and he may believe that was fiscally irresponsible given her wealth at the time of that decision. (Of course, if the market has significantly reduced the client's estate and the costs of long-term care have been horrific – as they often are – and you convinced mom to buy and hold long-term care coverage, you'll have been a hero.) Again, we must carefully document any situation in which the client decided in favor of an intangible benefit versus greater wealth.

Zaritsky's fifth and final principle is to avoid malpractice suits by avoiding fee disputes. In his profession, at least, most malpractice suits begin as fee disputes. Often the client disagrees with the fee the attorney has charged and, when pressured to pay it, makes a counterclaim against the attorney. In most cases, this is not likely to affect the financial planner – at least not if the planner employs a fee structure whereby the client can anticipate his fee. The advisor that bills hourly and surprises his client with a high bill based on hours the client couldn't anticipate is asking for trouble. Perhaps that is why there aren't many veteran planners whose clients don't know approximately or exactly what they're going to be charged.

However, this is not to say that charging lower fees insulates us from fee disputes. If we quote a certain number of hours of work and find we've underestimated the time necessary to do the job right, we may cut corners. In this instance, we are more likely to make serious errors in judgment, says Zaritsky, implying we should either learn to quote the job accurately, or do the job right and "eat" the difference.

Of course, following these principles will not guarantee us absolute protection from lawsuits. According to Vessenes, we should all be devoting major resources to client education. It seems there will always be some clients who expect to invest significant sums in equities yet avoid the losses that must necessarily occur in a down market. Investing, either directly or indirectly, is still the one activity that gives rise to most suits.

Nowhere is this truer than in the highly unpredictable arena of alternative investments – investments that we hope will further diversify portfolios that may be too heavily skewed to the domestic and foreign stock and bond markets – all of which seem to move more in tandem, as one Global Economy becomes a reality.

Yet alternatives like privately owned real estate, oil and gas drilling, hedge funds, windmill farms and even racehorses, usually pose the highest risks to our clients. Most E&O insurers judge these risks so great as to refuse coverage of the losses or lawsuits resulting from such investments. The few insurers who do cover alternatives charge what most advisors would deem to be exorbitant premiums for the privilege of using these vehicles.

The company Bud Bigelow represents, First Specialty of Overland Park, Kansas, markets its reasonably priced E&O product to the mass advisor market and, therefore, does not cover alternatives. Says Bigelow, "There's been little change in our position on alternatives since 1994 when we first excluded them from E&O coverage. We believe advisors can achieve the rates of return they're seeking through alternatives without taking the risk *associated* with alternatives. Some insureds who've taken issue with the fact that we don't insure alternative investment activity say we're going to be out of business as a result [of this gap in coverage]. It's simply not true. We target the small advisor market with revenues under $1,000,000. If we fiddle around with our target market definition, we run the risk of sacrificing the good of the many for the interests of the few [i.e., those who do alternatives vs. those who don't]. This vision has allowed us to survive when other insurers have gone out of business. We've been financially stable for years. Our revenues are telling us that a majority of our policyholders want us to do exactly what we're doing. Many of the positions we take are to protect our policyholders as well as ourselves. We're the ones who see the claims coming in. Let me add ... most advisors [who have to defend investments in alternatives] don't do well on the witness stand."

Should you not recommend alternative investments? It's your call. Some advisors do them without E&O coverage because they consider their inclusion in client portfolios essential for proper diversification. Others don't do them because they aren't covered, or because they feel they're more trouble than they're worth. Being a financial advisor – a small businessperson – is a matter of managing business risks. This is one of them.

Notice we haven't spent much time talking about E&O insurance, per se. As with any other insurance product, there are technical details you need to know about how this insurance operates, your choices *vis-à-vis* deductibles, special contract provisions that might be present or absent in your policy, limits of liability, and so on. While this information is no doubt important, it's readily available elsewhere (see below, "Where to Get Technical Information on E&O Insurance").

What few planners appreciate are the many risks we've discussed that must be managed *even though you have E&O coverage.* Without making reasoned decisions concerning the use of alternative investments, without developing some type of relationship with clients' children, and without protecting clients' principal in down markets, the E&O coverage you already have will get put to use.

What's wrong with this, you ask? It's not only your money on the line – it's your reputation. Having E&O coverage may save you $15,000 in legal defense costs, but it can't repair a good reputation destroyed by the frivolous lawsuit of a greedy and misguided client or his children. Perhaps the single best long-run way to avoid lawsuits and to keep your E&O coverage premiums down (as well as to sleep much better at night and spend less time in courtrooms as a defendant) is to know when *not* to accept and when to "fire" a client. (See Chapter 11, "Problem Clients.")

WHERE TO GET TECHNICAL INFORMATION ON E&O INSURANCE

The Cambridge Alliance (http://www.cambridgealliance.com/) offers the following articles:

- "Insuring Your Financial Planning Practice"
- "Perils of Group Sponsored Broker Dealer E&O Insurance Programs"
- "Surviving in the Liability Jungle"
- "Are There Differences Among Policies"
- "Selecting a Limit"

CHAPTER ENDNOTES

1. Stephan Leimberg and Howard Zaritsky, *Tax Planning with Life Insurance* (Boston, MA: Warren Gorham & Lamont, 2002).

Chapter 24

"WHAT'S THE NEXT STEP? DO I GO OUT ON MY OWN, OR LOOK FOR A JOB?"

Let's say you're a CFP® candidate, reading this book as part of your CFP® curriculum. You haven't yet decided whether to use these "Tools & Techniques" to create your own firm, or to just keep in the back of your mind as you seek work as a CFP® employee of someone else's firm. (The CFP® mark is used with permission of the Certified Financial Planner Board of Standard, Inc., at: http://www.cfp.net/certificants/markuse.asp).

Here are some things to think about as you make your decision:

First, let's discuss the ways in which you might practice as a financial planner, and what will be required of you. As has been discussed in other chapters, the novice CFP® will probably consider a wirehouse, an independent broker/dealer (BD), or an independent Registered Investment Adviser (RIA) firm as the basis for employment. ("Independent RIA firm" is being used here to describe a firm not affiliated with a broker/dealer, although many independent broker/dealer representatives set up their own RIAs).

In fact, these three venues, in the order we listed them, often form the career path taken by financial planners. The reason why is because they represent three stops on the business ownership continuum – from full support and no ownership (i.e., the wirehouse) to do-it-all-yourself (i.e., the independent RIA firm).

If you work in a wirehouse, you have a well-known and well-advertised brand name, an office, office equipment, assistants, back-office support for trading and all of its related functions, a built-in compliance department, approved investment offerings, and a tried-and-true blueprint for growing your practice. But a "practice" is about all you really have. The clients you attract, cultivate, and help prosper *might* be yours to take to another wirehouse, should you someday move, but they aren't yours to sell. And if you can't sell them, you don't "own" them – even in the most professional sense of the term.

As the representative of an independent BD, you will operate your own firm with support from your broker-dealer. Your payout, less than 100% of the total revenues you generate, will reflect the degree of support you receive from your BD. However, you will be free to set your own fee structure and make many other entrepreneurial decisions that reflect your way of doing things. And you will own your clients. An independent BD representative strikes a compromise between the wirehouse representative and the independent RIA.

The owner of an independent RIA must create his/her own brand. The BD rep can at least say he clears his securities through Securities America, or Raymond James, but the independent RIA (even though he might use a recognizable discount brokerage operation for clearing) must really forge a distinct identity and brand. And, not only will an independent RIA be self-reliant for marketing and brand-building, he'll also design and create all of his own internal operating systems, buy his own computers and software, arrange for his own accounting and legal work, do his own hiring and firing, and much, much more.

Why would you select one option over another? There are probably two primary considerations motivating you: one is know-how, and the other is money. Traditionally, CFP® curriculums have focused primarily on the technical knowledge needed to be a financial planner, not the business skills. As a young, independent CFP® building a fee-only RIA firm, I found early on that I couldn't *just* be a financial planner. I had to wear three hats in pretty much equal proportions: (1) financial planner; (2) marketer; and (3) administrator. In other words, when I wasn't working on clients' plans, I was looking for new clients or doing administrative work (e.g., preparing and filing my ADV, comparing E&O policies, renting office equipment, hiring an assistant, typing and mailing correspondence to a client, and so on).

This combination of activities can be intimidating – and even overwhelming – to a new CFP® graduate. You are bursting with ideas on planning, on asset allocation, on all of the things you've learned in your CFP® program. But, unless you've got an MBA, or grew up working in your parents' business, and unless you have a great deal of capital or financial backing, you probably feel ill-equipped to run your own shop right from the start. You know you want to start out as an employee, not a business owner. The question is ... which of the three choices should you make?

At this point in your decision-making, it's important to take a long-range view. What do you want your involvement in financial planning to look like 10 or 20 years from now? Do you see yourself as a planner running your own firm? Do you want to know how to be an expert marketer, how to get clients, how to establish a workplace that keeps employees happy and loyal? Do you want the financial rewards that accrue to the owner of a successful advisory firm? Are you willing to invest the time, energy, money, and willpower?

If so, then your initial employment should be geared to this end. Ideally, you should work in a venue where you will learn not only to be an expert planner, but also pick up the necessary practice management skills you need. In conjunction with the information in this book, you can then plan to strike out on your own at some point. Except for the wirehouse, any of the venues will encourage this experience. In a wirehouse environment, you will be taught to sell products, not to run your own business. As mentioned earlier, some planners begin their career path with the wirehouse but, if they successfully move beyond the wirehouse to an independent BD or RIA, they are more likely to have been motivated by a need for freedom than any business acumen they picked up in the wirehouse environment. Many successful planners have achieved their goals after leaving wirehouses because they were fueled by the desire to use better products than the wirehouse could offer, or work with clients on a fee basis doing a more objective style of financial planning – or both.

So if you want to run a successful advisory business of your own someday but aren't prepared to do it from the start, look for an employer that can teach you the ropes correctly. This is easier said than done, because most quality planning is being done these days in boutique shops (either by independent BD reps or RIA advisors). Read financial planning publications while you are studying for your CFP® so that, by graduation, you will have a sense of which planners have good reputations and are running firms admired by others for their quality of client service and/or innovative practices.

Don't be afraid to ask practitioners you meet if they can suggest good firms where you can intern. Go to conferences conducted by the Financial Planning Association (FPA) or the National Association of Personal Financial Advisors (NAPFA) when you are within a year of graduation to network and seek employment possibilities. At this stage in your career, also keep in mind that you will have greater likelihood of interning in a quality shop if you have the freedom to relocate.

What if your deepest desire is to do a little financial planning but, more important, to make a lot of money? Do you have sales skills that were apparent to you and those around you from an early age? Could you "sell ice cubes to an Eskimo" as the saying goes? If so, you may be better off in a wirehouse than in either of the other venues. In spite of advertised changes to a new culture of fee-based planning, wirehouses still compensate their reps primarily on commissions earned, with (at best) a secondary nod to the end-client's success as an investor or financial planning client. While a wirehouse career can't yet be considered the same as a financial planning career, it *is* a place where someone with a CFP® who also possesses strong sales skills can build a successful and prosperous career.

But if you want to be a business owner, to put into practice all of the Tools you've learned in this and the other *Tools & Techniques* resources, you'll need to take a more entrepreneurial path than the wirehouse can give you. Below are some additional resources to help you make your decision.

WHERE CAN I FIND OUT MORE?

1. John E. Sestina, *Fee-Only Financial Planning: How to Make It Work for You* (New York, NY: Wiley, 2000).

2. Nancy Langdon Jones, *So You Want to Be a Financial Planner* (Sunnydale, CA: AdvisorPress, 2002).

3. Jeffrey H. Rattiner, *Getting Started as a Financial Planner* (Princeton, NJ: Bloomberg Press, 2000).

Chapter 25

CREATING A PLAN / FINDING CLIENTS

YOU NEED A PLAN

Any business, whether new or old, should have a business plan, which is updated periodically. Many readers of this book are no doubt capable of putting together a plan with general purpose software such as a word processor and a spreadsheet; however, we have found that it is cost effective to purchase a specialized business plan program for this task. Good software saves a considerable amount of time. The better packages include wizards, templates, sample plans, and advice.

One software package that we have found particularly useful over the years is Business Plan Pro from Palo Alto Software. An enhanced version of the program, Business Plan Pro Premier, offers additional features such as collaboration, customization, and enhanced reporting.

Bplans.com, which is also published by Palo Alto, is an excellent source of business planning resources online. Other sources of business planning software and/or information include PlanWare (www.planware.com), Center for Business Planning (www.businessplans.org), bpVision (www.bpvision.com), and PlanMagic Corporation (www.planmagic.com).

Creating a separate marketing plan is extremely helpful for new businesses. A number of the providers mentioned above, including Palo Alto and PlanMagic, offer separate, dedicated marketing programs. We think that investing in one is money well spent. If the additional time and money you spend result in the acquisition of just a couple of additional clients over your first year in business, you will have reaped an excellent return on your investment.

FINDING CLIENTS, ETC.

Advisors, both novices and veterans, have a number of tools at their disposal to help bring prospective clients through the door. The purpose of the remainder of this chapter is to offer readers an overview of some technology-related marketing ideas.

The Web

Advisor websites can serve a number of purposes, but the two most prominent ones are marketing and client service. We'll discuss website providers and the client service aspect of websites in Chapter 27, "Communication Tools: Web Sites," so for now let's look at how a website can help attract prospects.

Do you ever go shopping on the web for services? So do a great many other folks. If a prospective client in your town is searching for, say, a Certified Financial Planner® (CFP) licensee in your town with your specialty, will your name be displayed prominently in the search engine results? It had better. If prospective clients can't find you, they cannot find out about the wonderful service that you offer.

Journalists often "shop" for sources the way prospective clients shop for advisors. Local papers and periodicals often prefer to quote local sources. They are often eager to work with a new source, particularly one who can offer a fresh angle. A well executed website will help reporters find you. Alternatively, if you initiate contact with a reporter, you can add legitimacy to your image, and offer easy access to more information about yourself and your firm with a good website. Your authors, who both write for financial planning publications, regularly check out potential interviewees on the web.

Perhaps you meet a potential referral source at a mutual friend's birthday party. After chatting amicably for a few moments about your profession, you hand the person a business card. Rest assured that before the person refers any business to you, they will check you out on the web. Don't have a website, or worse yet, have an unprofessional one? The odds of you ever seeing a referral from that source just dropped dramatically. If the content is high quality and professional, however, you've just increased your chances.

In many instances, your website will be the first contact that a prospective client has with your firm; and we all know how important first impressions are. Because your website will play a crucial role in building your business, sufficient resources should be allocated to it. What constitutes a professional website? The short answer is one that projects your firm's core values, and one that is easy to navigate.

If, like most of us, you have problems refining your core values into a few sentences, or portraying them effectively on the web, you are a prime candidate for some marketing help. At least one web service company that we profile in Chapter 27 offers such consultations, as do a number of independent consultants.

Helping People Find You on the Web

If potential clients, journalists, and others will be trying to locate you on the web, it is important that you do what you can to make sure that they find you. One obvious first step is to make sure you are listed on all of the major search engines; however, this is becoming increasingly more difficult and expensive to do. Currently, many of the important search engines, with the exception of Google, charge a fee for business listings. SearchEngines.com is a good source of information to guide you through the submission process.

Getting listed, however, is not enough. You must use the proper keywords. When we recently conducted a Google search for the keywords "financial planner," Google returned about 360,000 results. "Financial advisor" returned about 712,000 results. If you solely use broad terms such as these, you and your firm will become the proverbial needle in a haystack.

If you live in a small town, or one without much competition, geography may be enough to set you apart from the crowd. For example, when I ran a Google search for "financial planner" and "Paris, Texas," only 15 results were returned. If you live in a more densely populated or competitive market, you will need to find other methods of differentiation, such as a specialty niche or other unique identifier.

In some cases, paid listings on search sites can help the right people find you. The trick is to target your ads properly. If you use a broad keyword like "financial," it will be displayed and clicked on often, and it will cost a great deal of money; however, it will bring few qualified prospective clients to you. If, on the other hand, only people searching for your specialty, plus your town, plus financial planner see the ad, the cost can be quite modest, and the results more productive.

Overture, Inc. and Google are two companies that offer paid listings or ads. Both allow users to create targeted ad campaigns on a limited budget, sometimes as little as $25 per month. If you are looking for a more prominent presence on the web, particularly to a local audience, paid listings can be effective.

Being Quoted in the Local Press

If you are quoted in the local press, it is increasingly likely that an online version of the article will find its way onto the search engines. Whenever this occurs, it creates another free "presence" for you on the web, making it that much easier for someone to find you. If the article you are quoted in contains your firm's website, its value to you increases substantially, so ask reporters to include it. If the story contains a hyperlink to your firm's website, it may have a positive influence on your firm's overall search rankings.

Online Referral Sources

Online referral sources can be an excellent source of new business, but the quality of the referrals varies greatly from source to source. Your authors have never received an inquiry that actually resulted in an engagement, which we can specifically attribute to one of the many paid or "free" commercial listing services that have solicited us over the years. We can, however, directly attribute qualified referrals, some who became good clients, to the websites of organizations that the public holds in high regard.

Without a doubt, the best source of qualified referrals we have come across is the referral service of the National Association of Personal Financial Advisors (NAPFA). In 2003, qualified NAPFA members received over 36,000 referrals through the NAPFA Referral Service (www.napfa.org). For a small fee, NAPFA members can further enhance the value of the referral service by linking their own website to their NAPFA referral listing, so that prospects can click through to their site from the NAPFA site.

The Financial Planning Association (FPA) offers a similar referral service through its FPA Planner Search tool (http://www.fpanet.org/PlannerSearch/PlannerSearch.cfm). For a nominal fee, members can purchase an "enhanced" listing, which includes additional information about their practice, as well as a link to their own corporate website.

While not strictly speaking a referral source, the CFP Board (www.cfp-board.org) allows consumers to locate CFP® licensees using a number of different criteria at their website. Here, consumers can check on the status of a licensee, including any disciplinary history.

Other Organizations

The Garrett Planning Network, Inc.

Sheryl Garrett, CFP® has been the nation's leading proponent of hourly financial planning for a number of years. She is the founder of the Garrett Planning Network, Inc. (http://www.discovergarrettplanning network.com/), which offers a turnkey hourly fee-only financial planning business model for a fee.[1] The package includes coaching, training, marketing, practice management, a peer network, and vendor discounts.

The Garrett Planning Network leverages the web in a number of ways that benefit its members. Garrett (and other more visible members of the network) is often quoted in the press. This leads to substantial traffic on the network's website. The consumer portion of the site offers a referral service similar to those offered by NAPFA and FPA, where consumers can locate a fee only hourly planner in their neighborhood. The site offers a separate section devoted exclusively to journalists. Here, reporters can easily locate members by geographic location and/or specialty, as well as view a "featured story idea." The prominent placement of the journalist section of the site insures that it will be noticed and used, increasing the press coverage members receive.

Cambridge Alliance of Advisors, Inc.

The Cambridge Alliance of Advisors, Inc. (www.cambridgeadvisors.com) is another organization offering a turn-key financial planning practice. Founded by Bert Whitehead, J.D., MBA, a true pioneer in the field of bringing professional financial planning services to the middle market, Cambridge offers coaching, training, templates, a peer network, and vendor discounts. Like the Garrett Planning Network, the Cambridge site offers a referral service and a journalist section.

For those just starting out in the business or those transitioning from a large firm to independence, organizations like the Garrett Planning Network and the Cambridge Alliance of Advisors can significantly compress the learning curve. They offer a wealth of proven, useful business information, as well as the credibility of being associated with a respected "name" brand.

My Financial Advice

Since the advent of the web, entrepreneurs have been trying to devise methods of bringing consumers and qualified professionals together virtually. Until recently, each attempt that we have been aware of has ended dismally. My Financial Advice (www.myfinancial advice.com), a relatively new entrant into the field, looks much more promising, however. The site attempts to match pre-screened, qualified advisors with those looking for help regarding a specific financial challenge. Advisors offer consultations over the phone or by email, and consumers are charged by the minute for the work advisors do. Advisors set their own hourly fees, which are published on the site. My Financial Advice makes its money by charging advisors a listing fee, and retaining a portion of all planning fees generated on the site.

My Financial Advice offers a number of advantages for newer advisors in particular. First, it can help you reach qualified prospects that need your help. Second, it can help you fill empty hours profitably as you build your practice, particularly if you set your price competitively. Third, since this is more of a "virtual" consulting process, it allows advisors to reach consumers nationally. In short, My Financial Advice is an interesting new technology platform, which offers benefits to both consumers and advisors. If there is sufficient consumer traffic, this concept looks like a winner.

Drip Marketing

Earlier in this book (see Chapter 7, "Marketing"), we told you that direct mail might not be the most effective marketing technique. Perhaps we need to clarify that a bit: bulk mailings (as described in Chapter 7) may not be effective, but another type of direct mailing may be: follow-up mailings to those who have already expressed an interest in you services.

Drip marketing can work effectively if used as a follow-up to those who have requested information online or through a referral source. The good news is that drip marketing has never been less expensive. Email has lowered the cost of drip marketing to almost nothing. A few short years ago, drip marketing was expensive. We had to create content (or buy it), do a mail merge, print it, stuff envelopes, and mail it. The cost in paper, printer supplies, mailing labels, envelopes, and postage was substantial. Now, essentially the only marginal cost is the content.

Prospective clients are busy people, and they are often easily distracted. One day they decide they should look for a financial planner, but then some other task takes priority. It may be several weeks, or several months, before they are actually ready to take the next step. Drip marketing keeps your name in front of them during the period between the initial contact and the point when they are actually ready to hire a planner. In order for drip marketing to work, you must send the prospect something of value, not a sales pitch.

When we receive a referral or a request for information, we respond as quickly as possible with introductory information, by email, about our firm. We also include an invitation to schedule an introductory phone call. We then send out follow-up pieces on a regular basis for a predetermined period of time. Perhaps the second piece would be a piece on how to select a financial planner, followed by general information about the financial planning process, then a copy of our monthly newsletter, etc. If the prospective client recognizes the value of the information you are sending, he or she will be more inclined to eventually engage you; if not, the prospective client will probably request to be removed from the list, which should be done immediately.

Drip marketing does not guarantee success, but it does increase your chances of success. We've had a number of clients tell us over the years that they eventually decided to engage us because we were the only advisor who contacted them multiple times in a user friendly, non-invasive manner. In the past, cost was an impediment for novice advisors, but with technology, the costs are minimized. We think that electronic drip marketing is definitely worth trying.

CHAPTER ENDNOTES

1. Sheryl Garrett is the author of *Garrett's Guide to Financial Planning: How to Capture the Middle Market and Increase Your Profits* (Cincinnati, OH: The National Underwriter Company, 2002) and *Just Give Me the Answer$: Experts Address Your Most Pressing Financial Questions* (Chicago, IL: Dearborn Trade Publishing, 2004).

Chapter 26

COMMUNICATION TOOLS: EMAIL

Email is one of the true workhorses of the modern financial planning practice, but this was not always the case. In the late 1990s, many financial planning firms resisted the idea of using email as a client communication tool. Many thought it too impersonal; others thought their clients were not receptive to the idea of using email.

Your authors were early proponents of leveraging email as a client communication tool. We saw it not only as a way to lower costs, but also as a way to significantly improve client service. In fact, we so firmly believed in the benefits of email that we both encouraged and aided clients without email accounts to establish them.

Our opinion of email has not changed much over time. We think it can be used effectively both as a marketing tool and a communication tool. We still know of advisors who conduct "drip marketing" campaigns using snail mail. ("Drip marketing" is a proven prospecting technique whereby the advisor sends a number of messages, traditionally letters, to a client at predetermined intervals of time). For the newer, smaller advisory firm, drip marketing can be effective, but it can also be costly. The cost of paper, printing, and postage can add up, and it takes time (a labor cost) to stuff the envelopes before finally mailing them. An email drip marketing campaign can be just as effective, and the cost is minimal by comparison. No paper, printing, or postage costs. No envelopes to stuff. No trips to the post office. And it's easier for the client to respond to.

Email, if used properly, can vastly improve client communications. Many clients are otherwise engaged during "normal business hours." They may be hesitant to telephone you other times. Email removes these communications impediments. Clients can send you an email message when it is convenient for them to do so, and you can respond when it is convenient for you to do so. Your authors often respond to client email from airports, hotel rooms, and even taxis when we are on the road. When it is convenient for us to do so, we will respond to clients on evenings and weekends. Email, when used properly, actually increases our flexibility while reducing response times.

Email avoids the annoyance of "phone tag," and it often allows advisors to respond more effectively. For example, if a client asks you about a specific mutual fund, a written response with supporting documentation is probably preferable than some remarks over the phone.

Email can also provide a written record for compliance purposes. Consider the case of a client who insists upon selling a poorly performing foreign bond fund. You advise holding the fund because you believe that it is a good portfolio diversifier and because you believe the United States dollar is about to fall (so the fund should benefit from the exchange rate differential, assuming it is not hedging the currency exposure). At the client's insistence, you sell the fund, and a year later it performs brilliantly. The client, who has a short memory, now claims that you insisted on selling the foreign bond fund. If all communications took place over the phone, it is your word against his; however, if the discussion took place through email, everything is documented (including your own mistake, if you've made one).

EMAIL SOFTWARE

Ironically, in a few short years, the main objection to email among advisors was that all of their clients did not use it. Now, we have the opposite problem: many advisors are having trouble dealing with email overload. One of the keys to productivity in the modern financial planning office is the effective processing and management of email.

The tools and techniques of managing email are somewhat dependent on the email program one uses. Since the vast majority of planners we come into contact with use MS Outlook, we will focus much of our discussion on that particular product, including third party utilities that can increase Outlook's usefulness. Later, we'll provide a brief overview of some alternative email programs.

Microsoft Outlook 2003

Outlook 2003 does a much better job of dealing with email than previous versions did. Most financial professionals are grappling with a deluge of email. Outlook

Figure 26.1

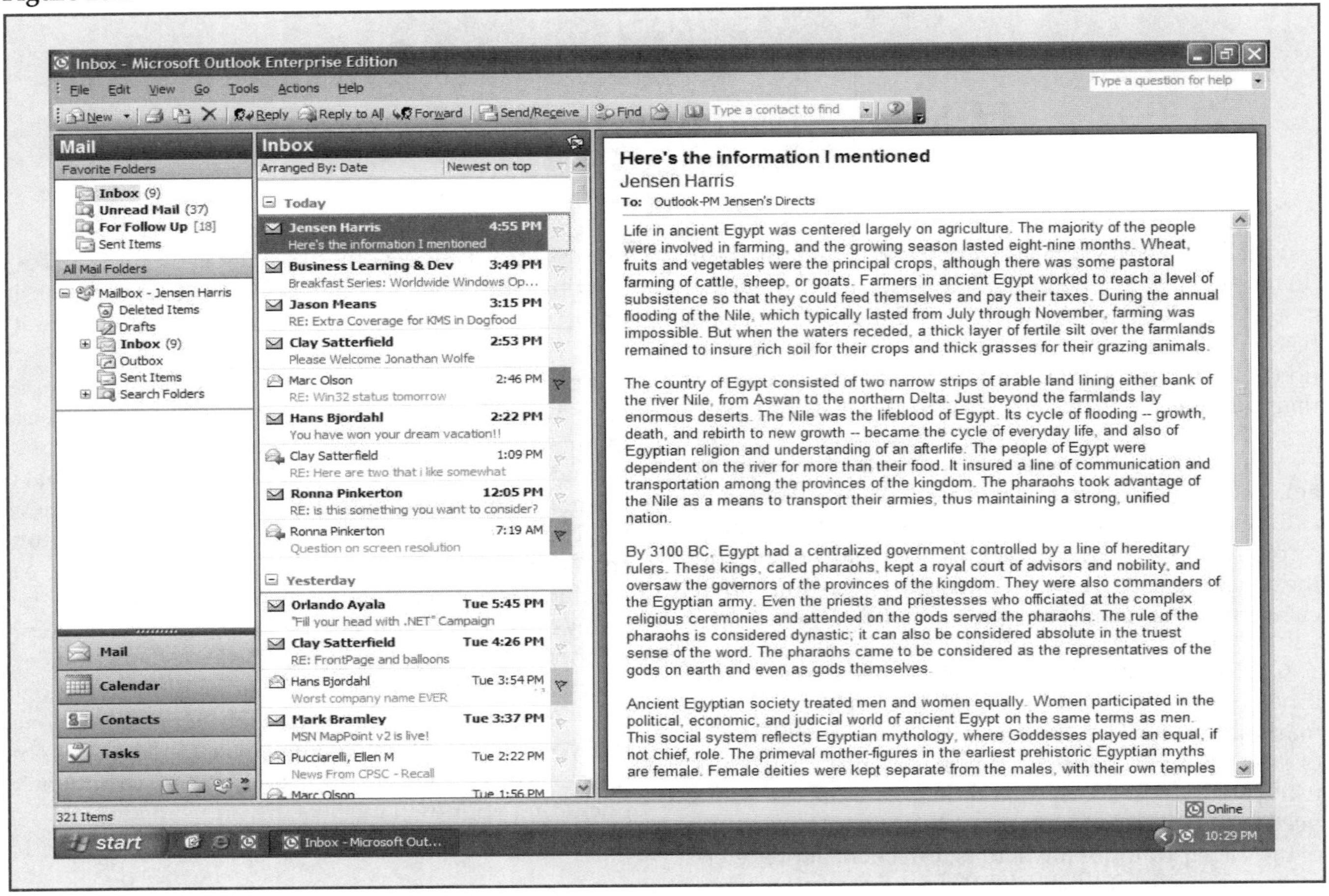

2003 contains a number of enhancements designed to better manage the high volume of email that we receive.

One enhancement is the new default view. According to Microsoft, the new vertical pane (the center column above) combined with the new reading pane (at the right) makes it possible to see nearly twice as much data when compared with previous versions of Outlook.

The vertical view now offers multiple lines of information. Messages are arranged by date. Research indicates that users decide what to do with an email based on who sent it, so the sender's name and the time stamp are displayed in bold type, to help draw reader's attention to this important information. The subject of the email is displayed below in a lighter typeface.

The vertical view has built in "Intelligent Groupings." One type of Intelligent Grouping is a grouping by date. Rather than just listing messages chronologically by date, the program goes a step further and groups them into logical sections such as Today, Yesterday, Last Week, and Last Month. These groupings make it easier for users to locate messages when scrolling.

Another new feature, Smart Dates, modifies the format of the date as it ages. Here's how it works: the Today grouping receives a time stamp only, because the user knows the message arrived today. Messages received within the past week display the day of the week and the time received. Messages more than 10 days old display the date only.

Outlook also offers virtual groupings. Virtual groupings do not cause a message to move, but rather to appear in multiple listings. For example, Outlook automatically scanned all of my email messages, and grouped the largest ones in a virtual folder called "Large Mail." When I clicked on the large mail folder, all of the largest email messages in my inbox were listed, from largest to smallest. This list was further divided into categories such as Huge, Very Large, and Large. Another virtual folder contained all of my unread emails, arranged alphabetically.

Perhaps the most important new virtual folder is the "For Follow Up" folder. Essentially, there are three things that you can do with an email message: act on it immediately, delete it, or store it for action at a later date.

Figure 26.2

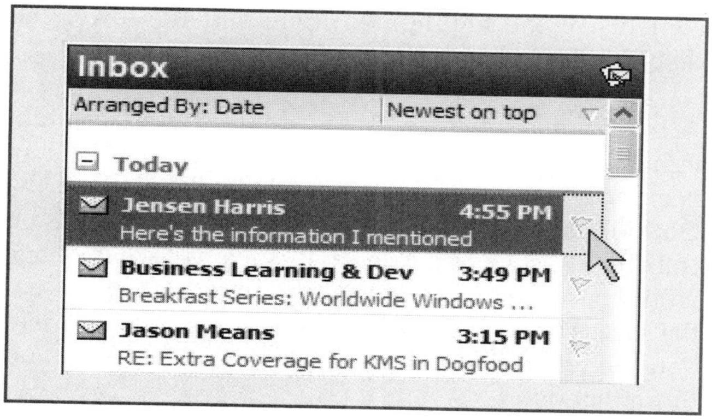

Figure 26.3

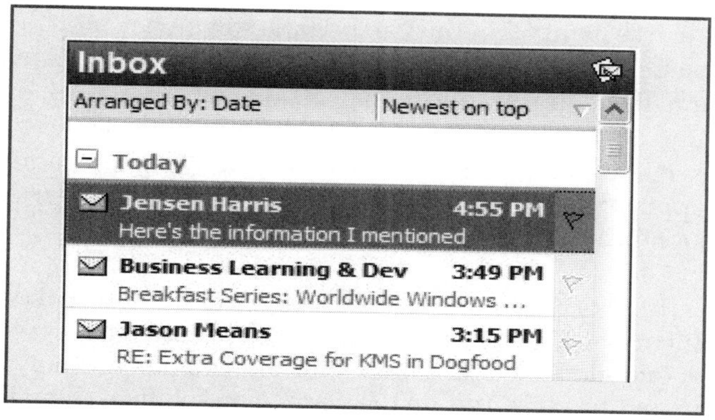

The "For Follow Up" folder is designed specifically to deal with the latter.

By single clicking on the grayed out flag next to any email, users can attach a flag to it. The program supplies six flag colors, so that flagged items can be grouped according to user needs.

As email items are flagged, they are automatically added to the virtual "For Follow Up" folder, with the messages grouped by color. In effect, flagging a message creates a virtual to do list. Later, all the user has to do is go to the folder, take action, and single click the flag again. This will produce a check mark, designating that the task has been completed. MS Outlook adds a "completed" stamp to the formerly flagged email, which included the date and time action was taken.

As you work with virtual folders, and come to appreciate their power, it is highly likely that you will want to create more of them. MS Outlook makes it easy to do so. From within the Mail section of the program, click on "File," then "New," and then "Search Folder." A dialog box appears that allows you to create a virtual folder from one of 12 pre-defined templates. You can also create your own customized virtual search folders here (it is also possible to save any Find or Advanced Find search into a customized virtual folder).

For the first time, Outlook 2003 has added a fairly intelligent junk mail filtering capability. The junk mail filter uses a combination of lists and artificial intelligence to determine which incoming messages are spam (Microsoft periodically updates the spam list; updates can be found at the MS Office Update site). Messages identified as junk mail are routed to a special junk mail folder, where they can be reviewed or deleted. Users can chose from a number of protection settings. Higher protection levels filter more messages, but they generate more false positives (legitimate mail wrongly identified as spam). Lowering the protection level cuts down on false positives, but some junk may slip through, although the system improves as you identify spam it did not initially catch by either adding offensive senders to a list, or clicking on an email you have received then selecting the option to block future messages from that sender. Our experience indicates that the highest setting is too restrictive for a financial service business. It allows through only email from senders that you specify (you can import lists of approved senders).

In a policy change from the previous version, Outlook 2003 blocks HTML images embedded in email from downloading on to your computer by default. The primary reason is security: images from unknown senders can contain malicious code. An added benefit, however, is that plain text email downloads faster than HTML, which is easier to read. If you receive a legitimate message, and you want to download the graphics, you just click in a gray box at the top of the email that says, "click here to download pictures," and the images will appear.

There are a number of obstacles that prevent advisors from achieving optimal email productivity. They range from program limitations, to organizational problems, to spam. The next section provides an overview of some email utilities designed to boost productivity.

EMAIL ENHANCERS

Nelson Email Organizer Pro Version 3.0 (NEO Pro 3.0)

MS Outlook is a very good program, but it could be even better. Two areas where MS Outlook falls short are search capabilities and the ability to organize email in different ways. One program that can help in these areas, and in many others, is Nelson Email Organizer Pro. For those of you unfamiliar with the program, NEO Pro 3.0 is an MS Outlook add-in that does only one thing, but it does it very well: it helps users organize and interact more effectively with their email.

NEO Pro 3.0 doesn't replace Outlook; it works in conjunction with it. Users have access to both the NEO views and the regular Outlook views from right within NEO. A single mouse click allows users to toggle back and forth between the two interfaces.

Outlook has many powerful features, but most people never make use of them. One common problem among MS Office programs, including Outlook, is that they contain a lot of powerful features, but the average user only employs a fraction of them. There are a number of reasons that this is the case. One is that some features are hidden; it takes time and dedication to uncover and deploy these tools. Another is that some of the "tricks" that Outlook is capable of performing require professional programming or customization skills. NEO, like some other add-in programs supplies "customization in a box." Simply purchasing and installing the program relieves NEO users of the customization burden. Once installed, the program not only configures itself automatically, but also immediately begins performing a number of tasks, such as sorting email, in multiple ways.

When NEO Pro is launched for the first time, it creates an index of all email messages. This index is then used to create what the company calls "unified views of messages across Outlook folders." This means that NEO is not bound by the Inbox/Outbox/Sent folder structure of Outlook. With NEO, multiple links can be created to a message, so the message is instantly accessible through multiple views.

Notice that a number of tabs now reside above the main screen. As illustrated above, NEO automatically sorts email into various "baskets." These baskets are accessible by clicking on the tabs that run across the top of the screen. The "Hot" tab is a place to store folders that you want to monitor closely. Typically, this would include incoming email, "Active Mail," and your "To-Do" list. The Hot tab can also contain folders for your most important contacts and correspondents. Folders can easily be added to the Hot tab by right clicking and selecting "Make Hot" from the menu. Current Hot folders can be removed from the "Hot" tab by right clicking and selecting "Remove from Hot."

The main part of the screen is divided into four quadrants. The upper left quadrant contains the NEO folders. The content of the active folder is displayed in the upper right. The lower right quadrant displays the contents of the highlighted item, and the lower left displays the Outlook folders.

In Figure 26.4, the "Active Mail" folder is highlighted. It acts as a staging area for email that has not been acted upon. The Active Folder differs from the Outlook Inbox as follows: With the Inbox, users typically read, act on, or delete email. Ideally, each message would be acted upon immediately, but often, this is not the case. The Active Folder serves as a tool to differentiate between items that require further action, and those that don't.

Many people use MS Outlook 2003 flags to mark "active items," but this can became somewhat cumbersome. The "Active Folder" is a better solution. Any emails requiring additional action, whether read or unread, can be stored here. The Active Folder serves to keep the pending items front and center. Flags are more appropriate for messages with medium to long-term significance.

Each of the additional tabs represents another sort or filter. The Correspondent tab sorts each email by correspondent. All email to and from a given person shows up in this view. Within the Correspondent view, email can be sorted by priority, date, attachment size, etc. Both messages to and from the correspondent appear in this view, but they are color coded, so it is easy to distinguish incoming mail from outgoing mail.

The Correspondent's tab is a great timesaver. Rather than using Outlook's sluggish search feature, all email to and/or from a given contact can be located immediately. NEO includes a number of preconfigured filters, located on the toolbar, so a single correspondent's messages can be further filtered if necessary.

Generally speaking, NEO is not smart enough to recognize that some correspondents may be emailing you from multiple email addresses, so it treats each email address as a separate correspondent; but NEO can learn. With a few mouse clicks, you can teach NEO that two or more email addresses represent the same person. Once NEO knows this, it will group all existing and subsequent messages as a single correspondent.

NEO filters differ from MS Outlook filters in a couple of important ways. First, they are indexed, which means that searches take no more than seconds, as opposed to Outlook filters, which can take several minutes. Second, NEO filters can operates across folders, so you can filter all messages, no matter where they reside, with one action.

Figure 26.4

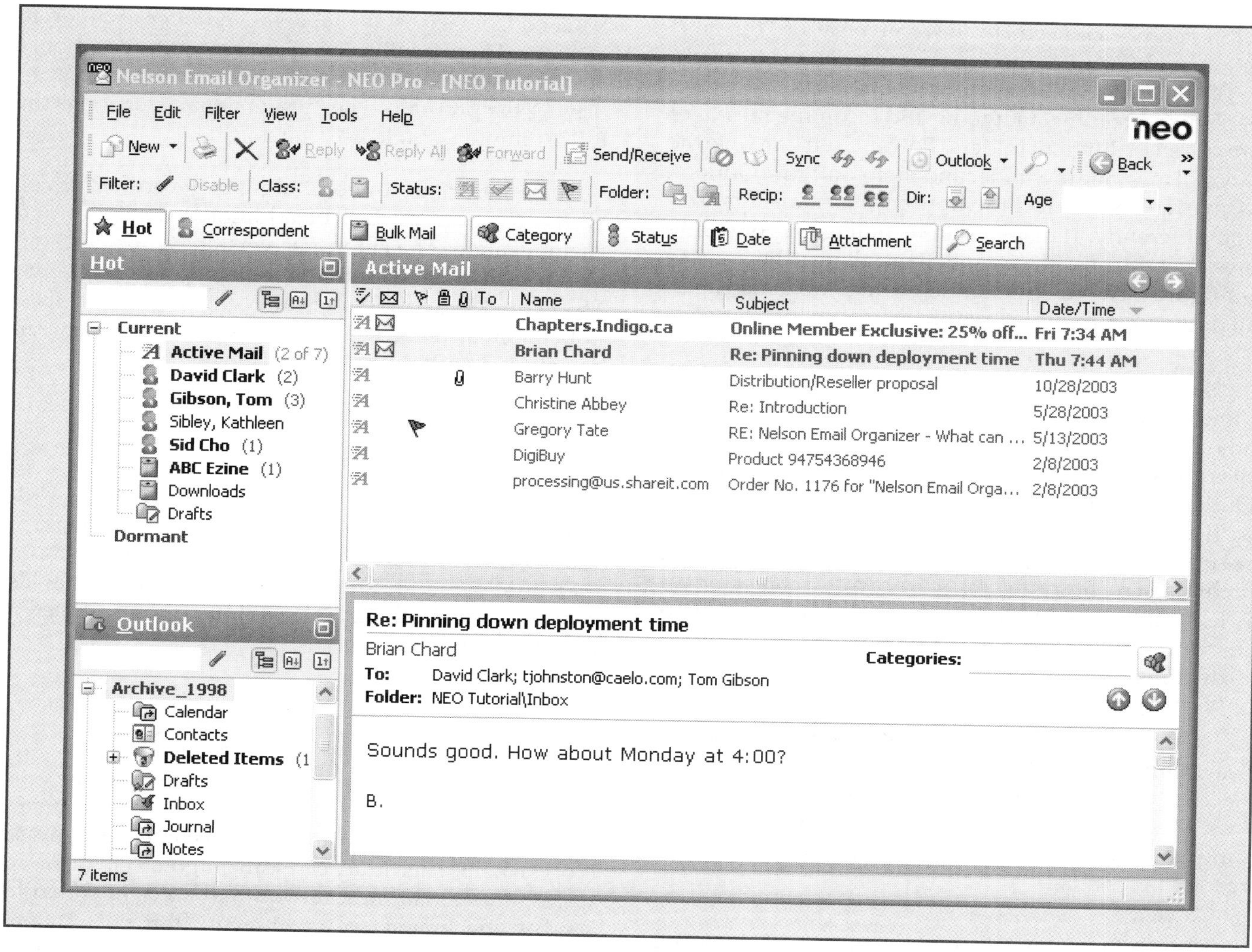

If you receive email alerts, or if you subscribe to electronic newsletters [such as Steve Leimberg's LISI (Leimberg Information Services, Inc.) at www.leimbergservices.com, which provides updates on recent cases, rulings, regulations, and legislation] or participate in other sorts of email lists, NEO's automatic bulk mail detection and handling is a godsend. Outlook offers the ability to create folders for your various "subscription" email, but each time you subscribe to a list, you must manually create a new folder, along with rules so that Outlook knows where to route the subscription to. NEO does a much better job of handling bulk mail.

Within NEO, all bulk mail is automatically detected and sorted under the "Bulk Mail" tab. If you receive a large volume of subscription mail, you can create a unique folder for each subscription. NEO assumes that bulk mail is less important, meaning you may not want to view it right away. By default, all mass mailings are placed inside the bulk folder. This folder can be hidden, or it can be viewed when things are less hectic. The bulk folders can be customized, however, so, for example, if you receive important alerts that require immediate attention from one or more sources, those folders can appear in the "Correspondent" tab or in the "Hot" tab for faster action.

MS Outlook users are probably familiar with "categories." Outlook allows users to assign one or more categories to each contact listing, so they can be grouped or sorted in useful ways. For example, tax preparation clients can be assigned to a "Tax Prep" category; so only they receive communications related to tax preparation clients.

NEO makes it easy to apply Outlook categories to email messages. As you can see in the lower right of Figure 26.4, the open email message had a black "category" line. A category can be assigned to an email by clicking on the icon to the right of the category line, then selecting from a drop-down menu. Categorized email can is then sorted and accessible through the "Categories" tab.

Sometimes it is useful to view conversation "threads" (all incoming and outgoing messages related to a subject). Generally speaking, Outlook does not offer conversation threading. Outgoing and incoming messages are stored in different folders (Power Users can save the original message to a folder and then configure Outlook to save replies with it). NEO approaches email organization differently. It displays all incoming and outgoing messages in one place, and then allows the user to configure the view so he can see all incoming messages, all outgoing messages, or both.

Many advisors tell us that the single most annoying thing about MS Outlook is its inability to deal with large amounts of data. As time goes by, personal Outlook files grow. The larger the files become, the slower Outlook's performance becomes. Microsoft's solution to the performance problem is to urge users, on a regular basis, to archive their email. Unfortunately, archiving creates problems of its own. Archived email is less accessible. Outlook does not allow the user to search multiple files at the same time, so the archived file(s) must be searched separately.

NEO Pro 3.0 provides a solution. It allows users to search for and view messages across multiple folders. In effect, working with archive folders becomes seamless. Messages can be archived to keep Outlook running smoothly, but the archived messages are still readily accessible.

As email volume continues to increase, financial advisors are spending more and more time organizing, searching through, and responding to email. For MS Outlook users, NEO Pro is the most effective tool we've come across to handle large volumes of email effectively. We highly recommend it.

Keeping Contact Information Current

Good Contacts is an application that helps keep your contact list up to date. Good Contacts creates an email to everyone in your address book, and provides them with a link to a webpage where they can update their contact information. All updates are received back at your computer, where the software processes the responses and automatically updates your address book. The outgoing message to contacts can be customized, as can the list of recipients. Users can control how often update requests are sent out. The update requests can be staggered over time, or they can all be sent out at the same time.

Good Contacts is available in a number of different versions. There is a "lite" version that limits the amount of outgoing update requests. This is a good way of test-driving the program. The "professional" version is the full, unlimited, single user version.

For enterprises, there is a custom verifier, which allows for a great deal of additional flexibility and customization. The enterprise version can be used not just to verify contact information, but also for seminar RSVP tracking, surveying, and creating opt-in lists. Both the email and websites of enterprise customers can be branded with the purchaser's logo.

PocketKnife

PocketKnife is little utility that offers access to Outlook contact information without opening Outlook. A little icon sits on the computer's system tray. Clicking on the icon allows users to grab information from Outlook's contact list and use that information to send a letter, a fax, or an email.

Attachment Forget Me Not

Have you ever been embarrassed or lost precious time because you forgot to include an email attachment with your message? If you have, Attachment Forget Me Not can help. This utility can scan outgoing email for up to 15 phrases that indicate you may have intended to send an attachment (see attachment, draft, etc.). Whenever one of the phrases is detected, it asks the user if an attachment is required and offers the ability to add one before the email message is sent out.

Anagram

Anagram is a time saving utility that captures information and moves it to Outlook. When you receive an email that contains a person's contact information, you simply highlight the information and click on the hot key to launch anagram. The program analyzes the text, launches Outlook, and places the text in the appropriate Outlook fields.

Personal Folder Backup

This free program, available for download at the Microsoft website, installs a "backup" button on the "File" menu in Outlook, and automates the backing up of personal Outlook folders (the .PST file).

Email Saver Xe

If you need a backup for client email other than MS Outlook, Email Saver Xe may be able to help. It supports Outlook Express, Netscape Navigator, Opera, and Eudora as well as earlier versions of MS Outlook.

OTHER EMAIL PROGRAMS

Microsoft Outlook Express

Novice computer users often confuse Outlook and Outlook Express. Outlook Express is a free program that comes pre-installed on many computers along with MS Internet Explorer. MS Outlook is a more powerful program that is part of the MS Office Suite of products. It can be purchased as part of an Office Suite "bundle" or it can be purchased separately. Outlook does much more than manage email; it can manage contacts, calendars, to-dos, etc. It also integrates tightly with other MS Office programs.

Outlook Express has more basic email functionality. It generally has limited customization options and more limited privacy controls. It does not include automatic built in junk mail filtering (you can manually create a blacklist of blocked senders). Outlook Express does have some organizational features, like the ability to create subfolders and message filters, but overall, Outlook Express is probably a bit underpowered to the frequent email user.

Eudora

Eudora has been around for many years, and it has a good reputation for usability and functionality. The full version is highly customizable, powerful, and relatively easy to learn. Built in spam filtering is included. Eudora is available in three versions: a free "lite" version, an ad sponsored version, and a "full" paid version. The lite version lacks some key features. The sponsored version includes all features except the automatic spam blocker.

Bloomba

Bloomba is an interesting alternative to most other email programs. Unlike most other out of the box programs, this one has fast search capabilities built in. Bloomba indexes all incoming email, allowing the user to later search by multiple criteria and obtain rapid results. Searches can be saved, so they can be used over and over again. Bloomba is available in two versions: Personal and Professional. Personal enables quick searches of email and attachments. Both versions include a calendar and a contact list. Professional adds shared calendaring, scheduling, and meeting alerts. It also enables the exporting of contacts, the ability to publish calendars, and Palm Pilot synchronization. Both versions include automatic spam protection.

Web Based Email

Many practitioners find it useful to maintain one or more web-based accounts. Yahoo, Hotmail, and others offer such accounts, often at little or no charge. Advisors typically use these accounts when they participate in online forums, or when they sign up for "free" newsletters. This is a good business practice. Email addresses that are published on the Internet are more likely to be harvested by spammers. Since Google announced its intention to offer free web based email accounts, others, including Hotmail and Yahoo, have responded by significantly increasing online storage and adding other enhancements.

Using a separate address allows the advisor to limit the spam in their primary inbox. The trackers offered by Mailblocks, described below, offer another, better alternative for dealing with mailing lists and online forums.

DEALING WITH JUNK MAIL

Spam, or junk email, is a problem of major proportions. According to Postini, a company that processes over 1.3 billion email messages per week for over 5 million email users worldwide, on the day we accessed their website, spam accounted for 79.6 % of the 83,282,296 emails they tracked. The percentage was almost identical to the 79.7% they reported the last time we checked a few months earlier.

A less well known, but equally troubling, problem is that many legitimate messages are not reaching their destination, usually because they are being blocked by a corporate or ISP filtering system .What types of email are most likely to be blocked? Those with attachments of various sorts, email that has been carbon copied (i.e., cc) or blind carbon copied (i.e., bcc) to multiple recipients, e-newsletters you've subscribed to, and electronic statements are just a few examples.

Some corporations and ISPs block outgoing email traffic. Many of the largest ISPs in the country, including AOL, Yahoo, and EarthLink screen, and sometimes block, outgoing messages. If you send email to a large list of people, or if an ISP believed to be doing business with spammers provides your email service, there is a higher likelihood that your message will not reach its intended recipient. If you are sending legitimate email, (perhaps an electronic newsletter to clients and prospects), it is possible to have the newsletter whitelisted, which will prevent it from being blocked, but this entails dealing with numerous ISP's which can be time consuming. Some advisors decide to outsource the task of distributing e-newsletters in part because they'd rather have the distributor deal with the whitelisting headaches and the bounced emails.

In general, ISP's and corporations have been increasing the level of spam protection, which means that more email is being rejected. The better corporate and ISP filters allow users to view questionable messages in order to reject or accept them, but not all systems allow for this. As a result, messages sent through many systems today end up lost in space.

User-friendly email systems offer much more control at the individual user level than others do. For example, some services only offer an on/off switch. If you turn the filters on, you may never know what you missed. Others have the same on/off switch, but the filtered email goes into a "junk" folder, where you can review it and decide whether or not it really is junk. The better services allow you to set up your own rules with the touch of a button. If they initially filter something as spam, and you click a "this is not Spam" button, all future emails from that sender will automatically be allowed.

Unfortunately, it does not appear that financial professionals can rely upon their corporate systems or the filtering systems employed by their ISP's blindly to filter their email. Readers would be well advised to take as much control of the filtering process as possible. We have no problem with virus screening that is done at the ISP or corporate level; in fact, we encourage it; however, when it come to determining what is spam and what is useful information, the end user must become proactive.

If email is being filtered at the corporate level, and no control is offered at the individual user level, it is essential that you work with your IT department and check often to make sure you are receiving all of your incoming mail. If you subscribe to e-newsletters, for example, you might ask your IT department to allow traffic from the server the email originates from, or to create an email rule based on some other criteria so that your mail can get through.

A better solution, if it is available, is to have suspected junk routed to a "junk" email folder, where you can review it, move the good emails to your inbox, and destroy the rest. Many corporate email systems are capable of providing a "junk" box to users, but sometimes it is an option that must be enabled by the system administrator. If your email system does not offer this capability, request it. Generally speaking, sorting through the "junk" folder only takes a few minutes a day, and it is time well spent, because you will occasionally recover an important message from there.

Another option might be to have the filters turned off at the individual user level. This will obviously increase the amount of junk mail that reaches the end user, but there are ways of dealing with this. You can use MS Outlook 2003 or a third-party program to get rid of most of the junk by routing it to the junk folder. There, the user can periodically review the messages, catch the few "good" messages, and delete the rest. Outlook's filtering system works fairly well out of the box, and it improves over time as the user trains the filters. There are numerous third party systems for filtering email. One system your authors have used is Norton AntiSpam 2004 from Symantec, one of the leading antivirus companies.

Whitelist (accept) / blacklist (deny) applications have proved an effective solution for many practitioners we've spoken with. With most of these tools, you can create a whitelist, and/or a blacklist upon installation. Messages from whitelisted correspondents will be routed immediately to the inbox. Messages from blacklisted senders will either go to the junk mail folder or be deleted. All other incoming email from new senders or questionable parties is placed in a "pending" folder. The software then sends out a challenge message. In almost all cases, if a response is received to the challenge, the sender is legitimate, because a human is required to respond. Most spam is generated by machines, which are incapable of responding to the challenge.

Whitelists and blacklists are highly effective, but the initial challenges can sometimes be annoying to your correspondents, and your e-newsletters will initially be quarantined. In some cases, you can eliminate these issues by regularly browsing through your "holding" box, and manually moving desired emails into the inbox or approving them through some other mechanism. Two desktop whitelist applications worth investigating are ChoiceMail (www.digiportal.com) and Qurb (www.qurb.com). Mailblocks is a web-based email service that offers similar capabilities.

Since Mailblocks is not as widely used as some of the other web based services, it seems to attract less spam. It can download mail from other POP3 and IMAP accounts, so you can use Mailblocks as a whitelist program for other emailboxes if you wish.

Mailblocks offers disposable email addresses (also known as "trackers") to help ward off future junk-mail flows. Tracers are disposable email addresses. These tracers are ideal for ordering at an online store, subscribing to newsletters, etc. If my normal address is joel@mailblocks.com (it is not), then I might set up an address like joel123@mailblocks.com and annotate the account so I know what I am using it for (to request information from ABC Corp.). Once I receive the information I've requested, I can dispose of the email box for good, or, I can leave the mailbox in place for a while to see if I receive additional mail, either from ABC Corp. or from others. If I receive email from others, odds are they got my email address from ABC Corp!

As this chapter indicates, there's more to using email effectively than meets the eye, but with some thought, some planning, and the proper tools, it is possible to optimize email to suit your needs.

For our analysis of the impact of SEC Rule 206(4)-7 (effective October 5, 2004) on email compliance, as well as brief explanations of the software solutions that are now available, see "E-maelstrom" in the September 2004 edition of *Bloomberg Wealth Manager.*

Chapter 27

COMMUNICATION TOOLS: WEBSITES

In Chapter 25, "Creating a Plan and Finding Clients," we discussed how a website can serve a marketing function. Now, let's take a look at how it can serve as a communication tool. A good website allows you to communicate with visitors, and it allows others to communicate with you.

Your website should tell your story. It should present an image of your firm that speaks to how you want others to think and feel about you. In other words, it should convey who you are and how good you are – for them. As with all your contact with clients and prospective clients, it should be representative of and reinforce your central marketing theme.

Ideally, you would like your website to be your client's portal to the web. In order for clients to be attracted to and make frequent use of your site, the information must be perceived as both useful and fresh. That means you must offer new, timely helpful content on a regular basis. Quality financial planning articles should definitely be part of the mix. You may also want to offer news, stock quotes, and other up-to-date material.

In addition, your site should perform a client service function. If a client requires a transfer form, account application, or any other similar document, they should be able to access it online, whether you are in the office or not. Posting downloadable forms or fillable PDF forms to your website are proven delivery methods.

One basic feature that all advisor websites should contain is a "Contact Us" page. In its simplest format, such a page would include some text, and a hyperlink that launches an email program, with a message addressed to you. If you have different people at the firm responsible for different aspects of the business (general inquiries, business planning, etc), or if you just want to pre-sort the mail according to topic, you can set up a different email address for each. For example, info@xyzplanners.com for general inquiries and businessplanning@xyzplanners.com for business planning.

Many firms set up a form to facilitate incoming email that originates at their website. The form can then offer drop down menus with a list of topics, email addresses, etc. It can also require information from the visitor in order for them to send you a message. Required information might include name, address, phone number, email address, etc. The advantage of using forms is that it can simplify use for visitors, route the email correctly, and collect useful information for the firm. The flip side of the coin is that some visitors resent having to enter information, and they can become frustrated if the drop down menu choices don't match their needs.

Some type of instant messaging can also be incorporated into a website. This offers visitors the ability to reach someone immediately. In order for this to work, it is usually necessary to outsource the monitoring of the service, since the advisor or staff will not always be available to respond.

ONLINE MEETINGS

There are a number of services that allow you to interact with clients and prospects – either one on one, in groups, or over the web. Providers include WebEx (www.webex.com), AdvisorSites Conferencing (www.advisorsites.com), Microsoft Office Live Meeting (http://main.placeware.com/), and GoToMeeting (www.gotomeeting.com). With one of these services, you can conduct online seminars and interactive client meetings. They allow you to communicate effectively with a group of people without leaving your office. The primary advantages of web conferencing are that they eliminate travel time and bring you together with your audience, no matter where they might be.

GoToMyPC, is not, strictly speaking, an online meeting service, but we know of many advisors who use it to conduct one-on-one virtual sessions with their clients. Through GoToMyPC, a client can be invited to "share" the advisor's desktop. This allows the advisor to show the client reports, PowerPoint presentations, etc., while each is at their own respective desk. Conversely, an advisor, if necessary, can view a client's desktop, perhaps to see a Quicken report that the client has generated, for example.

SOME PROVIDERS SERVING OUR INDUSTRY

There are exceptions to every rule, but the general rule when it comes to advisor websites is: "Engage a professional web provider that specializes in the financial service industry." The best of these firms are intimately familiar not only with the technological aspect of web design, but also with the unique requirements of financial service professionals. When shopping among those with the expertise to cater to advisors' needs, there are a number of other criteria deserving of your attention.

One criterion for selecting a web creator is an extensive technology platform. If you decide to start out small, will the platform be able to support your firm's growth? Can you transition seamlessly from a limited template site to a robust custom site with all the bells and whistles? Can you integrate data feeds, performance reporting, custodial interfaces, and the like?

Another factor in selecting a web provider is service. If your website is to play a key role in your business strategy, it must be reliable. You want a firm that delivers on time and as promised. If problems occur, or if you simply require help, your provider must respond promptly. One of the most important aspects of prompt response is a system to alert both you and the provider that your web site is "down" – and it WILL go down! The trick is an alert system that not only resets the site automatically, but also alerts by phone – both you and the web provider – that the site is down.

Ease of use matters too. A well-designed intuitive interface makes updating and maintaining a site less time consuming and, hence, more cost effective. Over the course of a year or two, a good interface can save untold hours of labor costs.

Figure 27.1 – Marketing Copy Before Professional Editing

Reprinted with permission of AdvisorSites.com.

Figure 27.2 – Marketing Copy After Professional Editing

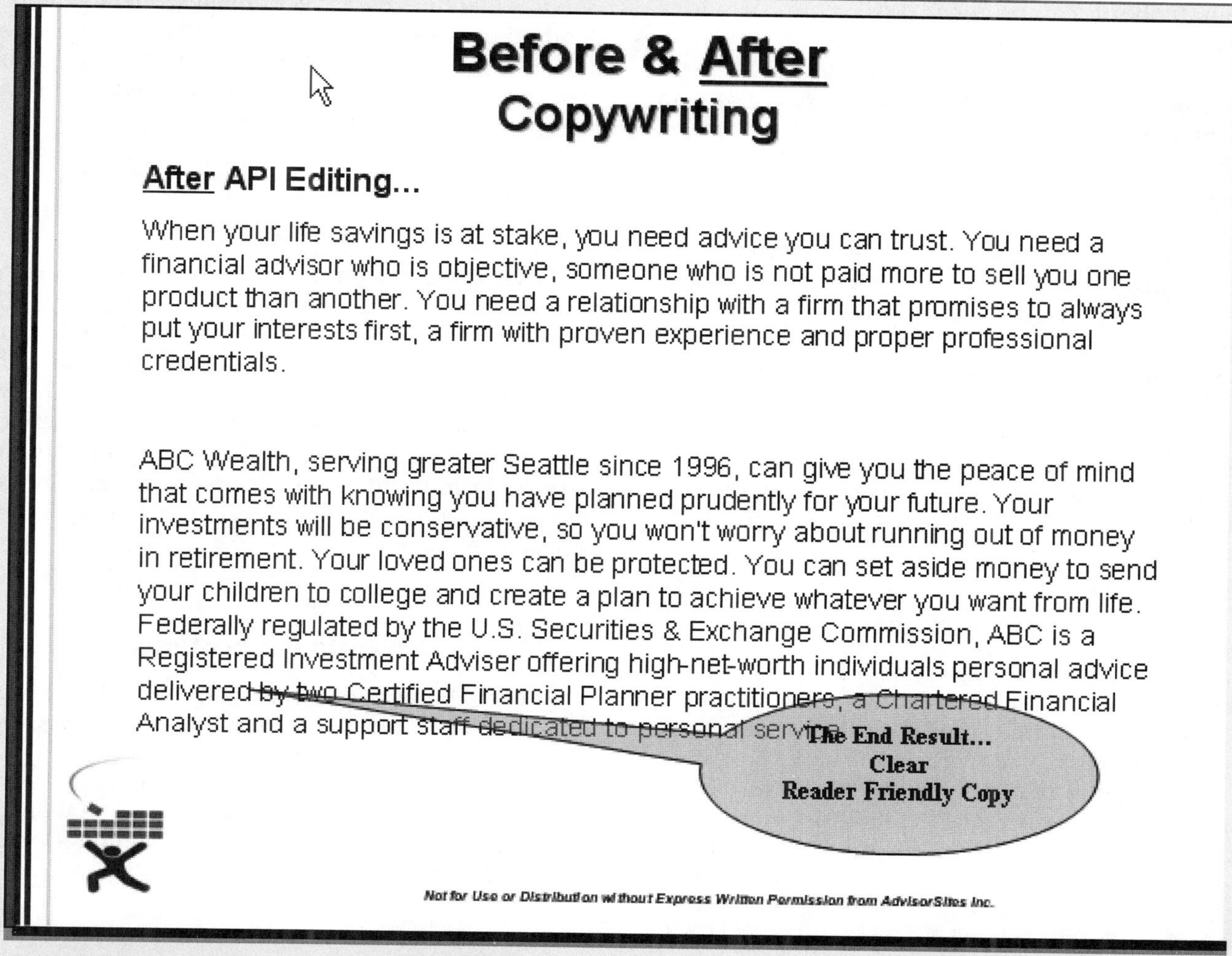

Before & After
Copywriting
After API Editing...
When your life savings is at stake, you need advice you can trust. You need a financial advisor who is objective, someone who is not paid more to sell you one product than another. You need a relationship with a firm that promises to always put your interests first, a firm with proven experience and proper professional credentials.
ABC Wealth, serving greater Seattle since 1996, can give you the peace of mind that comes with knowing you have planned prudently for your future. Your investments will be conservative, so you won't worry about running out of money in retirement. Your loved ones can be protected. You can set aside money to send your children to college and create a plan to achieve whatever you want from life. Federally regulated by the U.S. Securities & Exchange Commission, ABC is a Registered Investment Adviser offering high-net-worth individuals personal advice delivered by two Certified Financial Planner practitioners, a Chartered Financial Analyst and a support staff dedicated to personal service.
The End Result...
Clear
Reader Friendly Copy
Not for Use or Distribution without Express Written Permission from AdvisorSites Inc.

Reprinted with permission of AdvisorSites.com.

Pay careful attention to content. Content available for purchase varies greatly in quality. Many advisors create their own interfaces, but you should think long and hard about how much original content you can reasonably create on a regular basis, and whether or not that is the best possible use of your time. Also, honestly assess your ability to generate optimal content versus the ability of a professional.

Figure 27.1 is an example of some advisor-generated copy, contrasted with an example of a version reworked for us by AdvisorSites, an advisor-centric web service provider.

Before

Notice that in the "before" example, there are numerous subliminal messages that the advisory firm probably does not want to project. The copy starts off by discussing the firm's location. Is that really the most important message to convey first? The next sentence sounds self centered. Clients don't want to hear about that, they want to know what the advisor can do for them! And on it goes....

After

Now let's examine the "after" slide (see Figure 27.2). The opening grabs the reader's attention. It talks about advice, trust, objectivity, and relationship. Aren't those the kind of messages a client wants to hear first? The second section reinforces the message. "We understand your concerns," it says. "You worry about running out of money, educating your kids, and protecting your loved ones." Based on the copy alone, which advisor do you think the prospective clients will be more favorably disposed to?

What about compliance? Will your provider capture and save a snapshot of your site each time you make a change so that it can be archived? If not, you will have to find an alternative means of doing so. Can you integrate your email compliance into the package, so that all outgoing and incoming email is archived as well?

Finally, consider breadth of services offered. Your website should be a part of your unified brand image. As mentioned above, it should integrate with all of your other branded materials, including your logo, business cards, printed brochures, newsletters and other marketing materials. If one can find a single source for all of the above, the odds of generating a consistent look, message, and image are greatly increased. Purchasing a "package" of goods and services can usually result in cost savings too.

AdvisorSites

Your authors have investigated numerous web service providers over the years, and we have both, independently, come to the conclusion that AdvisorSites, based in Westbury, New York, is one of the best, if not the best provider of quality websites and services to financial service professionals (we both use them for our author websites: www.joelbruckenstein.com and www.david drucker.com). Apparently, others have come to a similar conclusion. Some of the most prominent independent RIAs in the business, including Harold Evensky & Deena Katz, Lou Stanasolovich, Elissa Buie, Sheryl Garrett, Ross Levin and Gregory Friedman, to name but a few, have turned to AdvisorSites for their website needs.

One of the keys to AdvisorSites success is Andrew Gluck, a veteran journalist who has covered both personal finance as well as the financial planning profession in his long and illustrious career. This background has given Gluck insights into the needs of both the advisor and the end client. Another plus is the fact that the firm started out designing highly customized solutions for very successful firms. As a result, they were able to standardize some of the lessons they learned and incorporate those lessons into their template products.

Another thing we like about AdvisorSites is the breadth of their service. In addition to website creation and maintenance, they offer high quality content, marketing services, client surveys, public relations, newsletters, web reporting, account aggregation, and much more. AdvisorSites offers various package deals of multiple services that can save advisors money, but more importantly, there are synergies among their business lines; so, for example, lessons they learn from their marketing research will be reflected in the newsletter and web design aspects of the business, benefiting all clients.

AdvisorSquare

AdvisorSquare is another web company with a large presence in the financial service sector. Like AdvisorSites, AdvisorSquare offers both template and custom designed websites. They offer financial planning articles through an arrangement with third-party providers, and they offer account aggregation services through an arrangement with ByAllAccounts. Other services include online calculators, news, stock quotes, maps, a calendar of events, and an online lockbox to store client documents.

Emerald Publications

Emerald Publications, a company with a long history of providing seminar materials and newsletters to financial service professionals, also offers web services. Emerald Websites offer: articles; calculators; a glossary of financial terms; eSeminars (brief presentations on demand covering general financial planning topics); and market information.

Financial Visions, Inc.

Financial Visions, Inc. caters to both the insurance industry and financial advisors. They offer template driven websites at reasonable prices. Their services include articles, news, stock quotes, insurance quotes and client portfolio tracking.

NEWSLETTERS

Newsletters are another avenue of communication. A well written newsletter can project a good image. It can be used as a client communication tool, a prospecting tool, and a public relations tool. Design matters, but content must be king. As is the case with website design and content, advisors must decide whether to do it themselves or outsource it.

Generally speaking, we think that advisors are better served outsourcing most, if not all of it. From a design perspective, it is almost always better to get professional help. A good designer can make sure that the newsletter presents a consistent image that matches your website, stationery, etc. With regard to content, it is also better to outsource provided that you can find a provider that understands both financial planning and writing. We have seen some lousy canned content over the years, but we have also seen some excellent work. If you can find the right provider, you will have an excellent product, and you will free up more time to acquire new clients and service existing ones.

Each advisor must decide what medium they will use to deliver their newsletter. Some readers still prefer paper copies, but producing quality newsletters and mailing them out can be expensive. An electronic newsletter that can be emailed to recipients is much more cost effective. If you are not sure which method is best for you, a compromise might be in order. You might want to try emailing a monthly newsletter, and send out a printed newsletter quarterly. After a year or so of using both delivery mechanisms, it should be easy to determine if one, the other, or both are most appropriate for your particular situation.

LISTSERV

A listserv is essentially an electronic mailing list. There are two types of listservs: announce and discussion. If you need to send an announcement, press release, or newsletter electronically to a large group of people, an announce listserv is an effective way to do it.

If you have a large list of potential prospective clients who want to hear from you, a listserv can be a good method of reaching them. If your firm frequently sends out press releases to a national audience, a listserv would be appropriate. Using an electronic newsletter to reach a large group? A listserv may be the most effective method of distributing it.

It is highly likely that the company hosting your site will be able to provide you with the listserv functions you need. If not, ask your web service provider for recommendations. Since your provider will be somewhat familiar with your business, they should be able to point you in the direction of the appropriate listserv to suit your needs.

Chapter 28

SECURITY

We live in perilous times. These days, all business owners should be concerned about security, but financial service professionals bear an added responsibility. Not only do we have to worry about safeguarding our data; we also have a responsibility to exercise care in the handling of our client's information.

How much security is enough? There is no precise answer to this question. The answer is dependent upon many variables, including the size and nature of one's business, but at the very least, an advisory firm should create written policies and procedures that cover the following:

- The protection of client information and records;
- Maintenance of client privacy;
- Safeguards to protect the inappropriate use of client assets by employees; and
- A disaster recovery plan.

Increasingly, client information is being maintained in digital format, so in order to protect client information, records, and privacy, advisors must possess at least a basic understanding of the threats to data integrity, as well as the tools available to counteract those threats.

THE THREATS

Unfortunately, there are so many potential threats to your business that we cannot possibly offer a comprehensive discussion of them all. We will, however, look at three of the most common problems you are likely to confront: unauthorized access to client data; malicious code (aka computer viruses); and physical damage.

Unauthorized Access

Unauthorized access can take a number of different forms. It could be as simple as a delivery person or someone else who gains access to the premises stealing your files. While an employee is away from his or her desk, computer files could be at risk. The best method of guarding against this type of attack is strong password protection. Password protection can also help guard against certain types of remote attacks.

Password Protection

All computers and business files should be password protected. At a minimum, users should be required to log on and off their computers. After a period of inactivity, computers should automatically lock down until a password is reentered.

A higher level of security can be maintained by deploying software that allows the administrator greater granualarity when granting permissions. Some software producers allow different levels of permission, so that some employees can only view documents, while others can view, print, forward and/or change them.

Short, common passwords are much easier to break; in fact, inexpensive software is readily available which does just that. Good passwords are long (at least eight characters), and they contain a combination of letters, numbers, and other characters ("!," "?," "&," etc.). The problem with strong passwords is that employees often forget them. It is all too common to see employees jot down passwords on a sticky note posted to their computer monitor in order to remember complex passwords. Unfortunately, that sort of defeats the whole purpose of using strong passwords in the first place. One way around this problem is to use a biometric device that accepts a fingerprint, for example, as a substitute for a password.

A growing number of companies manufacture biometric security devices for use with computers. We have long been partial to the U.are.U line of fingerprint sensors from Digital Persona, Inc. (http://www.digitalpersona.com/).

U.are.U sensors are well designed and durable, but it is the software that really sets U.are.U products apart. U.are.U persona is designed for home users and small

Figure 28.1

U.are.U 4000 Fingerprint Scanner

businesses. It allows users to log on to their computers, as well as password protected websites, with the touch of a finger. In addition, it allows users to encrypt and decrypt files with a single touch. In conjunction with Windows XP fast user switching, the application allows a new user to log on to a shared computer effortlessly.

The Pro version can provide double authentication (fingerprint plus a password). An identity lockbox is created which stores a user's password for all applications, which can then be accessed by a finger touch. As an option, the program can create a random password for each user application, which even the end user does not know. The applications are then accessed through the user's fingerprint.

Recently, Digital Persona released a new consumer version of their software called Password Manager. This software will ship with a number of new Microsoft hardware products including Microsoft Optical Desktop with Fingerprint reader (includes optical wireless mouse and a keyboard containing the fingerprint reader), Microsoft IntelliMouse Explorer with Fingerprint reader (a wireless optical mouse with seperate fingerprint reader), and the Microsoft Fingerprint Reader (see Figure 28.2).

Figure 28.2

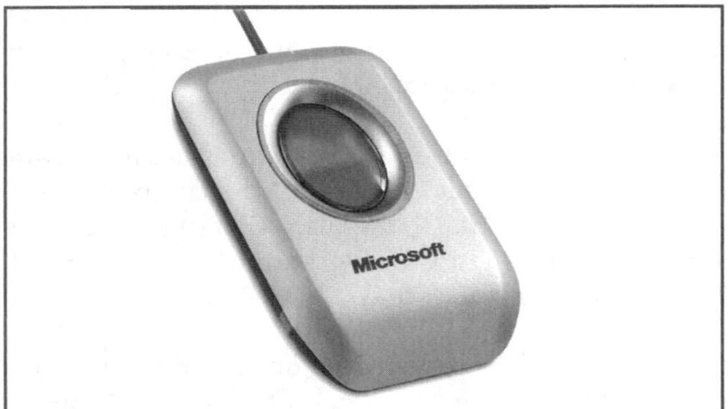

Microsoft Fingerprint Rreader

APC (www.apcc.com) makes a device that is very similar in functionality to the Digital Persona product that goes by the name of APC Personal Biometric USB Pod.

The Targus DEFCON Authenticator may appeal to users of mobile computers. It is small, light and portable, so it is easy to stash in a laptop bag. Other manufacturers of fingerprint readers include Sony and Key Tronic.

Iris scanners are another type of biometric security device. While they are not commonly used in conjunction with computers at the moment, there is no reason that they could not be in the future, provided that the price became more affordable. Manufacturers of these devices include Panasonic and LG Electronics.

Theft

Another type of unauthorized access advisors should guard against is computer theft. An enterprising thief might decide to break into your office, steal a computer or server, then hack into it. While it is beyond the scope of this book, advisors should give some thought to making sure their computers are stored in a safe environment. In the event that a computer is stolen, strong password protection and/or encryption can help minimize the damage; however, we are sure most readers never want to have to wonder whether their password protection is sufficient after a theft has occurred.

Malicious Code

Many readers may be familiar with terms such as virus, worm, and Trojan Horse, but very few people we meet really understand what the terms mean. Here are some useful definitions we accessed from the website of McAfee, Inc., the company that sells the popular McAfee line of security products:

> *Virus*–A computer program file capable of attaching to disks or other files and replicating itself repeatedly, typically without user knowledge or permission. Some viruses attach to files so when the infected file executes, the virus also executes. Other viruses sit in a computer's memory and infect files as the computer opens, modifies or creates the files. Some viruses display symptoms, and some viruses damage files and computer systems, but neither symptoms nor damage is essential in the definition of a virus; a non-damaging virus is still a virus.

Worm – Worms are parasitic computer programs that replicate, but unlike viruses, do not infect other computer program files. Worms can create copies on the same computer, or can send the copies to other computers via a network. Worms often spread via IRC (Internet Relay Chat).

Trojan Horse – A Trojan horse program is a malicious program that pretends to be a benign application; a Trojan horse program purposefully does something the user does not expect. Trojans are not viruses since they do not replicate, but Trojan horse programs can be just as destructive. Many people use the term to refer only to non-replicating malicious programs, thus making a distinction between Trojans and viruses. (http://uc.mcafee.com/virusInfo/default.asp?id=glossary.)

Viruses, worms, and Trojan horses are not the only malicious code threats advisors face. Adware and spyware are increasingly worrisome as well. The glossary published by Symantec, makers of the Norton and Symantec product line, defines these threats as follows:

Adware – Programs that secretly gather personal information through the Internet and relay it back to another computer, generally for advertising purposes. This is often accomplished by tracking information related to Internet browser usage or habits.

Spyware – Stand-alone programs that can secretly monitor system activity. These may detect passwords or other confidential information and transmit them to another computer. (http://securityresponse.symantec.com/avcenter/vinfodb.html.)

Adware or spyware can be downloaded from Web sites (typically in shareware or freeware), email messages, and instant messengers. A user may unknowingly trigger spyware by accepting an End User License Agreement from a software program linked to the adware or spyware.

Preventing Malicious Code Attacks

Firewalls

Firewalls are, or should be, your first line of defense against malicious attacks. Firewalls can help prevent malicious code from attacking your network over the Internet. There are two types of firewalls, and we suggest that you use both. The first type of firewall is the hardware firewall. This firewall sits between your networked computers and the Internet. If it works flawlessly, it will prevent any malicious code from breaching your network over the Internet. Many routers have built-in firewalls today, even very inexpensive ones. For example, some inexpensive routers from companies such as Linksys (www.linksys.com) and Netgear (www.netgear.com) include basic hardware firewalls. Routers targeted at small businesses often include more sophisticated firewalls and/or virtual private network (VPN) capabilities. Larger firms should consider using an Internet Appliance, which offers more sophisticated capabilities. Manufacturers include Cisco (http://www.cisco.com/), Sonicwall (http://www.sonicwall.com/), Symantec (http://www.symantec.com/) and WatchGuard (http://www.watchguard.com/).

Software firewalls protect individual computers behind your hardware firewall. Not only do software firewalls act as a second line of defense against Internet borne attacks, they also protect other points of entry within your network (an infected floppy disk, for example). There are a number of good software firewall programs on the market. Popular programs include those from Zone Labs (http://www.zonelabs.com/), McAfee, Inc. (http://www.mcafee.com/), Symantec, and Trends Micro.

Antivirus Programs

Antivirus programs protect computers from files that enter your system, typically as email attachments or downloads. The last time we visited the website of Postini, an email security company, they estimated that about 2.4% of all email messages contained a virus type threat. (This statistic can spike considerably when a new threat strikes.)

Some of the better know producers of antivirus software include McAfee, Symantec, and Trend Micro. Often, antivirus software can be purchased in a "bundle" that includes a software firewall, and possibly additional programs. The bundles are often an attractive option when compared with the cost of purchasing each product individually.

Software firewall products and antivirus programs rely primarily upon definitions supplied by manufacturers to identify threats. The definitions must be updated regularly. The best way to stay current is to have the software automatically check for and download new definitions as they appear.

Spyware and Related Threats

Antivirus programs generally do not protect computers from spyware. In order to protect against, detect and/or remove spyware, a dedicated anti-spyware program is required. Anti-spyware software protects against spyware, adware, tracking cookies, browser hijackers, and other pests. If your web browser's home page or bookmarks change inexplicably, you are probably the victim of spyware. If your web browser's performance turns sluggish without warning, you may be a victim of spyware.

Spyware programs that install ads, bookmarks, shortcuts, and the like on your computer can be annoying, but there are more dangerous varieties as well. Some spyware can capture passwords and other information stored on your computer, then transmit it over the Internet to a third party.

Some of the more common methods by which spyware can enter a computer include peer-to-peer networks and free software downloads, although there are others. You may exercise caution when surfing the net, but be sure to have policies in place to make sure that anyone else with access to your computers exercises caution as well. Employees, interns, and family members should not be using your firm's business computers to download "free" music, games, or videos.

Spyware protection tools work much the way antivirus tools do. They compare code on your computer to a list of definitions, and flag suspicious code. The better programs offer information as to the nature of the spyware threat. Like antivirus software, anti-spyware programs must be updated regularly to maintain their effectiveness. Some of the better programs in this category include Ad-aware (www.lavasoftusa.com), Spybot Search and Destroy (www.saver-networking.org) and Spy Sweeper (www.spysweeper.com).

Updating Your Microsoft Programs

While we are on the subject of updates, make sure that you regularly check for updates to your other programs as well. Programs from Microsoft, since they are so widely used, are a favorite target for hacker attacks. Operating systems, such as Windows XP, are prone to attacks, as are MS Internet Explorer and MS Outlook Express. Updates for all of these can be found at the Windows Update website (http://windowsupdate.microsoft.com). Components of the Microsoft Office Suite, such as MS Outlook, and MS Word are also targets. Updates for these programs can be found at the Microsoft Office update site (http://office.microsoft.com/OfficeUpdate).

Backups

Despite your best efforts to protect data, the unexpected can happen. A virus can get through your defenses. A hard drive can fail. A fire, flood, hurricane, or earthquake can strike your office, damaging your records beyond repair. There are an almost unlimited number of scenarios that might make your office temporarily or permanently uninhabitable.

Should a disaster strike, you must be able to access your data. Selecting the best backup scheme(s) entails an analysis of numerous variables, including the size of one's practice, number of employees, and the amount of data to be stored, and cost. Each firm's backup plan should be tailored to its specific needs; however, we will attempt to provide some useful guidance.

First, we think there is an analogy to be drawn between backups and property & casualty insurance: insure against the greatest risks first. In this case, that means a total loss of your primary office and equipment. How important is it to protect this data? According to a May 2003 study by the London Chamber of Commerce (http://www.londonprepared.gov.uk/business/lcc_disaster_recovery.pdf), 90% of businesses that lose data from a disaster are forced to shut down within two years of the disaster; and 80% of companies without a well structured recovery plan are forced to shut within 12 months of a flood or fire. These statistics apply to businesses in general.

For financial advisory firms, the failure rates could be much higher. In addition, financial firms face the specter of regulatory action, not to mention civil suits if they have not made a good faith effort to protect client data.

One way to protect against the possibility of an inaccessible or destroyed office is to make use of an online backup service. These services allow advisors to backup their data over the Internet onto a remote server on a regular schedule. In the case of a disaster, the data can be retrieved and restored over the Internet, or, in some cases, by alternate means. For a more detailed discussion of online backup services, please see Figure 28.8.

For smaller businesses, external hard drives are another attractive option. All data can be backed up to the external hard drive and moved offsite daily. Ideally, advisors should purchase two hard drives, so one is always off the premises.

External hard drives are portable, inexpensive, and convenient. They are available in sizes ranging from about 40 GB to at least 1 TB (1,000 GB). External hard drives can be attached to a computer through a number of relatively speedy interfaces such as USB 2.0, FireWire and SATA.

The less expensive external hard drives do not ship with their own backup software. Good backup software is important, because it allows the user to customize and automate the backup routine. For example, the software could be set to do incremental backups on a daily basis and full backups at the end of the week. Two backup programs we recommend are BackUpMyPC (http://www.stompinc.com/bump/) and Dantz Retrospect Professional (http://www.dantz.com/).

Some of the slightly more expensive external hard drives are more convenient to use and they come packaged with backup software. Maxtor OneTouch drives (www.maxtor.com), Western Digital's Media Center (www.westerndigital.com), and a number of drives from CMS Products (www.cmsproducts.com), including the ABS Plus drives and the Velocity series of drives, are representative of this class. The ABSPlus series is particularly attractive for those who use a notebook as their primary PC.

Removable or swappable hard drives are another interesting option. These drives have been available from third party manufacturers for some time, but recently, at least one major manufacturer of PC's, HP, has started to offer a slot that holds a removable hard drive as an option on some of its mass marketed machines. Swappable drives are a little more convenient to use than an external drive. You simply push them into the slot, and you are ready to go. If a swappable hard drive can be configured in a RAID array to "mirror" the primary hard drive, the user will have an exact copy of the primary drive that can be removed and taken off site at the end of the day. If not, a backup program will be needed to schedule and perform the backup operation.

Figure 28.3

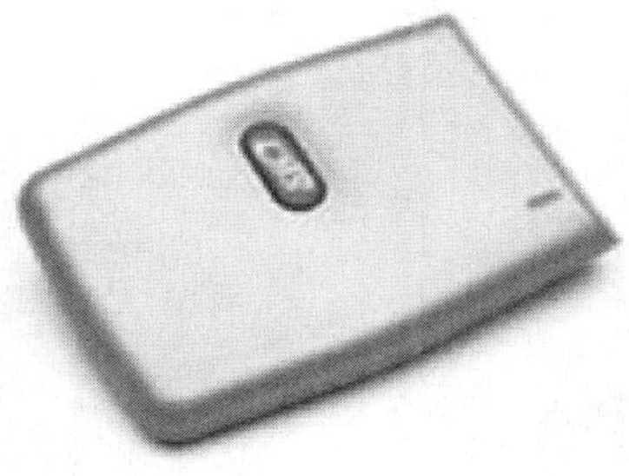

80 GB USB 2.0 ABSPlus

For larger offices, the equivalent of backing up to a hard drive is backing up to a network attached storage device (NAS), which is, in effect, a basic portable server. Snap Appliance, a division of Adaptec, Inc., (www.snapappliance.com) offers a number of packages that include one of their Snap Appliance servers bundled with software to provide a seamless solution. Adaptec, Dell, EMC, and Iomega are among the companies that offer NAS storage solutions.

Figure 28.4

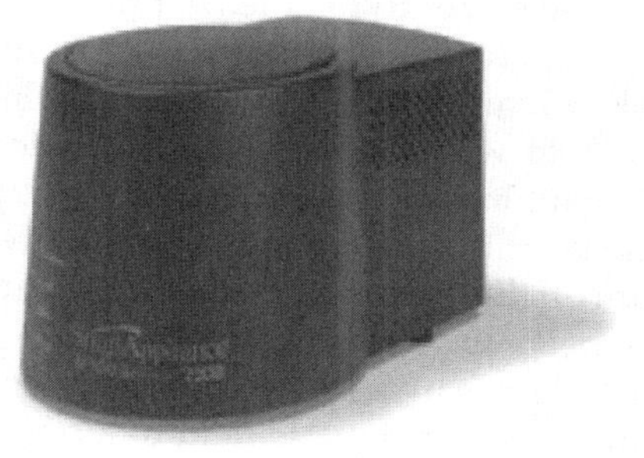

SnapServer 2200

Other Backup Solutions for Small Offices

Sole practitioners and other small offices have other, inexpensive backup options. These include CD, DVD, and Iomega's Zip drives. In the case of CD and DVD backups, we recommend that, for business use, readers spend a little more and purchase quality disks from well-known brands.

Other Solutions for Larger Offices

Tape is still a popular backup medium. Tapes are inexpensive, portable, and they can store relatively large amounts of data. Some of the newer technologies are appealing, but tape is still a reasonable option for those on a tight budget.

Archiving

So far we have discussed backing up in the context of disaster recovery; however, most advisory firms also create archival backups. The purpose of archival backups is to create a more permanent record of one's business at a point in time, for both business and regulatory purposes. Since longevity of the media is a more important consideration in the case of archival backups, some thought must be given to the shortcomings of commonly used backup media. Magnetic media, such as hard disks and tape, are vulnerable to dust, magnetic fields, and contaminants. Optical media, such as CD and DVD, are vulnerable to physical damage, light, and poor quality control. Our research indicates that one of the most reliable solutions available today is the magneto-optical disk (MO disk).

MO disks are less vulnerable to deterioration. With the exception of DVD-RAM (probably the least popular DVD format), CD's and DVD's do not have built in error correction; MO drives, on the other hand, do have error correction.

According to Fujitsu, a manufacturer of portable MO devices: "The secret to magneto-optical is that during the recording process, an intense laser beam is focused on a disk containing an alloy material that retains a magnetic field when heated above a critical temperature. By changing the magnetic field and pulsing the laser, data is written, and by reflecting a lower intensity laser beam off the disk, the drive can read the data. Once data has been written to a MO disk, it is virtually indestructible because it requires the combination of intense heat and a magnetic field to alter the data. An added benefit is that magneto-optical disks are infinitely rewritable and come up in many different capacities ranging from 128 megabytes up to 2.3 GB." (http://www.fapl.fujitsu.com/modrive/about_mo.html.)

MO disks are ideal for archiving, because they remain stable for long periods of time. Fujitsu claims they are good for over 30 years. Others claim reliability over 50 or even 100 years. MO cartridges are available in sizes up to 9.1 GB; those who require more storage can purchase a "jukebox" which write to multiple disks. At least one manufacturer we know of, HP, currently offers jukeboxes with capacities of up to 2.2 TB.

Mirra Personal Server

The Mirra Personal Server is an inexpensive, bare-bones server that operates on the LINUX operating system, which helps keep costs low. It is an inexpensive backup device, but it also offers the ability to remotely access data as well as the ability to share data with others.

To install the server on an existing network, the user simply connects a cable from the Ethernet card on the server to a port on the network router. Once the Mirra PC Application software is installed on a Windows XP or Windows 2000 computer, the Mirra system automatically detects networks settings and configures itself. Then, the software will recommend folders that you may want to backup. After the initial backup is complete, Mirra monitors files as they are opened, edited, and closed. Each time a file is altered, Mirra makes a copy. By default, Mirra retains the most recent eight versions of the file.

Mirra offers good insurance against a hard drive failure. It is also good insurance against malicious code that targets the MS Windows OS. If you accidentally delete a file, Mirra can restore it; if you alter a file by mistake and realize your error when you reopen it, Mirra can supply you with the previous seven versions.

Mirra is excellent additional data insurance, but as we went to press, it would not serve as the ideal primary backup mostly because, for now at least, the Mirra must be housed onsite, so it does not provide disaster protection (the company told us they are working on an offsite solution which may be available by the time you read this). Mirra also has problems accessing MS Outlook, as well as some database programs, while they are running. So, for example, if you keep MS Outlook open most of the day, Mirra won't back it up until you shut it down.

Figure 28.5

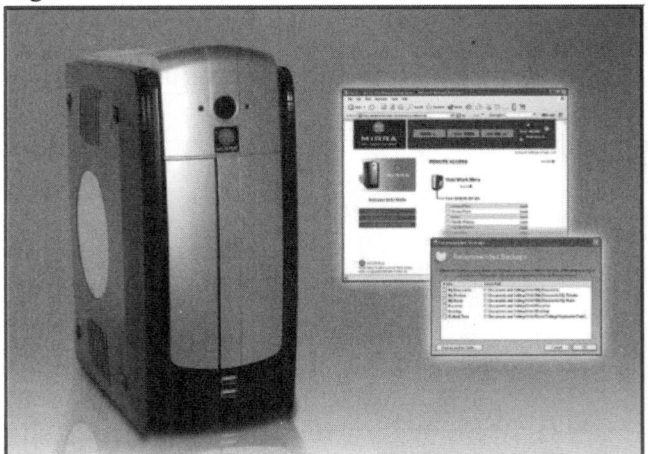

Mirra Personal Server

Mirra also offers remote access and file sharing. Both operate in a similar fashion. When you first configure Mirra, you designate folders that are subject to remote access. Your Mirra server then registers itself with the Mirra website. When you are out of the office, you can access the Mirra website. Once you have been authenticated, a secure connection is established with your Mirra server. You can then download any files or folders that have been designated for remote access. In the case of file sharing, you designate a folder to be shared, and identify the person you want to share it with. Mirra then sends the person an invitation to visit the Mirra site for authentication and registration. Once the person is registered, he or she can access the shared folder through the Mirra website.

While we would not rely on Mirra today as our sole backup solution, we think the device offers an added layer of protection and a great deal of convenience. In addition, it offers remote access and file sharing capabilities that are extremely easy to configure and use. Mirra represents an excellent value for the sole practitioner or small firm.

Smaller Backups

Disaster can often strike on a smaller scale. Perhaps you are traveling across town or across the country to make a presentation to a new, potentially lucrative prospective client. Could your laptop be stolen? Might the hard drive fail? Of course they could. That is why one must always be prepared for the unexpected.

Whenever your authors are invited to speak at a meeting or a convention, we always carry backup copies of our presentations and notes on a separate device. For a number of years now, our preferred medium for this type of backup has been a USB flash memory device. These devices are now widely available from multiple manufacturers, and they are sold under numerous brand names, but their basic design characteristics are similar. They are generally no more than a few inches long, they have a USB connector at one end, and they house anywhere from 64 MB to 1 GB of flash memory. The DiskOnKey Classic 2.0 (www.diskonkey.com) pictured below – a current favorite of ours – is one of the fastest on the market, but almost any brand will do, particularly when purchasing a device at the lower end of the memory scale.

The above devices are great, but some advisors worry that their data could be stolen if they were to lose one of

Figure 28.6

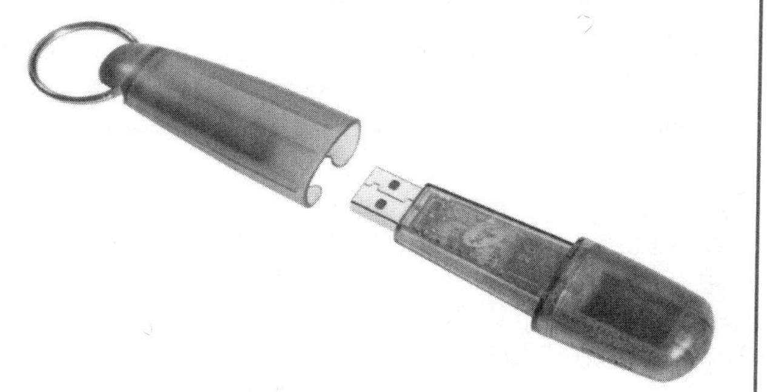

DiskOnKey Classic 2.0

these small devices. Just to put you at ease, we should point out that many of these devices include software that allows the user to password protect the drive. Third-party software is also available.

What about the password problems we talked about earlier? Not to worry! For a small additional charge advisors can purchase a USB Flash memory device that includes a biometric fingerprint reader. The Trek ThumbDrive Touch (www.thumbdrive.com) is one such device. Another is the Sony Micro Vault with Fingerprint Access pictured in Figure 28.7.

This particular drive includes some interesting software. Much like the U.are.U persona device discussed earlier, this drive can store user names and passwords for frequently visited websites on the drive. Once a website's information has been entered on the drive, simply touching it allows the user to enter a site. A number of additional utilities are provided as well.

The Sony Micro Vault PRO is very different from the regular Sony Micro Vault. Rather than relying on flash memory for storage, the Pro stores data on a 1 inch, 2 GB hard drive. Sony's Auto sync software comes pre-loaded on the PRO. It offers the convenience of one-click synchronization between designated folders on your computer and Micro Vault Pro. The software can be set to store up to the last ten versions of a saved file.

Figure 28.7

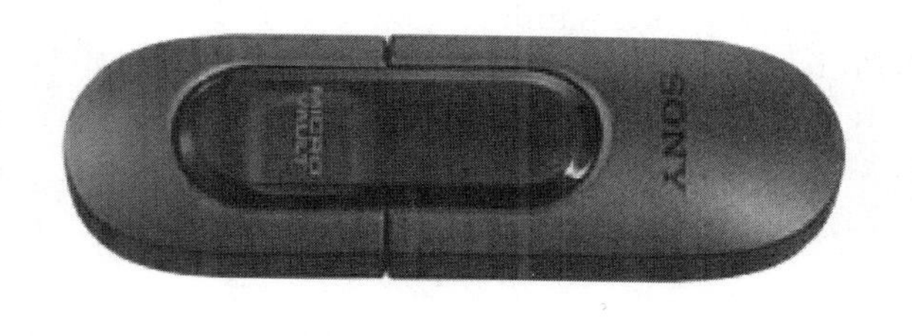

Sony MicroVault with Fingerprint Access

Computing in Public Places

Computing in a public place presents some additional unique threats. Ever try to access your office computer(s) from a client's office, an Internet café, or some other computer that is not under you direct control? Beware! Even if you are taking precautions, they may not be enough. For example, many advisors believe that accessing their office computer through a virtual private network (VPN) is totally secure. While using a VPN is a good idea (a VPN offers security and encryption), it is not foolproof. Some information may be stored on the computer you are using, and often that information is not encrypted. If you surf the net on an unsecured PC, you may leave behind other types of information that could be used against you by a malicious person, such as temporary files containing sensitive information, a list of URL's you visited, etc.

One way of dealing with the threat of leaving information behind on a public computer is to store that information elsewhere instead. This can be accomplished by using a program called P. I. Protector Mobility Suite (http://www.imaginelan.com). PI Protector is typically installed on a USB Flash memory device (but it also can work with other flash devices, including FireWire capable digital cameras). Before accessing a public computer, the user connects the flash device to the public computer, and then all Internet related files, including browser history log, cookies, and temporary/cached files are loaded onto the flash device, as opposed to the host computer's hard drive. Additionally, PI Protector prevents spyware, such as registry-based key logging programs from accessing passwords and account information.

PI Protector offers some additional functionality. It allows users of popular email programs to store their email on the flash drive. Data can be stored on the flash drive and synchronized with other computers. Internet settings can be stored and transported, so that users have their favorites, bookmarks, etc. available to them wherever they go.

Another option is Migo (http://www.4migo.com) from Powerhouse Technology Group, Inc. Migo is a flash drive that is sold with the Migo software pre-installed. Migo's capabilities are very similar to those of PI Protector. It offers secure Internet access, the ability to store data, and the ability to synchronize files.

Improper Disposal of PC's

Many people are clueless on the subject of PC disposal. They will commonly delete their files, and then throw their computer away or donate it to their favorite charity. Financial advisors who do not take proper precautions before disposing of a computer that has outlived its usefulness are potential lawsuits waiting to happen. In the May 2003 issue of *PC World* magazine, "Hard Drives Exposed" author Tom Spring quotes David Burns, who regularly scavenged PC's at the Needham, MA dump as saying "On almost every hard drive I pull, I find a tax return or a resume." The article goes on to recount the story of a Boston computer store that sold a hard drive previously owned by an accountant. The drive was crammed with four years' worth of his clients' payroll and tax information and employee Social Security numbers. Don't let this sort of easily preventable disaster strike you!

There are only three reliable methods of sanitizing a hard drive. The first is to physically destroy the drive. This method works, but some view it as wasteful. The second method, degaussing, involves exposing a magnetic media, such as a hard drive, to a strong, alternating magnetic field. Degaussing leaves the media in a randomized magnetic state. In other words, the disk is cleared, and probably useless. Since degaussing should be done professionally, and since other alternatives exist, degaussing does not seem to be the best route for most financial planning firms.

The third option is to overwrite the existing data on a hard drive so that it cannot be recovered. This allows a hard drive to be donated or repurposed. Deleting files won't accomplish this. Reformatting the hard drive may not destroy all data either. There are, however, a number of relatively inexpensive commercial programs that can do the trick. They include:

- CyberScrub (http://www.cyberscrub.com/);
- DataGone (http://www.os2.co.za/products/datagone24.htm);
- OnTrack DataEraser Professional (http://www.ontrack.com/dataeraser/); and
- WipeDrive (http://www.accessdata.com/Product07_Overview.htm?ProductNum=07).

BUSINESS CONTINUITY PLANNING

As we stated earlier in this chapter, all advisors should have a written disaster recovery plan. Backups, and some of the other topics we have covered in this chapter should certainly be part of a disaster recovery plan, but there is more to it than that. The best resource we know of to help advisors create a plan of their own is the Business Continuity Plan Template (http://www.protracker.com/BusinessContinuity.asp) published by ProTracker Software. (For more on the BCP, see Figure 28.9.

Figure 28.8

ONLINE BACKUP PROVIDERS

What are some of the factors that you should look at when selecting an online backup service? Price is one obvious factor, but comparison-shopping is not as transparent as one might expect. If one provider compresses files and charges only for the space you use on their server, while a second charges based on uncompressed file size, the former, while apparently more expensive at first glance, could actually turn out to be much less expensive. One provider, DATABarracks, claims that their technology compresses files by an average of 75%. If this is true, a reader requiring 8 GB of monthly storage with a provider charging per uncompressed GB would only require about 2 GB per month of space with DATABarracks.

Compression and encryption are desirable, and the more control you have over the process the better. Default settings often work fine, but if you usually transmit your data over a high-speed connection, and you are suddenly forced to use a dial-up connection, the ability to increase compression ratios will come in handy. As for encryption, DES with 128-bit encryption is common, and probably sufficient for all but the truly paranoid. Some providers, however, offer additional options, such as Triple DES (192-bit encryption) and Secure Blowfish (448-bit encryption).

Ease of use should be considered, but all of the products we looked at appear to be easy to install and use. Some offer the ability to access data through any web browser, while others require an applet be downloaded and installed.

Let's look at a sampling of providers.

Connected.com

Connected offers a range of plans to choose from. Home Office/Small Business Plans are available in the following sizes: 250 MB ($79.00 per year); 500 MB ($99.00 per year); 2 GB ($164.95 per year); 4 GB ($189.95 per year); 10 GB ($279 per year); and a 30 GB plan (for $799.95 per year).

There are some differences among plans besides the storage limits. The two least expensive plans are designed primarily for the home user. Subscribers can only back up files in the My Documents folder, plus Quicken and QuickBooks folders automatically. Any file type residing in these folders can be backed up automatically, but if it resides elsewhere on the hard drive, it must be backed up manually.

Plans from 2 GB up generally allow you to back up all data files automatically, regardless of where on the hard drive they reside, with a few exceptions (audio, video, other backup files and temporary files). This service provides versioning, so the 10 most recent backups of a file are retained for 90 days. Files deleted from your computer are also retained for 90 days. Connected.com's software recognizes files that have already been backed up, and if no changes have been made to the backed up files, it does not back them up again, which improves performance. When backing up files that have been changed, the software is smart enough to capture and back up only the changes to a file.

Figure 28.8 (cont'd)

Connected offers a good balance of utility and price; the authors have spoken to numerous advisors who use Connected.com, and the feedback has generally been favorable. In case of an Internet outage, Connected.com can supply files on disk for an additional charge.

Vital Statistics

Type of Backup: Scheduled / Manual (cheaper plans limit scheduled backups to select folders).

Access from a web browser: A qualified yes. But, there are some limitations.

Compression/Encryption: Yes / Yes.

Price for 2 GB/10 GB: $14.95 mo; $164.95 annually; 2 GB/ $24.95 per month, or $279.95 annually 10 GB.

Pricing based on: Uncompressed file size.

DATABarracks

There's always a chance that a nationwide emergency could adversely affect some domestic based online backup providers. Just when advisors need their data most, their storage provider might be suffering under the same conditions that they are. One possible solution is DATABarracks (www.databarracks.com).

One thing that differentiates DATABarracks from the competition is their physical location. DATABarracks warehouses data in a former NATO nuclear bunker located in a remote area of the English countryside. The site offers electrical redundancy, long lasting emergency power generation, electro magnetic pulse protection, protection against electrical eavesdropping, automatic fire detection and suppression, and, of course, superb physical security. The unique character of the physical plant, combined with the British address, minimizes the likelihood of a simultaneous outage.

According to company spokesperson Peter Groucutt, "DATABarracks deals with businesses and entities of all sizes, but their emphasis on security attracts a lot of financial related companies and government entities".

The system uses encryption and compression. Three different encryption schemes are offered (the default choice is Blowfish 448-bit encryption). According to the DATABarracks website, "Blowfish encryption is faster and more secure than DES, another widely used compression type." The initial backup takes longer than any subsequent backup is likely to. Like Connected.com, DATA Barracks uses technology to recognized changed data since your last back up, and it only saves the changes.

Pricing is based on the compressed file size. The firm says compression averages 75%, but compression ratios vary greatly depending on the type of file you are backing up. Assuming that the user achieves compression somewhere in the neighborhood of the average, DATABarracks pricing is quite attractive.

Unlike most other services, DATABarracks archives all files daily, and saves a copy for seven years. The archived data is not immediately available online, but if a customer requires an archived file, they can contact DATABarracks, and it will be made available in about six hours.

"If the Internet does go down, we will supply data back to our clients on DVD, CD or whatever media best suits them. We send these by courier to any place in the world, a service for which we, unlike our competitors, do not charge. The disks are still encrypted for safety and can only ever be unencrypted by the client (not even we can do it)", says Groucutt. "If the client is a large company with lots of data then we will send technicians

Figure 28.8 (cont'd)

on site, again with no charge. We have U.S. resellers and partners who we can rely on to assist our direct clients in the event of an emergency."

Vital Statistics

Type of Backup: Scheduled / Manual.

Access from a web browser: No, but software can be downloaded to any computer for access.

Compression/Encryption: Yes / Yes.

Price per month for 2 GB/10 GB: $33 per month / $143 per month.

Pricing based on: Compressed File Size.

@Backup

SwapDrive, the parent company of @Backup actually offers two distinct services: @Backup, and the SwapDrive service, which is discussed below. Right now, @Backup is targeted at users with relatively modest storage needs. (Plans start at 50 MB for about $4.16 per month, and top out at 2GB, although larger storage plans are scheduled to go on sale soon.) @Backup offers a 90-day rolling history, so users can always access earlier versions of their files. This utility is appealing, but it adds somewhat to the cost of the service. For those who want them, CD's are available on a regular basis or on demand for an additional charge.

Vital Statistics

Type of Backup: Scheduled / Manual.

Access from a web browser: Yes.

Compression/Encryption: Yes / Yes.

Price for 2 GB/10 GB: $995 annually (not currently available).

Pricing based on: Uncompressed File Size.

SwapDrive

SwapDrive offers features that @Backup does not, and it is cheaper, but @Backup looks to be a little more convenient as a "backup only" solution. In addition, @Backup offers a 90-day rolling history, but SwapDrive does not.

However, SwapDrive does offer the ability to share files with colleagues online. Users can drag and drop files to the Shared folder, where others can view them. Shared files can even be accessed wirelessly with a Palm PDA and some Blackberry devices.

This product is available in single user and "corporate accounts" versions. The corporate accounts allow you to purchase blocks of storage, then create and manage unlimited users in your own domain. CD backups are available.

Figure 28.8 (cont'd)

Vital Statistics

Type of Backup: Scheduled / Manual.

Can access from a web browser: Yes.

Compression/Encryption: Yes / Yes.

Price per month for 2 GB /10 GB: $50 per month, $500 annually for an individual plan; $65 per month, $650 annually for a corporate plan; 2 GB / N/A individual, $280 per month $2,800 annually for 10 GB.

Pricing based on: Uncompressed File Size.

Xdrive

Xdrive offers two services—Xdrive Plus and Xdrive for Workgroups. The difference is that the later allows a company to buy space in bulk, and then manage accounts of multiple employees. Administrators can generate usage reports. The service provides both online backups and file sharing capabilities. Xdrive can be operated from either a web browser or a software applet; the applet is used to schedule automatic backups; it also simplifies other tasks such as file sharing. With the applet installed, users can use "save" files directly to Xdrive or "drag and drop" files to Xdrive.

Xdrive does not offer to ship backup disks as part of their service.

Vital Statistics

Type of Backup: Scheduled / Manual.

Can access from a web browser: Yes.

Compression/Encryption: No / Yes.

Price per month for 2 GB/10 GB: $29.95 per month or $299.50 annually for plus service / $337 per month or $3,370 annually for workgroup with 15 GB of storage and up to 50 users.

Pricing based on: Uncompressed File Size

E-Vault Small Business Edition

E-Vault looks to be a better choice for those backing up networked devices, as opposed to individual PC's. The service looks to be fairly priced; it is not the cheapest, but it is not the most expensive either. E-Vault generally does not offer to ship data on disks, but in a severe emergency they can send out all of your data on an NAS (a Network Attached Storage Device) for an additional charge. For those backup servers, this is an appropriate alternative.

Figure 28.8 (cont'd)

Vital Statistics

Type of Backup: Scheduled / Manual.

Can access from a web browser: No.

Compression/Encryption: Yes / Yes.

Price per month for 2 GB/10 GB: $85 for up to 5 GB; $165 per month for 10 GB.

Pricing based on: Uncompressed File Size.

LiveVault

LiveVault is more expensive than some competing services, but it offers come additional perks. LiveVault provides continuous back ups and a 30-day history (with the option of expanding that to a full year at an extra charge). The MyLiveVault Web Portal allows users to monitor and control the backup process from any web browser. Like a number of other providers, LiveVault software detects changes to files, and only backs up the incremental changes. The firm uses a three-layer security system to transmit data over the Internet. This includes a VPN tunnel, encryption, and digital certificates. In addition, a professional monitoring staff monitors the back up process to make sure that all is functioning smoothly. Of course, this level of service comes at a price: $199 per month for "up to 10 GB".

If disks or an NAS are requested, the company will supply them at an additional cost. The current price for an NAS is $400; disks cost $25 per GB.

Vital Statistics

Type of Backup: Continuous

Can access from a web browser: Yes

Compression/Encryption: No / Yes.

Price for 2 GB/10 GB: $199 per month for up to 10 GB.

Pricing based on: Uncompressed file size.

FileShuttle.com

FileShuttle is an intriguing option for the mobile planner, and possibly those who employ virtual work partners as well. The service is targeted at individuals, with storage offerings of as little as 100 MB ($5.95 per month). 500 MB will cost you $15.95 per month, and 2 GB service is available for $30.95 per month. FileShuttle backs up files to a server as the other services do. Backups can optionally be encrypted.

FileShuttle claims that you can retrieve your data from "any computer or handheld device" using a web browser and an Internet connection. More importantly, FileShuttle allows users to synch files on multiple computers remotely, provided an applet is installed on all of the machines being synchronized.

Figure 28.8 (cont'd)

Here's how it works. Suppose that you are out of the office. You change existing files or create new ones, and then you back them up to the FileShuttle service. Assuming your other computers (at home or at work) are online, they will automatically be synchronized with the updated data on your laptop.

FileShuttle is based upon servers powered by Novell iFolder technology. Without going into the technical details, only the iFolder is monitored and synchronized. So if data is stored in the iFolder, changes are automatically reflected on the other connected computers. Files stored elsewhere on a user's hard drive are not automatically backed up.

For readers who work from multiple locations, FileShuttle provides a way to back up the data when they are away from their primary location, while insuring that all important files remain synchronized.

FileShuttle could also be used in conjunction with a virtual work partner (VWP). The VWP would be given access to an iFolder created for them, and as either the advisor or the VWP makes changes to the data, all computers linked to the iFolder will be automatically synchronized. Assuming that only a couple of projects are being worked on at any given time, it might cost as little as $5.95 per month for this convenience, a reasonable cost indeed!

This service is not necessarily the ideal primary online backup solution, but it may be sufficient for some. If you occasionally take work on the road, however, and you want a secondary backup solution, this service looks to be a cost effective solution, because you will only be backing up and synchronizing a limited number of files. When you consider the added utility of the synchronization feature, and the ability to access files from any web browser, FileShuttle represents a good deal for the road warrior.

Vital Statistics

Type of Backup: Manual sign-in to the service/constant synchronization while connected to the service.

Can access from a web browser: Yes.

Compression/Encryption: Yes / Yes (optional 128-bit Blowfish).

Price for 2 GB/10 GB: $30.95 per month. For 2 GB / 10 GB, the price is negotiable.

Pricing based on: Uncompressed File Size.

RECOMMENDATIONS

Initially, all online backup providers may appear very similar; however, if you dig a little deeper, differences are revealed. Some providers charge based on the amount of compressed data stored, while others charge based on uncompressed data. A number of providers archive data for varying periods of time; some don't. LiveVault offers continuous backups, but you do pay a premium for this service.

We suggest that you judge providers primarily on their backup and recovery prowess. By that measure, of all the providers we looked at, DATABarracks, a relative unknown, stands out. It has a uniquely secure physical plant, excellent encryption and good compression technologies. Its pricing is very reasonable, especially since you are only paying for the actual space you use on their servers. They offer seven years of archiving at no additional cost, and, in the case of a disaster, they will supply disks, and in some cases a technician, at no extra charge.

Figure 28.8 (cont'd)

Quite a few colleagues use and recommend Connected.com. The feedback on this firm was positive. Their pricing is reasonable, and their service should be sufficient for many advisors, so we think they are worthy of consideration as well.

Xdrive appears to be a good value for those who will make use of their file sharing and collaborative capabilities. FileShuttle's file synchronization features could be a real godsend to the road warriors among us, but we do not view it as the ideal primary online backup solution.

In summary, there are a number of good, reasonably priced online backup options available to readers. The firms that we have profiled are only a sampling of the services available to advisors, and we encourage you to do your own comparison shopping.

Figure 28.9

DISASTER PLAN

Here's an easy way to comply with the SEC's most complicated new requirements–and protect your business as well.

By Bob Veres

Okay, listen up. Next time the SEC comes to visit, they're going to be asking for a comprehensive business continuity plan, which tells them exactly how you're going to get up-and-running, with all relevant client records, if ever you should return to your place of business in the morning to discover that terrorists spent the evening blowing up your office building and melting your computers. Your plan needs to cover the potential failure of networks, theft of your computer equipment, tornado or hurricane disasters, and outline how you would go about reestablishing communications with clients, contacting and finding alternative worksites for employees and a whole host of things that you now have to think through in grisly detail.

If you don't have this plan on your shelf–and copies in alternative locations–then you're going to get written up.

Wouldn't it be nice if somebody created a template that would lead you through all the issues you need to consider, offer suggestions on how to handle a variety of disasters, and let you basically fill in the blanks for a customized disaster recovery plan that you could confidently hand to the SEC examiners when they walk in your door? One that was actually tested in actual SEC audits, and passed without a deficiency letter? And while you're fantasizing, let's keep the cost down to about the same price as dinner, a movie and a pair of sneakers.

You can stop fantasizing; the product actually exists. It costs $150 and it's called the Business Continuity Plan template, created by Warren Mackensen. Mackensen is better known as the president of ProTracker, Inc., one of the two client relationship management tools that virtually own the planning marketplace. (http://www.protracker.com/OrderInformation.asp#anch) He also runs a planning practice, and as an engineer and former submarine officer, he decided that if he needed to have a business continuity plan, it as well be a thorough one. "The best thing I can tell people," he says after several weeks of effort, "is that you do NOT want to spend the time I spent on this."

The starting point of the BCP template is imagining the worst. "If you went back to your office tomorrow, and it's gone, where would you be?" Mackensen asks rhetorically. "That is the event that we are planning for. Can you run your business? That, basically, is what the SEC wants to know."

Figure 28.9 (cont'd)

So how do you plan for the worst? Mackensen started by identifying off-site locations that can become alternative offices. For him, the primary alternative location is a ski cabin 100 or so miles north of his home and office. For you, it might be home, or the home of a key employee. The BCP offers letters you can send employees listing these alternative office locations with directions on how to get there, so they know you have a backup plan and can regroup more or less immediately.

Next? Identify the important documents in your office and the software that you're currently using. What if the hard copy is all burned, the CDs have melted and the software is gone? Mackensen offers some examples of business-critical functions that you would need to be able to perform off-site, like downloads from custodians. The BCP has to have the custodian's phone number and download protocol. Do you have copies of client file folders, the signed original contracts with clients, your personnel files and your corporate books and records (if your firm is a C corporation)? An appendix would include the names and contact information of all clients, so you can call everybody immediately after the disaster, and the names and phone numbers of all employees, so everybody can get in touch. Mackensen also recommends that you copy the corporate tax returns, the SEC and state filings, the IARD file, and the insurance policy that covers the contents of the office. "I don't even know the name of my insurance company," Mackensen admits. "I would have to go to the file and pull it out. But it's in the backup materials that we have off-site."

In addition, the document includes an office management manual, the compliance manual, and a manual that talks about how to download files from the custodian. There are backups of the software–which includes, in Mackensen's case, the Microsoft Office suite, database software, ProSeries for tax preparation, Peachtree Accounting and Naviplan.

The BCP also asks for a description of your facilities. "When you put pen to paper and actually document how your systems are arranged and configured," says Mackensen, "it reminds you of where your weaknesses are. So it's a good exercise to go through." In most cases, this will include a server computer and some files that are on employee computers, which are not on the server, which may, as a result, never get backed up. You need to list all the replacement equipment you will need to get back up to speed, and a list of real estate firms that can offer office space, with their phone numbers.

You are also asked about your alternative telephone capabilities, fax, e-mail, and banking considerations. Do you have checks offsite, so you can PAY employee salaries?

And what happens if you happen to be working late when the building goes down? Who would take care of your clients? There's space in the document where you can list other planners who might sign an agreement that in the event one of you dies or is disabled, the other will take care of the clients of both firms–the conservator of the other business.

The BCP is physically kept at several locations, in a recovery box, which also includes the basic office supplies that would be needed to set up a new office. The list comes from whatever is in the supply cabinet at the office: pens, sticky post-its, paper, and staplers. "We just use big plastic bins you can get from any office supply place," says Mackensen.

Finally, the plan has copies of a training log, so that your firm can record the fact that you conducted training on this business continuity plan. "It shows the regulators that you take this seriously enough to train every year and revisit the plan," says Mackensen.

When Mackensen went through the process with his own office, he learned some things that could be fixed fairly simply. One important thing he learned is that the telephone system required AC power. As a backup, he bought a cheap little Princess telephone, and had the telecommunications consultant put it ahead of the private branch exchange box, so that if the power went out, they still had a working phone.

Figure 28.9 (cont'd)

But how should your company back up its computer system? This may be the most complicated part of the plan, but it's actually pretty logical. Mackensen has a digital audiotape backup drive, which spits out a cartridge smaller than a pack of cigarettes. He uses Veritas backup software that is totally automated; it starts at 11:00 PM and backs up the entire server drive. "We do it only five days a week, and we use what is called a verified feature," Mackensen explains, "where the tape is recorded from the hard drive to the tape, and then it rewinds and plays it back and compares it with the hard drive. It has to get a one-for-one correlation to be successful." The backup process takes three hours, but changing the tape takes about 30 seconds in the morning. You open the door, pull the tape out and put another one in.

Organization of the tapes required a bit of thought. Mackensen originally bought 36 different tapes. 24 of them were labeled Day One through Day 24. "If you look at the calendar, there are never more than 23 business days in any given month," he says. The other 12 tapes are labeled by month and year: January 04 through December 04.

Each business day, one of the monthly tapes is inserted in the backup drive, and the old one comes out and is stored at a remote location. When D-24 is used, then you start back up again with D-1, without regard to the actual day of the month. The five oldest tapes from the previous month are returned to the site to be used (overwritten) that week. On the last business day of the month, that month's tape is inserted into the machine, and it is stored permanently, so that you always have a January 04, a February 04, etc. going back as long as the system does. The following day, you use the next daily tape.

At the end of the year, you take the daily tapes 1-12, and you convert them to monthly tapes; you relabel them January through December 05, which takes them out of circulation, and you buy 12 new tapes. At the end of year two, daily tapes 13-24 are converted to monthly tapes, and you buy 12 more. As a result, no tapes are used for more than two years or more than 25 times, and you have tapes that include all your server information at the end of every month. "If a regulator says to me, how many clients did you have two years ago, versus how many you have now?" I can answer that kind of question by popping in the relevant monthly tape and looking at our client list," says Mackensen. "Those monthly tapes never get overwritten."

The idea of a backup recovery plan is one of the new initiatives at the SEC that actually makes sense, although if you practice in West Virginia or South Dakota, you're probably not hiding under your desk all day in fear of a terrorist attack. But there are other natural disasters, including, in Mackensen's home state of New Hampshire, severe blizzards, and elsewhere tornados, hurricanes and wildfires.

You can obviously customize the BCP in a variety of ways; for example, Mackensen doesn't have a server that is analogous to what he has in the office, believing that he will take the business risk of having to buy a new one and being down for several days until it arrives at his home or new office location. Similarly, he doesn't have a redundant tape drive; he would have to purchase a new one in order to back up the information on the server if his office computers were melted or stolen. If you decide that being back online the same day as the disaster is important, you could have a server and tape drive installed at your home.

Mackensen recommends that you have printed copies of the BCP at several locations, arguing that the paperless concept is great until the computers go down and you can't get access to the information that you so carefully stored. This can lead to challenges—as you change procedures, or update processes, the information may be hand-written into the procedures manual, which then needs to be input into the master BCP and then printed and the pages replaced with new ones. Mackensen apparently does these updates regularly, but the minimum would be once a year. The important thing is to have a procedure that gets it done on a regular basis.

Personally, I think this is exactly the sort of thing where you want to delegate the framework thinking to an outside entity, and spend your valuable time answering specific questions about your practice–in hours instead of two weeks reinventing the wheel. At $150, ProTracker's business continuity plan seems like one of the best compliance bargains on the planet, So far as I know, it is the very best insurance against receiving

Figure 28.9 (cont'd)

a deficiency letter because you haven't prepared your offices for survival in case the unexpected happens to decide to hammer your firm. And if you DO encounter a disaster, you'll be grateful for more than simply passing an SEC audit.

This article is from the June 2004 edition of *Inside Information*. Reprinted with permission of Bob Veres (www.bobveres.com).

Chapter 29

OFFICE HARDWARE

If you are going to start your own financial planning practice, you will need to purchase office equipment. In this chapter, we will provide an overview of some equipment you will need, particularly in the realm of technology.

COMPUTERS

Computers are the lifeblood of the modern financial planning practice, but what exactly do you need? The correct answer depends on the size of your firm and the nature of your business.

Let's assume that you are starting off small – just you and an administrative assistant. Let's further assume that you are on a limited budget. In this case, you will probably not want to set up a dedicated server. A peer-to-peer network, one that allows each of you limited or full access to the files and folders on each machine should do.

You will have to decide whether to use a laptop or a desktop computer as your primary machine. You will most likely want a desktop for your assistant. The case for purchasing a desktop computer is that you still get more computer for your money; the downside is that it is not very portable. If you absolutely, positively need portability, get a laptop; if not, consider a desktop PC.

If we were to set out specific recommendations with regard to the exact configuration of the computer you should buy, they would be obsolete before they ever got to the printer, so let us supply some general guidelines instead. For mainstream financial planning applications, the latest and greatest processor is never required. You don't necessarily want to purchase the cheapest processor available, but something a couple of steps removed from the top of the line will always be fine. Don't skimp on random access memory (RAM). Many less expensive computers don't contain enough, and RAM is one of the most cost effective upgrades you can purchase.

When Windows XP first launched, we remember seeing claims that it could run on as little as 64 MB of RAM, with 128 MB recommended. Perhaps it can run on 128 MB, or even less, but we don't recommend that you try it. Once you load some of your other programs (which also use RAM), and decide you want to have numerous applications running simultaneously, you will have issues.

Your friendly computer supplier may forget to mention that inexpensive computers often lack a dedicated video card, in which case you will be relying on "integrated graphics." There isn't anything necessarily wrong with integrated graphics, but you must be aware that integrated graphics make use of system RAM, which means that you need even more RAM than the stated minimums. At the very least, we believe that a desktop computer today should have 256 MB of RAM, 64 MB - 128 MB more if there is no dedicated graphics card. If you are constantly multitasking, 512 MB is a better bet.

Don't skimp on hard drive capacity either. It often costs very little to upgrade to a larger hard drive, and experience tells us that users often underestimate their storage needs. As we discuss in the section on backing-up (see Chapter 28, "Security"), one should at least consider a RAID array, with two drives that mirror each other.

As for the operating system, go with Windows XP Pro, or the current equivalent. It costs a little more, but it offers better security and remote access features. If you purchase an LCD monitor, you will want at least a 15-inch screen; 17 inches would be better. If you purchase a CRT screen, you should get at least a 17-inch screen, although a 19-inch screen would be even better. LCD screens cost more, but they are lighter and consume less space. They are also relatively energy efficient. CRT screens are larger and bulkier, but the initial outlay is considerably less.

You will want at least one optical drive. We suggest a DVD-RW; and make sure you have an ample supply of USB ports so that you can connect peripherals. Many users prefer to order two optical drives as an added convenience. In the case of desktop computers, the additional incremental cost is small, so we think it is a good idea.

Don't overlook your keyboard and mouse. Better-designed keyboards are more comfortable to use, and they include additional shortcut keys that improve efficiency. Good mice are comfortable as well, and they are more accurate. Deluxe models have programmable buttons, which can be set to speed frequent tasks. A number of manufacturers produce innovative mice and keyboards. We've reviewed a number of products from Logitech (www.logitech.com) over the last several years, and have found them to be well designed and durable.

If you decide to go with a laptop as your main computer, and you are on a budget, you will probably have to make some trade-offs. The laptops with the largest screens and the fastest performance tend to be heavy, so they are not an option for those constantly on the go (although they work fine if you are taking them back and forth in your car). They also tend to have limited battery life. So-called mainstream laptops offer a good balance between size, functionality, and price. They can offer decent battery life as well. Those constantly on the go may want to consider an ultra portable. These are lightweight, and they often offer decent battery life; however, compared to the other categories, you pay more for an equivalent amount of computing power. Screens tend to be smaller, which can be an issue for some, and some require an external optical drive, often at an additional price.

If you decide to purchase a laptop, and you will be using it at home or in the office most of the time, consider a docking station, which allows you to easily employ a full sized keyboard, mouse, and perhaps a monitor when you are at your primary location.

For your assistant, an inexpensive desktop computer is usually sufficient, particularly if that person is primarily doing word processing, email, and other tasks that are not computer intensive. Even on the budget machine, make sure you purchase sufficient RAM.

NETWORKING

Even the smallest office will want to set up some sort of basic network, if only to share an internet connection. Inexpensive routers from companies from Linksys and Netgear are sufficient for many small businesses. The choice here is between wired and wireless. Wired is fast, secure (if configured properly) and inexpensive. Wireless will most likely cost a little more, but it is more convenient, particularly if the computers are far apart or if you want access throughout the office. Wireless networks, if configured properly, are relatively secure, but many users never read the router manual, stick with the default settings, and forego the opportunity to insure their network is as secure as possible.

Offices with more than four or five users will almost certainly want to use a dedicated server. Servers for small offices performing basic tasks are very inexpensive these days, but depending on your needs, additional software might be required. Deploying and maintaining a network often requires professional IT help; however, there are a number of companies that are beginning to offer "network in a box" solutions. Essentially, these products are a combination of hardware and software that are supposed to be easy enough for the average person to set up. You plug it in, and a wizard walks you through the configuration process. One manufacturer of these boxes, Axentra, (www.axentra.com), claims that a novice can set up one of their servers in as little as 10 minutes.

PRINTERS

For even the smallest office, laser printers are the way to go. They cost a little bit more, but they are durable, and much more cost effective in the long run. Prices of entry level color laser printers have dropped to the point where they are an option for even the sole practitioner. If you regularly produce reports for clients with color graphs and charts, get a color laser. We would encourage you, however, to save trees whenever possible by emailing color reports as PDF files. Doing so improves client service, saves money, and protects the environment.

If you only require an occasional color print job, consider purchasing a monochrome laser printer. As this chapter is being written, a few national retailers are closing out perfectly good discontinued models from major manufacturers for under $100; purchase a color inkjet for the occasional color report, and you're all set.

FAX MACHINES

Our advice with regard to fax machines can be boiled down to three words: Just say no! We can't think of a rational justification for owning a fax machine today. Transmission quality is not as good as competing technologies (email attachments or file sharing technologies), they take up space, and they require an additional telephone line. Whenever possible, encourage others to email you attachments; when that is not possible, use a service capable of sending and receiving faxes as an email attachment.

Probably the best-known service of this type is eFax (www.efax.com), but there are others, such as MaxEmail (www.maxemail.com) and VoiceFaxEmail (www.voicefaxemail.com). With plans starting at under $2 per month, these services assign each subscriber a virtual fax number, which can be supplied to contacts. Whenever someone sends you a fax, it is converted to an email attachment and emailed to the address you specify. The service offers a number of benefits. There is no fax machine or consumables to buy. No additional phone line is required. You can receive faxes from any location that allows you to download email. Best of all, if you don't need to print out the fax, you can just delete it. Outgoing faxes work in a similar manner. Usually, you email the document to a pre-specified email address, where it is faxed to the end recipient. Let's review the benefits: More efficient, less costly, better quality, portability. Need we say more?

COPY MACHINES

As is the case with fax machines, our first inclination is to just say "no." We favor minimizing paper files, not creating more of them. On the rare occasion that we do need to produce a copy, we simply scan a document and then print it. Some scanners come with a utility that allows the user to scan and print with a single mouse click. If yours does not, think about adding a third-party program such as Photocopier or Photocopier Pro, which allows you to effortlessly scan and print.

TELEPHONE SERVICES

Before you invest big bucks in sophisticated telephone systems, consider the "virtual switchboard" approach. Known by various names (the most common being "unified messaging system," "virtual switchboard," and "universal office"), we are referring to a service that, at its core, provides a single telephone number for all incoming telecommunications, a unified voice mailbox, and telecommunication routing capabilities. Depending on the firm and level of service chosen, additional features are available as a bundle or a la carte. The two companies profiled below are representative of the services currently being offered.

Freedom Voice Systems

Freedom Voice Systems (www.freedomvoice.com) offers three service bundles that can be further customized with add-on features at an additional cost. The entry-level service, FreedomLITE, includes the following:

- *Nationwide toll free telephone number* – Inbound calls, as well as outbound services such as call-back, paging, and fax back, are charged at 7.5 cents per minute, in 6-second increments.
- *Follow-me-live call transfer* – Routes calls to wherever you are (home phone, office phone, cell phone). Caller must announce name, then you accept the call, or route it into voicemail without them knowing you have done so.
- *Multiple voice mailboxes* – This feature is particularly useful if you have a virtual partner in a different location. Create a different voice mailbox for each partner, but one unified number for all to call.
- *Call return* – Return calls from within the voice mailbox.
- *Cardless card calling* – If you access your messages from a public phone or a hotel, this service allows you to return calls at a rate lower than that of many credit card calling plans.

The FreedomPRO bundle includes all of the above, plus the following:

- *Voice on demand* – Allows you to create menus and an unlimited number of extensions with recorded messages. For example, for additional information about our financial planning services, press one; for information about managed accounts, press two.
- *Fax mail* – Allows anyone to send faxes to your primary phone number. From there, they can be forwarded to the fax machine of your choice.
- *Group voicemail* – Leave a message and then automatically send it to everyone in your organization.
- *Call blocking / call limiting* – Block or limit calls from any incoming phone number.

Options that can be added to either package include:

- *Fax back* – Does a client need a transfer form or an application? Allow them to call in to your unified number, and they can have the document faxed to them automatically.
- *Email delivery* – Allows voice mail and faxes to be delivered to you by email.
- *WebLink access* – Check voicemail and faxes from any computer with Internet access.

EasyTel

EasyTel (www.easytel.net), a Nevada company, is a subsidiary of InfoUSA. Their mission is to integrate telecommunications, the Internet, and electronic banking – an interesting combination. EasyTel offers a number of different "universal office" packages.

One service that sets EasyTel apart is the electronic banking feature. This system allows people to call in, place an order, and pay by credit card, and receive instant verification. There are no set-up fees and no upfront costs for this service. Other financial services, such as payroll, ATM cards, and check cashing are available too.

EasyTel offers a Professional/SOHO one user package with an extensive list of features including the following:

- *Nationwide toll free telephone number* – Both incoming and outgoing calls are at highly competitive rates.
- *Two local numbers* – Incoming calls to local numbers are free (they can be in different area codes), so if most of your incoming calls originate from one or two locations, these two phone numbers, which all feed into the same line, will save you a bundle.
- *Conference calls* – Host a conference call on the fly at low rates.
- *Follow-me-live call transfer* – Routes calls to wherever you are (home phone, office phone, cell phone). Caller must announce name, then you accept the call, or route it into voicemail without them knowing you have done so.
- *Call return* – Return calls from within the voice mailbox.
- *AudioGrams* – Record a message and have it delivered to as many people you want at a time you specify.
- *Message alert* – Have the system alert you when new messages arrive by pager, cell phone or email.
- *TelePaging* – No need for a pager. The system will page you by phone. If you are offline, it will leave you a message.
- *Fax mail* – Allows anyone to send faxes to your primary phone number. From there, they can be delivered to a fax machine or by email. Emailed faxes arrive as a TIF file, so they can be easily forwarded to others if you wish.
- *Voice mail forwarding* – Voice mail can be forwarded to another voice line or by email.

Additional services available at an extra charge include:

- *Fax on demand* – This fax on demand service, which costs about the same as the Freedom Voice service, can be assigned a separate phone number, but can only send one fax per line.
- *Voice on demand* – Like the fax on demand service, this service can record voice information, but is limited to one message per phone number.
- For businesses with 2 - 99 employees, EasyTel offers the Small Business Plan. Under this package, each employee receives his or her own professional / SOHO plan.

VoIP

When we first covered VoIP (Voice over Internet Protocol) in the September 2003 issue of *Virtual Office News*, a few of our readers thought the article was a science fiction piece. Since that time, the technology is spreading rapidly.

VoIP allows users to transmit their telephone conversations over the internet, as opposed to traditional telephone lines. We are not going to delve into the details of the technology here, but suffice it to say that with a special phone (or another piece of equipment), a high-speed internet connection, and perhaps a router, customers can avail themselves of a revolutionary telephone service.

A number of new companies, as well as some familiar telephone companies and cable companies are now offering VoIP. Vonage, probably the best known of the new VoIP providers, offers unlimited local and domestic long distance plans for as little as $29.95. That is a significant savings over what the local phone companies generally charge, but it gets better: since your service is not tied to a static phone line, you can take your phone number and telephone service with you. If you go to your vacation home, or a hotel room with broadband access, you can use your VoIP service as if you were at home (or office). As the next version of WiFi deploys, it may be possible to use VoIP the way we now use cell phones.

Free features include voicemail over the internet or by email, caller ID, call waiting, 3-way calling, free in-network calling (even internationally), area code selection, call transfer, and more. For example, a downloadable software application turns any PC or laptop into a telephone. There's real time billing information and real-time online account management too. This is a new telephone service and there are some minor drawbacks (if your electricity goes out, so will your phone service; the 911 service has some limitations and requires registration); but overall, it is well worth investigating. Substantial savings should be possible, even if you install a traditional phone line as a backup.

SHREDDERS

A shredder is a good inexpensive security tool. You don't want a thief picking up confidential client information by sorting through your garbage. Personal models start at under $50, but you will probably need to spend at least double that for even a light duty office model. Unless you want to sit around feeding one or two sheets of paper at a time into the shredder, get a recommendation from a friend before you buy, or get a demonstration at your local office supply store to make sure the product performs as promised.

A WORD ABOUT FURNITURE

We are not interior designers, nor do we aspire to be, but we would be remiss if we did not at least touch on the subject of office furniture. Pay for "look" if you like, but be sure not to skip on comfort. You will be spending a great deal of time at your desk. Make sure it is comfortable and of sufficient size to hold both your computer equipment, as well as whatever else you will need to get your work done. We'd recommend erring on the side of too much, rather than too little desk space. Be sure to purchase a comfortable chair with arm rests, a high back, pneumatic height adjustment, tilt control, 360' swivel, lumbar support, and, of course, wheels.

Chapter 30

GENERAL OFFICE SOFTWARE

SOFTWARE SUITES

If you are going to be in the business of financial planning, some software programs, such as a word processor, spreadsheet program, presentation software program, and possibly a database program will be required. It is almost always less expensive to purchase these general purpose programs in a package, which is commonly known as a "suite." At one time, at least three suites, Microsoft Office, Lotus SmartSuite, and WordPerfect Office engaged in a fierce struggle for market share in this sector. All three are still around today, and there are other alternatives available as well, but for all practical purposes, the only rational choice for a financial planning professional is Microsoft Office. There are a number of reasons we believe this to be the case.

As of this writing, Microsoft Office clearly dominates the field, with a market share in excess of 90%. Among the planners that we've come into contact with over the last few years, the number probably approaches 100%. If you want to share a document with others in the profession, or with your clients, the easiest way of doing so is by using the program (s) that they use. Many competing programs can read MS Office files or output to MS Office file types, but, unfortunately for the competition, the only way you can be assured of 100% compatibility at all times, without any additional complications, is to jump on the MS Office bandwagon.

Another issue is integration. Some industry specific programs you may require often integrate with, or work in concert with, an MS Office component. For example, Junxure-I works in conjunction with MS Access, a database program. Might it work with some others? Perhaps, but since almost all of Junxure-I customers are using MS Access, that is where they devote most of their energies. StockOpter Pro, a very fine employee stock option analysis program from Net Worth Strategies, Inc. (www.netwworthstrategies.com) requires both MS Word and MS Excel. WealthMaster, a high-end financial planning package from WealthTec (www.wealthtec.com) also requires MS Excel; and we could cite many more.

The more analytically minded advisors among us like to export data from one program and manipulate it in another. For example, an advisor might export data from a portfolio management or financial planning program for further analysis in a spreadsheet or a database. Since MS Office is the industry standard, it is the Microsoft programs that vendors strive to offer compatibility with.

Microsoft Office and You

Okay, so you've read the above section, you're sold on the fact that MS Office should be your software suite of choice, and you're on your way out the door (or onto the web) to buy a copy. Wait just a minute! It's not that simple.

This may sound crazy, but before you go out and spend a considerable amount of money on MS Office, you'd better think about which version you want, and how you should buy it. MS Office comes in a number of different configurations, and it is sold in a number of different editions: retail; pre-installed; volume user licenses; and academic. Once you are out of school or not teaching, you can rule out the academic editions. If you are acquiring five or more licenses, volume users' licenses may make sense. For everyone else, the choice is between pre-installed and retail.

Microsoft's pricing policies may change over time, but historically, if you are in the market for a new computer, and you do not currently own software that allows you to purchase the current MS Office edition at the upgrade price, as opposed to the full retail price, you will reap significant savings by purchasing MS Office pre-installed on your new computer. If you already own a software package that entitles you to an upgrade, it pays to comparison shop. Sometimes, but not always, it will be cheaper to purchase the upgrade as opposed to purchasing a pre-installed version. Price, by the way, may not be the only determining factor.

All versions are not available through all channels, and sometimes versions with the same name can include a different mix of programs depending on the channel. For example, MS Office Small Business Edition includes:

- Excel (spreadsheet);
- Outlook (contact management, calendar, email, etc.);
- Business Contact Manager (enhances Outlook's contact management capabilities);
- PowerPoint (presentations);
- Publisher (publish newsletters, flyers, etc.); and
- Word (word processing).

Identical version are available pre-installed or through retail channels. However, if you are in the market for the Standard edition (Excel, Outlook, PowerPoint, and Word), you will only find it through retail channels. The Basic Edition (Word, Excel, and Outlook) is only available pre-installed.

The retail and pre-installed editions of Microsoft Office Professional Edition include the same programs as the Small Office Edition plus one additional program: MS Access, a database program. The volume license version of MS Office Professional includes one additional program, MS InfoPath (information gathering and management); Business Contact Manager is only available upon request with the Microsoft Office Professional Edition purchased through the volume license program, and a fulfillment fee applies.

Are you with us so far? Good, because we are not quite done yet. The version of MS Word and MS Excel that you purchase with the Professional version of MS Office is not exactly identical to the same programs offered in the other versions. In MS Office Professional, MS Word and MS Excel have enhanced Extensible Markup Language (XML) capabilities. This means that versions other than the Pro versions can make use of the XML capabilities built into the program (for example, a smart tag that can update stock prices in Excel), and it can read tags created in the Pro version, but you cannot create your own XML tags or XML schema in non-Pro versions.

For those of you not familiar with XML as it relates to MS Office, XML allows applications to integrate both internal (corporate) and external (over the web) data sources in new and exciting ways. Two examples you may be familiar with are Smart Tags and Smart Documents.

So, now that you are thoroughly schooled in the ins and outs of MS Office editions and versions, what should you choose? First, if you are a small firm, I would not worry too much about creating XML and XML schema today unless you are capable of creating your own; so, for most readers, enhanced XML authoring is not a reason in and of itself to select the Professional version of Office. This technology is still in the early stages of development, at least with regard to the financial planning profession, so I don't anticipate that many practitioners will be creating their own tags and schema right now. As development tools improve, and it becomes easier for the layperson to work with XML, possibly with the next version of MS Office, you may want to re-evaluate the feasibility of integrating your own Smart Tags and Smart Documents into your practice.

What the purchasing decision really comes down to, then, is the programs you are likely to need. MS Excel, MS Word, and MS Outlook come with all versions, so the question is: what else do you need? PowerPoint, in our opinion, is a necessity; that rules out the Basic edition. If, after reading Chapter 31, "Client Relationship Management (CRM) Software," you decide to rely upon MS Outlook for your CRM needs, we would strongly recommend that you get an Office version, which includes Business Contact Manager. Since the Small Office edition costs only marginally more than the Standard or the Basic versions, and it includes the Business Contact Manager as well as Publisher, it is a good choice for many readers. (Those who decide to publish their own newsletters, or even an occasional printed client communication, will be glad they have a copy of Publisher handy. It is the easiest to use program we are aware of capable of generating professional looking results.)

The other version worth considering would be the Professional version, which includes Access (the database) in addition to the programs discussed above (if after reading Chapter 31 you plan to purchase either Junxure-I or ProTracker, you will want to purchase MS Office Professional). If you decide that you would like to have a database program, but integration with other MS Office or industry programs is less of an issue, look at some of our other database recommendations at the end of this chapter. They are much easier to use, and integration may still be possible.

OneNote – An Additional MS Office Application

OneNote is a relatively new addition to the MS Office line of products. While it is officially considered part of the Office lineup, it is not currently included in any of the suites; it must be purchased separately. The program is designed specifically for note taking. It will work with both desktop and laptop computers, and it has some additional functionality designed to work exclusively with tablet PCs.

Unlike a word processor that is designed primarily to produce structured documents, OneNote allows users to take free form notes, organize them, move them around within the program, share them, and search through them. OneNote defines "note" broadly. It can include typed text, handwritten text (if using a tablet PC), diagrams, research cut from a web page, or even audio files (video files are coming soon).

Unlike many other programs, OneNote automatically saves whatever you put in it. By default, the program saves your work every 30 seconds or when the program is exited, whichever comes first.

The file structure is simple: it is comprised of folders, sections, and pages. The program ships with one default folder (called My Notebook). Within that folder are two sections: General and Meetings. Pages are added to a section by clicking on the add page tab or by using the "new page" command. Each page is dated and time-stamped automatically.

As with regular paper, the user can just click and start writing on any part of the page. Each section that is started with a mouse click is held in its own separate container.

It is possible to rearrange text within an individual container, or to drag and drop the containers from one part of the page to another. Sections can be color coded, which makes it easier to find things later.

OneNote includes templates for meeting notes, to-do lists, and lectures. Organizations can design their own layouts and save them as templates if they wish.

Note flags are one method of locating information. Note flags can be a symbol (a star, for example), a font color, or highlighted text. The program comes with a total of nine flags, five of which are preformatted, and four that are user defined.

OneNote includes something called the "Note Flags Summary Pane." This task pane allows users to view all of the flags in one place, and it provides a hotlink to each flagged item. The summary pane is customizable, so flag searches can be filtered by date or notebook location.

Keyword searches are also available. When the user types a keyword into the "Find" box, OneNote searches through every page in the active notebook and highlights each instance of the keyword. The page tab of every page that contains an instance of the keyword is also highlighted. One can easily scroll through each instance of the keyword by pressing the "next match" arrow or by hitting the "Enter" key on the keyboard.

Audio Note both records conversations and automatically synchronizes with typed or handwritten notes. The program knows exactly where in the audio track you entered a written comment, and you can later listen to the part of the audio associated with a note by placing your mouse cursor over the note and activating the audio playback; this is very handy for recording client interviews.

OneNote's research capabilities are promising as well. It is fairly simple to cut and paste items, be they text or graphics. When information is cut and pasted from a web page, the program automatically inserts the source URL information for future reference.

Side Note, an applet included with OneNote, which can be launched from an icon on the Windows taskbar, is a good substitute for the paper sticky notes many advisors still rely upon. It allows the user to create smaller notes on the fly, without launching OneNote. If desired, the side note can be "pasted" to a position on the screen with a virtual pushpin, where it will remain visible at all times. Side Notes are accessible from within OneNote when it is next launched, so they can be edited and stored.

One advantage of digital notes over paper notes is that the former can be easily shared. OneNotes can be e-mailed from within the program with a single mouse-click. They can also be printed to a number of popular paper sizes.

We think OneNote is a worthy addition to your software toolkit.

Quicken

We do not suggest that you maintain your business books with Quicken; QuickBooks is much better suited to the task. Why consider Quicken then? Because, presumably, a lot of your prospective clients and clients are maintaining their personal financial records using the program. As a courtesy and a service to them, you should maintain a current copy of Quicken so that they can supply their data files to you, rather than creating reports for yourself. The cost of Quicken is modest, and the payoff in client satisfaction, not to mention undiscovered information could be substantial. This is a "must have" as far as we are concerned.

QuickBooks

QuickBooks is an excellent choice for managing the financial transactions and records of your business. Like Microsoft Office, QuickBooks now comes in a constantly expanding array of versions. All versions can perform basic accounting tasks such as creating invoices, checks, and reports. All versions are compatible with additional QuickBooks services, including payroll processing and direct deposit.

While the basic version will probably prove adequate for those on an extremely tight budget, we'd suggest that you pay a little bit more and move up to the Pro version. Pro adds a number of useful features such as the ability to print labels, the ability to email invoices and reports (and save them as PDF files), integration with MS Office applications, form customization, the ability to customize prices, budgeting, time tracking, asset tracking, and many more. The Premier edition adds some additional functionality, but we don't think that the incremental functionality is worth the additional price for most firms.

askSAM – A Free Form Database

Databases are great for storing information. Things like contact information, Knowledgebases, IM archives, research notes, journal clippings, a list of all hardware and software in the office, etc. The problem is many people do not find the creation and maintenance of databases particularly intuitive. Often, the help of a programmer is required to achieve the desired results.

The askSAM (www.asksam.com) program is somewhat of an exception to the normal database rules. This program is easy enough for many non-programmers to use. Better yet, the askSAM website features a good collection of database templates, pre-designed databases that can be deployed immediately using the latest version of askSAM. Two versions are available: the Standard version and the Professional version. The more expensive Pro version includes full text indexing, which produces faster search results; however, the Standard version is more than sufficient for beginners. askSAM offers a free trial version, which can be downloaded from their website.

If you can benefit from a database program, and you want something that is easy but effective, askSAM is worthy of your consideration.

FileMaker Pro

FileMaker is another easy to use database program. Like askSAM, the company offers a number of database templates that are free to users at its website (www.filemaker.com). Those of interest to a financial planning practice include contact management, event planning, expense reports, performance management (tracking goals for you and your employees), research notes, Knowledgebase builder, and a task manager. Additional templates and add-ins are available from third-party providers. FileMaker Pro offers a free trial version, available for download at its website.

Voice Recognition Software

If you are a lousy typist, you may want to think about investing in voice recognition software. The primary utility of this software is that it allows you to dictate your letters, notes, etc., into a word processor. It can also be used to issue voice commands to your computer and perform some other tricks. Microsoft Office includes a basic voice recognition application, but it may not install by default (try doing a custom install instead).

The Microsoft application is a decent tool to familiarize yourself with voice recognition, but if you really want to use it on a regular basis, we recommend that you purchase a copy of either Dragon Naturally Speaking or IBM Via Voice. In our trials, we found both of these products more accurate and easier to use than the Microsoft application. Dragon is offered in a number of different versions. We would only consider purchasing

Preferred or Professional. Via Voice is also offered in various flavors. We would only consider the Pro USB edition or the Advanced Edition.

If you decide to use one of these products, there are a few keys to success. One is training. You must do some initial reading into the system so that it recognizes your voice. Once that is accomplished, you must make corrections to your documents so that the program can further refine its understanding of your speech.

The other key to success is a good microphone. We have heard from a number of experts that many customer failures are do to the poor microphones that they use. One advantage of the Pro version of Via Voice is that it comes packaged with a good microphone. If you do not have one, get one. It could be the difference between success and failure.

Many users become frustrated with the software and give up too soon. This is a mistake. If you stick with it, you can achieve a high degree of accuracy. Just be aware that even high accuracy does not equate to perfection. If you achieve 95% accuracy, for example, there will still be some words that require correction in most documents that you create. Spend time on training, and approach the software with realistic expectations, and there is a good chance that you will become a satisfied customer.

Chapter 31

CLIENT RELATIONSHIP MANAGEMENT (CRM) SOFTWARE

Client Relationship Management (CRM) software is arguably the most important piece of software in a financial services practice. As any experienced practitioner will tell you, ours is a "people" business. In order to be successful, one must nurture client relationships through a constant flow of communications. In addition, you must be organized so that all tasks are completed on schedule and no "to-do" item is overlooked. Good CRM software can help you provide excellent client service, and some can do much more.

At its most basic level, CRM software can help you store information about your clients and contacts, organize the information, and rapidly retrieve the information when you need it. Some of the more advanced packages go way beyond the basics. They can help with scheduling, marketing, workflow management, document management, compliance, and much more.

In order to facilitate the discussion of programs that organize client data, let's divide them into three categories:

1. General purpose programs, such as:

   a) MS Outlook (http://www.microsoft.com/office/outlook/default.asp),

   b) ACT! (www.act.com), and

   c) Goldmine (http://www.frontrange.com/goldmine/);

2. A middle group, which includes some add-on programs that we will discuss shortly; and

3. The highly specialized, industry specific programs, such as:

   a) Junxure-I (http://65.243.105.162/), and

   b) ProTracker Advantage (http://www.protracker.com/).

We'll also look at one high-powered practice management program that is in a category of its own.

MS OUTLOOK 2003

MS Outlook 2003 is probably not the ideal contact manager for financial service professionals; however, there are a number of reasons to discuss it. First, it comes bundled with some versions of MS Office that so many readers already have MS Outlook installed on their computers, making it their least expensive option. Second, a number of more robust CRM packages either use MS Outlook as their email client, or provide the ability to email through MS Outlook as an option. Third, MS Outlook integrates well with other MS Office products such as Word, Excel, and OneNote.

This latest iteration of Outlook greatly improves some existing features, and it adds some important new ones. Whole books have been written about Outlook, so we really cannot discuss it fully here. We've already discussed MS Outlook's email capabilities earlier. Now, we'll highlight the Business Contact Manager, an add-on generally packaged with MS Office versions targeted at small businesses. The added capabilities of Business Contact Manager enhance Outlook's attractiveness to financial service professionals. We'll also briefly discuss a topic that generates a lot of questions among readers: calendar sharing in MS Outlook

MICROSOFT OUTLOOK WITH BUSINESS CONTACT MANAGER

Those who purchase a retail version of MS Office Professional Edition 2003 or MS Office Small Business Edition 2003 (either shrink-wrapped or pre-installed) receive an Outlook add-on called Business Contact Manager (Figure 31.1), which is designed to enhance Outlook's ability to deal with business information and sales opportunities.

Business Contact Manager can store information about Accounts (companies you do business with, for example a company whose 401(k) plan you are managing), Business Contacts (persons you do business with at a company), and Opportunities (a potential additional sale to a prospective client or existing client, which is then linked to an Account or Business Contact).

It appears that the idea behind the Business Contact Manager is to give MS Outlook some of the functionality that has long been present in CRM products such as ACT! and Goldmine. While MS Outlook with Business Contact Manager falls far short of the power that ACT! and Goldmine provide, it does increase Outlook's overall usefulness to the financial professional.

With regard to relationship management, Outlook's greatest weakness for most financial professionals is its inability to create a history of interactions with an account, business contact, or opportunity. Business Contact Manager fills this void by automatically linking email messages, meetings, appointments, and tasks to the relevant account, business contact, or opportunity. Other types of information, such as notes, documents, and phone logs can be manually linked to the same records.

Like most popular CRM packages designed for businesses, Business Contact Manager enables grouping and the ability to assign categories to a record, which in turn greatly enhances reporting capabilities. The add-on can be used with Microsoft bCentral List Builder to distribute newsletters to clients or create an email marketing campaign.

In short, Business Contact Manager provides entry level business CRM capabilities to Outlook 2003, along with some nice ties into other Microsoft products, like bCentral, that are appropriate for smaller businesses. It is not going to challenge ACT! or Goldmine, but it will be useful for those currently only using Outlook, and it may be enough for novice advisors working on tight budgets.

Note: The Business Contact Manager is not designed to be an enterprise solution. It only works with POP3, IMAP, and HTML email. The Business Contact Manager functionality is not enabled when used in conjunction with MS Small Business Server or MS Exchange Server configured for MAPI email.

Figure 31.1

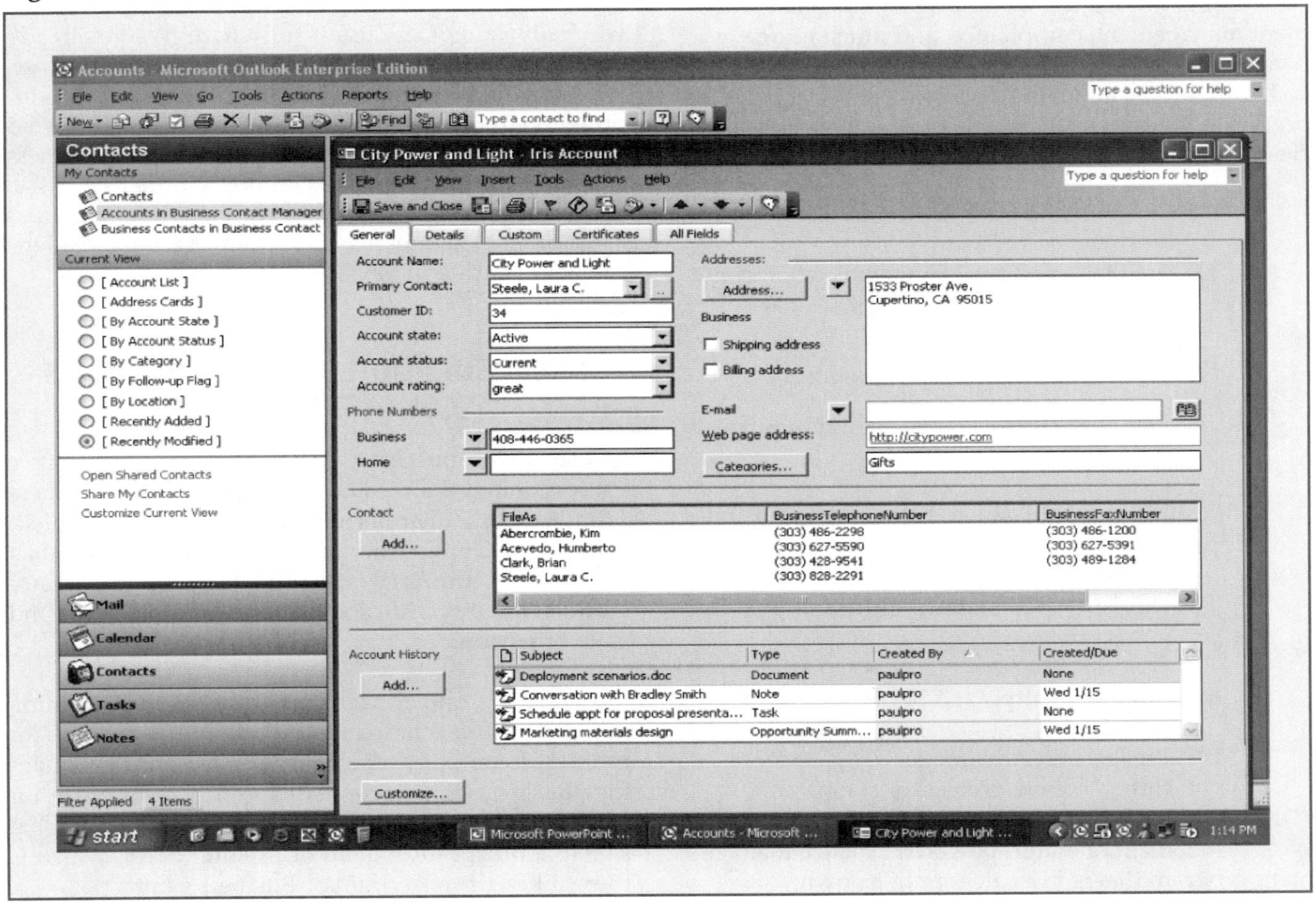

SHARING YOUR MS OUTLOOK CALENDAR

In previous versions of Outlook, you could not share calendars in an office unless you were running Microsoft Exchange Server. The same is generally true about Outlook 2003; however, there are alternatives. Those who purchase Windows Small Business Server 2003 will receive both Exchange Server and an edition of Windows SharePoint Services. SharePoint enables the sharing of calendars, as well as other types of MS Office information. There are also other options. Advisors can rent SharePoint space online through an ISP, and share information there. If all employees use MSN as their ISP, they can share their Outlook calendars through MSN. If none of the above solutions are suitable, third-party programs such as Public Outlook and Schedules4Teams provide additional calendar sharing options. For sharing among a small group, for example a sole practitioner and an assistant, Punch Networks WebDrive Synch Engine is another possibility.

ACT! VERSION 6.0 – AN OVERVIEW

ACT! Version 6.0 is one of the most widely used general purpose contact relationship managers. Much of ACT!'s popularity, no doubt, can be traced to its intuitive interface. It takes a while to become an ACT! power user; however, novices can learn the basics rapidly with the help of the short, but well-written user's guide. Additional help is readily available for those who need it. Numerous books, newsletters, user groups, consultants, and add-ons are available to help with ACT!

Figure 31.2

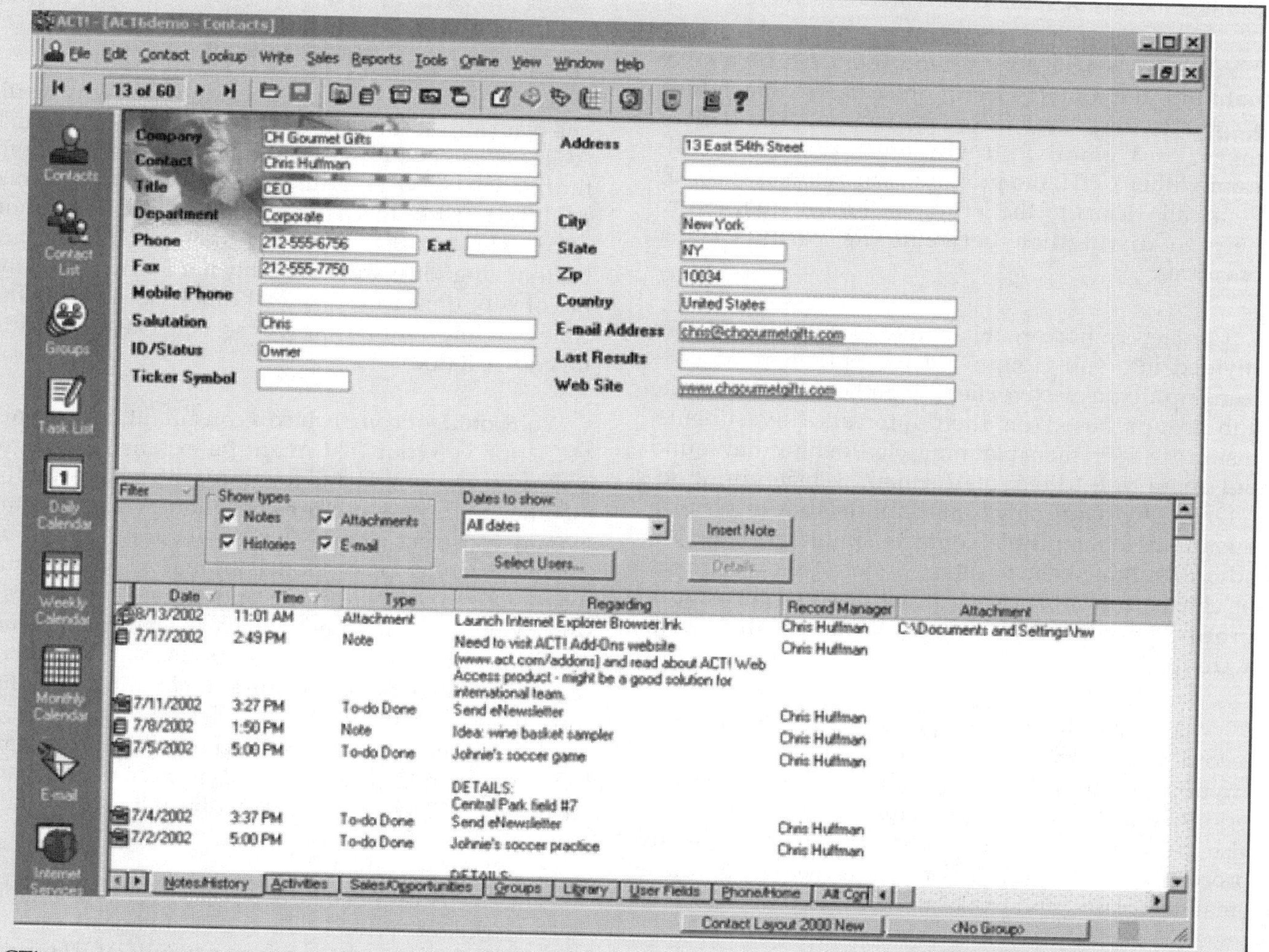

ACT! screenshot reproduced with the permission of Best Software SB, Inc. ©1993-2004 All rights reserved. ACT! is a registered trademark of Best Software SB, Inc.

ACT! packs a lot of power into an inexpensive package. Like most other contact management systems, ACT! has the ability to track contacts, view your calendar, schedule appointments, and track tasks, but it can do much more, as I will demonstrate shortly.

ACT! is client-centric, which means that every action you take in the program revolves around a contact record in the program.

As you can see in Figure 31.2, the ACT screen is divided into two sections. The top section holds the type of information that would typically appear on a business card. The bottom half of the screen displays the information associated with the tab on the bottom of the page (in this case Notes/History). The toolbar at the left of the screen allows you to navigate from the contact record to other parts of the program (contact list, groups, to do list, calendar, email).

At the Notes/History section users can type notes right into the contact record; one can also attach files, assign "to-dos," and record correspondence (letters, faxes, and emails). If you initiate phone calls from within ACT!, the program will automatically log your calls. Icons to the left of each individual record help to distinguish between the various types of entries.

Contacts can be organized into groups, and further divided into sub-groups. For example, it is possible to group all prospective clients together, and then create sub-groups based on their interests (investments, insurance, retirement planning, etc.), or how they found out about you (direct mail, email, website, print ad, referral, etc.). Grouping contacts allows one to perform operations on multiple contacts simultaneously. An advisor might want to attach a note to a sub-group of clients, for instance, or attach a spreadsheet to a group. Emails or faxes can be associated with a group.

ACT! makes it easy to organize your schedule and record your activities. Tracking calls, meetings, and "to-dos" becomes almost effortless. You can set alarms, prioritize tasks, and create activity reports. You can also create letters (using either ACT!'s built-in word processor, MS Word), perform mail merges, produce email templates, and track sales.

ACT! will synchronize appointments, tasks, and "to-dos" with MS Outlook. ACT! Link, available for a small additional charge, allows you to synchronize your ACT! data with your PDA (both Palm and Pocket PC versions are available). As we went to press, a company spokesperson for Best Software (producer of ACT!) informed us that ACT! 2005 had been released. Act4Advisors and Brokers*ACT work with the prior version, ACT! 6.0. For more information, go to www.bestsoftware.com.

THE MIDDLE GROUND = ADD-ONS

For those of you unfamiliar with the add-on concept, they are really nothing more than computer code that enhances an existing product, such as ACT! The ACT! add-on products discussed below add some or all of the following customization features: a customized ACT! Database, specialized macros, screen layouts, reports, and search capabilities designed specifically for financial service professionals.

Act4Advisors

If ACT! is such a great product (and it is), why would one want an add-on? The answer is really quite simple: ACT! is designed for general sales, not specifically for the financial services industry. Sure, you can customize ACT! yourself, so that a financial advisor can use it more effectively, but that would be time consuming, and customizing software is probably not the most effective use of your time. Doesn't it make more sense to use that time building your business or serving existing clients? Of course it does!

You could, of course, hire a consultant to customize ACT! for you, but that might be expensive. Imagine instead if you could band together with a large number of other advisors and hire a consultant. This consultant would construct a semi-custom version of ACT! for financial service professionals so that all of you could use it. Due to cost constraints and the needs of others in the group, you might not get every feature you want, but it would probably come pretty close, and the others just might suggest some features that you yourself had not thought of. When you purchase Act4Advisors, or one of the other add-ons profiled below, the process and results are similar. (*Note*: Act4Advisors currently works with ACT! 6.0. A version compatible with ACT! 2005 is due in early 2005.)

The Act4Advisors main contact screen and Personal tabs are better suited to the typical financial advisory firm's needs than are the generic default ACT! screens. The Act4Advisor screen prominently displays the spouses name on the top portion of the screen, so it is

Figure 31.3

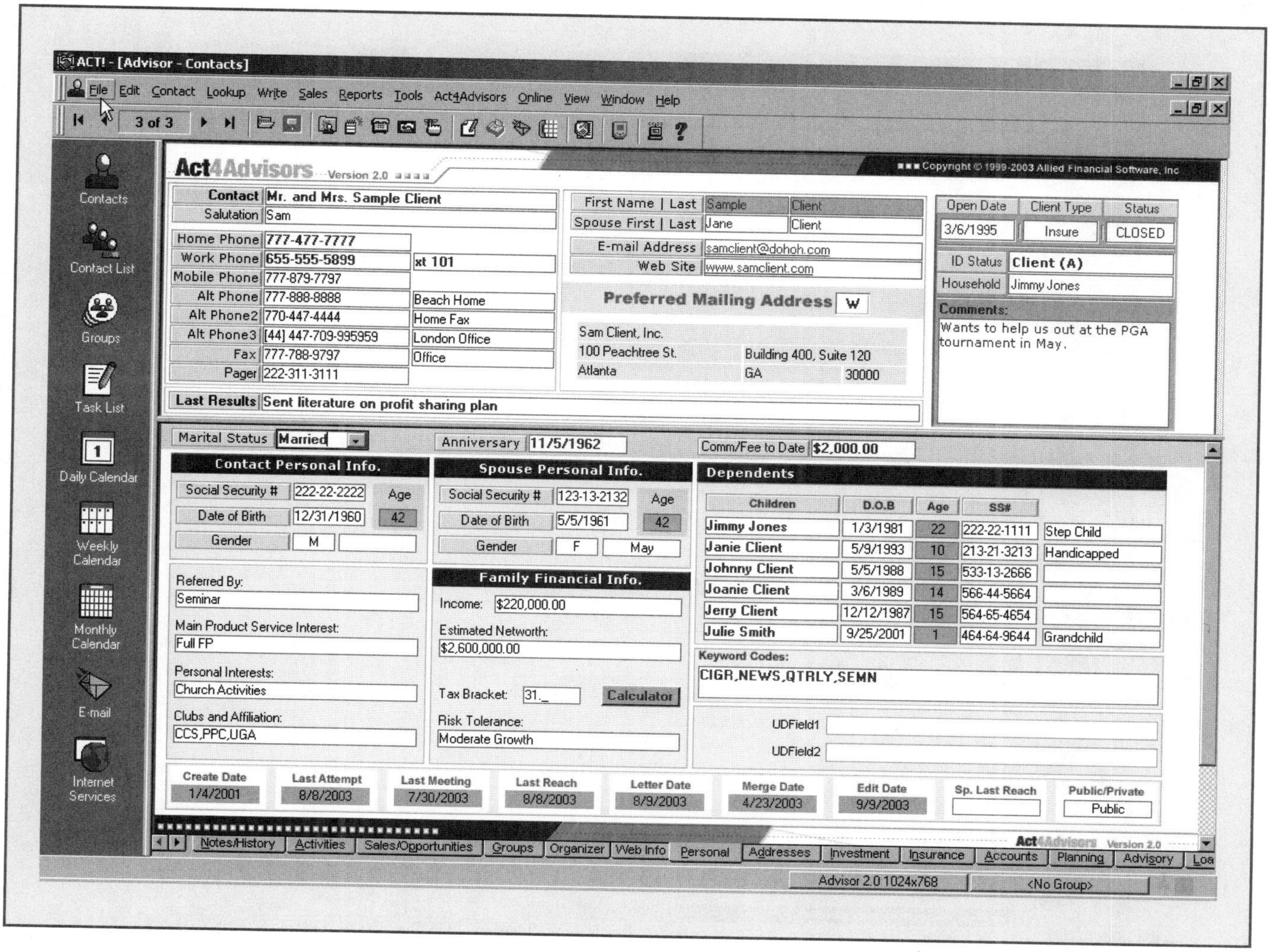

viewable regardless of the tab one is viewing. The Personal tab offers fields for important information such as children's names, dates of birth and Social Security numbers for all family members, main product/service interest (comprehensive financial planning, asset allocation, insurance, etc.), risk tolerance, tax bracket, estimated net worth, commissions/fees to date, personal interests, referral source, and clubs/affiliations. That's a great deal of useful information in one view.

The standard Act4Advisors layout displays the client's home information on the top half of the screen so it is always visible, but since some advisors prefer client's business information as the default, the program offers an alternate layout to accommodate them.

The Insurance screen (Figure 31.4) is another customized view that many advisors find useful, either as a sales tool, or to just to track coverages.

The "Security Quote" field on the Investment tab is very useful for those advisors who have clients phoning in and asking for stock quotes. It enables advisors to obtain a quote from right within the client record.

The primary advantage of Act4Advisors is that you receive a highly customized version of ACT! at a very affordable price. As of this writing, Act4Advisors 2.0 was selling for $199.00 for a single user license ($299.00 for two, $499.00 for five) That's quite a bargain. It is important to note that you can further customize the program, if necessary, by either engaging the Act4Advisor staff or hiring an independent consultant.

In addition, you already own ACT!, so you can make use of the entire set of underlying ACT! features. This means that you can record every client contact, share information within the office, coordinate schedules, perform mail merges, and download information into PDA's.

Figure 31.4

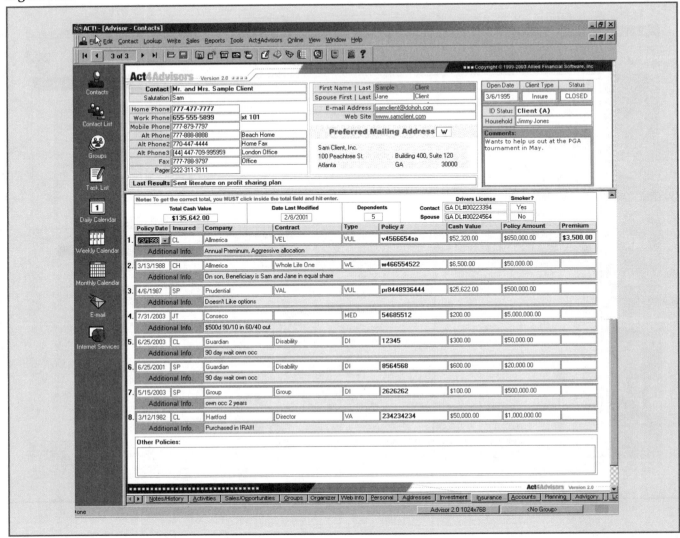

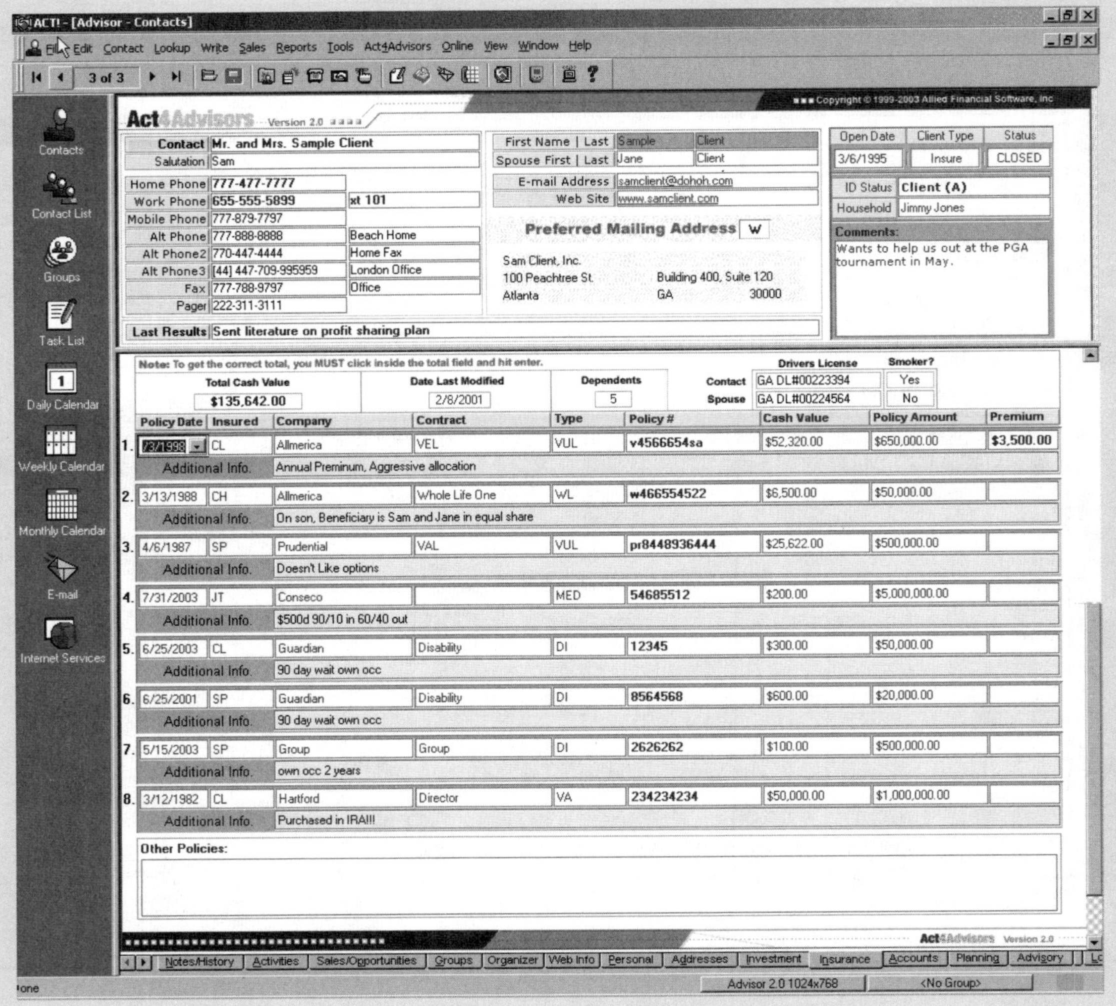

With ACT!'s large user base, there's a good chance that some of your staff are familiar with the program, which means that your training cost will be minimized. Finding competent temps or virtual work partners to perform various tasks (data entry, mass mailings, etc.) within ACT! shouldn't prove much of a challenge either.

There are no major disadvantages to speak of. This firm, like its competitors, is a small company (five employees) and thus, is dependent on the skills of a few employees. Usually, this would concern me, but it is likely that if a problem were to occur, another ACT! consultant would be interested in taking over the task of serving Act4Advisor clients.

Another minor concern I'd heard voiced a few times is that the program is geared towards commission-based rather than fee-based planners. A recent conversation with company spokesman Scott Aboud reassured me that the program has been updated making it equally useful to fee-based and commission-based planners.

Act4Advisors Bundle

Act4Advisors offers a bundled product that includes ACT!, Act4Advisors, and Scan & Organize for ACT!, which helps manage client documents by automatically navigating to the client's folder on the network or local PC from within Act4Advisors. It has an optional scanning feature to scan documents directly into the client folder. The bundle currently sells for $399.00 for a single user, with discounts available on multiple license purchases.

CYBERBROKER

CyberBroker, like Act4Advisors, is an add-on product for ACT!, which means that in order to use it, ACT! must be installed on the computer or network running CyberBroker. The price for a single user installation is $95.00 or $295.00, depending on which plan you choose. CyberBroker is appropriate for those who want a CRM package targeted specifically at the financial service profession. It is particularly well suited to those who like ACT!, but who do not have the time or the inclination to customize it for their practice.

Installation

The CyberBroker installation process is somewhat different than that of other programs. Usually, downloading and installing programs is a self-service proposition. In the case of CyberBroker, the user is offered one-on-one help, making it especially well suited for those who feel uncomfortable around computers. CyberBroker support (via telephone) walks users through the whole download and installation process, which does not take very long.

Figure 31.5

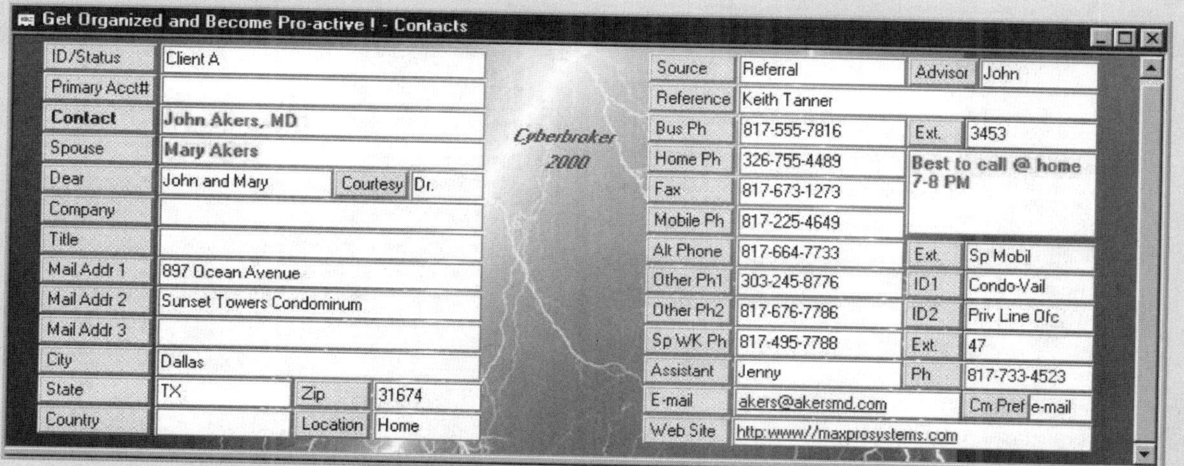

Reprinted with permission of MaxPro Systems (www.maxprosystems.com).

Figure 31.6

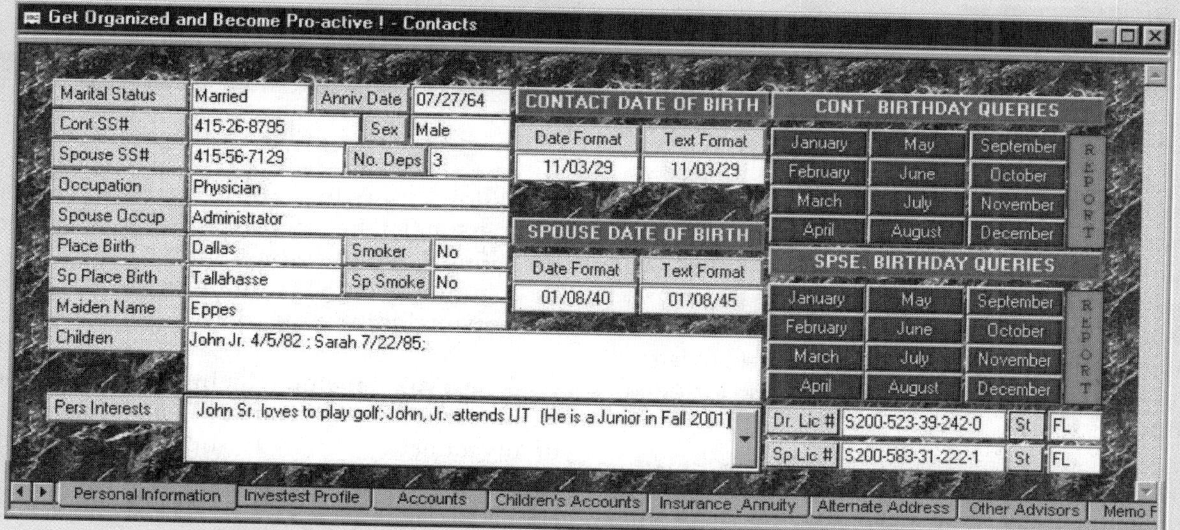

Figure 31.7

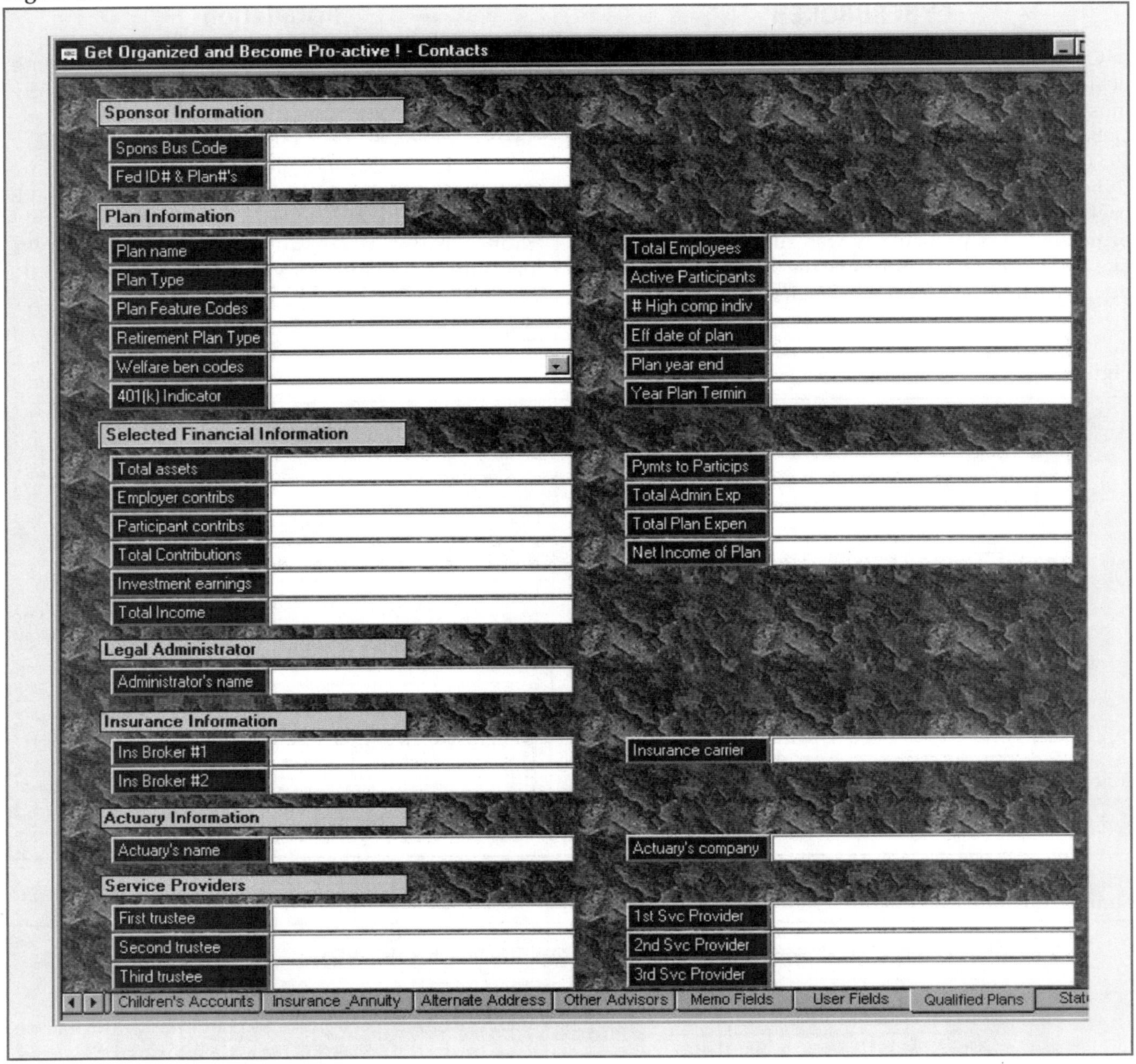

When compared to Act4Advisors, CyberBroker provides more information on the primary user screens. The main contact screen pictured in Figure 31.5 contains fields for multiple mailing addresses, while Act4Advisors contains only one. There are fields for eight phone numbers versus two for Act4Advisors. Assistant's name and phone number are also included on the primary screen.

CyberBroker includes some health information on the personal tab that Act4Advisors does not (whether each spouse smokes or not). CyberBroker also allows users to perform birthday queries from the personal tab. Act4Advisors does not include these fields and functions, but it does include fields for a summary of the family's financial condition on the personal tab.

CyberBroker includes an Investment Profile tab, a feature that Act4Advisors does not have. In the area of investments, Act4Advisors offers fields for an asset allocation summary, which CyberBroker does not have. It also contains fields for liabilities (mortgage, credit card debt, etc.).

Both programs provide fields to enter individual account information. Both programs can track insurance and annuity policies, but CyberBroker offers more in this area. Advisors who have clients taking regular periodic distributions from an annuity will value the monthly distribution field, which is not included in Act4Advisors. CyberBroker shines with respect to qualified retirement plans.

Those advisors who offer such plans as part of their practice will love the ability to record trustees, administrators, actuaries, plan tax ID's, and important plan information (plan type, number of highly compensated employees, etc).

Templates

No two advisors use their CRM software in exactly the same way, but most advisors primarily require the ability to store information and the ability to communicate effectively with their clients. The inclusion of letter templates facilitates such communication. Many readers will want to customize their letters, or obtain approval from their compliance departments, but templates for general prospective clients and client service issues can save considerable time, as can birthday letter templates, thank you letters, etc. CyberBroker includes quite a few letter templates aspart of the package.

Training and Consulting Services

MaxPro Systems, the developers of CyberBroker, offer training, marketing, and consulting services. Productivity classes are offered by teleconference at reasonable rates. They are probably a good investment for those unfamiliar with ACT! or CyberBroker. A separate marketing class, which includes about 20 additional marketing report templates, is designed to help advisors obtain the maximum value from their databases. The marketing course with templates is priced at $300. Advisors can order a package, which includes CyberBroker, the productivity classes and the marketing class (with the report templates) for $468 or $39 per month for 12 months. Those who opt for the monthly plan receive a $39 credit for each new client they refer to CyberBroker.

CyberBroker might be a slightly better choice for those new to ACT!, or those new to the financial service profession. The less you know about ACT! or the profession, the more you are likely to benefit from the productivity training. Those looking to build a new business, or expand an existing business, will probably find the marketing class a good value.

BROKERS*ACT

Brokers*ACT (www.brokersact.com) is the latest ACT! add-in for financial professionals we've come across. Brokers*ACT shares many similarities with Act4Advisors and CyberBroker. For example, all provide a customized ACT! database, customized layouts, letter templates, report templates, and the like; however, Brokers*ACT is distinct in a number of ways. (*Note*: As we went to press, Brokers*ACT had not yet released an ACT! 2005 compatible version. We expect one to be released within a few months.)

Installation

When we tried it, Brokers*ACT was the easiest to install. The process was totally automated. Upon purchase, the company sends out an email that contains a link to the download site, a user ID, and a password. The user simply clicks on a hyperlink within the email that points to the download page. Once the file is downloaded, you double click on the file, and it installs itself. The set-up process was very fast when compared with Act4Advisors and CyberBroker.

Some Typical Screen Layouts

Of the three add-ons, Brokers*ACT has the most modern and professional feel to it. The primary user screens (Figure 31.8) more closely resemble those of Act4Advisors than those of CyberBroker, but they are more polished.

All three products probably contain the information advisors would like to see on their primary screens: name; addresses; multiple phone numbers; spousal information; SS number; driver's license; and email address. Most other information is available by simply clicking one of the tabs along the bottom of the screen, but if a particular firm requires specific fields, they should either purchase the product that offers the fields or talk to one of the three vendors about customization.

Brokers*ACT takes a slightly different approach to its asset allocation screen (Figure 31.9). Assets are logically grouped into three columns: (1) fixed income; (2) equity; and (3) others.

Figure 31.8

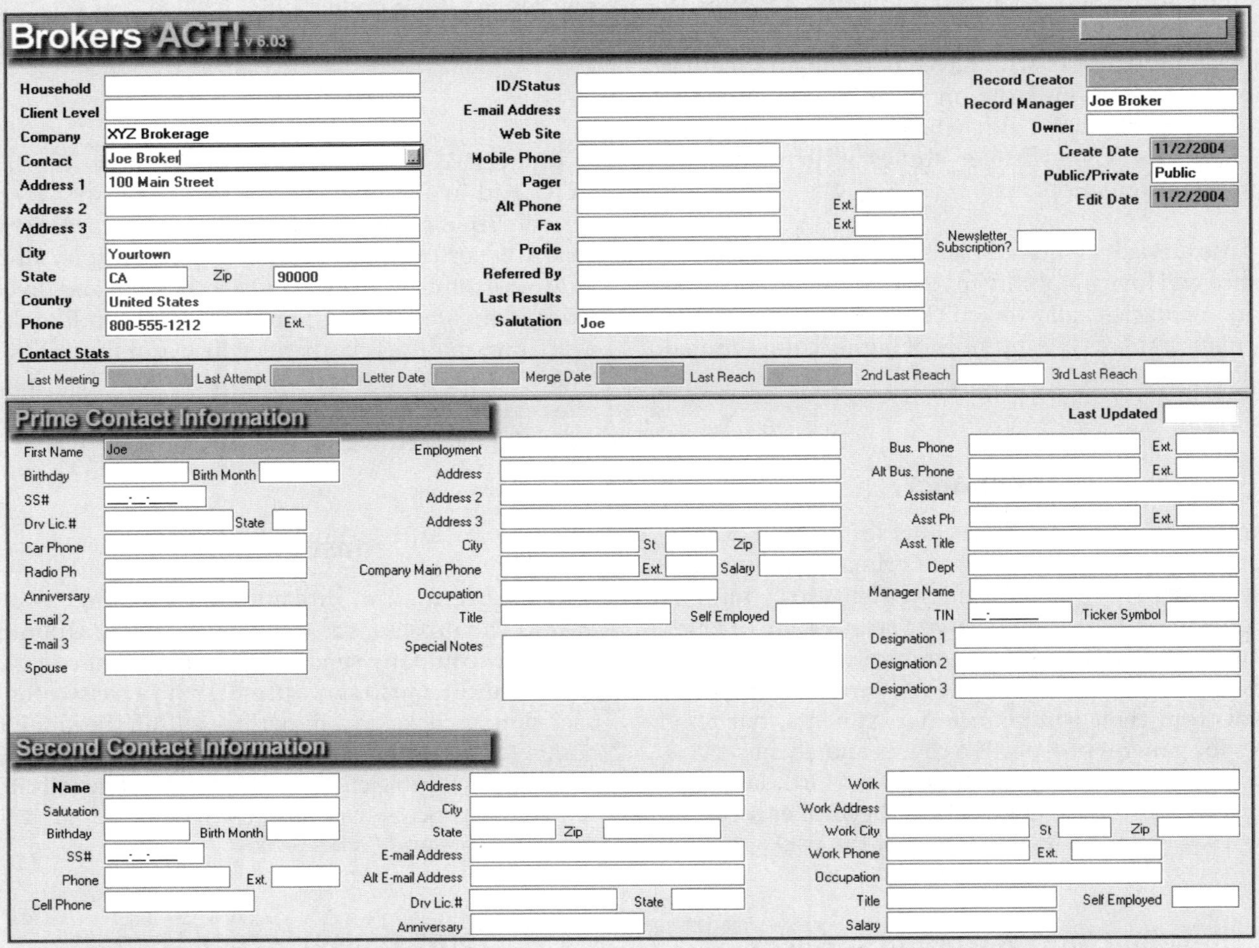

Reprinted with permission of Brokers*ACT.

Rather than try to build asset allocation capabilities into their contact management software, the developers leave that task to another software package. They use this layout simply to record the allocation at a specific point in time, the last rebalancing date for instance, and use it for later reference.

According to the Brokers*ACT website "With the SEC breathing more and more down your backs, you need to make sure your client's investments are suitable, not just at the time you open the account, but during the management of and yes, even after the account is closed." We agree; however, the information provided on Figure 31.10 may not be sufficient. It is a good start though, for novices who are not using a more detailed suitability tracking system.

Brokers*ACT can track life insurance policies, disability policies, and annuities (Figure 31.11). Overall, the design of the insurance and deferred products tabs is very good.

Client Road Map

Another somewhat unique feature is the Client Road Map (Figure 31.12). This screen is based upon ideas the developers picked up from two well-known authors: Bill Bachrach and Scott West.

Essentially, this screen tries to capture a snapshot of client values, and relate them to both short and long term goals. It also documents a client's "investment style."

Templates

Brokers*ACT comes with a reasonable assortment of letter and report templates. In almost all cases, users will

Figure 31.9

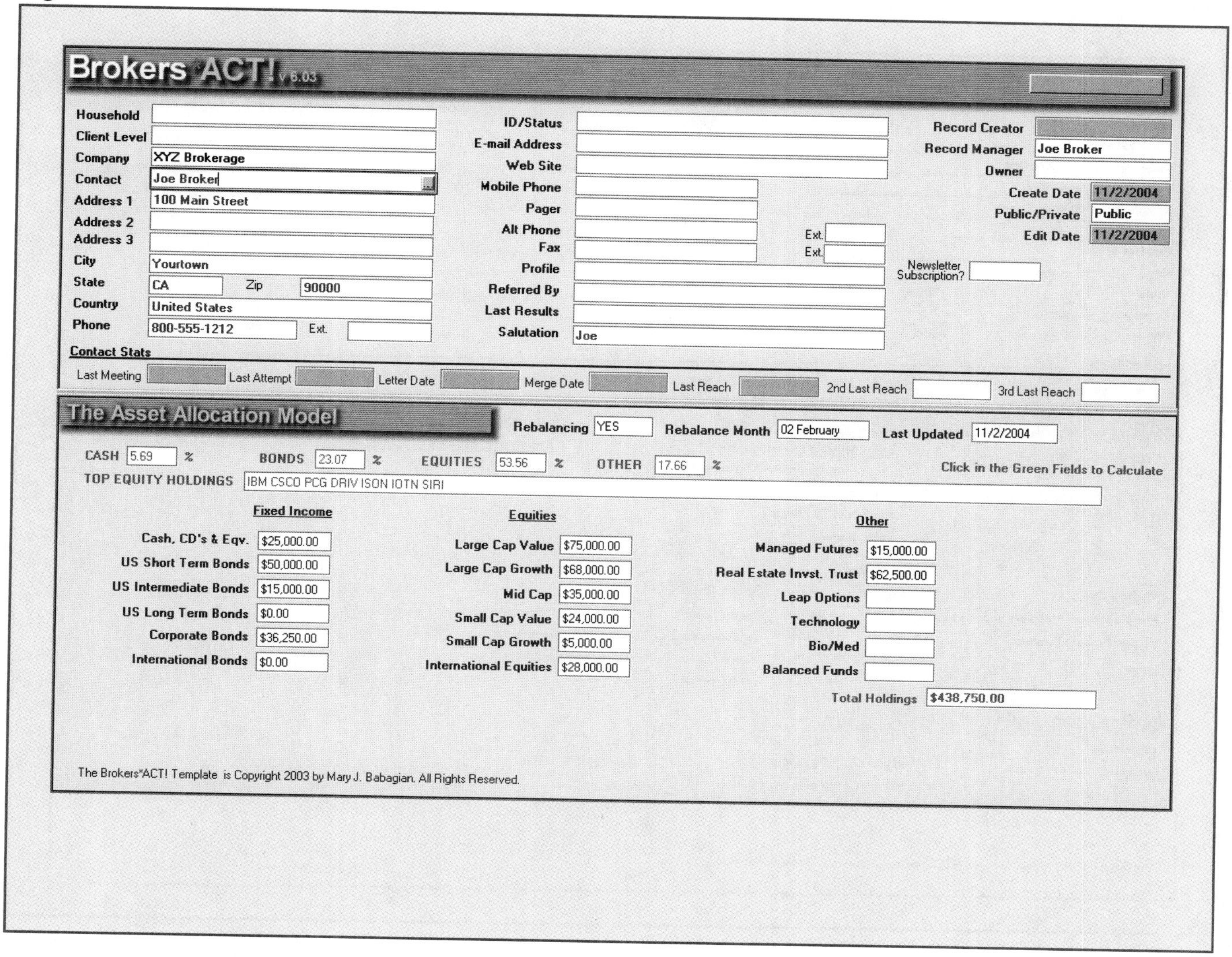

want to add their own personal touch to the letters in particular, but it is much easier to work from an existing template than to start from a blank document. According to the developers, numerous additional generic letters will be added to the program in the near future. All licensed users will be able to download them and use them at no additional charge.

Other Features

Brokers*ACT has a screen to facilitate drip marketing campaigns and shorter marketing blitzes. There is an Estate Planning tab to track wills and trusts, as well as information relating to them. The Qualified Plan section tracks clients' retirement accounts.

Brokers*ACT is the only one of the three add-ons available in a Canadian edition. The Canadian version differs primarily with regards to retirement accounts and insurance.

As we went to press, a company spokesperson for Brokers*ACT informed us that the screen had recently been enhanced. For more information, go to www.brokersact.com.

Summing up Add-on Products

All three of the products discussed above, Act4Advisors, CyberBroker, and Brokers*ACT are solid products. Most potential purchasers will be happy with whichever one they choose. Before you buy, try to determine what specific features, fields, templates, and reports are most important to you. Select the product that comes closest to satisfying all of your needs. If more than one product still qualifies, look at issues such as

Figure 31.10

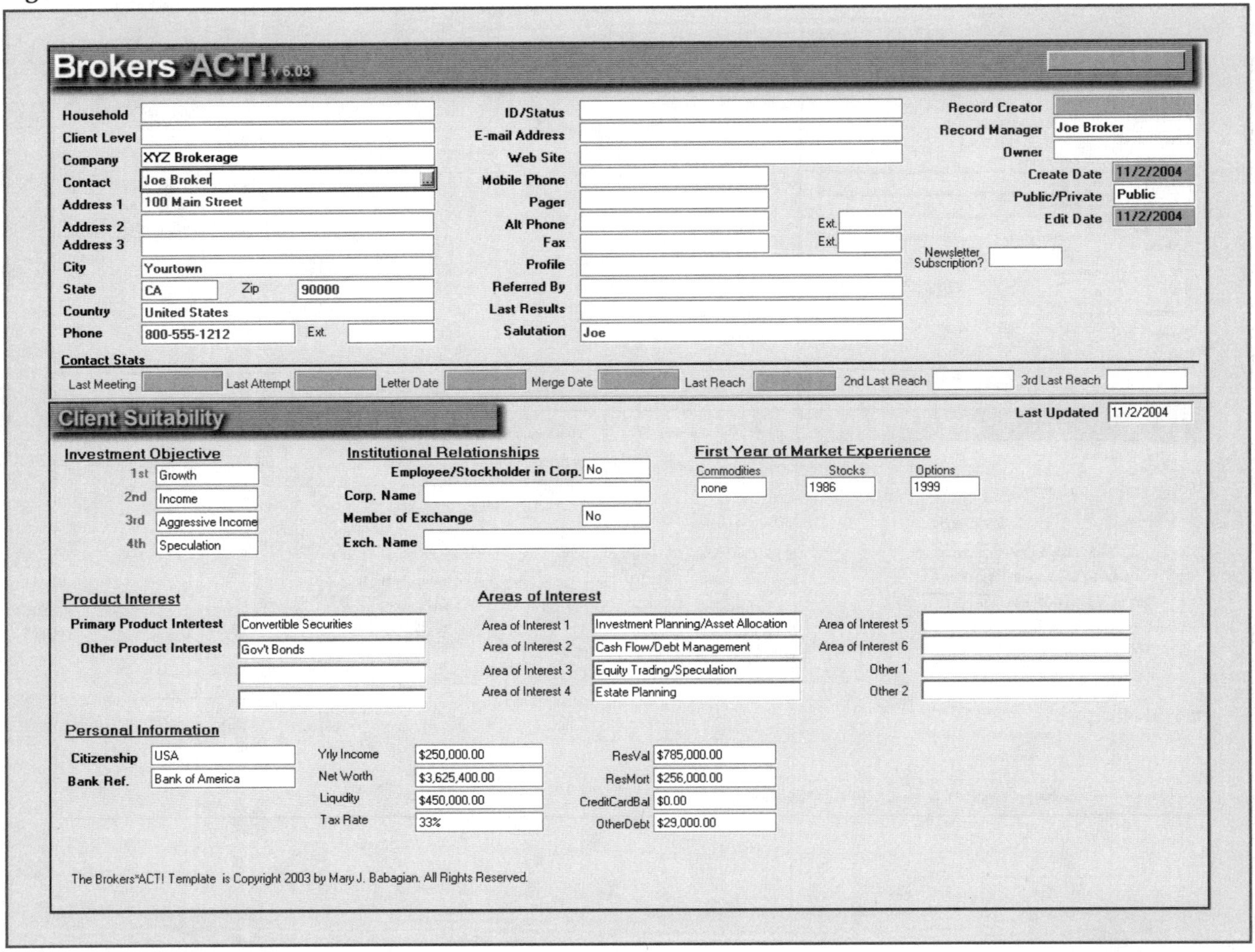

training, integrations with other programs, additional features available at an additional cost, etc.

Don't forget that none of these programs will do you any good if you do not set aside the time to learn them and use them. It takes a while to become familiar with these add-ons and to use them effectively, but eventually it becomes second nature. Before long, you will begin to reap the productivity gains and profitability rewards that these programs provide.

GOLDMINE

Goldmine is another highly popular general purpose CRM software package. Goldmine is much more powerful than ACT!, but we tend to come across more people in our industry who use ACT! rather than Goldmine. We believe the reason for this is that ACT! is easier to learn and use. Many users of both of these programs initially try to do some simple customization on their own. The feedback we have received seems to indicate that those using ACT! are more successful. In addition, those using Goldmine in a networked environment are more likely to require expert assistance than those using ACT! Nevertheless, Goldmine holds great promise for those advisors willing to commit to it and configure it properly.

As one would expect, Goldmine does an excellent job of managing contacts, schedules, and "to-dos." Like ACT!, Goldmine is client centric, so all actions and histories can be linked to the client record. But rather than discuss the similarities, let's discuss a few of the features that set Goldmine apart.

Goldmine allows users to set up automated processes. An automated process is a conditional response to one event. For example, any time you log an initial call to a prospective client, Goldmine can be pro-

Figure 31.11

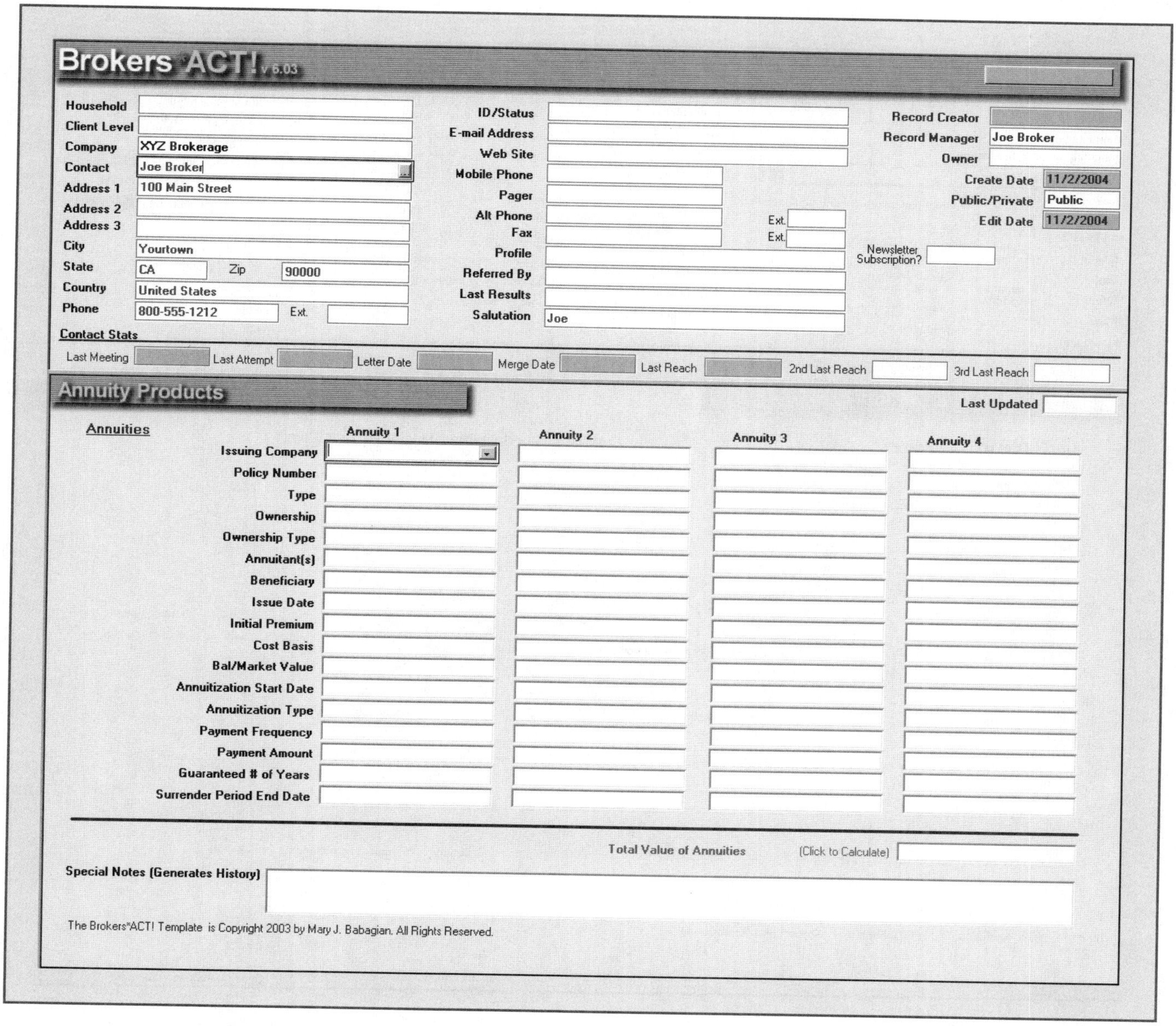
Brokers ACT! v 6.03

Household:
Client Level:
Company: XYZ Brokerage
Contact: Joe Broker
Address 1: 100 Main Street
Address 2:
Address 3:
City: Yourtown
State: CA Zip: 90000
Country: United States
Phone: 800-555-1212 Ext.

ID/Status:
E-mail Address:
Web Site:
Mobile Phone:
Pager:
Alt Phone: Ext.
Fax: Ext.
Profile:
Referred By:
Last Results:
Salutation: Joe

Record Creator:
Record Manager: Joe Broker
Owner:
Create Date: 11/2/2004
Public/Private: Public
Edit Date: 11/2/2004
Newsletter Subscription?

Contact Stats
Last Meeting | Last Attempt | Letter Date | Merge Date | Last Reach | 2nd Last Reach | 3rd Last Reach

Annuity Products
Last Updated

Annuities

	Annuity 1	Annuity 2	Annuity 3	Annuity 4
Issuing Company				
Policy Number				
Type				
Ownership				
Ownership Type				
Annuitant(s)				
Beneficiary				
Issue Date				
Initial Premium				
Cost Basis				
Bal/Market Value				
Annuitization Start Date				
Annuitization Type				
Payment Frequency				
Payment Amount				
Guaranteed # of Years				
Surrender Period End Date				

Total Value of Annuities (Click to Calculate)

Special Notes (Generates History)

The Brokers'ACT! Template is Copyright 2003 by Mary J. Babagian. All Rights Reserved.

Figure 31.12

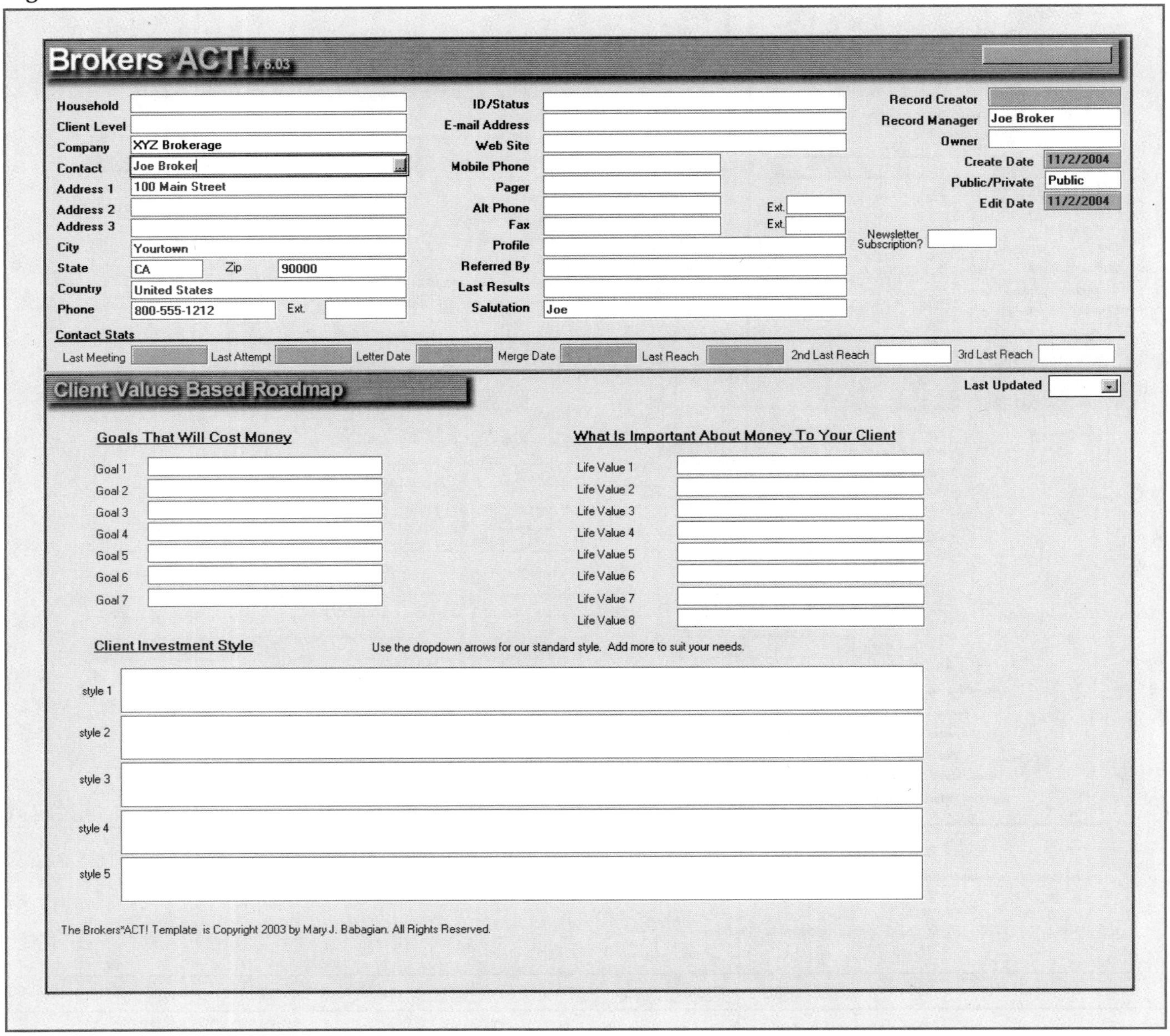
Brokers ACT! v 6.03
Household
Client Level
Company XYZ Brokerage
Contact Joe Broker
Address 1 100 Main Street
Address 2
Address 3
City Yourtown
State CA
Zip 90000
Country United States
Phone 800-555-1212
Ext.
ID/Status
E-mail Address
Web Site
Mobile Phone
Pager
Alt Phone
Ext.
Fax
Ext.
Profile
Referred By
Last Results
Salutation Joe
Record Creator
Record Manager Joe Broker
Owner
Create Date 11/2/2004
Public/Private Public
Edit Date 11/2/2004
Newsletter Subscription?
Contact Stats
Last Meeting
Last Attempt
Letter Date
Merge Date
Last Reach
2nd Last Reach
3rd Last Reach
Client Values Based Roadmap
Last Updated
Goals That Will Cost Money
Goal 1
Goal 2
Goal 3
Goal 4
Goal 5
Goal 6
Goal 7
What Is Important About Money To Your Client
Life Value 1
Life Value 2
Life Value 3
Life Value 4
Life Value 5
Life Value 6
Life Value 7
Life Value 8
Client Investment Style
Use the dropdown arrows for our standard style. Add more to suit your needs.
style 1
style 2
style 3
style 4
style 5
The Brokers'ACT! Template is Copyright 2003 by Mary J. Babagian. All Rights Reserved.

grammed to automatically follow up with a letter or email containing "canned text" that you create: an invitation to visit your office, for example. Automated processes can even be set up to capture and process leads from a website.

The Details tab is designed to house random information for which you may not want to create a customized field, because it will not be used for all contact records. The program comes pre-populated with a number of "detail names," and you can add additional ones to suit your needs.

The Referrals tab is another feature that can be useful to the financial professional. This tab allows you to create a relationship between a number of different accounts. You could use it to "link" all clients that you have referred to a specific CPA firm, or you could use it to track all prospective clients that a law firm has referred to you.

Goldmine incorporates some powerful sales forecasting tools. For those readers who are trying to grow a business, these tools can help project growth, and help analyze where new business is coming from. Users can create sales goals, create forecasts, and track results both tabularly and graphically.

The InfoCenter is another noteworthy feature. The InfoCenter is a place to store information in digital, searchable format so that it is available to all members of the firm at all times. The InfoCenter contains three tabs: (1) Knowledgebase; (2) Personal Base; and (3) What's New. The Knowledgebase can be used to store things like the employee manual, general company rules and procedures, disaster recovery procedures, compliance procedures, etc. Individuals can use The Personal Base to store their personal information. What's New is a chronological list of additions and changes to the Knowledgebase.

Armed with the features listed above, and many others that are too numerous to detail here, an advisory firm can become highly automated using Goldmine. In order to harness Goldmine's full potential, it will probably be necessary to hire a consultant, preferably one with experience serving financial advisors. One such firm that a number of our readers have used is Trumpet, Inc (www.trumpetinc.com). There are some individual advisors who have harnessed Goldmine's potential without the help of a consultant and made it work (for a profile of one such adviser, see Figure 31.24 at the end of this chapter).

JUNXURE-I 3.0

Some of the better CRM packages available to advisors these days go far beyond managing client contacts. The best systems can help you market, manage data, store and retrieve documents, manage employees, control workflows within the office, monitor virtual work partners, and much more. In other words, a good CRM system, if used correctly, can contribute directly to your practice's efficiency and profitability. Junxure-I is definitely one of the better CRM packages available to financial service professionals today.

A More Powerful Product

There are a number of things that set Junxure-I apart from lesser programs. The primary distinguishing factor is that a financial planner originally designed it for his own office. Since that time it has incorporated literally hundreds of suggested enhancements from other experienced advisors. Since Junxure-I was built by financial planners for financial planning practices, it contains fields for almost every type of information a planner is likely to require, including, but not limited to, personal information, family information, client goals and objectives, investment information, estate planning information, and insurance information. Used properly, Junxure-I can document not only every client interaction, but also every action taken within your office on behalf of a client. The documentation produced by Junxure-I can be used to meet compliance objectives, improve productivity, improve profitability, and measure employee performance.

Let's look at a few examples of how Junxure-I differs from other programs. The main menu screen provides access to all of Junxure-I's powerful features.

The main screen also offers a summary of important information, such as clients and pending actions. The views are customizable, so advisors can view information in a way that is most convenient for them. As illustrated in Figure 31.13, there are two rows of buttons above the list of pending actions. The bottom row allows the user to control how pending actions are displayed. The user has a choice of filtering for and displaying only overdue actions (of which hopefully there are none); those due within the next one, two, or three weeks; or those due in the next one, two, or three months. If no filter is chosen, all pending actions are displayed. The top row of buttons offers users the ability to further fine-tune the way "to dos" are displayed. The view can be displayed chronologically in ascending or descending order, by client, or by priority.

Figure 31.13

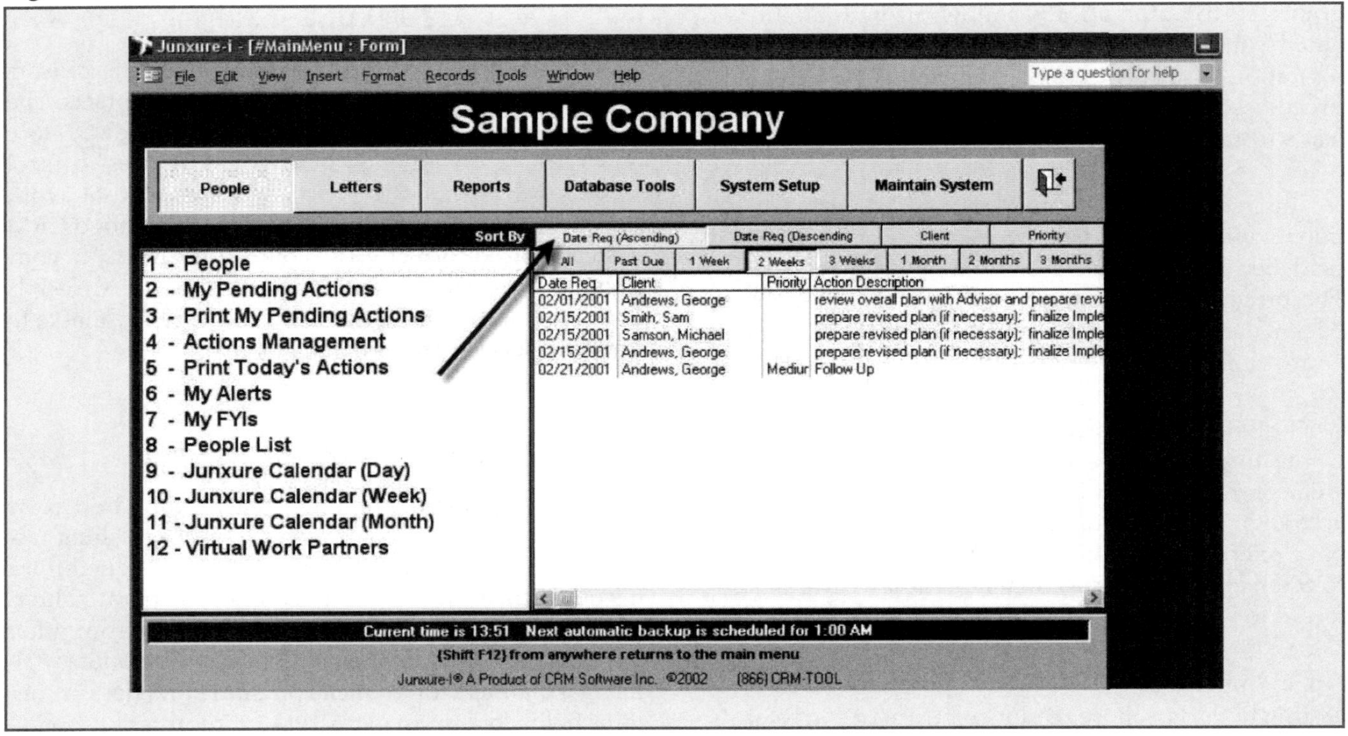

On the main contact screen, users have access to fields capable of storing extensive client contact information. Loads of additional information is accessible by clicking on one of the other tabs (personal information, profile, actions, etc.).

The information field labels in the phone section can be easily edited by double-clicking on the label. So, for example, if one wanted to change the "car" phone number label in Figure 31.14 to "mobile" or "cell", it could be easily done. Any changes made to a label apply only to the individual client record. The advisor must remember that the field will retain its original label when running reports.

Junxure-I offers fifty user defined fields for customization for each client record. User defined custom fields are fully searchable, so reports can be run on them, and they will appear with the field labels that users assign to them.

Custom fields can be used as merge fields. For example, let's say you decide to offer account aggregation to your clients. Once the system is in place, your firm could create individual user names and passwords for each client, enter the information in Junxure-I within custom fields that you create, and then construct a form letter to all clients that would draw the account name and passwords from the field you created, automating the whole notification process. The benefits of this process are threefold: (1) the information is stored for future reference within Junxure-I; (2) the mailing to clients is highly automated, and it can be repeated at any time; and (3) a record of each mailing is linked to the individual client record automatically.

The "Tax & Suitability" subsection of the "Profile" tab offers easy access to a snapshot of the clients' income tax situation, including state tax liabilities, short-term loss carryover, and long-term loss carryover. The subsection even provides a space to jot down tax and suitability notes right within the section (Figure 31.15).

Recently, the insurance section received a complete makeover. The insurance detail screens are context-sensitive. Rather than displaying every possible field on every detail screen, Junxure-I will only display the fields relevant to that policy type.

Financial planners can now track the following types of insurance policies: life, disability, LTC, health, dental, home, auto, and umbrella. Data entry in this section has been greatly simplified. Junxure-I makes generous use of drop down menus here, so users can select an item with a single click mouse click. Drop- down menus improve productivity because: (1) they speed up data entry; (2) they reduce errors; and (3) they make it possible to delegate data entry to a subordinate.

Figure 31.14

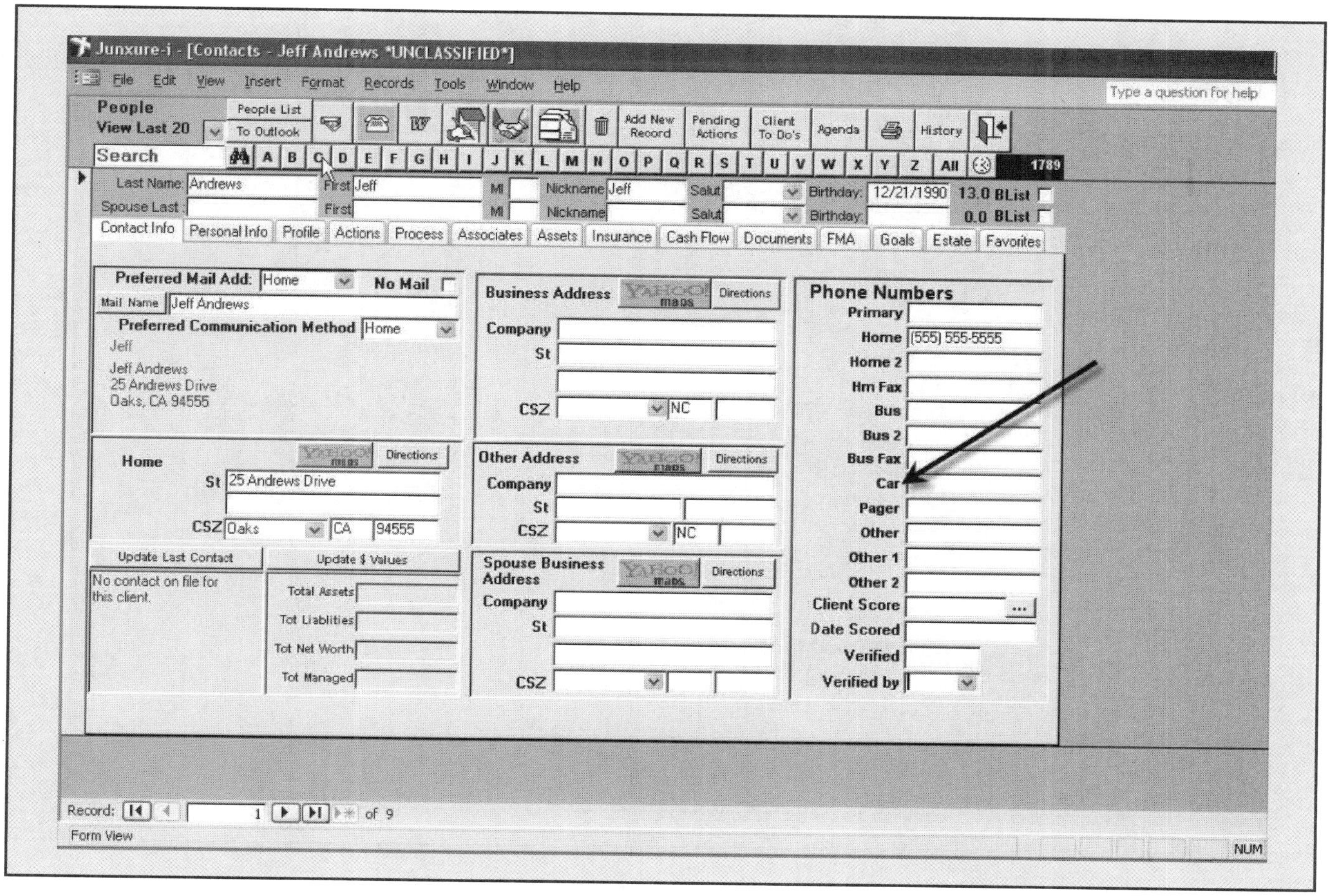

An options report, accessible from the "assets" tab, provides a quick and easy way to view all of a client's employee stock option holdings. Fields include grant date, current stock price, exercise price, vesting date, expiration date, number of units, and current value. If the underlying stock is publicly traded, the stock price can be updated (15 minute delayed) from Yahoo.

Automation

There are a number of ways that Junxure-I helps automate a financial planning practice. One that we've already touched on is the mail merge. Many programs can do simple mail merges, which grab a client's name, address, and other "basic" information, in order to create form letters. Junxure-I, because it stores so much detailed information, can create much more effective mailings which draw upon the stored information. A letter wizard is included to help users put together highly customizable mailings. A report wizard allows users to create highly customized reports tailored to their own business needs.

One of Junxure-I's most powerful features is the ability to create and track "processes." A process is a collection of pre-mapped tasks, which insures uniformity and enables tracking. For example, each time a prospective client contacts your office for the first time, you will want a number of things to happen. First, a record of the call, with the prospective client's contact information, should go in Junxure-I. That will trigger a "prospective client" process. This process, which is user defined, could include the following steps: a follow-up letter thanking the prospective client for the call and confirming an appointment date; second, the emailing of a checklist of things to bring to the meeting; third, an email two days before the appointment with a reminder of the appointment and a link to a website with driving directions to your office; fourth, a thank you for visiting and an invitation to become a client. All of the above individual tasks can be assigned to different members of your firm and grouped into a single "prospective client task." With the click of a mouse, the whole process can be initiated, assigned, and tracked. By creating processes for as many groups of tasks as possible (processing a new client, opening a small

Figure 31.15

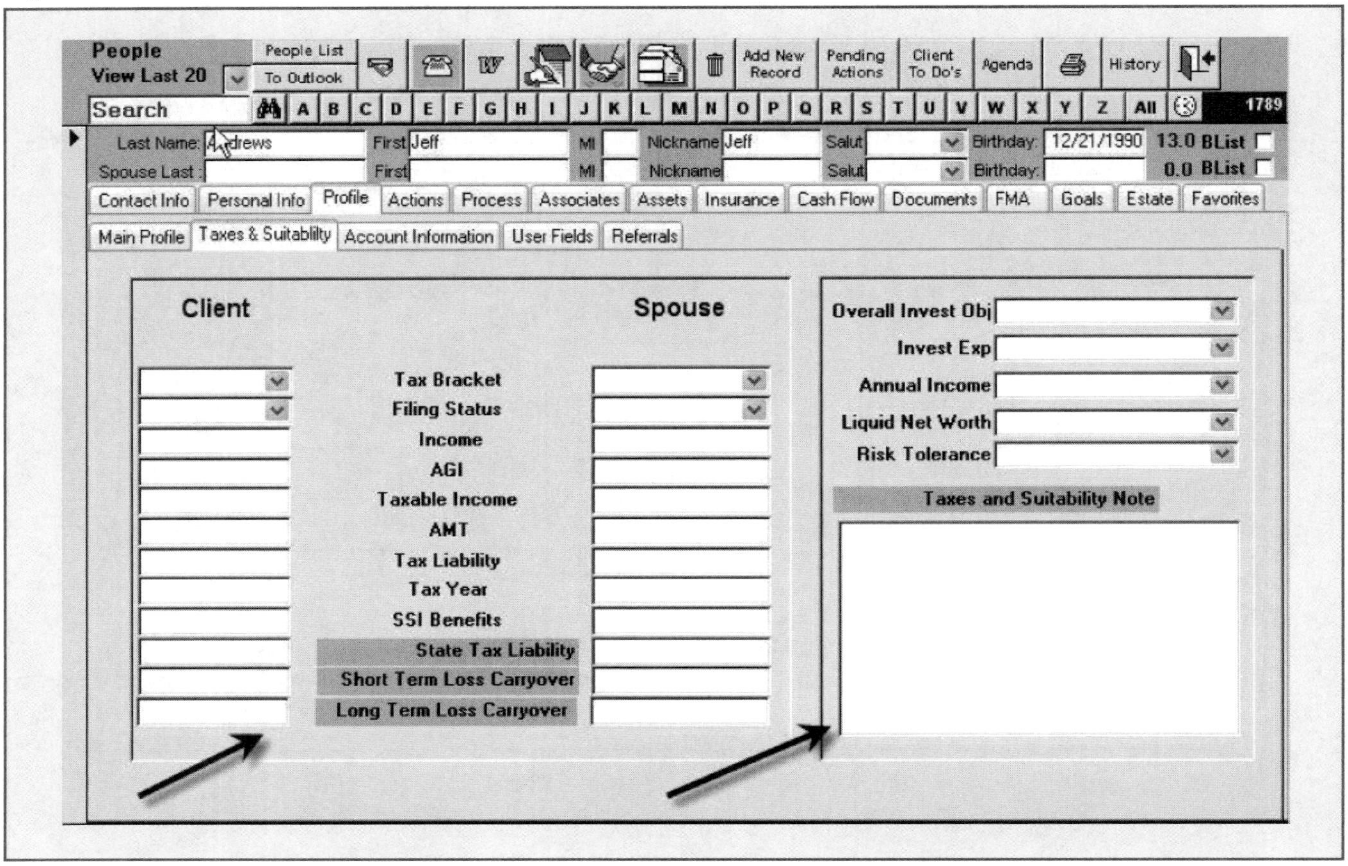

business retirement plan, etc.), users can reap huge productivity gains.

The program can be used to track email for compliance purposes. All email can be captured within Junxure-I and easily viewed. A "View email" button displays all emails sent to or received from the client, in chronological order. Emails can be sorted in a number of ways.

Within Junxure-I, any kind of document can be linked to an action (Figure 31.16).

The "View Edit Client Actions" screen contains a timer for those who bill clients hourly or for those who internally track the cost of servicing a client. An employee can start the timer while working on behalf of a client, and then make an entry, if desired, in the note, action, or follow-up action column. Whether a note is added or not, clicking on the "1" button will add the allotted time to the "Minutes" window in the "Notes" section. Buttons "2" and "3" perform the same action in the "Actions" and "Follow-Up" sections.

Advisors who choose to use the timer can generate a number of time reports. Armed with these reports, a firm can analyze how much time is being spent on certain clients and activities. This can lead directly to an analysis of how profitable – or unprofitable – some clients are and what activities are being performed in a less than optimal fashion.

Keywords can be assigned to actions (Figure 31.16). This makes it easier to search for an action at a later date. Junxure-I does not include any preprogrammed keywords, so you'll have to supply your own.

Junxure-I is one of the most comprehensive, easiest to use, industry specific CRM solutions available to financial service professionals. Its long list of CRM, workflow, and business management features, combined with a user-friendly interface make it an excellent choice for the serious financial service professional.

PROTRACKER

ProTracker is very similar to Junxure-I in many ways. It too was originally designed by a financial planner for his own business, and then marketed to other experienced advisors who offered feedback that

Figure 31.16

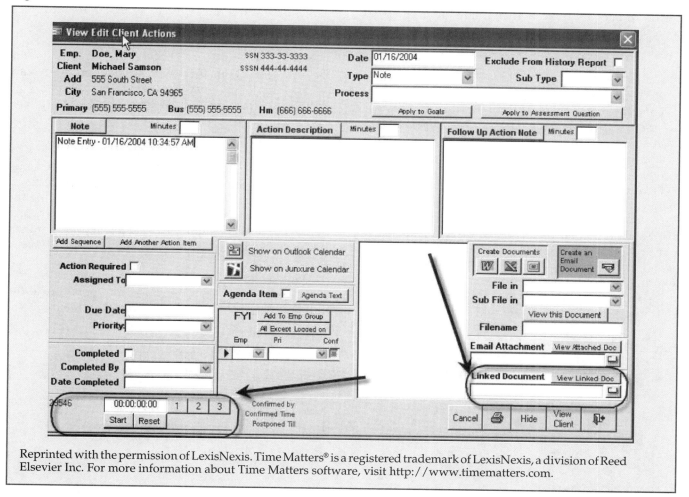

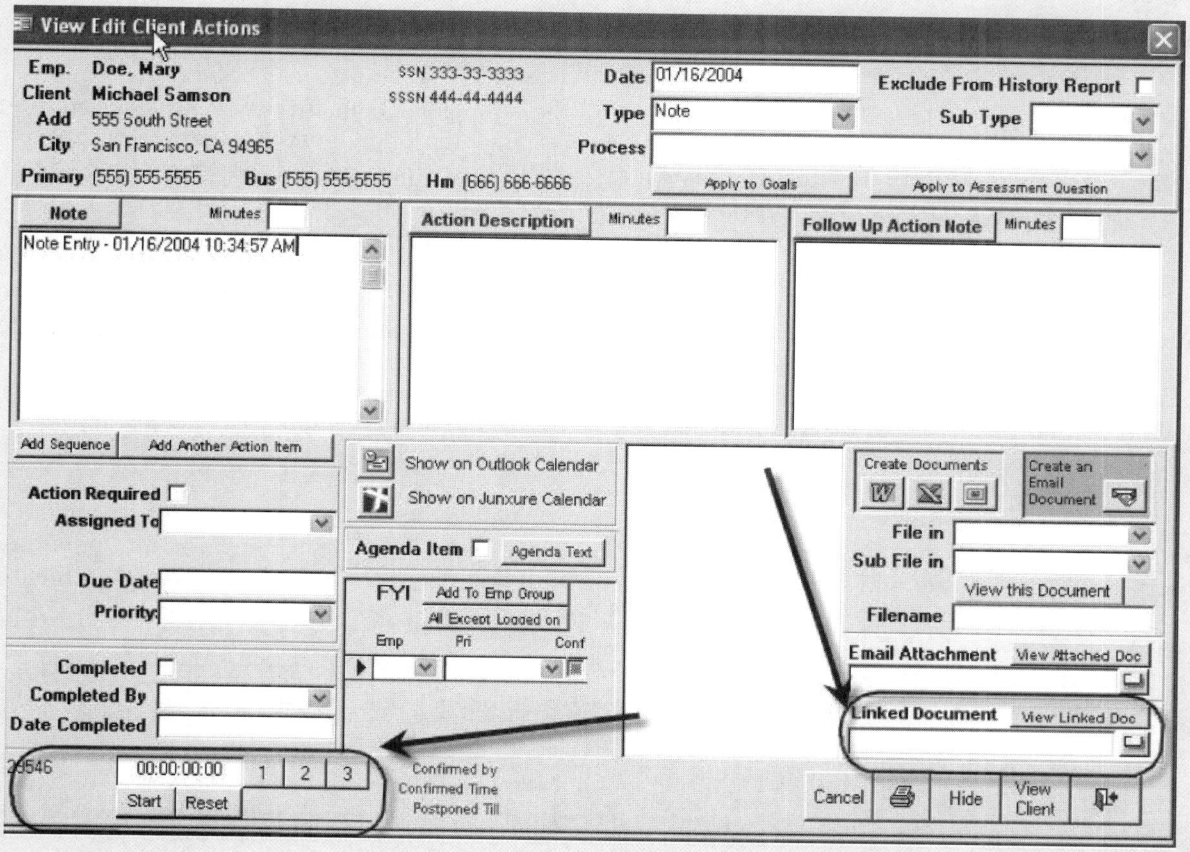

Reprinted with the permission of LexisNexis. Time Matters® is a registered trademark of LexisNexis, a division of Reed Elsevier Inc. For more information about Time Matters software, visit http://www.timematters.com.

led to substantial improvements. Unfortunately, as we prepare this chapter, ProTracker is putting the final touches on a major upgrade to the program. The new version will be dubbed ProTracker Advantage. Since we have not yet had a chance to test it, we will limit our remarks to some general observations.

In the past, based on overall feature sets, ProTracker and Junxure-I have been more similar than different. Both can track extensive amounts of client data, and both offer wonderful automation and productivity tools. Based on past versions, we generally had a slight preference for Junxure-I because we felt it was a bit more intuitive and easier to navigate. We've had a chance to preview the upcoming ProTracker Advantage, and we'd say that ProTracker is closing the gap with regard to the interface. We understand that the new version offers a number of new features, such as the ability to scan and capture information from business cards (and automatically enter the data in ProTracker), and a new module that calculates required minimum distributions for retirement accounts.

We believe that both ProTracker and Junxure-I are both excellent products, and that either one will pay for itself in short order provided that the purchaser takes the time to learn the program and use it properly.

TIME MATTERS 5.0

Time Matters (www.timematters.com), a practice management software program, has long been one of the most popular and widely used programs of its type in the legal profession. Time Matters is now offered in three product lines or series: Legal, Business, and …ccounting. We tried out the Accounting Series. All of the series are available in a Professional version for smaller offices and an Enterprise version (SQL) for larger installations. The product is feature-rich, customizable, and it has a loyal following in the legal profession.

Overview

There are four main sections to Time Matters: (1) events; (2) "to-dos"; (3) contacts; and (4) engagements. Each section can be accessed from the buttons on the toolbar pictured in Figure 31.17.

Pictured in Figure 31.17 is the default view of the main contact screen – the one you see when you push the "Contact" button on the toolbar. A contact list is displayed in the left pane, and primary details of the active contact are displayed on the right pane. The default sort on the left is by last name (notice the bold lettering in the column heading), but you can sort by any column. Simply click the column heading with your mouse, and the program will sort that column in descending order. Click the column again and it will sort in ascending order.

Notice the "quick tabs" above the contact list on the left. These tabs are user definable, and they can be used to "quick sort" contacts. For example, you could create tabs for clients, prospective clients, vendors, etc.

The right pane is a preview pane. It allows users to see some of the details a record contains without actually opening the record. The application includes a number of preformatted layouts, but the area is highly customizable. Basic layouts can be created in a word processor; however, it is also possible to create rather sophisticated layouts using an HTML editor.

Double clicking on a name in the Contact List displays the Contact Form (Figure 31.18). This is where you will find detailed information about the contact.

Figure 31.17

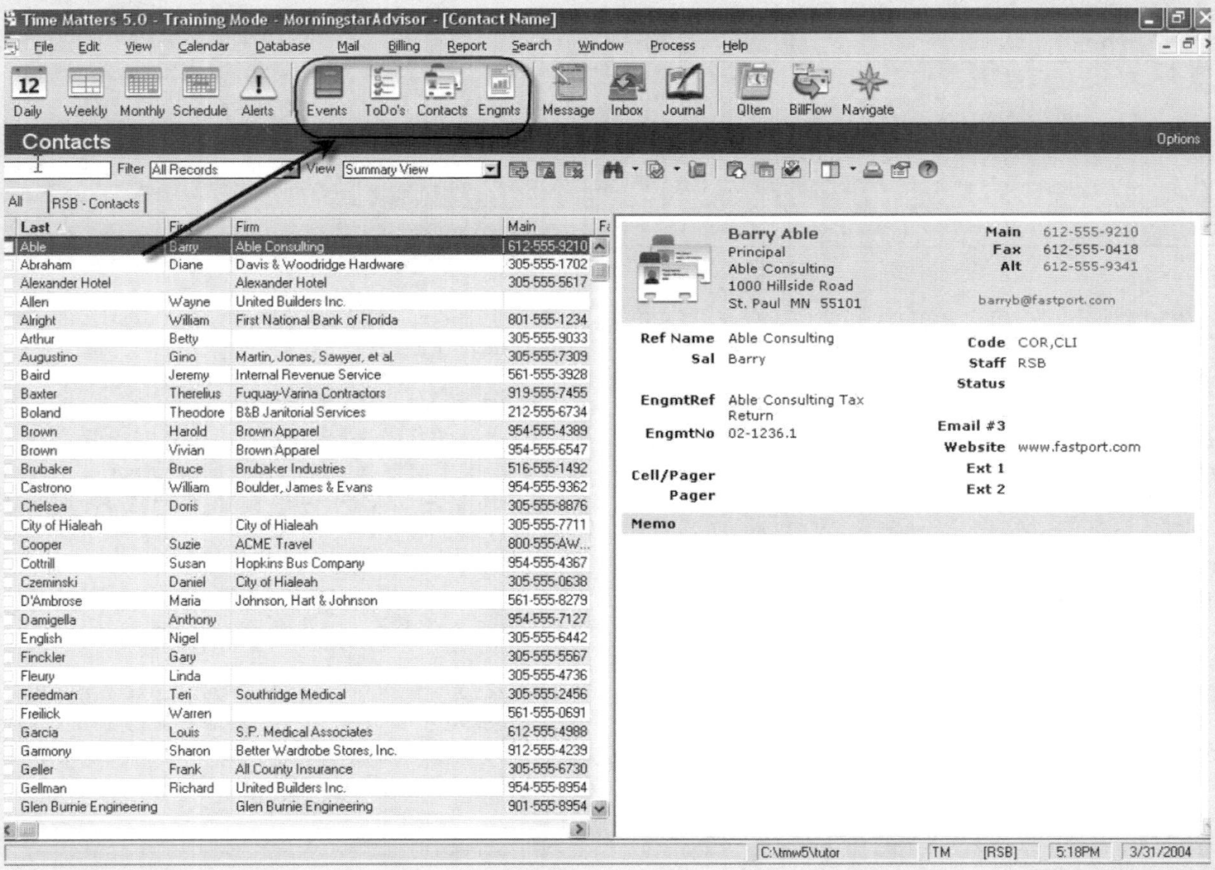

Reprinted with the permission of LexisNexis. Time Matters® is a registered trademark of LexisNexis, a division of Reed Elsevier Inc. For more information about Time Matters software visit http://www.timematters.com.

The main contact record offers sufficient room for the most critical information and is customizable. The next two tabs (here labeled "Officers" and "Additional") each contain about 38 additional, customizable fields by default. Fields can contain text and numbers; they can also contain caculations.

The Code field, in the upper right of the main contact screen, allows the user to divide contact records into helpful sub-categories (client, prospective client, mutual fund representative). Multiple codes can be applied to a contact record. Below the Code field is the Staff field. Here, a primary contact within the firm can be assigned to a contact, as well as five additional supporting staff.

Once a value is entered in the Code or Staff field, it can be searched upon, and quick tabs can be created based on the values. For example, if you create a code for clients, you can then create a quick tab for clients. All client records will be sorted, and contacts classified as clients will appear under the client quick tab on the main contact screen. After reading the manual, I was able to add a client quick tab to the main contact screen in less than a minute. The results are displayed in Figure 31.19.

When the Notify box is checked, as it is in Figure 31.19, it alerts someone else that the record should be reviewed. In this example, a recipient and message could be typed in the appropriate fields, or they could be selected from a drop down menu. Since the email box is checked, the notification will be sent by email. If the notification was going to another staff member, it could also be sent by instant message. Notifications can also be sent by auto message. This means that when a form is closed, the staff member(s) responsible for the contact in question will automatically receive a notification.

Engagements

Just about all of the widely used CRM packages in our industry are client centric; in other words, all of the

Figure 31.18

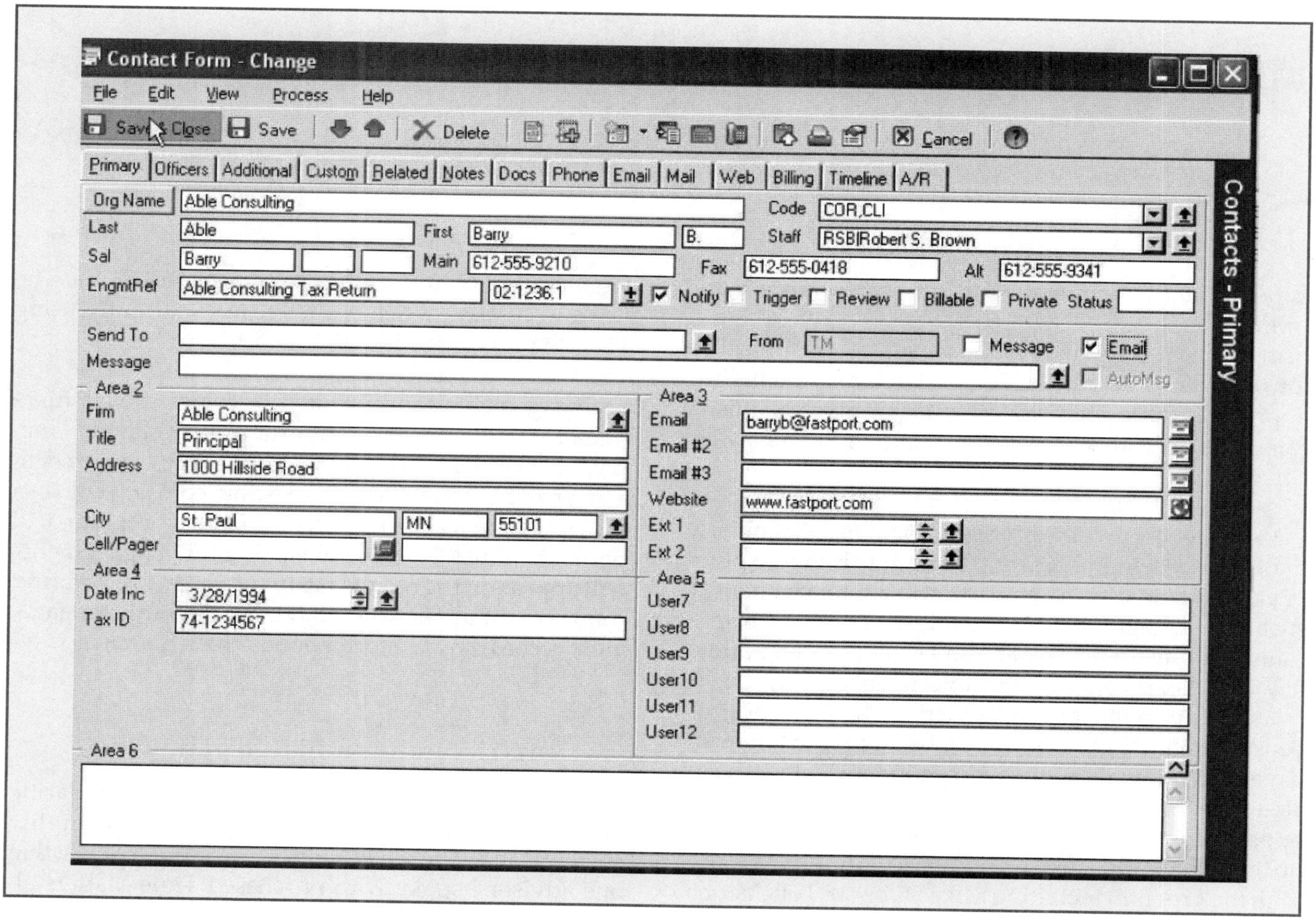

Figure 31.19

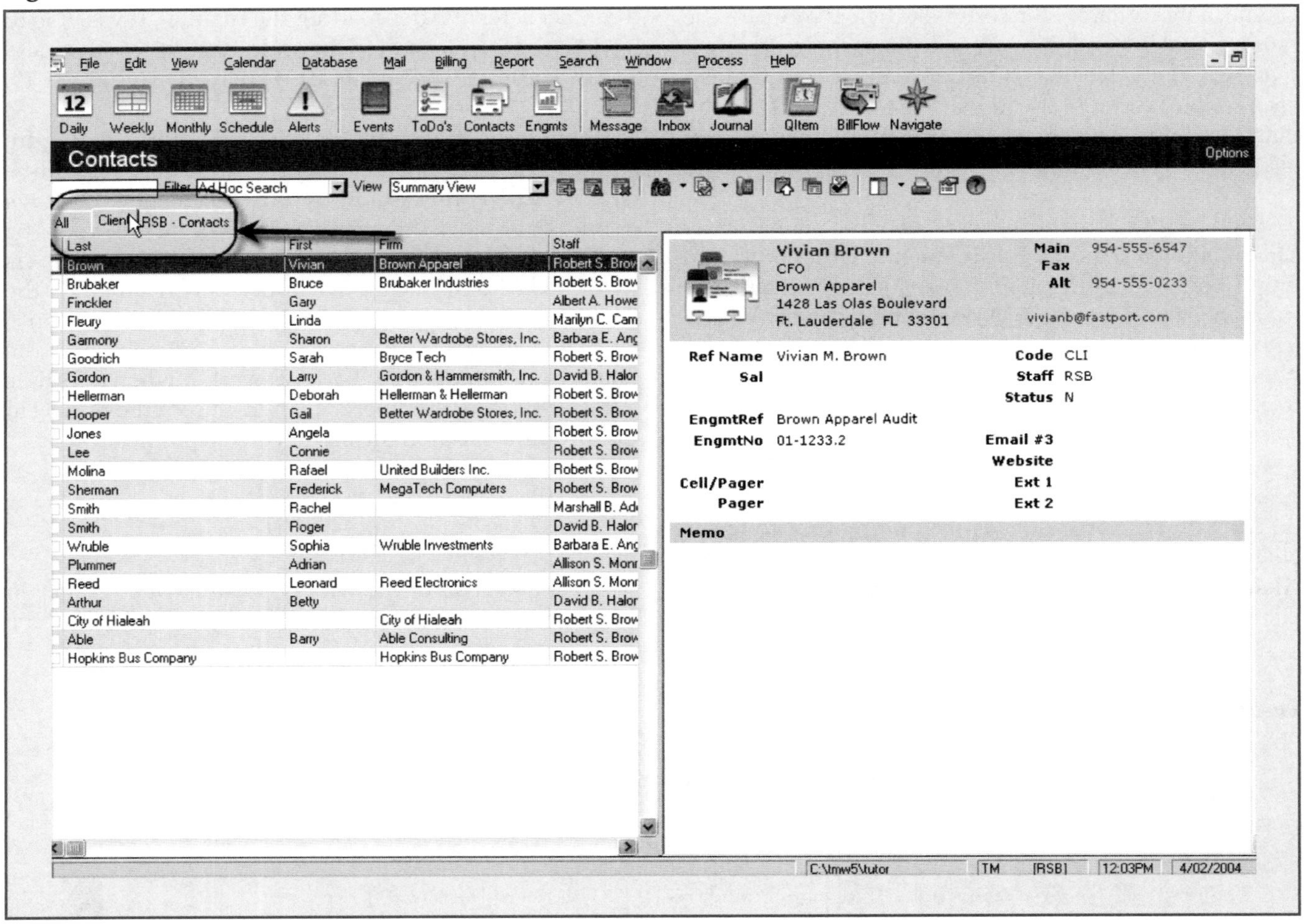

appointments, documents, and other records originate from and are stored with the client record. In small firms, or in larger firms where one person is responsible for the client engagement, this system may be highly appropriate; however, as firms grow more sophisticated and specialized, the client centric model may be constraining.

Consider the process of creating a financial plan for a high net worth individual at a firm comprised of experts in various fields. The construction of a financial plan at such a firm might include the following in house specialists: an insurance expert; an estate planning attorney; a CPA or tax attorney; an investment expert; a client relationship manager; and others. When a group of people are creating a plan, it may be more convenient to have all documents, notes, correspondence, etc., associated with the project linked to an engagement record as opposed to the client record. Time Matters allows you to do this, which appealed to a number of advisors familiar with the program including Mike Dubis, of Touchstone Financial, LLC and Tomas J. McFarland III, of The Darrow Company Inc. (Tom's firm is currently using Time Matters; Mike is still evaluating it.)

Engagements can be linked to contacts. This functionality provides two important advantages. First, it is not necessary to re-key information. If you begin a new engagement for an existing contact, you can select the contact from a list, and the program will populate most of the fields. Second, engagements will appear on the related tab in the contact record, and contacts will appear on the related tab of the engagement record, so all information is cross-referenced.

Time Management and Scheduling

Time Matters possesses very strong calendaring and group scheduling functions that are highly customizable. The scheduling features are so robust that one advisor I spoke with purchased Time Matters almost exclusively for its time management and scheduling capabilities. Charles E. Foster, of Blankinship & Foster in Del Mar, California told me that his firm uses ProTracker as their primary client management tool, because Time Matters is "not really designed for our business." Nevertheless, Mr. Foster finds Time Matters an invaluable scheduling tool: "We use it to manage the schedules of nine people. We also use it for managing our conference room schedule," he said.

Figure 31.20 illustrates the 21-day calendar view for one user. Double clicking on any of the blocked out time period brings up the event record for that time period. The view can be changed to daily, weekly, monthly, 5-day, 7-day, and/or 14-day with a mouse click. The multi-day calendars are customizable, so they can be set to a different number of days. Events can be moved from one time slot to another by simply dragging and dropping them. If a group event is rescheduled, the change will appear on all of the group members' calendars.

Assuming they are permissioned to do so, employees can bring the schedules of other employees onto the display by clicking on their names. The scheduler view (Figure 31.21) makes it easy to locate free time slots for multiple employees and schedule multi-person events.

As Mr. Foster alluded to above, schedule creation is not limited to people. Schedules can also be created for shared resources like conference rooms, LCD projectors, or corporate vehicles.

Timer

The program includes some nifty time-tracking capabilities. Time Matters can be configured so that whenever an employee begins a billable task in Time Matters, a timer launches. When the employee leaves the screen where work is being done, the program will either enter

Figure 31.20

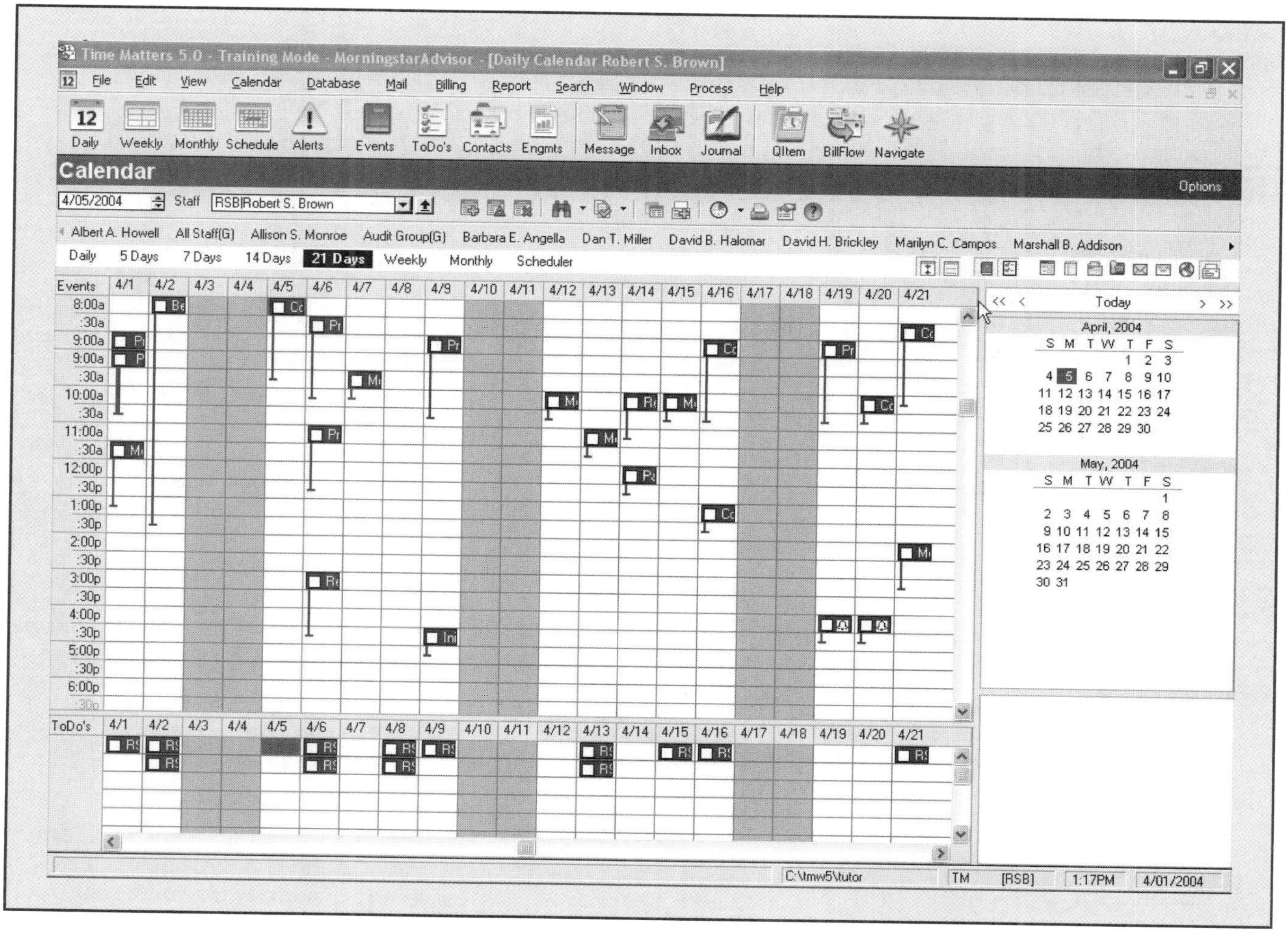

a time and billable amount, or prompt the user to do so (depending on configuration). Time Matters even offers multi-timer capabilities. For example, let's say that I start preparing a document for Mr. Smith, and I have a timer running. As I'm working, Mrs. Jones calls. As I shift my attention to the call, I'll minimize the Document tab (which will have been programmed to pause when minimized), and open a phone log, which will begin timing the call. When the call is completed, I'd relaunch the document, which will continue timing where it let off! This well designed time-tracker allows employees to "capture" more billable hours.

Personal Journal

The Personal Journal is a bit of a misnomer. Its real function is to allow users to create their own custom information view, sort of like a personal home page. The view displayed in Figure 31.22 below illustrates one "look." On the left, a weekly calendar is displayed. To the right, all of this user's recent phone calls, messages, notes, and emails are displayed. Users can set filters for the records, specifying the date ranges and types of information they would like to be displayed.

The little icons in the grey (on actual product screen) area below the green (on actual product screen) stripe are context sensitive. They change depending upon which section you are working in, in order for you to have the proper tools for a given section. For example, since the notes section is highlighted here, there are icons to add, change, or delete a record, followed by icons to mark a record as done, or mark a record as not done.

The Personal Journal has a nice usability and customization feature, but it is more than that, because managers can view the records of other employees here to see what they are up to. It is also possible to look at different time periods, so past and future records can be reviewed.

Figure 31.21

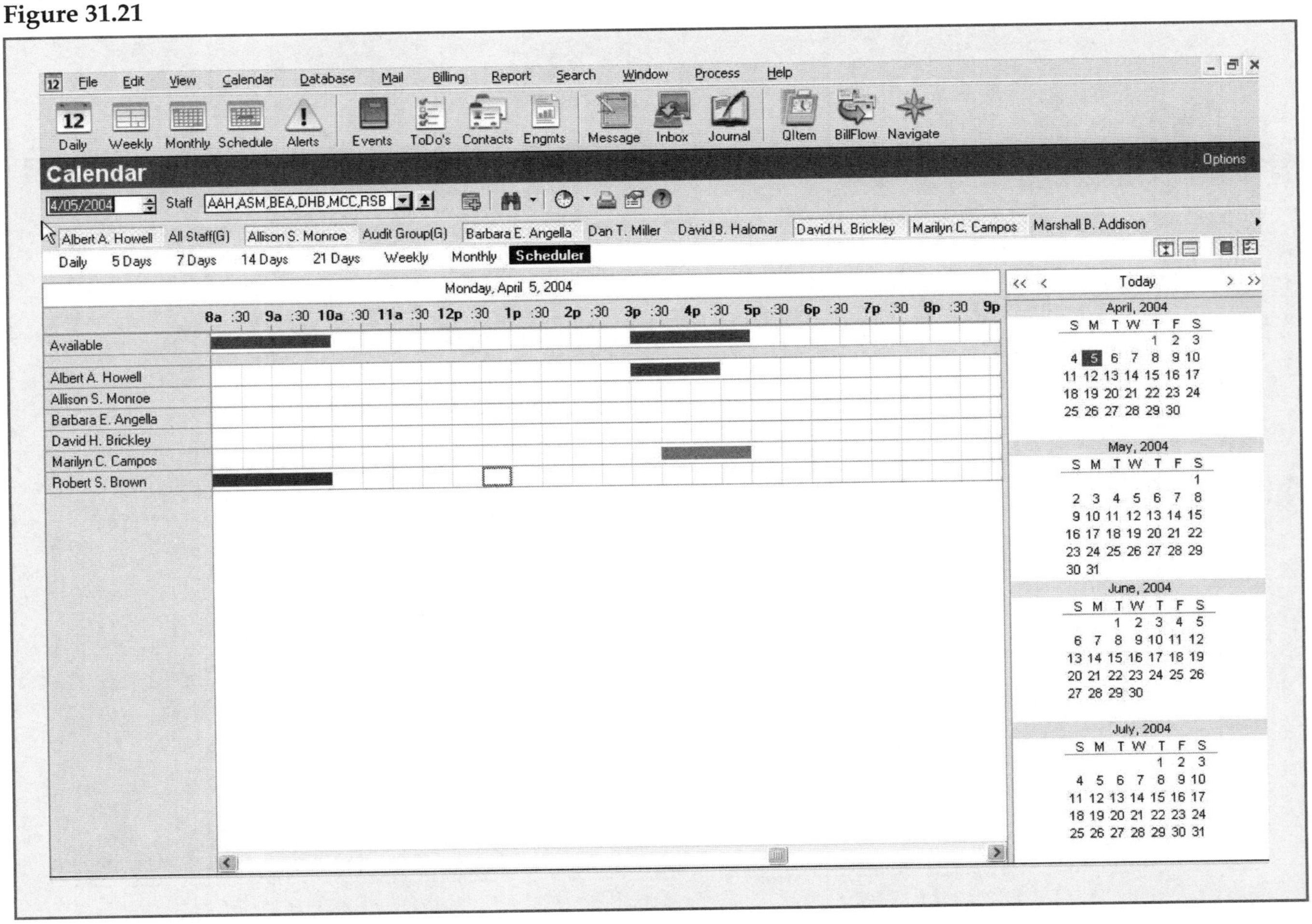

Figure 31.22

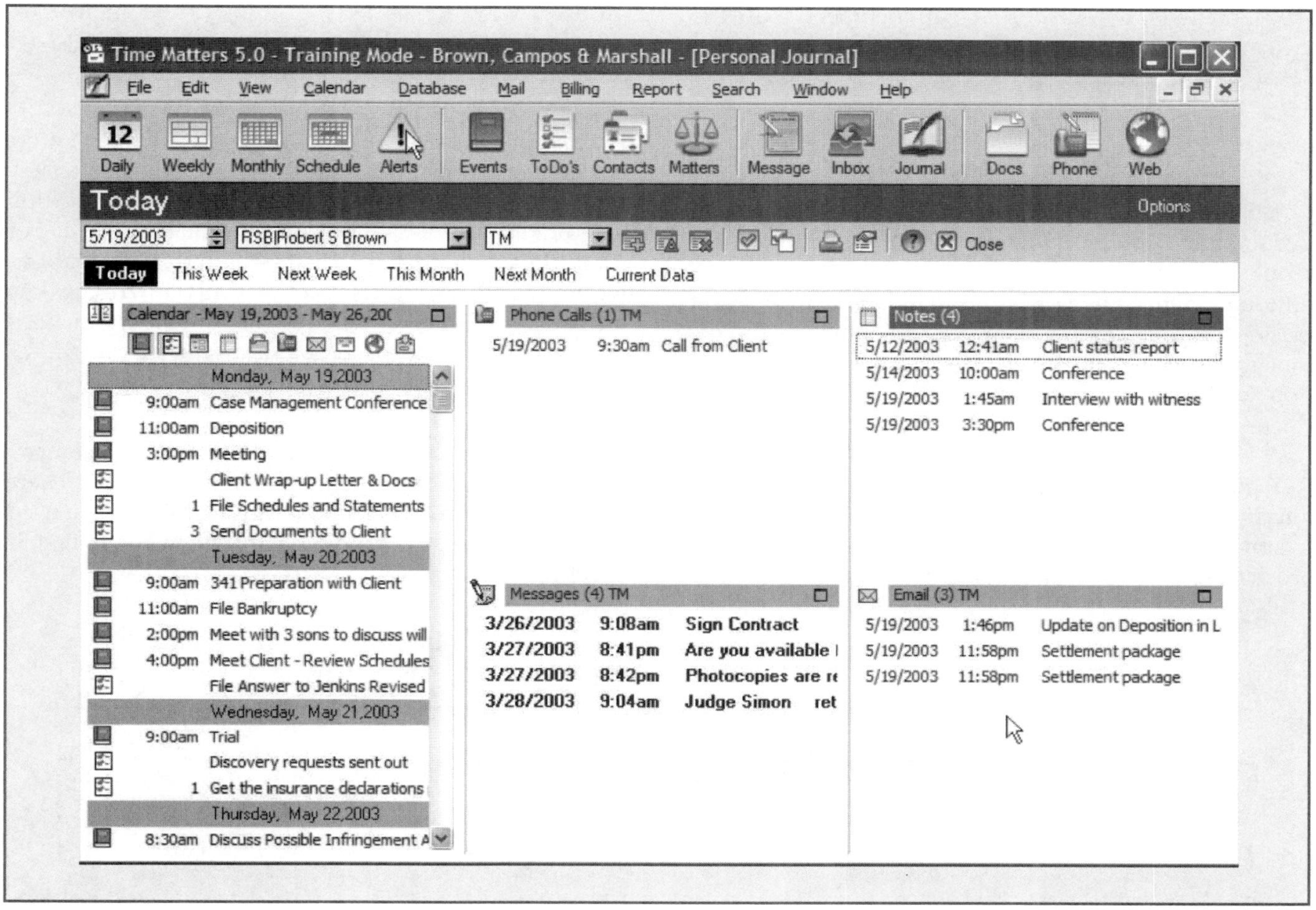

Triggers

Triggers are actions that automatically cause another action to take place. One obvious use of triggers is billing. A trigger can be set up so that as soon as an event or project is completed, a billing record is generated. Triggers can be used when new clients or prospective clients are entered into the database, or when a prospective client in the database is converted to a client. The triggers can cause one or a series of multiple subsequent actions to take place.

Chain Templates

Chain templates allow you to script more complex work flows. For example, if you wanted to script out multiple steps when a new prospective client is entered into the database – mail introductory letter; confirm appointment by phone, email, or mail; send directions; send appointment checklist, etc. – you might set up a Chain template. Each step of the operation would be scripted to a date, and each action would automatically be assigned to the appropriate staff person.

Custom Forms Templates

Custom forms can be used in a number of different ways. One use would be to create client documents that are used on a repetitive basis such as data gathering forms, checklists, risk profiles, and the like. Another way they can be used is to create additional fields for information you want to store about a client. Custom forms are displayed on the custom forms list, and they can be copied or linked to any main record. The advantages of using custom forms within the program are many. Let me highlight a few. First, the information goes directly into the system. There is no need to generate a paper form, fill it out manually, and then rescan it (unless a client signature is required, of course). Second, it is immediately part of the firm's permanent records. Third, some information, like the time, the client, the engagement, etc., will be automatically entered. Fourth, it becomes easy to notify other staff members, share the information with them, and initiate related actions right from the data-entry screen.

Document Management

Documents can be linked to contacts, engagements, events, and "to-dos." I would think that most users would primarily link them to contacts or engagements, although there could be reasons to link them to an event or "to-do" – for example, if you were planning an important meeting, you might want to link copies of documents you will be taking with you to the event record. The documents tab of a contact is displayed in Figure 31.23.

Figure 31.23 clearly illustrates how documents can be subdivided into topics through the use of tabs. In this example, there are tabs for general correspondence, worksheets, fax cover sheets, etc. There are a number of different ways to create tabs and sort documents. We won't go into details here, but there is quite a bit of flexibility.

Documents can be created from within Time Matters by clicking on the "Add" document record button. They can sometimes be created within the native application and linked seamlessly to Time Matters as well. For example, when I installed Time Matters, three buttons were added to my word processor (MS Word) that allow me to access Time Matters document related functions from right within MS Word, and to save documents as a Time Matters document.

Time Matters supports versioning, so that you can maintain multiple versions of the same document. There is also a check in/check out feature, which can be used to prevent changes to a document when someone has checked it out.

Figure 31.23

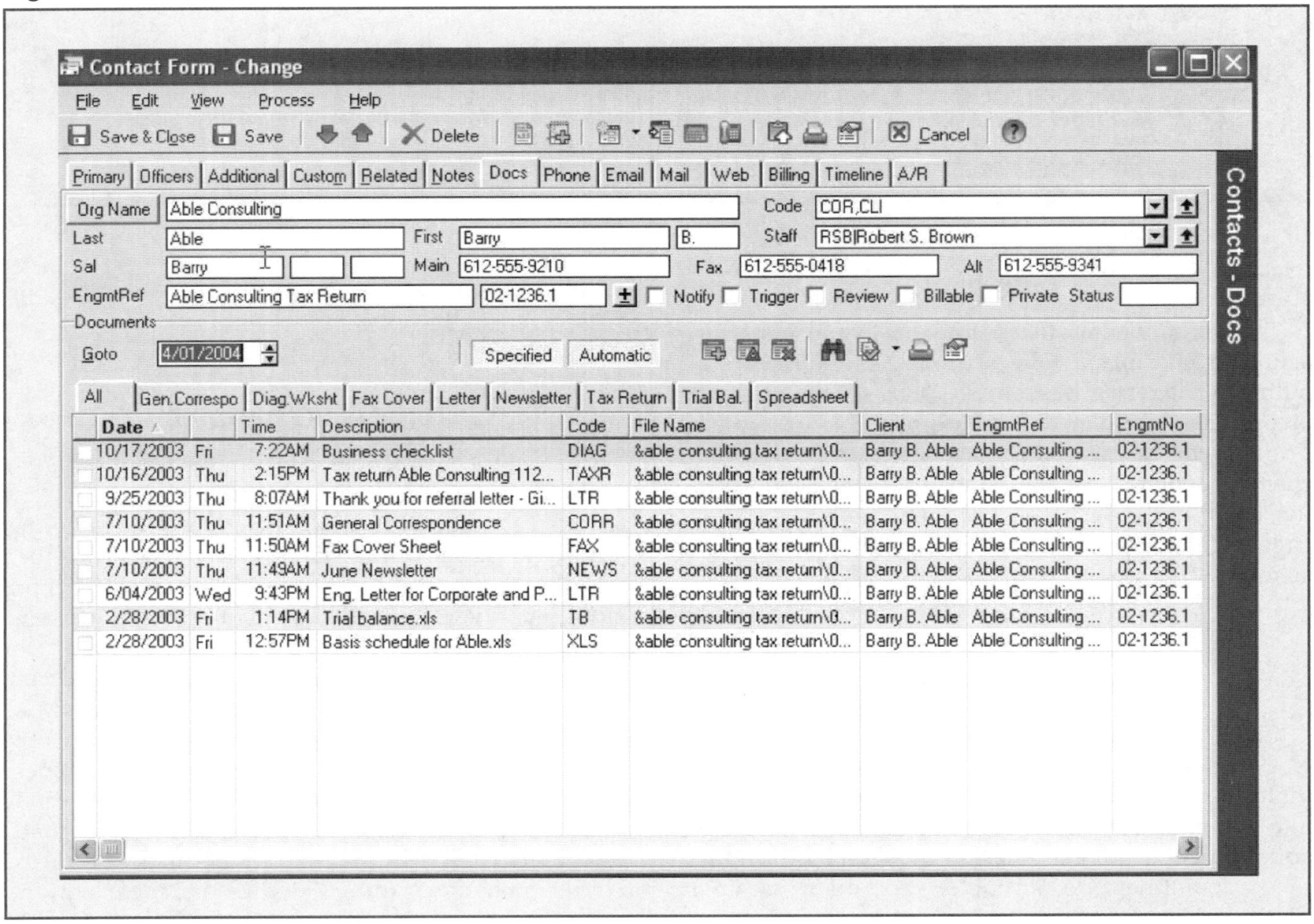

The program can be linked to Worldox, a powerful document management system that I discussed in my book *Virtual-Office Tools for a High-Margin Practice*. Time Matters possesses some fairly powerful search capabilities of its own, so not everyone will feel the need for Worldox, but there are a number of reasons one might want to add Worldox to the mix. One is that Time Matters users will be able to search for documents that don't reside within the Time Matters program. Another is that it may further automate the document naming and filing process. A third reason would be to maintain consistency for those who already use Worldox to manage documents.

In addition to the document tab on the main record types, there is a master document list, which includes every document in the system. The master document list can be tagged, sorted, filtered, searched, and processed.

Documents that reside outside the system can be brought in through various methods. For instance, you can drag and drop a single document from Windows Explorer to the main document list or to the document tab of a client record. You can also drag and drop multiple documents. When multiple files are brought into Time Matters, a document profile form opens. This form allows the user to supply information that is common to all documents.

Scanning

Documents can be scanned into Time Matters. The program offers a direct link with PaperPort, but unless one wanted to make use of the annotation features and other PaperPort tools, scanning directly into Time Matters should do the trick. The program supports scanners that use a standard TWAIN driver. ISIS and WIA drivers are not currently supported.

Formattable Clipboard

I am sure that most readers are familiar with the Windows clipboard, which allows users to "cut" text or graphics from one application and "paste" it into another one. Time Matters includes a very powerful clipboard that blows the Windows clipboard away! With this clipboard, it is possible to create, format and store text and fields for future use. For example, you could store an engagement letter for use with the personal clipboard. To send it to a new client, you would open a blank document while in the client record, and the boilerplate text, along with the contact's personal information, would all be displayed. Granted, you could get much the same result with a document template and a mail merge, but this is faster, and the Formattable Clipboard can perform one trick that a template/ mail merge cannot.

Conditional operations can be programmed into the Formattable Clipboard based on the contents of various fields. So, for example, if you generally used one letter for residents of New York, but New Jersey required different language or an additional paragraph, you could program the clipboard to make the changes if the "state" field in the client's home address equaled New Jersey. If you use different fee schedules based on the type of engagement, you can have the clipboard insert the fee schedule based upon the "type of engagement" field.

Phone Calls

For maximum office efficiency, Time Matters should be used to log all phone calls. The program can be set up so that employees dial phone calls from within Time Matters. It is also possible to configure the program so that it is notified of incoming phone calls. Time Matters will then attempt to identify the caller, and if the caller is identified, it will open the caller's main contact record.

Email and Fax and Instant Messaging

Time Matters has its own built in email system. It also works with MAPI compliant email systems (many commonly used networked email systems are MAPI compliant). The Time Matters email system offers rules to automate procedures, and it includes its own anti-spam tools. The advantage of using Time Matters for email is that everything can be organized and linked to a client or project. In addition, emails can be searched using the more powerful Time Matters search functions. If security is set so that emails cannot be altered, and if an audit trail is kept for all incoming and outgoing messages, Time Matters can go a long way towards solving email compliance headaches.

If WinFax PRO is installed, users can send faxes directly from within Time Matters. There's also an instant messaging system that allows communication between all users who are accessing the same Time Matters database.

Printing to PDF or RTF

Reports, documents, and templates can be saved from within Time Matters as either PDF or RTF files. For most users, PDF will be the format of choice; however, RTF might be useful on the odd occasion that you have to send a non-confidential communication to someone with very limited computer skills (someone who can't open a PDF file). This is a very handy feature if your firm emails documents to clients or others. PDF files can be created, stored, password protected (if desired), and emailed all from within Time Matters.

Synchronization

Clones of the Time Matters database can be created on other computers, and later synchronized with the host database. This might be useful, for example, when employees are on the road and are not connected to the host computer. Basic Contact, Event, To-Do, and Note fields can be synched with PDAs using the Palm OS.

Security

Time Matters has rather impressive security features. Security can be set at the company level and at the individual user level. The security feature is turned off by default; the administrator must activate it. Security settings can be applied at the application level, the record level, or the field level. In the case of program areas (things like permission to backup, import, or export), the only choices offered are to grant permission or not. In the case of fully controlled program areas (calendars, contacts, engagements, etc.) permissions can be granted to view, add, change, or delete. Even if users are granted access overall, they can still be restricted from certain records or fields. For example, a user might have complete access except the permission to alter a billing code field. The program will also track changes. An audit can be generated by login code, record, or field.

The security controls offer a great deal of flexibility. For example, the administrator can decide whether or not to require employees to log on each time they open time matters. If a login is required, Time Matters can easily be set so that employees can use their Windows logins and passwords to log onto Time Matters if desired – this eases the "password burden," but lowers security somewhat. If multiple users within an organization are to be assigned the same permissions (all members of a department, all interns, etc.), security templates can be created, so that a group of settings can be assigned effortlessly. Time restrictions can be set so that employees can only access files during their normal business hours.

What's Hot?

It should be obvious by now that Time Matters has an extremely rich set of features. It is really impossible to do full justice to its capabilities. Out of the box, the program offers a great deal of power, but to really get the full benefit of Time Matters, some customization will be necessary. The good news is that many types of customization, such as adding quick tabs, are relatively easy to accomplish.

Time management and scheduling are clearly strong points. Time Matters' strength in this area is all the more notable given the fact that the CRM packages typically used by financial service professionals fall far short in comparison.

Tomas J. McFarland III, of The Darrow Company, Inc., was one of the few advisors I talked with who has fully implemented Time Matters into a financial planning practice. When Tom's firm decided to install Time Matters, they installed Worldox and World Server (discussed below) for maximum flexibility. One aspect of the program Tom really likes is the ability to create engagement-centric, as well as client-centric records. He also likes the fact that Time Matters allows his firm to store and archive everything, including documents, phone calls, and emails in one place.

World Server, available at an additional cost, allows secure, browser based access to Time Matters from any Internet connection. It does not require a "virtual private network" (VPN). In order to use World Server, firms must be using the Enterprise Edition of Time Matters, and they must meet certain other hardware and software requirements.

Security is another strong suit. With Time Matters, the firm can control who has access to what information. The firm can also control the level of access with a high level of granularity. Employees can be blocked from access except during normal business hours. They can be granted limited or full access to various types of records and/or parts of the program. It is hard to imagine a security configuration need that Time Matters could not meet.

The timers could lead to greater profitability at many firms. As the focus of more and more firms turns from product to advice, it is important to receive appropriate compensation for whatever time is expended on a client. Whether you charge clients based on an hourly fee, a retainer, or assets under management, it is essential to understand the firm resources that are expended on each client or engagement, so that management can evaluate the profitability of those relationships. Time Matters gives users the tools to measure the true cost of each relationship, which empowers users to charge accordingly.

Billing is another strength. Time Matters has good billing capabilities. When used in conjunction with the timer, and a link to QuickBooks, Time Matters should meet the needs of many firms. For those who require more robust billing tools, DATA.TXT Corporation offers Billing Matters, a companion program that integrates with Time Matters to offer truly robust billing capabilities.

What's Not

For some, I fear that the very comprehensiveness of this program may be a disadvantage. CRM installations often fail because employees do not "buy in" to the new system. In some cases, new technology can intimidate employees; others are just uncomfortable with change of any sort. In order for Time Matters to produce the maximum benefit, all employees must be incentivized to adapt the new system and educated on how to use it properly.

This leads to my next point: many readers will underestimate the cost of installing and implementing Time Matters properly. A casual glance at the Time Matter website might lead one to believe that Time Matters is quite inexpensive – for the professional version, the first user currently costs $300, each additional user is $150. However, I suspect that for almost any multi-user installation, the SQL version, which is double the price per user, would be a better choice.

Training costs must be budgeted for. You will probably want at least some hands-on training. DATA.TXT Corporation offers it, as do consultants. Prices will vary depending on the level of service required.

Tom McFarland told me that he would never dream of recommending that anyone implement Time Matters without the help of a qualified consultant, and I agree with him 100%. To reap the full benefits of this program, it must be customized to your needs, and many of the more sophisticated customizations require professional help.

Unfortunately, finding the right consultant may be problematic. Since very few financial professionals are currently using the program, you may have trouble locating someone who both understands the program and your business. Expect to spend a fair amount of money for customization.

In short, for a 10-person installation, a total price of $10,000 would not surprise me. If one were to add all the bells and whistles, including Worldox, World Server, more extensive customization, etc., I could envision a bill double or triple that amount. If used properly, the money will be well spent; but don't fool yourself into believing that you can do this on the cheap.

Integration with other programs is somewhat of a question mark. Since the program does not currently cater to the financial service industry, there are no packaged links to portfolio management and financial planning applications. I'm assuming that a consultant could create some of those links without too much difficulty, but for now, each financial advisory firm is forced to do it independently, which adds to the overall cost.

As I was preparing this chapter, it was announced that LexisNexis is acquiring DATA.TXT Corporation, the developers of Time Matters. Potentially, this could be good news for the firm, if more money and resources are devoted to the program; however, there is also a chance that the new owners will decide to concentrate on their core legal market, or that other changes could take place that negatively impact the program's attractiveness to financial advisors. When I asked company spokesperson Charlie Rogers about this issue, he told me that any changes would be positive. According to Rogers "We've had a contractual relationship with LexisNexis for almost three years. Our President Bob Butler is still in charge. The new relationship will allow us to better serve our clients."

Service and support are somewhat of a question mark as far as I am concerned. In most cases, when a firm is aware I am working on a review (as a representative of this firm was), they tend to be very responsive. That was not the experience I had here. Maybe it is due to the recently announced sale of the firm, but maybe not. I received a couple of emails from advisors who told me that service at DATA.TXT Corporation left something to be desired. A number of random calls I made to the sales line yielded a recording as opposed to a person. My calls were returned, however.

The firm does offer a useful detailed manual (in print and electronic form). They also offer a CD that demonstrates many capabilities of the program. The website contains additional useful resources, including a Knowledgebase.

Bottom Line

Time Matters is a very impressive program. If implemented correctly, I feel certain that it will pay for itself in a very short period of time. That's not to say that it is appropriate for everyone; it probably isn't. While even a firm of just a few persons can take advantage of the automation capabilities that Time Matters offers, the workgroup capabilities may be more than they need. Since a small installation would require almost as much customization as a larger one, the cost per employee might be too high to justify the investment for firms of fewer than 5-10 employees.

I'd feel much more comfortable recommending Time Matters if the company exhibited a genuine interest in servicing financial service firms, but apparently they are relying on resellers to fulfill that function, which will ultimately increase the cost to financial advisor end users. However, since I've yet to come across anything this comprehensive that is specifically geared towards advisors, I think Time Matters is worthy of serious consideration by those firms who can benefit from its features and who are willing to pay the price to implement it correctly.

Note: The Time Matters® section of this chapter was adapted from an article that first appeared on MorningstarAdvisor.com.

Figure 31.24

CASE STUDY: HOW A CONTACT MANAGEMENT SYSTEM FUELED 400% GROWTH

By Joel Bruckenstein, CFP®
July 22, 2003

A commitment to technology and client service helped one financial advisor do better than weather the bear market—he grew his asset base 100% in four successive years.

Four years ago, Raymond D. Mignone, CFP®, didn't have much of a practice. A sole practitioner specializing in portfolio management and retirement planning, Mignone opened his shop at the height of the tech bubble—only to face one of the worst bear markets in recent history.

Prospecting was a particular struggle. Compounding the challenging market, Mignone, a firm believer in drip marketing, was having trouble getting his prospect letters out. For starters, his multiple mailings required too much of his time. The mail merge process (which actually generated the letters) was automated, but everything else required manual intervention. Prospect names had to be input one by one. Then, as the different mailings went out, names had to be copied and pasted from one tickler list to another. Determining who received what and where prospects stood in the series was often difficult. As a result, the whole drip marketing campaign was executed in an ad hoc fashion.

Client service was also a problem. There was no easy way to document every client interaction. Copies of letters and e-mails were retained on Mignone's hard drive, but they were not linked to one central client folder. Important phone calls were documented, but calls and contacts that were less critical were often overlooked.

The Challenge

Technology was the source of most of his problems, says Mignone. "When I started out, I used Microsoft's Office suite of products," he remembers. "In the beginning, this combination appeared to be all I needed. MS Outlook could communicate with the other programs I used, and there were templates available for various needs. I quickly discovered, however, that performing many routine tasks, such as tracking client data, documenting client contacts, and creating mail merges, seemed clunky and cumbersome."

Mignone wanted a program that could help him build his practice in two ways. First, he needed software that would automate his efforts to market his services to new prospects. Second, he wanted to establish a world-class customer service system that would help him retain clients and pick up a few referrals as a result.

The Strategy

Mignone began searching for alternatives to his clunky system by asking friends and colleagues for recommendations on client relationship management (CRM) programs. He looked at a couple of products specifically developed for financial planners, but was wary of getting involved with small software companies. Finally, he found a promising program at a local financial planning meeting, where a practitioner demonstrated how he used Goldmine to run his practice. "By the end of the meeting, I was sold," says Mignone.

Mignone immediately went out and purchased the program. (Note: Other popular contact management programs include ACT!, Maximizer, Junxure-I, and Protracker.) Although he was anxious to start using the software, he decided to take it slow and read the manual thoroughly. As he studied the program, Mignone began to see how his various office tasks could be automated. Before long, he began to develop a plan for automating his workflow.

Figure 31.24 (cont'd)

Step 1: Establish a drip marketing process

The first area Mignone wanted to automate was prospecting. He had leads—as a member of NAPFA, Mignone receives a list of qualified referrals every week. He also participates in the TD Waterhouse AdvisorDirect referral program. But he didn't have a good system for following up on inquiries and converting these prospects into clients.

So Mignone developed an automated drip marketing campaign consisting of nine mailings: an introductory letter that includes his firm's brochure, a special edition of his newsletter that doubles as an evergreen informational and marketing piece, and further letters that are designed to be both informative and inviting. The first three letters mail at three-week intervals; subsequent letters mail at six-week intervals. Once the marketing letters were in place, all Mignone had to do was program the mailing sequence and apply it to a given prospect.

Referrals from clients or professionals are handled—and coded—differently. These referrals receive one letter, followed by a phone call. After the phone call, they are usually ready for an initial meeting. If a good prospect does not become a client after the meeting, he is put on a separate drip cycle for one year.

The results have been impressive. Mignone estimates that 60% of his new clients came to him either directly or indirectly from the drip marketing campaign. The other 40% originate from his referral system.

Step 2: Develop a client management system

Given the success of his prospecting efforts, Mignone was anxious to put his software to work in the client service area as well. Rather than overwhelm himself and his assistant with an overnight revolution, he decided to move slowly. The first order of business was to start tracking each and every client interaction (phone calls, letters, and e-mails) and to document them in one central location. This required some new input processes. "Like anything else, it's all about creating good work habits," he says. "Once you get used to it, working with CRM software becomes second nature."

With the initial set-up complete, Mignone and his assistant entered additional information into the client records. Rather than customize manually, Mignone downloaded a free financial services template from the Goldmine website, which he tweaked to suit his firm's needs.

Some of the client details Mignone tracks include: names of all family members, marital status and length of time married, retirement account beneficiaries (including whether distributions to multiple beneficiaries are per capita or per stirpes), marginal tax brackets, tax-loss carryforwards, client health issues, and information on executors and powers of attorney.

As client records grew, reports were generated and analyzed. Almost immediately, certain patterns emerged. The reports indicated that the firm was manually performing a number of repetitive tasks, so Mignone targeted those activities for automation. For example, Mignone found he was spending a lot of time preparing prospects for the initial meeting. He would explain over the phone the information he wanted clients to bring with them. Later, his associate would call to provide driving directions to his office. Now, those tasks are automated. Mignone created e-mail templates that include a pre-meeting checklist for clients and driving directions to the office.

Mignone also developed a procedure for updating client records. First, he filters all of the fields in a client record; selects the ones he wants updated; and pastes them, with the current field values, into an e-mail, which he sends to the client. The e-mail requests that the client review all information, update it where necessary, and return it. This approach serves the following purposes:

Figure 31.24 (cont'd)

- Obtains the information needed to provide high-level service;
- Provides written documentation of the client's response; and
- Serves as a record that the firm has performed its due diligence by requesting the information regularly.

Step 3: Provide world-class service

As his business grew, Mignone automated a number of other processes that both he and his clients value:

1. **Quarterly estimated tax reminders.** Mignone has many clients, primarily small business owners and retirees, who are required to make estimated payments. Each quarter, his CRM program generates a pop-up reminder 10 to 15 days before estimated taxes are due. Mignone then filters his client list for all estimated tax clients (the filter is saved, so all he has to do is hit a button) and reviews the list. Next, he selects the estimated tax reminder template and creates a mail merge. The client is then sent an e-mail reminding him to pay his tax on time. The whole process is completed in a matter of minutes.

2. **Commentary.** Once a month, Mignone sends out a brief review of the market to keep clients apprised of economic developments.

3. **Short-term sales.** Mignone rarely makes short-term trades, but on some occasions it is necessary. He learned from system reports that short-term trades generate a high number of client inquiries, so now he takes preemptive action. Whenever a short-term trade is executed, the software automatically alerts the client and provides a brief explanation. The result has been higher client satisfaction and fewer client calls.

4. **Tax-loss harvesting.** When Mignone executes trades to harvest a tax loss, a letter (or e-mail) is automatically sent to the client explaining the motivation for the trades and the benefit to the client.

5. **Receipt of deposit.** Although clients receive confirmations from the custodian, elderly clients often call to check on the status of their deposits. Mignone now e-mails clients whenever a deposit has been credited to their brokerage accounts. Clients appreciate the high-touch service, and service calls are minimized.

6. **"Loving clients."** Depending on the account, Mignone puts each client on a 30-, 60-, or 90-day rotation. At the stipulated time, the software reminds him to initiate a personal touch. To Mignone, a personal touch is a face-to-face discussion or a completed phone call—e-mails and voicemails don't count. Once the contact occurs, the timer is automatically reset and Mignone can generate reports tracking the progress and results of his high-touch campaign.

The Results

While technology may have cost most investors money over the last three years, Mignone's investment has paid off big time. Business is booming. Assets under management have grown from $5 million to $80 million in the four years since he purchased the program—a 400% increase despite the bear market.

Mignone attributes almost all of his success to contact management. "It's been a godsend for me," he says. "It's allowed me to build a successful financial planning practice and manage it efficiently. I feel confident that I can, with one assistant, provide a higher level of customer service than most so-called full-service firms. CRM software has significantly reduced my service costs, improving my profitability. There is no way we could operate without it."

Chapter 32

UNDERSTANDING THE NEED FOR DOCUMENT IMAGING AND MANAGEMENT

Traditionally, in the financial service industry, it has been difficult to avoid paper. Comprehensive financial planning, investment related activities, insurance, estate planning, and the like all require that information be gathered and shared. Until recently, these tasks were performed with paper forms and paper reports. Investment accounts were opened through the use of paper forms, and all confirmations arrived in the mail on paper. To this day, most insurance applications are generated on paper, as are the resulting insurance contracts.

Client correspondence is another area that results in huge amounts of paper over time. The requirements as to exactly what must be retained vary. Federally registered investment advisors who are regulated directly by the Securities and Exchange Commission (SEC) must conform to one set of rules and regulations. Those under the primary jurisdiction of the National Association of Securities Dealers (NASD) must conform to a different set of rules. Advisors registered at the state level and insurance professionals may be governed by yet another set of rules. Whatever your exact case may be, it is generally considered good business practice to document client communications, and to retain records of those communications, whether it is required by regulation or not.

In order to operate efficiently, each firm must establish policies to efficiently deal with the deluge of documents they are required to process and store. The authors believe that the best method of dealing with paper is to avoid it whenever possible. Eliminating paper, to the extent possible, saves space, saves time, improves workflows, and ultimately lowers costs.

Dealing with paper is an expensive proposition. Paper costs money, as does ink. If you regularly produce or pay to produce marketing letters, color reports, brochures, etc., costs can quickly add up, especially when you factor in the costs of envelopes and postage. But there's more. If you store hard copies of all the documents you produce, before long your office will be overrun by filing cabinets full of records. These filing cabinets also cost money. They also take up space, which necessitates the rental of space to house them. Regulators generally require that your more current documents be housed onsite. Older documents may be moved off site to a storage facility. In either case, there is a cost involved in housing your paper records, often a substantial one.

Financial advisors incur additional costs whenever they are required to retrieve a document. An employee may have to go to another part of the office to remove and return files. This only requires a small unit of time, but as each employee repeats the action numerous times over the course of days, weeks, months and years, those small units of time add up. If a record stored off site is required, additional time and cost is involved. All this assumes, of course, that each required document is filed properly, and that it can be accessed without further complications when needed. If only life were so simple! Files do get misfiled, misplaced, and sometimes even lost. Whenever someone goes looking for a paper document, and has trouble locating it, additional costs are incurred.

Financial professionals have another consideration to deal with: workflows. Essentially, what we are talking about here is the flow of paperwork back and forth among the various people who must handle it before an operation is complete. Generally, we find that advisors working in medium to larger sized offices readily grasp this challenge, but those working in smaller offices and sole practitioners have a more difficult time understanding the need for work flow management. Let's be clear: this is an issue that all financial planning professionals must come to grips with.

Offices housing more than a few employees, or those working with Virtual Work Partners (VWPs), will often have a number of different persons involved in a process. For example, if a change is required to a client's investment portfolio, numerous staff persons could be involved. If a client made a request due to a change in circumstances, a note of the request would go out to other staff members. An administrative assistant would schedule the appointment and confirm it with both the client and the planner. A new investment policy statement might be required, a portfolio proposal generated, a report printed, trades would have to be made, etc.[1]

Each step of the way, team members would be performing work on documents, then forwarding them to other team members and the client for review. Good software can facilitate the flow of documents, make sure that nothing "slips through the cracks," and maintain a complete record of the process.

While sole practitioners face slightly different circumstances, they still have the need for this type of document workflow management. For example, when a new client engages an independent Registered Investment Adviser (RIA), investment accounts must be opened and client signatures obtained. The forms must then be forwarded to the custodian, and replies will be forthcoming confirming the new accounts or requesting additional information. In some cases, the sole practitioner will be performing all of these tasks and interfacing with the custodian; in other cases, the practitioner will hire a virtual assistant to perform some of these tasks. In both cases, the process will be more efficient if software is used to monitor and document the process.

While disaster recovery is addressed fully in Chapter 28, we'd be remiss if we did not at least mention it in the context of the "paperless office." If all of your files were paper based and stored in filing cabinets, what would happen if your office were to burn down, or if your files were otherwise destroyed? What would happen if other circumstances prevented you from accessing your paper files for an extended period of time?

Regulators are increasingly posing the above questions to advisors, and they are requiring coherent answers. Suffice it to say that digital records are relatively easy to copy, transport, and access from alternate locations. They should almost certainly be a part of any disaster recovery plan.

Technology in general, and document management/imaging in particular, is one area where new entrants into the field possess competitive advantage over their more experienced counterparts. "Paperless" office technologies are still relatively new, and far too many established firms have been slow to embrace them. One probable reason is that the thought of converting years of legacy paper files to a digital format is enough to cause some industry veterans nightmares. New entrants into the field are not burdened by legacy paper files, so if they start off on the right foot, and minimize paper from the outset, maintaining efficient, orderly files will be easy to accomplish.

TOOLS OF THE TRADE

Broadly speaking, there are six components that advisors need to consider when purchasing a "paperless" document system. Today, three of the components are mandatory and three are optional.

The three mandatory components are:

- Hardware (a scanner);
- Document imaging software; and
- Document management software.

The three optional components are:

- OCR software;
- Rights management software; and
- Workflow management software.

It is rather unusual for advisors to purchase each of the components individually. Many of the products we recommend come in "bundles," and include two or more of the above, but for clarity's sake, let's briefly consider each item separately.

Scanners – Hopefully, at some point in the not too distant future, the financial services community will move to a near paperless environment. All documents will be generated, signed, and transported digitally, and all legacy documents will be converted to digital formats. When that day arrives, there will be little if any need for a scanner. Until that time, however, a scanner is essential. Documents that are received in a paper format must be converted to digital files before they can be stored, and a scanner is one of the tools necessary for the conversion to take place. In a later chapter, we will offer specific scanner recommendations that will help you locate the right equipment for your business.

Document imaging software – As you scan a document with a scanner, the image of the document must be captured by a software program. Notice that we said, "image." Scanners, and the software that works with them, produce an image, or photograph, of the scanned document. In order to recognize the text in a document, or to edit it, one further step is necessary. We'll discuss that step in a moment.

Document management software – Documents, whether they originate as paper, or a digital file such as an MS Word document, must be filed with a system that allows for easy retrieval at a later date. Good document management software facilitates this task.

OCR software – Optical character recognition software, or OCR software, is used to convert scanned images into editable text. If you want to edit a document image, or perform a full text search on one, you will need OCR software. OCR will be discussed further in Chapter 34.

Rights management software – In recent years, increased attention has been focused on the protection of client privacy and the security of client records. Rights management software, which can be supplied either at the operating system level or at the document software level, offers a much higher degree of document security, while at the same time providing an audit trail. Rights management software allows an administrator to assign different levels of permission to different employees with a high degree of granularity. Positions can be granted globally, at the drive level, at the folder level, or at the individual document level. Administrators can determine exactly who can access, read, edit, copy, print and delete what. If desired, a record can be maintained of each version of each document, and a record can be kept of every person who came in contact with a document and every action taken with respect to the document.

Workflow management software – Advisors commonly use CRM software to manage workflow related issues, but there are some document management systems that provide this capability as well. As we discussed above, workflow management software can facilitate, manage, and record the flow of documents within, and sometimes beyond, the confines of the office.

In the next chapter we will address scanners. Most scanners include at least some basic document imaging software; in some cases, you will find that your document management software includes superior imaging tools. We will not address imaging software at length, but in Chapter 34 we will give you a brief idea of what you can expect from this type of product.

CHAPTER ENDNOTES

1. For advice on investment policy statements, see *Creating an Investment Policy Statement* (Denver, CO: FPA Press, 2004).

Chapter 33

DOCUMENT IMAGING AND DOCUMENT MANAGEMENT: SELECTING THE RIGHT SCANNER

Scanners come in all shapes and sizes. They are usually categorized by their functions such as sheet fed, photo, business card, or document. Good document scanners include an automatic document feeder (ADF). Functionally, we will limit our discussion primarily to document scanners.

SCANNER BASICS

Some general rules of thumb can go a long way towards helping you select the right scanner(s) for your business: First, you must have an automatic document feeder. No matter how small your business is initially, you do not want to perform your scans one sheet at a time into a sheet fed or flatbed scanner. Second, if at all possible, purchase a scanner with a straight paper path; in other words, a scanner that allows the paper to pass trough the scanner without making any turns. A straight paper path reduces wear and tear on the scanner, and it reduces the chance of paper jams. Third, favor products capable of performing duplex scans. These scanners can create an image of both sides of a document with a single pass. The forth consideration is speed. Any decent corporate scanner today is rated at a minimum of 15 images per minute. Don't settle for less. If you plan on scanning a large number of graphic images, resolution may be an issue, but for document scanning, a corporate scanner will provide sufficient resolution.

Finally, think about how you will connect the scanner to your computer. Just a few years ago, virtually all scanners in the classes we recommend required a SCSI interface. This generally required the advisor, or an IT person, to open computers and install SCSI cards before scanners could be put into service. While SCSI scanners are still widely available, most manufacturers now offer their lower duty corporate scanners with a USB interface, which greatly simplifies the installation process. Unless there are other reasons to select a SCSI interface, we suggest that you purchase a USB model.

A scanner meeting all of the specifications laid out above will not be inexpensive. Technology prices are in a constant state of flux, so it is possible that things will have changed by the time you read this, but currently it is probably impossible to find a scanner that meets our minimum specifications for much under $500. Larger offices can easily spend several thousand dollars on an appropriate machine. This may sound like a lot of money, but we would strongly urge you not to be "penny wise and pound foolish" when it comes to scanners. A high quality scanner's longer lifecycle and improved speed will result in lower total operating costs over time.

CENTRALIZATION VS. DECENTRALIZATION

Offices with more than a couple of employees will have to decide whether to purchase one larger scanner for the group, or a separate scanner for each desktop. Some firms will prefer a decentralized system, with each person responsible for his or her own documents. Others will prefer a centralized system, with one or more persons responsible for scanning the documents into the system, and then making them available to others.

There really is not one right answer to this dilemma. It is more a function of the firm's management style. The important thing to remember is that the firm must make a decision first, so that the appropriate scanner(s) can be purchased.

THE ROLE OF A FLATBED SCANNER

A flatbed scanner can be useful from time to time for those who want to scan a page of a book, for example. Personally, I find that I rarely use a flatbed, but your experience may differ. If you believe that you will be doing a fair amount of flatbed scanning, by all means purchase a good scanner with that capability. If you will only be using a flatbed occasionally if space is tight, or if you are on a tight budget, purchase the best document scanner you can afford, and then purchase an inexpensive consumer flatbed scanner that can be stored in a closet, then pulled out and connected for occasional use.

DRIVERS

Drivers are the software that help the scanner communicate with the scanning software. The two most common drivers you will encounter are TWAIN drivers and ISIS drivers. TWAIN drivers are royalty free, so they are found commonly among less expensive products. Corporate scanning packages that use ISIS drivers often offer additional functionality, such as filters, that TWAIN drivers do not offer, but there is a cost associated with ISIS drivers, so they are rarely paired with less expensive products. It is not necessary for practitioners to become experts in the intricacies of drivers, but it is important for them to know which drivers their hardware and software support, so they do not create a mismatch. For example, you would not want to purchase a scanner that only supports TWAIN drivers while purchasing a software package only capable of using ISIS drivers. Under such circumstances, there would definitely be a problem, so be sure to check!

RECOMMENDATIONS

Below, we will offer some scanner recommendations. Some of the models we recommend may be replaced by newer ones by the time you read this, but our recommendations should nevertheless provide you with useful guidance during the selection process. Don't expect to find our recommended models at your local electronics or computer retailer. Most are classified as corporate scanners. You are more likely to find them at an online retailer or a corporate "reseller."

Fujitsu ScanSnap™ Scanner

Currently, the Fujitsu ScanSnap™ Scanning Solution is one of the least expensive scanners that meet our requirements outlined above, but it does have some limitations. On a positive note, it is a small, duplex scanner with adequate speed (15 ppm simplex color, 30 ipm duplex color). The automatic document feeder can hold 50 pages. It can automatically detect whether a page contains black and white or color print, and it adjusts to the appropriate settings. It will also automatically detect the size of the paper being scanned. Another capability, blank page detection, saves space by sensing pages that are blank and eliminating them from the stored document.

Figure 33.1

Fujitsu ScanSnap™ Scanner

The software package is quite generous. It includes Adobe Acrobat 6.0 Standard, and CardMinder, a program that scans business cards and feeds them into a database, which can be linked to some of the popular general purpose CRM packages.

The ScanSnap™ Scanning Solution is unique among the scanners mentioned here in that it is the only one specifically designed to work with Adobe® Acrobat as the document imaging software. The "One Step PDF" system utilizes Adobe® Acrobat to scan documents and store them as PDF files. This system may be adequate for small offices, but it may be too limited for larger firms. If you are a small firm, and are comfortable using Adobe® Acrobat as your scanning software, the Fujitsu ScanSnap™ Scanner is worth a look; however, those planning on using another document imaging/ document management system should probably look elsewhere.

Fujitsu *fi*-4120C Scanner

The Fujitsu *fi*-4120C is currently one of our favorite scanners, suitable for both the sole practitioner and the larger, decentralized office where multiple persons are performing their own scans. It produces high quality scans, and it is highly reliable. Like the Fujitsu ScanSnap™ Scanner, it has a small footprint, so it does not require much real estate on the desk. This color, duplex scanner is rated at 25 ppm simplex, 25 ipm duplex. It has a 50 page ADF and can work with both TWAIN and ISIS drivers.

The Fujitsu *fi*-4120C, like the other scanners to follow, is capable of working with many different software packages. When paired with the proper software, these scanners offer automatic paper size detection, color detection, automatic blank page detection, etc.

Figure 33.2

Fujitsu *fi*-4120C

Canon DR-2080C

The Canon DR-2080 is even smaller and more portable than the Fujitsu *fi*-4120C. It is a color, duplex printer with a 50 page ADF. It can operate with both TWAIN and ISIS drivers. The scanner comes bundled with Canon's CapturePerfect software. This program is fairly basic, but it allows the user for save files in a number of formats, including PDF. Overall, we judged the Canon DR-2080-C to be somewhat inferior to the Fujitsu *fi*-4120C in speed, paper handling ability, and scan quality, but it was still more than adequate for the needs of most firms.

Figure 33.3

Canon DR-2080C

The thing that sets this scanner apart from the competition is its portability. It is small enough and light enough to carry around with you. Canon offers an optional carrying case that is similar in size and shape to a laptop computer bag; so, if you are a mobile planner looking for a good balance of functionality and portability, the Canon DR-2080C is worth a serious look.

Fujitsu *fi*-4220C Scanner

The Fujitsu *fi*-4220C is the only scanner we have recommended so far that includes a flatbed. This scanner is essentially a version of the Fujitsu *fi*-4120C we reviewed earlier with a flatbed attached. There are two reasons that we have not recommended more: space and price. Flatbeds require more space, and space is often at a premium in the financial planning office. The Fujitsu *fi*-4120C, for example, measures 6.3 in. x 11.9 in. x 6.7 in. (H x W x D). By contrast, its stable mate, the Fujitsu *fi*-4220C, measures 9.0 in. x 11.9 in. x 22.4 in. It also costs several hundred dollars more than the Fujitsu *fi*-4120C, so it is difficult to justify the extra space and cost unless there is a real need for a flatbed on a regular basis.

Figure 33.4

Fujitsu *fi*-4220C

Panasonic KV-S2026C

This particular scanner does not offer a straight paper path, but in all other resects it appears to be an excellent value. While a bit larger than the Fujitsu 4120C, its specifications and price are comparable.

Figure 33.5

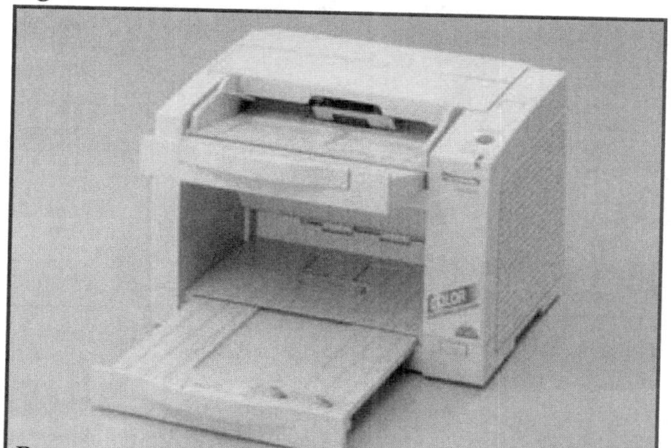

Panasonic KV-S2026C

It is rated at 23 pages per minute for B & W 200 dpi simplex scans, 42 images per minute duplex. The color ratings at 150 dpi are 10 pages per minute simplex, 18 images per minute duplex.

It is durable and works with either ISIS or TWAIN drivers. This unit ships with document scanning software and a copy of PaperPort SE.

Xerox DocuMate 252 Scanner

The Xerox DocuMate 252 bears a striking resemblance to the Fujitsu fi-4120. It is one of the newest and fastest USB 2.0 scanners we have tested, with a rating of 50 images per minute in the duplex mode. The scanner has a 50 page ADF and can work with both TWAIN and ISIS drivers. The DocuMate 252 comes with an outstanding bundle of software, which includes PaperPort Pro 9 Office, OmniPage Pro 12, Kofax VRS (an image enhancement product), and ArcSoft PhotoImpression 4.0, a photo editing program. In addition, you get QuickScan 3.0, a very impressive program that allows users to perform many operations, like scanning to PaperPort, or scanning to an email, with a single mouse click. In short, this product is a "document management solution in a box" for someone starting a small business. Since the DocuMate 252 is a new product, we cannot yet gauge its reliability, but assuming it meets expectations, this scanner/software combo is an attractive package.

Figure 33.6

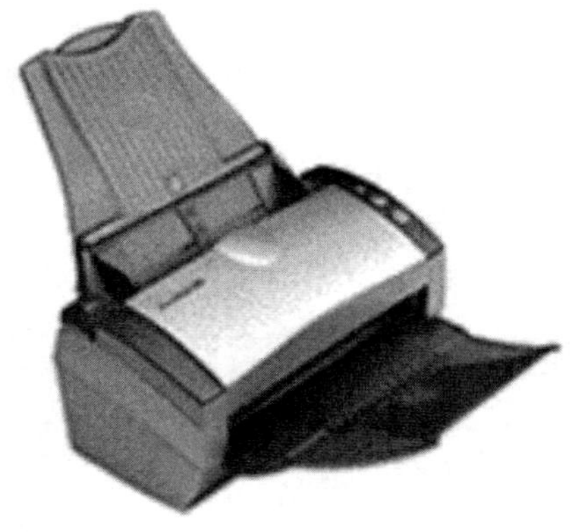

Xerox DocuMate 252
Courtesy Xerox Corporation

Fujitsu *fi*–4530C

If you need to share a scanner among a group of employees, or if you require a machine that can scan 11 x 17 sized pages, this scanner may be for you. The Fujitsu *fi*-4530C is larger and more powerful version of the *fi*-4120C. It is a duplex color scanner. The 4530C can process 35 ipm, has a 100 page ADF and it is the smallest scanner on the market capable of processing 11 x 17 sized pages (the *fi*-4120 maxes out at 8½ x 14). It's also manufactured to withstand more wear and tear, with a duty cycle roughly three times that of the 4120. This unit ships with Adobe® Acrobat software.

Figure 33.7

Fujitsu *fi*-4530C

Other Choices

Our list of recommended scanners is far from exhaustive, but it represents what we believe to be some of the best values at this time. In recent years, Fujitsu has been the dominant manufacturer of entry level corporate scanners due to their high quality products and aggressive pricing. Conditions do change however. For example, in the past, we did not recommend the Panasonic KV-S2026C simply because it was much more expensive than a comparable Fujitsu product. Now that Panasonic has seen fit to lower its price, we think it is a worthy contender.

Kodak makes some excellent scanners, but when we last looked at them, we thought its prices were too high. If Kodak were to lower the prices of select models, we would enthusiastically recommend them.

Conclusion

We've indicated the features you should be looking for and offered examples of some very good, attractively priced scanners. Before making a purchase, do your own research, using this chapter as a guide.

In the next chapter, we will examine document management software and OCR software. When the software products we cover include additional functionality, such as rights management or workflow management, we'll try to bring those additional features to your attention.

Chapter 34

DOCUMENT IMAGING AND MANAGEMENT SOFTWARE

INTRODUCTION

Broadly speaking, readers must contend with two types of documents: (1) those that originate in digital form (files that you have created on your computer, and those that were created on another computer and copied onto your computer); and (2) those that originate as paper and must be scanned (and possibly converted to text) before they can be stored on a computer.

While it may sound difficult, converting a paper document to a digital format is not difficult, provided that you have the right tools. Any scanner discussed in the previous chapter, combined with most digital imaging packages on the market, should do the job.

Dealing with files that originate in digital format is very easy. Your computer's operating system already provides one way of organizing and managing your files. For example, MS Windows XP includes Windows explorer and search capabilities. A number of third-party vendors offer utilities with additional capabilities.

The real challenge, however, is not collecting documents on your computer; the challenge is organizing them so you can rapidly find what you need, when you need it. That's where document management systems come in handy. The dedicated document management systems we will discuss below all offer the ability to import digital files from your hard drive, as well as the ability to "acquire" scanned documents that originate in paper form.

In order to facilitate our discussion of document management, we will arbitrarily divide the products into three categories: basic; intermediate; and advanced. However, before we delve into the various methods of organizing your documents, let's take a brief look at optical character recognition (OCR) software, since it may play a role in your document management system.

About OCR

Scanning merely creates a "photograph" of the scanned document. In order to edit the document or perform full text searches upon it, the page must be converted to text through a process known as optical character recognition (OCR).

If you only need to edit an occasional document, there is no reason to perform OCR on each document you scan. On the other hand, if you regularly want to perform full text searches on each document scanned into your computer, you will need to perform OCR on them first.

While novice users are often enamored with the idea of OCR, there may be other methods of finding what you need that are less burdensome. There are some negatives associated with performing OCR on each scanned document. The first is that it takes time to perform OCR on each scanned page, so it slows down the scanning process considerably and it consumes computing power. There's also the issue of accuracy. While OCR accuracy has improved considerably in recent years, it still is not foolproof. Perfectionists will often have to review documents manually to fine-tune the errors. Of course, if OCR is being used strictly for search purposes, 100% accuracy is not necessarily essential. Depending on the software employed, accuracy might range from 85% to over 98%, good enough for indexing purposes.

A number of software products we will discuss below offer some OCR capabilities. If you purchase a program that does not include OCR, and you wish to use it either for indexing or occasional editing, we recommend that you consider two products: ScanSoft OmniPagePro and Abbyy Fine Reader. Both products offer a high degree of accuracy, can recognize multiple languages, and both can output to a number of popular file formats. The latest version of OmniPage Pro includes an expanded dictionary of financial terms, so it may do a slightly better job for financial service professionals, but it retails for approximately double the price of Fine Reader; however, discounts may be available for those who own other ScanSoft products. Microsoft Office users may also qualify for special pricing.

For heavy users, assuming no discounts apply, OmniPage Pro is probably worth the additional cost, but occasional users should be satisfied with Abbyy Fine Reader.

File Formats

Adobe Portable Document Format (PDF) and Tagged Image File Format (TIFF) are the most widely used document image file formats by a wide margin. We strongly suggest that you confine your selection of document imaging and management software to those programs that can work with one, the other, or ideally, both of these formats.

BASIC PRODUCTS

The most basic method of organizing your files is to make use of your operation system's file structure and search capabilities. Under this scenario, you would use a software package and scanner to scan paper documents, and integrate those files with your current file structure. For the purpose of this illustration, let's use Windows XP.

Using Adobe Acrobat

If I chose this method, I might decide to use Adobe® Acrobat as my scanning package. By launching Adobe® Acrobat 6.0 and selecting ... "File" ... and "Create PDF From Scanner," I can scan paper documents as Adobe PDF image files. Then, if I wish, I can use Adobe Paper Capture (Abode Acrobat's OCR module) to convert the image into a searchable and/or editable PDF document.

Using Microsoft Office

Microsoft Office offers another alternative. My version of MS Office Professional 2003 includes Microsoft Document Imaging. It may not install as part of the default installation process, but it can be added using the custom install feature. Microsoft Document Imaging allows users to scan and perform OCR on documents with a minimal amount of fuss. When used in concert with Windows XP, the application defaults to Widows Image Acquisition Drivers (WIA) as opposed to TWAIN drivers. Unfortunately, WIA does not work with all scanners equipped with automatic document feeders (ADF). If the application does not behave well with your scanner, you will have to configure it to use the TWAIN driver.

Images scanned with this software can be saved as either TIFF images (one of the industry standards) or Microsoft Document Imaging (MDI) format. According to Microsoft, the MDI images are equivalent in quality to TIFF images, but they consume less disk space. However, the TIFF format is universal and compatible with a wide range of document imaging and management programs. Few programs other than MS Office applications currently support MDI.

Microsoft Document Imaging offers users only limited control of the scanning process, and its OCR capabilities are on the light side as well. These deficiencies make it unsuitable for most financial professionals; however, it may be sufficient for a small start-up operation with more time than money on its hands. Those that employ this system should plan to upgrade as their business and their bank account grows.

Bundled Scanning Software

Manufacturers of scanners often provide a basic scanning application with their product. Generally speaking, these applications allow users to scan documents in one or more formats and save them to the computer's hard drive. The programs range in utility from very bare bones to moderately useful.

For example, the Canon DR-2080C, discussed in the last chapter, comes bundled with CapturePerfect 1.0. This program enables basic scanning and viewing in JPEG and PDF formats. It offers "scan to email" and "scan to print" options. It can zoom and rotate images, but overall, I found it limited. In contrast, the Reliable Throughput Imaging Viewer (RTIV), which came bundled with the Panasonic KV-S2026C, offered a bit more control over imaging. Users could choose from four file formats (TIFF, PDF, JPEG, or BMP).

For those who plan to use third-party software, the bundled software is of little concern. But if you plan on keeping it simple and using your computer's directory structure, then the bundled software could influence your buying decision (all other things being more or less equal).

Filing, Indexing, and Searching Using the Operating System

Typically, I would set up a folder on my hard drive labeled "Clients." Under that I would create sub-folders for each client, and in each sub-folder, I might create additional folders by subject or year. Using this methodology, I would later search for documents either by navigating to the proper folder or by using Windows native search capabilities. I could enhance the search capabilities somewhat by manually assigning additional properties to documents (keywords, categories, subject, etc.), but doing so is somewhat time consuming.

This method has other limitations as well. Compared to dedicated software systems, scanning into one of the above packages and filing documents in using the Windows filing system can be cumbersome. Searches can sometimes be problematic. Files must be named individually, so there is no file naming continuity. As the folders containing client records grow, the search process can slow considerably. If care is not taken during the initial filing process, over time searches may return too many results, resulting in retrieval delays.

In the authors' opinion, filing and retrieving files through the operating system is possible, but it is impractical for all but the smallest of practices, and even they will most likely want to upgrade in the future. That being said, if you are just starting out, and if you have more time than money, this may be a temporary answer to your needs. If you save to a format generally used in the financial community, and you upgrade to a dedicated document management system in the future, you should be able to move your files into it without a problem.

CRM Products: ACT!, Goldmine, Junxure-I

A number of CRM products popular in the financial service community, such as ACT!, Goldmine, Junxure-I, and ProTracker Advantage (updated in June 2004) now have some sort of ability to manage documents. Typically, computer generated documents can be linked to a client record. Sometimes, scanned documents can also be linked to a client record, although an add-on product, like Laser App, may be required.

For those advisors who spend most of their day working within their CRM program, using it to manage documents has a great deal of appeal. The primary disadvantages we see with such a set-up are that searches may be limited, and users may have a problem deciding how to file documents that are not related to a client or contact.

Advisors seriously interested in managing documents through their CRM system should give careful consideration to Junxure-I. Junxure-I offers three distinct methods of managing documents. The most basic is the one described above – that is, where documents are scanned, or linked to the client record. A second, somewhat more robust method is to link Junxure-I with PaperPort, an inexpensive document management system discussed below (Junxure-I technical can supply instructions for doing this). The third, and most advanced method for managing documents within Junxure-I, is to purchase an add-in package that seamlessly integrated Worldox, a sophisticated document management system, with Junxure-I. With three different document management options to chose from, Junxure-I offers advisors a range of options that is currently unrivaled in the industry.

PaperPort

PaperPort is the least expensive, fully functional document imaging and management system the authors are aware of. PaperPort is currently available in two versions: PaperPort Deluxe and PaperPort Pro Office. The former is targeted primarily at the consumer and home office user. The somewhat more robust Pro Office version is targeted primarily at small businesses and professionals. Pro Office includes better integration with MS Office applications, same more advanced PDF file capabilities, database links, a network digital copier interface, a MS SharePoint link agent, and DeskTop Delivery.

> Some scanners come bundled with a product called PaperPort SE. This product should not be confused with the full versions of PaperPort listed above. PaperPort SE resembles an earlier version of PaperPort with some functions disabled. Based on our visits to the PaperPort website, it appears that support for this product is virtually nonexistent. We think it is probably fine for home use, but we'd discourage you from using it in your office. To us, the main benefit of PaperPort SE is that it may allow you to purchase a current full version of PaperPort at the discounted upgrade price.

PaperPort contains a number of features we consider desirable, such as unlimited folder nesting, search capabilities, indexing, document thumbnails, and annotation capabilities. It also offers additional niceties such as OCR capabilities and a simulated desktop. Essentially, PaperPort allows you to acquire, file, edit, manage, and retrieve all of your documents and images.

Most novices find PaperPort easy to use because its nested filing system looks identical to a Windows directory tree; however, PaperPort offers some additional functionality that Windows does not. For example, like Windows Explorer, PaperPort offers a split pane view; the Directory Tree resides on the left pane. PaperPort folders can be color-coded, which makes it easier for users to locate the folder they are looking for.

The individual files reside in the right pane, and each is represented by a thumbnail (miniature version) of the document. It is usually possible to get a good idea of what the file contains simply by glancing at the thumbnail; if not, users can double click on the image and a full-sized version appears. A toolbar that runs across the bottom of the program links other applications to the PaperPort desktop. For example, if you want to perform OCR on a document, you can drag and drop it onto the icon for your word processor and PaperPort will perform OCR. Dragging and dropping an image onto the print icon will send it to your printer. Another icon, Web Capture, allows users to capture a copy of a web page and save it in PaperPort.

Drivers and File Formats

Earlier versions of PaperPort were sometimes criticized for their inability to manipulate files in formats other than PaperPort's proprietary native file format (MAX). MAX files are fine for one's own use, but they cannot be easily shared with others. Critics also voiced concerns about the advisability of archiving files in PaperPort's proprietary format because if the product were to be discontinued, they would have trouble moving their files to another format and/or system. Currently, images can be scanned into PaperPort as PDF files (an industry standard), so we feel more comfortable recommending PaperPort for business use. Once files are stored in PDF format, PaperPort can manipulate, edit, and annotate them.

PaperPort now offers better TIFF image support as well. In the previous version, you could bring TIFF files into PaperPort, but you couldn't do much more than rotate or crop them. Now, when you bring these images into PaperPort, you can annotate, edit, index, and file them. The only downside to annotating images in PaperPort is that the annotation overwrites the file itself – in other words, the original image is permanently altered. When working with TIFF files, we suggest that you copy a file and annotate the copy if you want to preserve the original.

Another nice PaperPort feature is the SimpleSearch index. This feature uses PaperPort's OCR engine to recognize words and phrases in PaperPort images so they can be searched at a later date. Items can be indexed individually, or PaperPort can automatically update the index. Index updates can slow down a user's computer, so PaperPort can be programmed to run index updates only when a machine is idle. Alternatively, users can manually set the index to update before they leave their offices in the evening.

Of course users can manually assign properties, such as author, keywords and comments to files, and many people do. This works particularly well when only one or two people are assigning the keywords; but as more people become involved, the process becomes less efficient due to the lack of uniformity.

PaperPort's search pane is very user friendly. Users can search by name, keyword, author, or they can search for text within an image, which results in slower searches. A simple drop down menu allows users to set search parameters on the search. PaperPort can be set with a mouse click to search all PaperPort folders, or the search can be confined to the current folder. The SimpleSearch index can be turned on or off. PaperPort can be instructed to return exact matches or approximate matches. Setting the whole search process in motion takes only a few seconds.

PaperPort Desktop Delivery (which is included in the Pro Office version, only) monitors a specified folder on a networked file server or a local hard drive for incoming faxes and scanned images. The program then transfers files from the monitored folder to the PaperPort desktop. TIFF files are converted to PDF image items; JPEG and PDF files are moved in their original format.

PaperPort is not right for every office. The larger you are, the more likely it is that you will want a more robust document imaging system. As one moves up in scale, we see two major disadvantages to using PaperPort: indexing and auditing. While PaperPort's indexing features are more than sufficient for small offices, they are not ideal for larger installations, particularly if you have many different people doing the indexing. For example, one person might assign the keyword "Social Security" to a Social Security Report, while someone else might assign "SS" as a keyword. Under such circumstances, you'll still be able to find the document using SimpleSearch, but things can quickly get out of hand. More robust systems allow the administrator to set indices in drop down menus, thereby preserving uniformity. That's a feature many offices will be willing to pay extra for.

The other issue is the audit trail. More expensive systems allow you to assign different levels of permission at the folder, sub-folder, and even the document level. Some actually track each time a file is opened, read, modified, etc. PaperPort cannot perform these tricks.

PaperPort can be an excellent investment, even for some who will never use it as their primary document management system. For those who are unfamiliar with scanning, document management, OCR, annotation and the like, PaperPort is a great educational tool. It is not unheard of for firms go out and spend thousands of dollars on an elaborate document management system without any idea of how the systems work or the features they need. If nothing else, PaperPort offers you an inexpensive introduction to document management. Before investing in an elaborate document management system, it can be instructional to understand the capabilities of an entry-level product.

If indexing and audit trails are of primary importance, you will probably be better served by a more robust document management system. Everyone else is a potential PaperPort customer.

INTERMEDIATE PRODUCTS

DocuXplorer Professional

DocuXplorer is available in three distinct versions, and it is difficult to classify. The Personal and Professional editions fall squarely in the intermediate category. The Enterprise version is scaleable enough that it can be classified as either intermediate or advanced, depending on how it is deployed. The Personal edition is a single user version that offers all of DocuXplorer's core functionality, minus the document tracking and security features. The Professional version is essentially a single user version of the Enterprise edition. It includes document tracking and security features. Enterprise is the highly scalable multi-user version. It can be deployed in an office of three or three thousand and it includes the full set of DocuXplorer features. The discussion below applies to the Enterprise version.

Application Design

DocuXplorer, like some of the other more intuitive programs we recommend, is modeled on the same physical dynamics you use in your existing office environment. Storing and finding documents is accomplished using standard Windows conventions and a familiar hierarchical tree structure in a Virtual Library that contains Cabinets. Cabinets contain Drawers; drawers contain Folders that hold sub-folders and/or Documents.

Drivers and File Formats

DocuXplorer uses no proprietary formats; instead, all documents are stored in the DocuXplorer database in their original format and can be exported from the database in their original format. DocuXplorer supports only the TWAIN interface for direct scanning; however, the DocuXplorer In Box can be used to import documents previously scanned into another document capture interface that supports ISIS.

The DocuXplorer scanning interface creates TIFF files exclusively. The company's position is that TIFF is the only truly universal file format that can be accessed on all computers without the necessity of installing additional software. (Windows and Apple computers include a TIFF viewer; in order to access PDF files, users must install Adobe® Acrobat Reader®.) DocuXplorer includes a PDF viewer; it can also index imported PDF files. However, DocuXplorer users cannot scan directly to PDF from within the program.

Indexing

The DocuXplorer Desktop is central to all interactions within the program. With DocuXplorer's ability to create an effective index structure, the program allows users to retrieve any document in seconds. Documents can easily be moved or copied using standard Windows conventions. The Desktop also contains powerful features to sort and group documents in a folder by simply dragging and dropping the folder's column headers.

Summary footer fields can be added to view the sum, minimum, maximum, count, and average of a column. These Folder and Query Views can then be printed as reports or exported as calculated Excel spreadsheets or as XML, CSV, or HTML files

User Definable Index Sets

The program allows users to profile documents with multiple user-defined index fields in an Index Set. DocuXplorer allows up to 33 user-defined index fields in each Index Set. Indexing can be accelerated with Auto-Indexing Variables, which allow users to populate index fields automatically. DocuXplorer's indexing capabilities are highly customizable. They should be able to meet the needs of any firm.

Automatic-Indexing with Multiple Index Field Controls

DocuXplorer provides Auto-Complete Static Data Fields to create lists of specific relevant data. It also provides Auto-Complete Dynamic Data Fields to enter data in a field once and automatically fill the field from the history list as you start to type. Auto-Indexing features can be used to input index data automatically based on a predetermined set of variables for a field including incremental numbering, date, time, document location, and more.

Extended Database Features

Index Information Only documents provide users with a method of storing and tracking data that does not have an image or computer-generated file attached. This feature can be used as a placeholder for documents that have not yet been received. For example, if you are waiting for a client to return a signed investment policy proposal, you can add an Index Only Information document, and then scan in the signed document when the client returns it to you.

Security

Security has become a key requirement under government regulation for the financial services industry. DocuXplorer is equipped to deal with that need by allowing you to choose who will have access to a document, folder, or drawer. Security permissions can be set to allow or disallow user rights, such as:

- Modifying or annotating documents or their indexes;
- Copying, deleting, or moving documents; and
- Exporting, emailing, faxing, or printing documents from within the program.

Adding Documents

Adding a document is easy and fast: First, scan in paper documents, individually or in batches; import electronic documents; or print images of documents from any Windows program. Next use the "Send To" command in Windows Explorer to open DocuXplorer and import the document to a DocuXplorer Folder, or use the DX In Box to import documents directly from any folder on your network or local drives by simply dragging and dropping the document to a DocuXplorer Folder. Then define those documents using "Heads up" indexing – that is, adding a document to DocuXplorer brings up a Document Window so that you can view image documents while you index them.

Retrieving

Quickly retrieve documents using the Find Dialogue, which can be reached by clicking the "Find Document" button on the Icon Toolbar. The Search Engine allows for full text searches or index searches.

OCR

DocuXplorer includes a built-in OCR engine. Full text searches can be performed on scanned images after they have been scanned and OCR'd.

Document Viewing

The Image Document Window is used to view documents that are image files, whether they were scanned or imported to the database. Computer-generated documents launch their native programs for viewing and editing just as they do in Windows Explorer. PDF documents open the PDF Document Viewer Window, allowing for speedy "heads up" indexing.

Annotation

The Annotation tools are another powerful feature of DocuXplorer. Users can annotate any TIFF image document while keeping the integrity of the original document intact. Annotation tools include the highlighter, virtual sticky notes, rubber stamps, and hyperlinks. Documents can be printed as needed with or without annotation. Other types of documents can be annotated in the program that created them.

Archiving

DocuXplorer does a nice job of making archiving painless. File drawer sizes can be set to coincide with the user's preferred back-up medium (a feature that is very handy if you are backing up to CDs or DVDs). For example, if the user wants to create backups to CD-ROM for compliance purposes, simply right click on the "File" drawer, select "Drawer Properties," then click on the "Drawer" tab and enter a maximum drawer size of 640 MB. The program will now limit the amount of information stored in the drawer to the amount of information that can be stored on the CD.

Versioning and Check-in/Check-out

When you make changes to a document, DocuXplorer can automatically save those changes with the time, date and author of the edited copy as a version of the original. When you "check out" a document from the Library, and make your edits, no other user will be able to access the document until the document is "checked in" again.

Global Access to Your Documents

DocuXplorer is suitable for use by remote offices. Here's how it works: DocuXplorer is client-server software. The server component is installed to the network server and each workstation installs the client component. A client can be installed to any computer including remote computers anywhere an Internet connection is present. To use DocuXplorer remotely, the server would need a static IP address. On the remote computer client setup, a user enters the static IP address, server name, login name, and password. Then, when they open DocuXplorer and have an Internet connection, the program will automatically open the shared library stored on that server.

Speed in accessing documents will be dependant on the type of connection one has. But with a cable modem or DSL line, you can get very respectable performance in searching for and viewing documents, although scanning documents from the remote computer would naturally be slower.

Workflow

Manual workflows can be created in DocuXplorer through the use of the Library Work Folder and subfolders. Workflows can be created based on each individual user to receive an item in the workflow, or tasks where multiple users can access documents that need to be acted upon. Expanding on its workflow abilities, DocuXplorer will soon introduce Folder and Document Notification Subscription Lists that allow users to be notified via email when a document is placed in a folder, or a date or event triggers a notification.

Interface Modes

The program offers a choice of Basic and Advanced interfaces. The dual interface allows users to begin performing basic operations rapidly, and then switch over to the advanced interface as their knowledge of the program grows. The Basic Mode Interface consists of two buttons that give users access to the most basic functions of DocuXplorer – adding a document and retrieving a document. The Advanced Mode Interface gives users access to the full range of DocuXplorer features and functions.

CEO Executive Assistant

Executive Assistant is a very interesting intermediate level document imaging and management system offered by CEO Image Systems, Inc. It is intended for use in offices of 10 people or less.

Executive Assistant is a slimmed down version of CEO's Image Executive program, which is designed for larger enterprises. Executive Assistant takes a different approach than many other products to document imaging and management process by breaking it down into three separate tasks. A separate module handles each task. The modules are Scan Documents, File Documents, and View Documents. Each module can be accessed through the Executive Assistant Toolbar.

The Executive Assistant Toolbar

Drivers and File Formats

The scanning applet can be used with either a TWAIN or an ISIS driver, but the ISIS driver offers greater flexibility and functionality. Images can be scanned to a number of popular formats, including TIFF and PDF. When used with ISIS drivers, document enhancement tools can be applied to scanned images. These tools are capable of performing numerous tasks, including border and hole removal. Before scanning, the user specifies which file cabinet documents will be filed in.

Indexing

Scanned documents reside in a queue, accessible from the filing module, ready to be indexed and filed. Digital files that already reside on a hard drive can be imported into the system. Users can set up their own file cabinet, file folder, and index structure, offering maximum flexibility to the user.

Advisors might create one cabinet named "Client Records," with a folder for each client residing within it. Indices would be customized based on how employees would search for documents at a later date. For example, if employees might search for a client by name, client type, or state of residence, you would create an index for each of these. Executive Assistant also allows for the creation of indices at the document level. Once the indices are established, the user selects an image from the queue, types in a description, assigns values to the indices, and saves it.

Retrieving

Retrieving documents through basic searches is easy. Click "View Documents" on the toolbar, type in your search criteria, hit the "Process" button, and the results will be displayed. Executive Assistant is also capable of more powerful, searches based on multiple criteria. So, for example, you could easily locate all clients who are 70 years old, reside in New York State, and own long term care insurance (provided you have an index for each of those criteria).

OCR Capabilities

Executive Assistant does not currently offer built-in OCR capabilities; however, OCR can be performed on individual documents with a third-party software package. Once converted to text, the documents can be imported into Executive Assistant.

Annotation

Executive Assistant ships with a fine assortment of annotation tools. They include:

- A highlighter;
- Virtual sticky notes;
- Watermarking (which can also be used to electronically complete blank forms);
- Redaction (used to block out a region of a document before printing, for example); and
- An eraser.

Security

Executive Assistant does not have security features built into the system; however, users can avail themselves of the security features built into their operating system. Technical support at CEO Image Systems, Inc. can help clients configure their operating system security features upon request.

Archiving

Executive Assistant's archiving works in much the same way as DocuXplorer does, although we did not find the process quite as intuitive. The user can set a back-up size that conforms to the back-up medium for CD or DVD copies. The complete directory tree can be backed up for off-site storage.

Another Feature of Note

Executive Assistant offers alternative methods of organizing and indexing your files. One thing you can do is create an HTML table of contents as your index scheme, with a hyperlink to each image. The index would then be posted to a password-protected section of your company's web site, providing users with access to the images residing on your hard drive from any web browser.

Executive Assistant is a good choice for any office of one to ten employees. Its modular format is ideally suited for firms that want to centralize the scanning and/or filing functions. If one person at the firm were responsible for scanning, and another one were responsible for filing, other employees would only be required to master the "View Documents" or retrieval module – which would reduce the learning curve and accelerate the adoption rate.

MORE ROBUST SYSTEMS

Cabinet NG

For a robust document management system, Cabinet NG is user friendly. The conventions employed by the program for organizing data are more intuitive than those of many competitors. Cabinet NG's three levels of virtual filing mimic the real world – that is, there are cabinets, folders, and individual documents within the folders. Because the filing conventions parallel those of the paper world, they are easy to grasp.

With Cabinet NG, users can file and manage all of their documents and images in one place. In fact, it is often possible to actually create documents from right within the program. Cabinet NG makes it easy to share information among employees and expedite workflows while controlling and auditing the process every step of the way. As an added bonus, Cabinet NG can be configured to perform some light CRM duties.

Drivers and File Formats

If you are forced to deal with old-fashioned paper instead of a digital file, you can scan it into the system. Currently, Cabinet NG only works with TWAIN drivers, but is expected to add support for ISIS drivers. It supports most popular file types, including TIFF and PDF.

Indexing

Like most of the more sophisticated document management systems, Cabinet NG allows users to create their own indexes. This creates uniformity throughout the organization because indexes are the tools employees will use to search for filed documents. Cabinet NG provides 24 totally customizable indexes per cabinet, the first ten of which (clearly marked with yellow fields) can be sorted at the main cabinet screen.

When setting up a cabinet, the administrator can create a rule that requires that the first index must be unique, a useful function when creating cabinets that will store client files. "Unique 1st Index" assures that each client will have a distinct identifier (e.g., account number or Social Security number).

Figure 34.1 is a blank index screen for a Cabinet labeled "Clients." A unique identifier will be assigned to each client folder. Figure 34.2 illustrates the indexes that were applied to this cabinet. Notice that we have chosen to use the Social Security number as the unique first index.

Since Indexes 1-10 can be searched from the main screen, we've populated those fields with identifiers that might be searched most often.

Next, let's look at some filing tabs, or sub-folders, that have been assigned to the client folders. In Figure 34.3, the administrator has set up the following filing tabs:

- Correspondence;
- Financial Plans;
- Tax Documents;
- Estate Plans;
- Investments; and
- Miscellaneous.

Retrieving

Pictured in Figure 34.4 is the main screen for the Client cabinet. Notice that the blue (on actual product screen) bar below the buttons provides important information including the name of the cabinet, the index currently in use, the folder count, and the number of folders marked. Below the bar we can see a visual representation of each folder. The last name of the client folder currently selected, "Burns," appears in red (on actual product screen). The index fields are displayed to the right of the folders, on a blue (on actual product screen) background. The current index is highlighted in yellow (on actual product screen).

Suppose we wanted to search for all clients residing in New York State. We would simply highlight the "State" index in the blue (on actual product screen) box, and type "NY" into the search field. The folders would re-sort alphabetically by state, and the first folder with "NY" in the state field would be listed in red (on actual product screen).

Figure 34.1

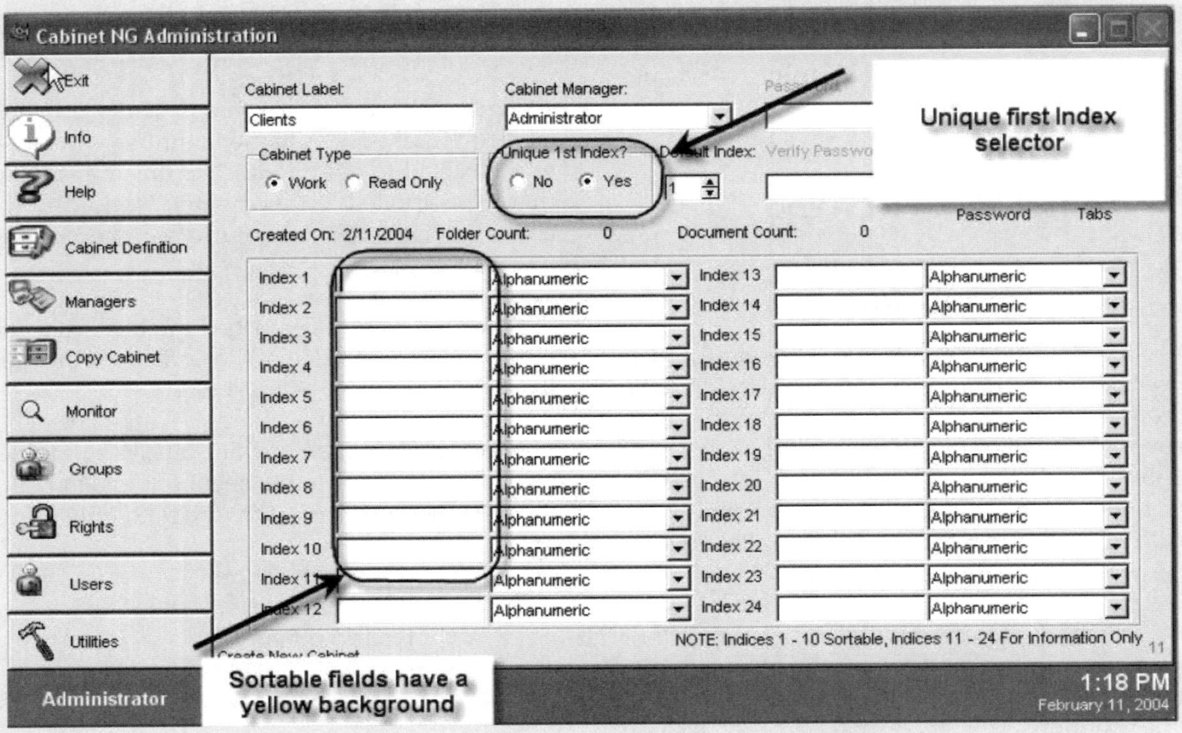

All screen shots reprinted with permission of Cabinet NG (www.cabinetng.com).

Figure 34.2

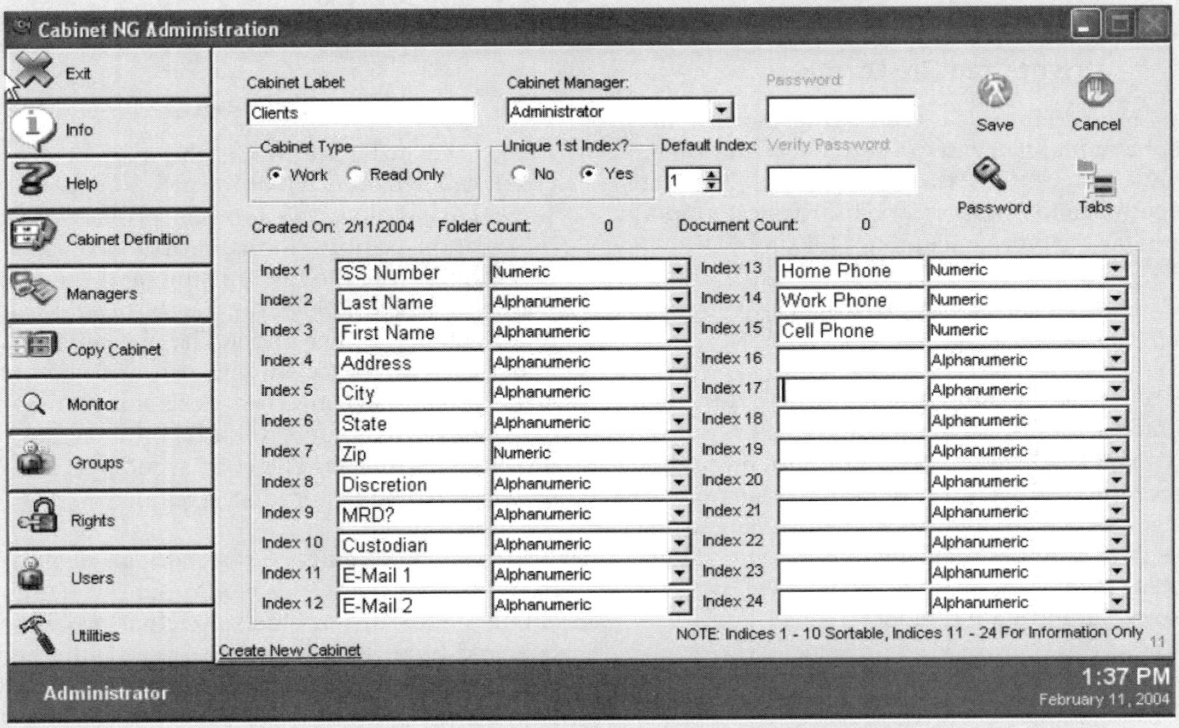

Figure 34.3

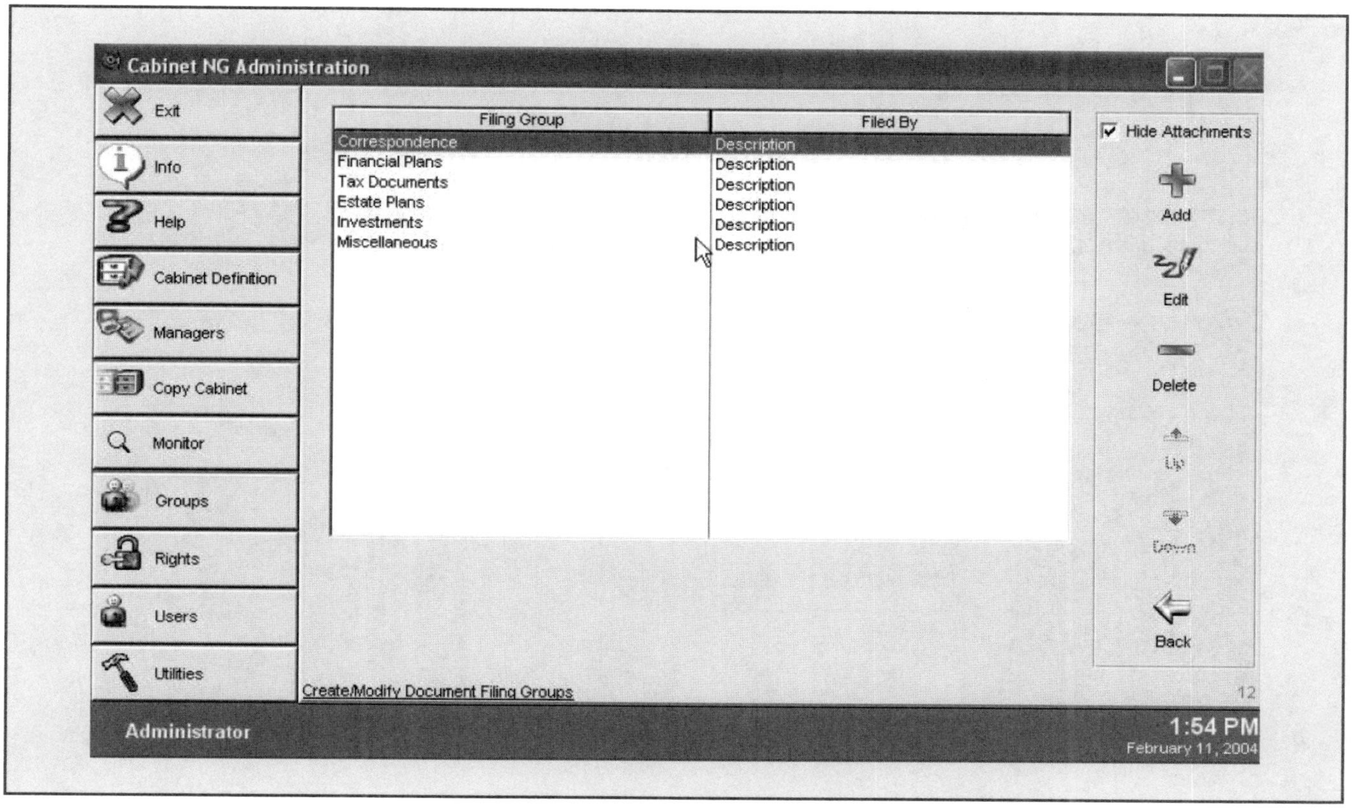

For more complex searches, the "Document Search" menu (above the "New button in Figure 34.4) is used. Document Search brings up a screen that allows users to conduct multiple keyword searches or full text searches. As an alternative, users can click in the "Marking" menu in Figure 34.4, select "Mark for Query," and search by any of the 24 indexes. For each match, a little red X will appear next to the folders containing a match. New folders can be created by clicking on the "New" button (see Figure 34.4).

Up pops the Folder Indexes screen where values can be entered for the various indexes (see Figure 34.5).

Opening a folder introduces you to some of Cabinet NG's other functions. An open folder is illustrated in Figure 34.6 below.

There are a number of different methods of moving documents into Cabinet NG. The "New" button allows users to create certain types of documents (e.g., MS Office and Adobe files) from within Cabinet NG. This requires an initial set-up procedure. Another method of getting things into the program is to move them or copy them by clicking on the "Files" button. One hundred files at a time can be moved or copied into the Cabinet NG folder.

Large firms can create "naming templates," which "force" users to file certain documents according to conventions so that there is uniformity. Naming templates are completely customizable. Cabinet NG can pre-fill certain information (e.g., date, time), and prompt the user to supply other fields.

OCR Capabilities

Cabinet NG can perform full text searches on digital text files; however, it does not include OCR software. This means that if you want to do a full text search of a scanned image, it must first be processed with a third-party OCR package.

Annotation

The version of Cabinet NG we tested does not include annotation features, but the company has assured us that they will be adding such features. Currently, it is often possible to work around the lack of an annotation tool by using other programs. For example, one can annotate a PDF file using Adobe Acrobat® or Microsoft® Word and still store the file within Cabinet NG.

Figure 34.4

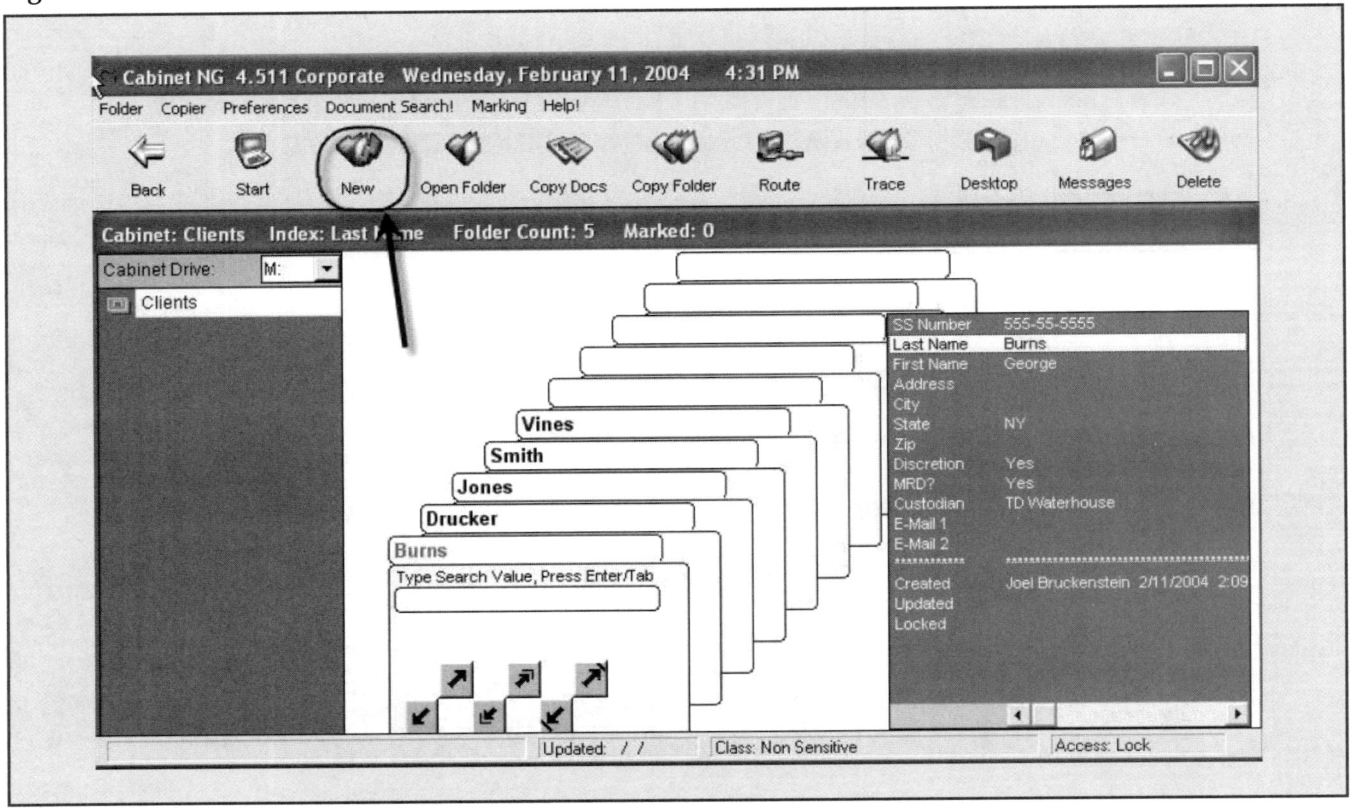

Security

Cabinet NG offers three levels of administrative privileges: local; cabinet; and system. The local administrator has administrative rights for the local drive on the computer. The cabinet administrator has administrative rights over an individual cabinet, regardless of where it resides. And the system administrator has rights over the entire system.

Various levels of permission can be granted at the folder and/or the individual document level. Permission levels are as follows:

- None (no access);
- View (read only access);
- Work (read and edit only access);
- Create (read, edit, and create new);
- Delete (read, edit, create new, and delete); and
- Lock (complete access plus the ability to lock a document or folder).

In short, Cabinet NG offers total control over your documents. You can set permissions, lock down documents or folders, copy, etc. It also provides a complete audit trail.

Archiving

Cabinet NG assumes that users have their own backup software, so it does not have automated backup utilities, and it does not offer the ability to set the size of the backup medium. However, it does contain some utilities that may be useful in the backup process. For example, Cabinet NG has a copy utility that allows users to copy whole cabinet structures or individual files to a different location. This might be useful, for example, in the case of inactive clients. One could set up a parallel file structure and just copy the inactive clients to it for archive purposes. For full backups, users can either copy the entire document storage structure to a separate drive, or use a third-party software package to customize backups.

Figure 34.5

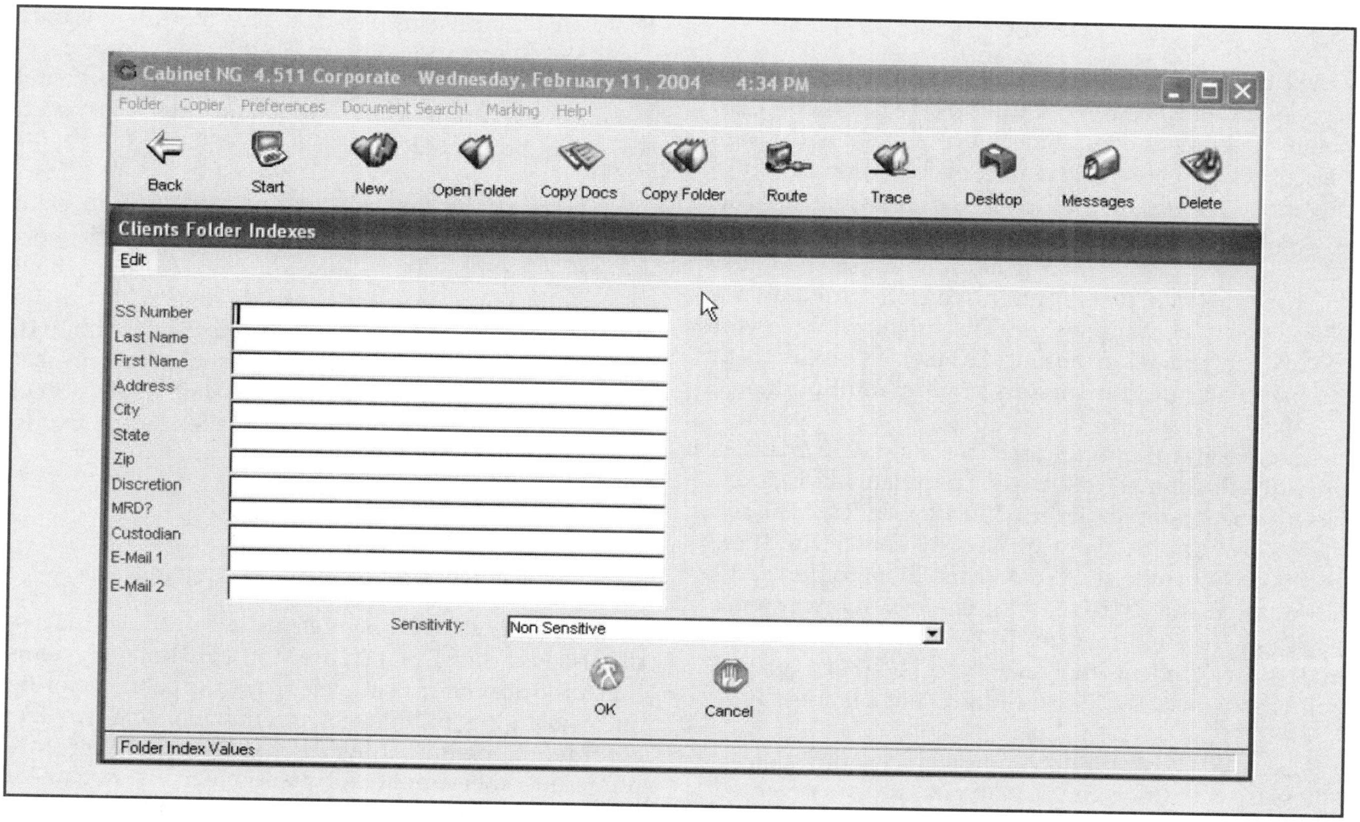

Figure 34.6

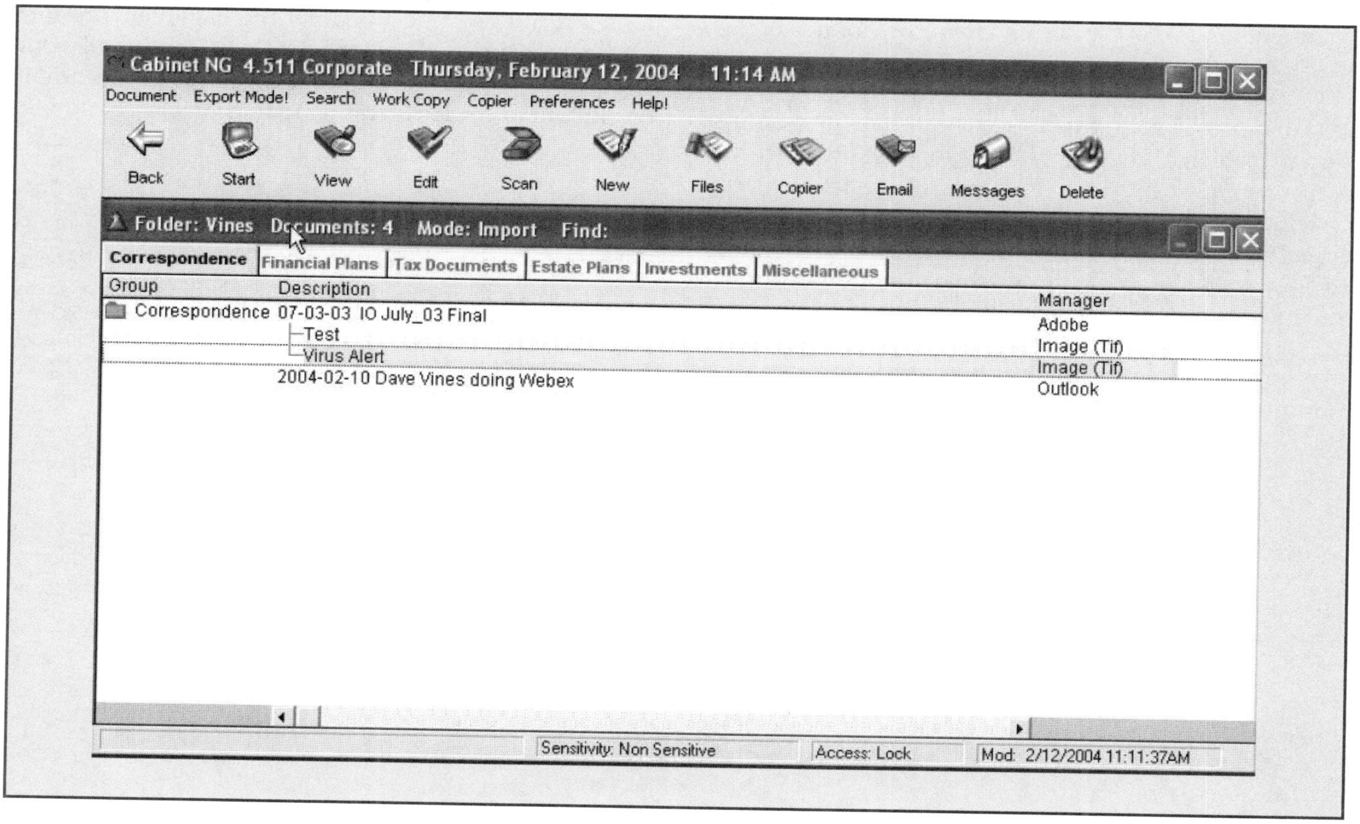

Other

The email button allows users to copy or move email correspondence from MS Outlook into Cabinet NG, a notable feature for compliance purposes. As with other files, users can chose to leave a copy in Outlook, or they can move emails to Cabinet NG and delete the file within MS Outlook.

There's also a "Copier" button, which controls Cabinet NG's internal copying system. This function allows you to copy documents from one Cabinet NG location to another. This function can copy single or multiple items.

The program can be used for light CRM duties provided that contact information populates the indexes. Here's one example: Set up an index called "Follow-up." Now suppose we want to touch base with three clients on December 1, 2005. In each client folder, at the follow-up field, "2005-12-01" is entered. At any time, a search of the field for "2005-12-01" will bring up the folders for the clients that are to be called that day. Each will have a little red X next to the client's name.

Users can "check out" folders, and route them to others so work flows can be managed and documented. When folders are routed to others, written comments, and even audio remarks, can be sent along with the folder. The system will either store the attached comments as part of the permanent record, or not, at the user's discretion.

Cabinet NG includes its own internal messaging system, which allows employees to send and receive both written and audio messages. A bulletin board system is included as part of the messaging system. The bulletin board can be used to circulate internal memos and document internal actions while providing an audit trail of who received and/or acknowledged the memo.

A forms module is available at an additional cost. The module provides an enhanced, customized version of ScanSoft's OmniForm package. This module not only facilitates the creation of forms, but it also allows users to "pull" information from Cabinet NG or an external database to automatically populate forms. Rule based forms can be created, too.

Cabinet NG appears to be best suited for offices of five or more employees, since they will benefit most from the workflow and communications features. But it is equally well suited for those dealing with off-site employees and/or Virtual Work Partners. Although small firms may end up paying for some features that they cannot take full advantage of, in general Cabinet NG's usability and functionality make it attractive to firms of all sizes.[1]

Other Enterprise Solutions

The two developers of intermediate products that we discussed earlier, DocuXplorer and CEO Image Systems both produce enterprise level software capable of storing and managing millions of documents, and we feel confident recommending both products. There are numerous other suppliers of quality enterprise document management solutions, but they are beyond the scope of this book.

Selecting the proper document management product for an enterprise requires knowledge and skill. Our suggestion would be to hire a qualified independent consultant to guide you rather than trying to go it alone.

CHAPTER ENDNOTES

1. Cabinet NG added several new third-party integrations in 2004. Planners can use these products daily in the course of doing business because they work in conjunction with Cabinet NG. An example of third-party integration support to Cabinet NG includes the following applications: (1) Laser App; (2) ACT!; (3) QuickBooks; and (4) Advisor Assistant.

Chapter 35

CLIENT SURVEY SOFTWARE

FINDING OUT WHAT YOUR CLIENTS REALLY THINK

When it comes to problems with clients, it is always better to be proactive rather than reactive. The challenge, of course, is that you may not always be aware of the fact that a problem exists until it is too late. One method of identifying problems before they reach a critical stage is to regularly survey your clients.

We don't mean to sound negative here. Surveys are not just about identifying problems. They can also help you pinpoint what you are doing correctly, so that you can accentuate the positive in the future. What is your unique value proposition? What made a new client chose you over the competition? What products and services do you offer that particularly please clients? Is there anything you could be doing that you currently are not? Survey software can help you find the answers.

It certainly pays to be aware of what your clients think. It is significantly less expensive to retain existing clients than to attract new ones, so there is a real financial incentive to invest some time and energy keeping our clients happy.

While current clients are our primary concern, they should not be the only one. In order to grow a practice, it is necessary to attract new prospects and convert them into clients. It would be useful to know what it was that persuaded some recent prospects to become clients. If new clients consistently point to certain factors that won them over to you and your firm, you could tailor your approach in the future to further emphasize those factors. It is also important to find out anything you can do that turns prospective clients off, so you can minimize any negative reactions in the future.

Surveys aren't the only method of obtaining information, but, if done right, they are quick, accurate, and inexpensive. Before the advent of modern survey software, collecting and analyzing data was a tedious and expensive proposition. But now, advisors can gather valuable information rather easily. There is a surprisingly wide array of survey software tools available in the marketplace, but we've identified a few that appear to be particularly well suited for financial advisors. They are SurveyMonkey, PollMonkey, and AdvisorSites Survey Kit.

SURVEYMONKEY

SurveyMonkey is a well-designed, capable product. This online tool makes it very easy to design surveys, collect responses, and analyze your results. SurveyMonkey offers a free basic service, for those who like to try before they buy, but some of SurveyMonkey's useful advanced features are disabled in the free version, and basic surveys are limited to 10 questions and 100 responses.

Making use of the free service to conduct a test run is perfectly acceptable, but in order to enjoy the full benefits of the program, advisors will want to sign up for the professional service, which costs $19.95 per month. The professional service includes an unlimited number of surveys, and each survey can include as many questions as you like. The monthly fee includes processing of 1,000 responses per month. If more than 1,000 individuals' responses are received monthly, the account will incur an additional charge of five cents per respondent.

As we mentioned earlier, creating surveys with SurveyMonkey is easy. The best way to start is to launch the sample survey that is provided with membership and use that survey as a template to create your own. Using the sample as a starting point, novice users should be able to construct a basic survey in less than 15 minutes.

Frequent SurveyMonkey users will rapidly come to appreciate the site's design flexibility. Users can select from a menu of question formats (multiple choice/one answer, multiple choice/multiple answers, matrix, open-ended, etc.) and design themes. Logos up to 50 kilobytes in size can be inserted as banners atop each page.

In an effort to improve data integrity, SurveyMonkey allows the user to randomize the order of the answers within a question, so that if you provide four answers to a multiple choice question, each answer will be listed as choice a, b, c, and d roughly 25% of the time. When appropriate, skip logic can be applied to questions so that a respondent will be guided to subsequent questions based upon the response to the current question. To further engage respondents in the survey process, the advisor can chose to program the software so that it will display a summary of the results to participants upon survey completion.

SurveyMonkey offers flexibility when collecting information. Most users feel that the easiest way to collect data is to email potential respondents with an invitation, providing a link to the survey that SurveyMonkey generates. The program includes email list management features, so the user can import email addresses and generate mailings from within the site.

The advisor's corporate website can be used as an additional means of driving traffic to surveys (SurveyMonkey provides the code required to generate a link on your corporate website). Another method that can be used to increase survey responses is the pop-up ad. Pop-up ads are somewhat controversial, but those who are comfortable using them can create two different types from within SurveyMonkey: one generates an invitation to take your survey when a visitor arrives at a specified webpage on your site; the second generates a pop-up of your survey when a specified webpage is visited.

Once the responses are received, they can be analyzed in various ways. The software provides total respondents per answer and percentage of respondents per answer. Information is provided as to how many respondents skipped an individual question. Filters can be used to isolate trends. For example, filters can be created to pinpoint respondents who answered positively or negatively to a certain question. If further analysis is required data can be exported to spreadsheets, HTML, or a relational database.

In summary, SurveyMonkey provides all of the functionality that most advisors desire in an easy to use package.

POLLMONKEY

The similarities between PollMonkey and SurveyMonkey are striking, but PollMonkey is actually a separate company with a distinct product. PollMonkey only does one thing, but it does it well: it creates single question polls that an advisor can use on his or her website.

There are a number of reasons that one might choose to use PollMonkey in addition to, or instead of SurveyMonkey. One reason is that PollMonkey works particularly well when you require rapid feedback with a minimal amount of fuss. For example, if the government proposed significant changes to the tax law, and you wanted to gauge your clients' reaction to the proposal, PollMonkey would be the tool of choice to do so. In a couple of minutes, you could post a Poll to your website requesting client reactions. Are you thinking about scheduling a series of seminars for clients? Why not use PollMonkey to gauge their interest in various potential topics of discussion?

A second reason for using PollMonkey is to create a series of quizzes for visitors to your website. Each week, a financial planning question can be posted to your site. Once the poll is completed, PollMonkey will display the correct answer. Quizzes are a nice way of educating and entertaining your clients, while encouraging return visits.

The service includes a utility called Poll Zones, which allows advisors to plan a series of polls or quizzes in advance and have them displayed on a pre-determined schedule. Poll Zone is a real timesaver. It alleviates the need to constantly visit PollMonkey's site to create updates.

Due to its limited scope, PollMonkey is not a replacement for SurveyMonkey, but it is a very useful supplement to it. At $19.95 for unlimited polls and up to 10,000 responses, PollMonkey is the fastest and easiest method of finding out what those visiting your website have on their minds.

ADVISOR PRODUCTS SURVEY KIT

All too often, circumstances conspire to derail the best-laid marketing plans of financial advisors. Despite the good intentions most of you have as you read this, many will never use the above mentioned products. Perhaps you are just too busy dealing with other issues. Maybe you're afraid you won't ask the right questions. Whatever the case may be, if you are hesitant about building your own surveys, AdvisorProducts Survey Kit is the service for you.

The kit, developed by AdvisorSites, the web development arm of AdvisorProducts, is similar in form and function to SurveyMonkey; but there are a number of notable differences. Specifically, AdvisorProducts Survey Kit includes three unique features that general purpose products do not: a series of financial services specific survey templates, branding assistance, and prompt live tech support.

AdvisorSites' survey templates are professionally designed by authors who have extensive knowledge in the financial services profession. Andrew Gluck, President of AdvisorProducts, oversees the survey writing process. Mr. Gluck is a seasoned journalist who has covered the financial planning industry for many years. Since a template library is available and ready to use, all the advisor has to do is select the survey template, fill in the firm name where required, and distribute the survey.

The importance of branding assistance should not be overlooked. AdvisorProducts will create a corporate banner for use on all of a firm's surveys so that a single, unique image is projected to survey recipients. If an advisor is already an AdvisorProducts customer, a firm's branding materials will already be on file, which will expedite the initial branding process. Advisors new to AdvisorProducts will have to submit their existing logos or arrange to have AdvisorSites create new ones for them.

Many financial advisors we have come in contact with over the years demand access to live, phone-based technical support, which AdvisorProducts offers. Both PollMonkey and SurveyMonkey worked flawlessly when we last tested them. Both offer online help as well as email help, but advisors who require handholding will find AdvisorProducts more to their liking.

The AdvisorProducts Survey Kit costs $600 per year, which is a bit more than the competition. The premium price is justified, however, when the templates, branding assistance, and live support are factored into the equation. In addition, the Survey Kit price includes an unlimited number of surveys and responses. It represents an excellent value for those who require professional design and content with a minimal amount of effort.

Chapter 36

FINANCIAL PLANNING SOFTWARE

If you are new to the financial planning profession, you probably don't have a clue with regard to the evaluation and selection of a suitable financial planning software program. Don't be alarmed! You are not alone. The topic list for the CFP® Certification exam does not require a financial planning software orientation, and as a result, many of the curriculums that prepare prospective CFP® licensees to sit for the exam do not see fit to address the software issue, either due to time constraints, or fear of appearing to favor one developer over another. If you are reading this chapter, your firm or educational institution is offering you information that was not commonly available to the average student at the time of this writing. Congratulations!

Many experienced practitioners constantly grapple with the same questions that are probably going through your mind right now.

A BRIEF HISTORY OF FINANCIAL PLANNING SOFTWARE

Affordable personal computers and professional quality financial planning software programs are a relatively recent development. Before the mid-1990's, many planning functions were performed on financial calculators or individually designed spreadsheets. To this day, prospective CFP® licensees generally receive their introduction to mathematical financial planning concepts with a financial calculator, like the H-P 12C, grasped in one hand.

Quite frankly, there is nothing wrong with this approach. A financial calculator can be both a wonderful educational tool and a practical tool for certain applications in a financial planning practice. The problem with calculators is that they have limitations. As the sophistication of financial planning models has increased, they have outrun the ability of calculators to perform the necessary calculations; and even if the calculations could be performed, it would take way too long, and the probability of input errors would be immense.

As technology advanced, PC's and spreadsheet programs started making their way into the mainstream. A number of technology savvy planners, often those who came from a corporate finance background, started constructing their own financial planning spreadsheets. Some, like this book's co-author David Drucker, realized that other financial planners could benefit from financial planning spreadsheets, but not everyone had the time, skill, or inclination to build their own; this was in the days of the DOS operating system, when the task of constructing spreadsheets was less intuitive and user friendly than it is today. As a result, Dave, and others like him, decided to market the spreadsheets they had developed for their own practices to others. Dave's spreadsheets evolved into a financial planning program called Integrate, which is still marketed today.

SPREADSHEETS

There was a time when constructing one's own financial planning spreadsheets might have been a viable option for practitioners, but the authors believe that, for most readers, this is no longer a realistic solution. There are a number of reasons that commercial software is preferred over home grown spreadsheets. For example:

1. A planner's primary job is to service existing clients and/or attract new ones.
2. Most successful firms are able to differentiate themselves from the competition. We know of few, if any, firms that successfully differentiate themselves based upon the financial planning software they have written.
3. Writing good software requires both advanced financial planning and advanced technological knowledge and the ability to integrate the two.
4. Home grown software must be de-bugged.
5. Financial planning software requires almost continuous updates, which continually updates the potential for errors and increases the cost of creating and maintaining it.
6. Home grown software offers no economies of scale.

7. There are good, commercial alternatives that can meet the needs of most financial planners. These programs range in complexity from basic to highly advanced.

8. Software prices and maintenance costs are generally reasonable, with prices ranging from a few hundred dollars per year per user up to a few thousand per year per user.

Even if no software package meets your exact needs, the odds are that you will still be better off with a commercial program than one of your own design. In almost all cases, the incremental improvement derived from a custom designed program will not be worth the investment of time and money required to develop it.

We base our conclusion on the fact that many of the largest financial institutions in the country are depending on third parties to develop and maintain their financial planning software. If these firms, with their large base of employees to spread costs over, are turning to outside vendors, it is difficult for us to fathom how small to mid-sized firms can design software with sufficient added value to justify the development costs; not to mention the costs of maintenance and upgrades.

EVALUATING COMMERCIAL FINANCIAL PLANNING SOFTWARE

When it comes to financial planning software, it is safe to say that one size *does not* fit all. Almost every serious financial planner adheres to the six-step financial planning process, but the similarities end there. It is not difficult to understand why: personal financial planning is, after all, highly *personal*, both from the perspective of the client and the planner.

Client bases vary from firm to firm. Many advisors, as part of their business and marketing strategy, target a market niche such as: small business owners; mid-level managers at one or more large local firms; high net worth entrepreneurs; younger middle class couples; or same sex partners, to name just a few. Each of these groups has some unique needs.

For example, planners who work with small business owners will want a software package that can value and track small business assets, as well as one that can illustrate tools commonly used for small business succession planning. Mid-level managers may have issues related to non-cash compensation, such as employee stock options, restricted stock, stock appreciation rights, and the like.

In addition to the hard core planning issues, there are "soft" issues that also must be considered. Soft issues include things like the look and feel of the program, ease of use, and the support policies of the vendor.

DIFFERENTIATORS

How does one go about differentiating between the numerous financial planning programs that are available today? We'll get into some of the details shortly, but before we do, let's discuss some categorizations that will serve as a jumping off point for the rest of the discussion.

COMPREHENSIVE VS. MODULAR

Comprehensive Financial Planning Software

A comprehensive financial planning program is one that offers at least some coverage of the major financial topics: goal setting; risk management; investments; education planning; retirement planning; tax planning; and estate planning. In a true comprehensive financial planning program, all of the input screens and calculation engines share a common database, so that information entered in one module of the program is immediately available to the rest of the program.

All things being equal, we find that most practitioners have a strong preference for comprehensive financial planning software. Comprehensive programs alleviate the need for repetitive data entry, facilitate navigation, and produce uniform reports.

Of course, all things are usually not equal. While the overall qualities of many comprehensive financial programs are quite good, an otherwise satisfactory program may be lacking in one or more areas that are critical to your practice. Commonly, a good program will provide some coverage in the required area, but it will not provide the depth and breadth of planning functionality that you need. In other cases, the program may totally lack coverage in an area due to weak customer demand. In such cases, practitioners will often turn to a modular software package.

Modular Financial Planning Software

Conceptually, modular financial planning software can be subdivided into two groups:

1. Software that focuses on one or more of the core financial planning topics mentioned above; or
2. Specialized modules dealing with topics that receive little or no coverage in most comprehensive financial planning packages.

The first group of software is designed primarily for those who specialize in a particular area of financial planning, such as estate planning or retirement planning. Comprehensive financial planning firms will sometimes buy these programs, as well, in order to expand the depth and breadth of their capabilities in selected areas. Most novice planners need not concern themselves with this category of software. Some readers may be tempted to construct an "all-star" comprehensive financial planning program by combining the "best of class" from a number of these core specialty programs, but, as a practical matter, this is difficult to do because transferring data from one program to the next is likely to be problematic.

In some cases, it may be possible to import/export data; in other cases, manual re-entry will be required. Under the best of scenarios, the cost of plan production is likely to increase and plan output will require reformatting; the worst case is that data will be manually re-keyed incorrectly, leading to all sorts of problems. Generally speaking, creating comprehensive programs from modular programs should be avoided whenever possible.

There are times, however, when it will be impossible to avoid deploying software programs in the second group. There are certain planning situations that many mainstream comprehensive programs do not address adequately, if at all (employee stock options are one that comes to mind). In such instances, the planner has little choice other than to work with multiple programs in order to produce the required result.

CASH FLOW VS. GOAL DRIVEN SOFTWARE

Cash Flow Driven Software

Some practitioners and their clients absolutely love cash flow driven financial planning programs. Historically, almost all of the most highly regarded comprehensive programs were cash flow based. The argument for these programs is:

- They offer the greatest level of detail.
- They are the most precise.
- They offer the greatest degree of planner control over the models.
- They are easier to audit.

Cash flow driven programs are particularly appropriate when one wants to do sophisticated income tax or estate planning, and they are fine for almost any other financial planning engagement as well. The primary disadvantages of cash flow models are that they generally require the most data entry, and the output can sometimes overwhelm clients. Cash flow models are sometimes also criticized because they portray a level of accuracy that is not achievable.

For example, if you take an anticipated cash flow, such as the dividend on a stock holding, and project it out 30 years, the program will tell you exactly how much money, to the penny, will be available to the client at the end of the period. Of course, we all know that the dividend rate will probably vary from our projections, as will the client's overall federal and state marginal tax rates. Factor in income tax deductions, tax credits, and a change in the way dividends are taxed, and we really have no idea what our after-tax return will be 30 years hence. Now assume that every cash flow in the model will be subject to the same variability. One can see how inaccurate our forecasts might be, particularly when we project far into the future. This is not to say that other modeling techniques do not have similar problems, they do; what troubles critics is that the clients might look at seemingly precise numbers and accept them at face value. It is incumbent upon the planner to understand the underpinnings of any financial software model, and to explain any shortcoming to the client.

Goal Based Financial Planning Software

For many years, goal based financial planning software was considered by many to be of inferior quality to cash flow based software, and, for the most part, that perception was probably true. Many of the goal based programs of earlier generations were either sales oriented, simplistic, or both. Thankfully, however, this is no longer the case. In recent years, a number of increasingly sophisticated, high quality goal based programs have entered the marketplace, and they have been warmly embraced by the financial planning community.

Probably the strongest argument for goal based planning is that it "thinks" like clients do. It has been the experience of the authors that prospects often initially approach a financial planner with specific questions such as: "How much do I need to save annually to retire comfortably?" or "How much should I save annually to fund my child's college education?" Goal based planning is well suited to these types of tasks, because they frame the financial planning "problem" very much like the client does.

As a general rule, goal based programs tend to require less data entry, which keeps production costs down. Also, as we stated earlier, goal based planning is also appropriate when projecting far out into the future, a situation in which detailed cash flow programs are of questionable value.

There are, however, times when goal based planning is not appropriate, such as when doing detailed tax planning over shorter time horizons for higher net worth clients.

There are situations that lend themselves to goal based planning, there are situations that lend themselves to cash flow based planning, and there are times when either approach will do the job equally well. Many mature practices make use of both types of programs, relying on their experience and the nature of the engagement to dictate the software used with a specific client. Initially, the novice planner should select the program type most likely to fit with his or her intended client base. The planner should make every effort to thoroughly master a single program before adding another, if necessary.

DESKTOP VS. APPLICATION SERVICE PROVIDER (ASP)

Desktop Software

In years past, software programs and any related data files, resided on each individual PC. Today, at many small to medium sized firms, the financial planning program, the related data files, or both, may reside on a networked file server. For the purposes of this discussion, we need to expand the definition of "desktop" to include all software and data files that reside within a financial planning office, and which are typically accessed on site.

Advantages

1. *Comfort* – Many people, including financial advisors, tend to find a "comfort zone" and stick with it until it can be clearly demonstrated that there is a meaningful reason to change. In the opinion of some planners, there is no compelling reason at this time to deviate from the "tried and true" software that they are currently using.

2. *Control of the data* – This is probably the most commonly cited advantage of desktop software. Understandably, financial planners are highly protective of their client data.

3. *Security* – Many feel that the only way to keep such data totally secure is to maintain it in-house.

4. *Configuration and customization* – While practices vary from one software package to another, desktop software tends to offer planners more configuration and customization options. For example, some ASP programs may only allow users to save or print reports in one file format (Adobe PDF is a popular one), while many desktop programs offer additional options.

5. *Self-contained system* – Internet access is not required.

Disadvantages

1. *Set-up and installation* – Desktop software must be installed and configured on multiple computers. The larger the firm, the greater the cost of installation is likely to be.

2. *Maintenance* – Each time a desktop software package is upgraded, it will again be necessary to access multiple computers; a potentially expensive proposition over time.

3. *Lack of continuity* – Within the firm, there may not be hardware and software continuity from one computer to the next. Lack of continuity will increase maintenance costs.

4. *Limited accessibility* – In order to use a desktop program, the planner must have access to it. If the planner is out of the office, and a laptop loaded with the current software and data files is not present, the planner will not be able to access the files.

5. *Inability to "share" data with clients* – Sharing information with clients electronically is more difficult and requires additional hardware or software.

6. *Security* – Housing client data in-house does not guarantee security. Data may actually be more secure in a remote location.

Application Service Providers (ASP)

In contrast, web-based applications reside on a web-server. For small to mid-sized firms, web-based applications will typically reside off-site, and they will be hosted by an application service provider (ASP). Large firms, such as the major wirehouses can, and sometimes do, chose to act as their own host. Today, it is rare to find medium to smaller sized firms hosting their own web applications, although we expect that future technological advances will make the practice somewhat more common in the future.

Advantages

1. There are minimal set-up requirements.

2. Maintenance is performed by the ASP, resulting in lower costs and improved efficiencies.

3. Continuity is maintained throughout the firm.

4. Client data is always accessible, as long as an Internet connection is present.

5. Advisors can conduct virtual planning sessions with their clients, no matter where they are.

6. Costs can be further reduced by encouraging potential clients to provide data online before an initial meeting.

7. Other trusted advisors can be granted access to information and/or participate in virtual planning sessions.

8. Client data is often more secure with an ASP provider than it is at individual planning firms.

9. The ability to outsource financial plan writing tasks to Virtual Work Partners is simplified.

Disadvantages

1. *Need for a fast, reliable internet connection* – Some applications can run over a dial-up connection in a pinch, but connecting over a dial-up connection is not recommended for daily use.

2. *Data off-site* – This is unacceptable to some, but most objections can be overcome through negotiation and documentation. Any vendor contract should clearly state that the planner owns the data, and there should be a provision that spells out exactly how, and in what format, the provider will return your data to you should either party terminate the relationship.

3. *Security* – Some observers cite security concerns as a disadvantage of ASPs, but their logic may be faulty. Application service providers are more knowledgable about security than the typical planning firm with regard to security measures, and their livelihood depends upon their reliability. As a rule, they are highly qualified and highly motivated to protect your data.

4. *Client access to data* – Not every financial planner wants to grant clients access to their data over the Internet, but this problem may be more a matter of perception than fact: many of the better financial planning ASPs allow the financial advisor to determine the degree of access clients are granted online.

5. *Conversion costs* – For established planners, the costs associated with moving from one financial planning program to another can be significant. The task of transferring data and training employees to use a new software package should not be underestimated.

BEGINNING YOUR SOFTWARE SEARCH

Now that we've laid out some of the big, "top-down" issues that differentiate one program from another, we are ready to explore the financial planning software selection process in greater detail.

The first rule when selecting financial planning software is the same rule that applies to just about every function financial planners perform – plan, plan, plan! Envision what you would like your practice to look like in the short, medium and long-term. Will you try to be a generalist, or will you focus on a specific market niche? Will you cater to the middle class, the mass affluent, or the high net worth client? Do you have any expertise advising entrepreneurs, or do you prefer to work with employees of large corporations?

Your business model will guide your software selection process to some extent. For example, if you deal with small business owners or entrepreneurs, you may require software capabilities that only a few commercial programs possess, thereby narrowing your choices for you. If you decide to work with the mid-market, clients' planning needs will be somewhat more limited, as will be their ability to pay. This might suggest the need for a program that can deal with core financial planning needs in a quick and efficient manner.

Who will be doing the actual data entry? If it is a qualified planner, the level of financial planning knowledge necessary to operate the program is a non-issue; however, if an assistant or the client will be entering data within the program, the data required for a given field must be readily apparent.

Philosophically, what is your approach to planning? Do you believe that you add most of your value by supplying extensive documentation and reporting to clients, or do you believe your primary function is consultative?

What do you know about your potential software vendor? Does the firm offer an open architecture platform, or is it a proprietary system, which could potentially make it more difficult for you to change vendors in the future?

SPECIFIC CAPABILITIES YOU MAY REQUIRE

Each planner has a unique set of capabilities that they insist upon, and others that are open to compromise. We'd suggest that you write down the necessities and the options you are looking for; don't rush this step or you will regret it later.

Almost any decent program will be capable of dealing with cash inflows and outflows. Cash inflows include items like salaries, self-employment income, Social Security benefits, pension benefits, and annuity income. Outflows include fixed and variable living expenses, debt service, and taxes.

The better programs will allow planning for both even and uneven cash flows; they will also allow you to automatically direct excess cash flows toward a goal or account (to pay down debt, or save for a vacation home, for example). If there is a short-term cash flow problem, can the planner set rules for how it will be funded? If assets are to be sold to fund a deficit, can the program be instructed to sell the highest cost-basis assets first, if desired?

Coming back to your client base, what types of assets are your clients likely to hold, and how capable is your program in those particular areas? For example, are your clients likely to hold employee stock options or restricted stock? Will they have assets denominated in foreign currencies; what about investment real estate? What about specific types of accounts, such as 403(b) or 457 plans? Not every program can deal with all of the above, and those that do may not provide the level of detail you require.

Those planners who offer tax planning and/or tax preparation may require more detailed tax reporting than those who don't, but all practitioners will probably want some reasonable indication of their clients' federal and state income tax situation. For some readers, the ability to plan for, calculate, and report the alternative minimum tax (AMT) will be critical.

Your client base may have fairly straightforward estate planning needs, but if your practice will recommend advanced estate planning strategies, you should be aware that modeling abilities in comprehensive programs vary greatly in this area.

Undoubtedly, there will be other specifics you desire. Some programs do an excellent job of number crunching, but their charting and graphing capabilities leave much to be desired. Some give advisors a great deal of control with regard to the format, layout, and content of client reports; others do not. In some cases, one can overcome a program's rigid output constraints by exporting the reports to another program and touching it up, but this process increases production time and cost, so be sure to factor such considerations into your decision-making process.

MAKING THE COMPARISON

Armed with a list of differentiators and a list of desired capabilities, construct a simple comparison spreadsheet. List the names of the programs under consideration (Appendix A will help you identify potential candidates) across the top of the page, and a list of functions/features along the left hand side of the page. You can either list the features in order of preference, or, if you want to be a little more sophisticated, assign different weightings to individual cells.

Once the spreadsheet is completed, it will become apparent that only a small group of programs, probably no more than two or three, are compatible with your needs. At this point, it is time to secure demo versions of the finalists and put them through a more thorough evaluation. (Most vendors offer free versions of the software that deactivates after a specified time period, usually 15, 30, or 60 days). Be cautious with vendors who do not allow you to try a full working version of the software before you buy it.

Load and use the software. In the case of desktop software, does it install effortlessly? In the case of ASP software, can you sign on quickly? Do the pages load properly? Is the program easy to navigate? Is it responsive, or does the program occasionally freeze up?

Try running one or more test cases. Spot-check some calculations manually, so you understand how the calculation engines are behaving. Print a few reports to ensure they look as good (or bad) on paper as they do on your screen. Determine how much control you have over the printed output, and find out whether reports can be edited from within the program or by exporting them to a word processor.

Undoubtedly, you will have a few questions about the way the program operates. Call technical support (not your salesperson), and see what kind of service you receive. Inevitably, you will require technical support at some time in the future. At that time, you will require prompt, competent service. It is probably fair to assume that if you are unhappy with technical support initially, the situation will not improve after the vendor has your hard earned cash.

While you're chatting with the support team, be sure to inquire about support policies, hours of operation, communication channels (phone, e-mail, IM, etc.), manuals, training materials, and frequency of upgrades.

SURVIVORS

At this point in the process, you may have already narrowed your choice to one survivor; if not, there is one final step you can take: if possible, participate in a live training seminar. A number of vendors offer seminars at various sites nationwide over the course of a year; sometimes they are held in conjunction with regional or national financial planning conferences.

Seminars offer potential purchasers the opportunity to work through case studies under the guidance of experienced instructors who have an intimate knowledge of the product. The best seminars make use of a wide range of program features, and offer attendees ample opportunities to ask questions. Seminars offer participants a chance to compare notes with colleagues, which may help uncover facts that you overlooked. In short, there is no better way to rapidly become acquainted with a program's strengths and weaknesses.

Selecting a financial planning software package will take some time and dedication on your part, but doing it right the first time will save time and money in the long run. Make sure that you do your own research and select a product that meets your needs.

Chapter 37

PORTFOLIO CONSTRUCTION AND MANAGEMENT TOOLS

For better or for worse, at many financial planning firms, "investment planning" is the most prominently featured portion of the financial planning process. There are a number of reasons this is so. One is that many of the early financial planners came from an investment background, so it was natural for them to feature their strengths. Another is visibility. Clients don't necessarily think about their retirement plan, risk management plan, or estate plan every day, but media coverage of the financial markets serves to keep investment planning in clients' consciousness at all times. And then there's the issue of money: the investment portfolio is where the money is, and money therefore becomes the gauge by which many clients measure their planner's performance.

Clearly, there is more to the financial planning process than investing. It is equally clear that investment performance should not be the primary driver of the financial planning engagement. However, many planners – through their own business practices, such as asset-based fees or quarterly investment reporting – only serve to reinforce clients' attitudes.

There has been a movement underway in the profession over the last few years to de-emphasize short term investment performance and focus more on a client's overall financial health and progress (i.e., holistic planning or "life planning"), but this movement has a long way to go. Those planners who truly believe in comprehensive financial planning would be well advised to examine their compensation structure and reporting practices to make sure those practices reflect their beliefs.

While many gurus believe that investment planning's role in the comprehensive financial planning firm will diminish over time, in today's world it still plays a prominent role. As a result of this reality, planners, unless they are prepared to outsource the whole investment management function, must become familiar with the portfolio construction tools, as well as the portfolio management/reporting tools.

This chapter is intended to provide the planner with an overview of tools that are commonly used by independent registered investment advisor (RIA) firms. However, it is far from comprehensive. Larger firms, whether broker/dealers, trust companies, or institutional money managers, often use third-party software from other providers or develop their own proprietary tools. The products covered in this chapter, are, for the most part, representative of the type of tools one is likely to encounter in a small- to mid-sized independent RIA firm.

Subjects covered in this chapter include: portfolio construction software; portfolio management and reporting software; outsourcing investment planning; and choosing an investment custodian.

PORTFOLIO CONSTRUCTION

A financial planner who is going to help clients manage their money had better have some tools available to help construct and analyze portfolios. The *Tools and Techniques of Investment Planning* covers some of the theoretical underpinnings of portfolio construction.[1]

It is important that a person doing investment planning understand such concepts. Also, spreadsheets or programs can often be built based on such knowledge. However, most practicing planners use commercial software for constructing and analyzing portfolios. Unless there is a compelling reason to do otherwise, the authors would suggest following their example.

What can portfolio construction and analysis tools do? Here are a few examples. In the late 1990s, it was not unusual for a prospective client to walk into a planner's office with a "diversified" portfolio of mutual funds. In many cases, most or all of the funds were selected from a list of last year's top performing mutual funds. Since large capitalization (large-cap) growth funds at that time were the market leaders, and the funds with the highest weighting of the largest capitalization – tech sector funds – had performed best, the client with the "diversified" portfolio of seven mutual funds was very heavily weighted in large-cap growth – often to the total exclusion of other asset classes. Furthermore, it was very likely that there was considerable overlap across the top five or ten positions in the seven mutual funds held by the client. With the right tool, a planner, with very little effort, could demonstrate to the client that his "diversified" portfolio of mutual funds was not only concentrated in the same asset class, but it was also concentrated in the same few stocks! Not exactly what the client expected to hear.

How can a diversified portfolio be built for a new client without subjecting the portfolio to unnecessary (unsystematic) risk? How can a planner insure that a defined process is followed? Spreadsheets can be built if one has the expertise, but they will need to be updated regularly with appropriate data feeds.

Is building investment models from the ground up the best way to add value to the client? For 99% of planners, the answer is probably not. Good tools are already available so there is no need to re-invent the wheel. Time would almost certainly be better spent building the business and consulting with existing clients.

There is no one best tool for all planners or all situations. The choice of constructional/analytic tools will be driven by a planner's business model, client needs, investment approach, and budget.

Both Morningstar® Principia® and Morningstar® Workstation Office Edition offer some portfolio construction and portfolio analytical tools. In the June 2003 Tiburon study, Morningstar® was ranked the most widely used asset allocation software package by survey respondents. It also garnered the highest satisfaction scores within this category by a small margin. It is interesting to note that at the time of this study, Morningstar® Workstation Office Edition did not exist, so Morningstar's products have gotten even better. An overview of several portfolio construction software products follows.

Principia®

Morningstar® Principia® allows planners to enter (or import) client portfolios and analyze them in various ways. For the sake of simplicity, assume a portfolio consisting exclusively of mutual funds. Once all of the portfolio holdings are entered, Principia® can display a summary of information such as current allocation to major asset classes, fund statistics (potential capital gains exposure, average fund expense ratio), risk/return statistics (standard deviation, Sharpe ratio), and MPT Statistics (Alpha, Beta, R-squared). By drilling down further into the program, planners can obtain detailed information about the portfolio as a whole, or about individual holdings within the portfolio. The asset allocation functionality is limited, however. Planners can view the current allocation at any time, and they can enter proposed changes to see how the overall portfolio composition will be effected by the change, but it is really not an asset allocation tool. Principia® does not include an optimizer (or anything else) to help the planner determine whether or not a portfolio is efficient or suitable for the client.

Morningstar®

In addition to offering all of the analytical tools that Principia® contains, Morningstar® Workstation Office Edition offers planners three methods of building portfolios. One method is tied primarily to the included risk questionnaire. This method suggests an allocation based primarily on the client's risk tolerance, while giving little if any weight to other factors. The second method is the goal-based method. This methodology is tied primarily to a stated goal (to have X amount of dollars X number of years from now). This method emphasizes first on solving for a portfolio that can achieve the goal, with a secondary emphasis on risk. For example, if a number of allocations will achieve the desired result, the one with the lowest projected risk would be recommended. The third method uses a mean variance optimizer to recommend allocations along an efficient frontier.

The Morningstar analytics are very good, particularly when it comes to mutual funds (their core competency). Their portfolio construction/asset allocation tools are not the most sophisticated on the market, but they are more than adequate for the typical financial planning practice. In the case of Workstation Office, the seamless integration of the analytics and the construction tools add to the product's appeal.

M-V Optimizer

Those planners interested in a relatively inexpensive product, or those who are comfortable working within Microsoft Excel, should consider M-V Optimizer. This program, an Excel based product, was developed for Strategic Financial Solutions by Daniel H. Wagner Associates, a leading operations research, mathematics, and software development firm.

M-V Optimizer is designed to handle up to 250 assets, and provides functionality for computing and displaying the entire efficient frontier, the optimal portfolio associated with user-supplied target volatility, and the optimal portfolio associated with a user-supplied target return. Both long and short positions can be entered into the program.

M-V Optimizer also requires the expected return and volatility for each asset and a correlation matrix. The planner has the option of specifying these qualities himself, or allowing M-V Optimizer to calculate these quantities from user supplied time series of returns for each asset.

M-V Optimizer is powerful and customizable, provided the planner is good with Excel. Based on the functionality it offers, it is reasonably priced. It offers a great deal of flexibility, provided the planner has a solid understanding of the process and access to the required data.

Ibbotson

Ibbotson's primary investment planning product for planners is Ibbotson Portfolio Strategist. This software package is designed to help planners determine the asset mix that offers the best chance of achieving the highest return for a given level of risk. It can take into account client needs and objectives, constraints, and risk tolerances. Portfolio Strategist is designed to deal with an individual's (or couple's) tax situation, and it can integrate with Ibbotson Fund Strategist (Ibbotson Fund Strategist is a program that uses returns-based style analysis to arrive at an asset allocation strategy for a mutual fund portfolio).

Ibbotson's EnCorr is a modular system that integrates historical data analysis, strategic asset allocation, forecasting, style analysis, portfolio attribution, and a wide array of statistical and graphical analyses into one family. Because it is modular, firms can purchase only the data and capabilities that they need.

Available modules include EnCorr Optimizer, EnCorr Optimizer Plus (an add-on product to Optimizer that adds Ibbotson Associates resampled optimization capabilities and latest capital market assumptions to EnCorr Optimizer), EnCorr Attribution (for attribution analysis), EnCorr Allocator (a program that helps planners implement a target allocation through the use of managers and benchmarks), EnCorr Analyzer (examine and analyze capital market data), and Ibbotson Scenario Builder (generate customized "what-if" scenarios).

SunGard

SunGard offers a number of asset allocation products for planners. Frontier AllocationMaster, the desktop-based portfolio optimization tool, is probably the best known of these. Frontier AllocatonMaster Web, a newer product, includes additional capabilities, such as tax efficient optimization and Monte Carlo simulation techniques (once a proposed asset allocation is selected, the program can run a probability analysis on the proposed portfolio).

FactMaster and FactMaster Web are companion products for AllocationMaster and AllocationMaster Web, respectively. They add information and historical data for individual mutual funds (and an extensive list of market indices), hypothetical illustrations, and return-based style analysis.

Skill Weighted Portfolio

Skill Weighted Portfolio (www.skillweighted.com) is a rather new and unique online portfolio construction tool. It is the first commercial tool the authors have come across that helps planners construct core/satellite portfolios.

The core/satellite methodology is predicated on the belief that some sectors of the market (e.g., large-cap equities) are efficient. If these market sectors are, in fact, efficient, it follows that they should be indexed, so that investors can at least capitalize on lower costs and greater tax efficiency. The satellite portion of the portfolio is invested in those market sectors believed to be less efficient, or opportunistically, to capture alpha. The skill weighted methodology takes the concept one step farther, dividing the non-core portion of the portfolio into two parts: an active ring, for asset classes such as small cap stocks, real estate, and high yield bonds; and an alpha rim, for riskier investments such as sector funds, emerging markets, private equity, and hedge funds. The skill weighted allocations and models were developed in conjunction with Standard & Poor's Investment Advisory Services LLC.

In addition to its portfolio building tools, the Skill Weighted platform offers a well defined workflow structure and some well designed marketing materials.

PORTFOLIO MANAGEMENT AND REPORTING

What is the most commonly asked question financial planners get from existing clients? It is the following: "How am I doing?" The clients are referring, of course, to their investment portfolio. What has their monthly, semiannual, annual, three-year, and five-year performance been for individual holdings, their taxable portfolio, their tax deferred accounts, and their total portfolio? Can the planner supply a consolidated report of performance over various periods for the holdings of the entire family? Portfolio management and reporting software allows a planner to do so. It also enables the planner to manage portfolios more effectively, and make tax aware portfolio decisions.

Until recently, almost all of the popular portfolio management packages for planners were desktop based. The software and the data resided on the planner's computer, and each day, transactional-information was downloaded from the planner's custodian to update the portfolio management system. Today, planners can choose between desktop software and ASP model. The advantage of the desktop system is that the planner maintains total responsibility and control over the data and the system. The disadvantage is that the system must be maintained (daily downloads, reconciliations, etc.). Through the ASP model, much of the maintenance can be outsourced to the provider. ASP providers generally download the data and perform reconciliations. In some cases, there is seamless integration between portfolio management systems and custodial platforms so that downloads are no longer necessary and planners can access intraday data from within the portfolio management system.

Before deciding upon a portfolio management and reporting product, there are a few things to consider. The first consideration is the capabilities that will be needed. All of the packages discussed below can handle equities and mutual funds well, but some of the less sophisticated products can run into problems with certain types of fixed income products, hybrid products, derivatives, assets denominated in foreign currencies, and some other types of assets. Make sure that the program chosen can accept the billing schedule needed. Some programs allow for an almost unlimited number of billing schemes. They allow the planner to set up multiple tiered schedules, charge different rates for fixed income and equities, and even exclude individual assets.

Next, consider whether a desktop system or an ASP system is preferable. A planner who is just starting out may not have much of a choice. The better ASP systems usually charge a base service fee, plus a per account charge; and there is usually a minimum number of accounts (or a minimum account charge). In some cases, it just may not be economically feasible for a new planner to hire the ASP provider he prefers initially.

Whether selecting an ASP or a desktop package, find out how the data will be stored and how easy it is to move the data in and out of a system. In order to maintain maximum flexibility, it is important that the system stores and/or outputs data in industry standard formats, not proprietary ones. Think about security. Can the data be protected with a password, and can different access levels be set for different employees?

Does the company have a reputation for innovation? Are they constantly improving their product, or are they resting on their laurels? What does their typical client look like? Are they very similar to the planner's clients, or are they much bigger or much smaller?

Ask for recommendations from colleagues or consultants. Moving data from one portfolio management program to another is a bit more difficult than changing financial planning software; it isn't something one wants to do more than once unless one has to. Spend a little extra time at the outset to find the right fit.

DESKTOP SOFTWARE PRODUCTS

Centerpiece (Portfolio Center)

Centerpiece has long been a favorite product of independent RIAs, particularly those who place assets with Charles Schwab & Co., Inc (and that is quite a few, since Schwab is the leading custodian of independent RIAs). Centerpiece has always offered a nice balance of price, power, and usability. For software of this type, it is fairly easy to learn.

So what's the problem? There are a couple. One is that the product has been aging, and not too gracefully. As some financial planning firms have grown and added additional users, the current database has had trouble keeping up. There have also been complaints about the data format. In addition, some planners prefer not to purchase their portfolio management software from their custodian (Centerpiece is sold by Schwab Performance Technologies, Inc., a subsidiary of Charles Schwab & Co., Inc.).

Schwab Performance Technologies is addressing two out of the three issues. They are rolling out Portfolio

Center, the SQL-based successor to Centerpiece. SQL is an industry standard database, which should enable the new product to share data more easily with other programs. Informal discussions with PortfolioCenter beta testers indicate that the new program is significantly faster than Centerpiece.

In short, if a planner is not worried about purchasing his software from a custodian, Portfolio Center is definitely worthy of consideration.

PowerBroker

PowerBroker (www.powerbrokertools.com) is a new, open-architecture, desktop-based portfolio management and reporting package from Cornerstone Revolutions, Inc.

It ships with Microsoft SQL Server 2000 Desktop Engine (MSDE 2000), the free, redistributable version of SQL Server for client applications requiring an embedded database. According to Cornerstone, a MSDE database can store up to 2 GB of information. Firms that require more than 2 GB of information storage will need to purchase a SQL database license. Firms already running SQL server can elect to deploy PowerBroker through their existing database architecture (this is the same architecture Schwab's PorfolioCenter is using).

Like PortfolioCenter, PowerBroker is easy to learn and use; in fact, the authors find it easier than Centerpiece to navigate. PowerBroker contains most of the core functionality that Centerpiece does, although it lacked the ability to interface with CRM packages when the authors tested it. It also lacked some of the billing flexibility that other programs provide (e.g., the ability to set fees at the individual asset level). It did, however, include a number of handy usability features not found in Centerpiece.

While PowerBroker is a new product, the authors were very impressed by it. The program is sold by an independent software company and it is attractively priced. It represents an excellent value, particularly for those just entering the field and who do not have to worry about converting data from another program.

CapTools

The authors have always found CapTools to be a bit more difficult to learn and navigate than some of the competition, but it is a capable package at a reasonable price. For as long as memory serves, CapTools Professional has been a price leader in the desktop software category. CapTools Professional Level 2, the current price leader, offers all of the functionality that a new practice requires. For an additional charge, Level 3 supports web reporting, rebalancing by asset class, rebalancing of margin accounts, advanced reporting, incentive fee billing, dividend accrual, and a number of other extras. Level 4 offers some more advanced features, such as margin adjusted reporting and large fund accounting.

Advent

Advent's Axys portfolio management and reporting system is widely used by larger financial planning and investment advisory firms. It can handle a wide range of investments including equities, fixed income, mutual funds, derivatives, multi currencies, mortgage backed securities, and variable rate securities. It also offers excellent reporting capabilities. Advent also offers Moxy, a trading and order automation module.

While the authors think Advent's products may be suitable for larger firms, they do not recommend them for emerging practices.

APPLICATION SERVICE PROVIDERS (ASPs)

Investigo

Investigo offers a service that combines outsourced download and reconciliation, portfolio management, portfolio reporting, and light CRM functionality in an ASP package. This means that the applications, and all of the data, reside on Investigo's servers. Planners, and their clients, gain access to information over the Internet through a standard web browser, such as Internet Explorer or Opera.

Investigo offers all of the core functionality that most planners require at a reasonable price. Of all the ASPs the authors have investigated that serve independent RIAs, Investigo is the most reasonably priced by a substantial margin. For a planner with an emerging practice looking for an ASP portfolio management and reporting provider, Investigo would be a good place to start searching.

StatementOne

StatementOne is an online provider of investment consolidation and portfolio reporting tools. They are still fairly new to the independent RIA market; however, they are well entrenched in the broker/dealer market. The authors have found that StatementOne's pricing is attractive on an enterprise basis. Representatives or RIAs affiliated with a firm that deals with StatementOne appear to receive a good service package at a reasonable price. When the authors last spoke with the firm, their pricing for independent RIAs was much less attractive, particularly for smaller firms.

Fidelity / IDS

Fidelity recently announced a strategic relationship with Integrated Decision Systems (IDS) to offer an institutional portfolio management and order generation system to planners doing business with Fidelity. The platform will eventually become highly integrated with the Fidelity advisor platform, offering a high degree of automation.

When the authors recently previewed the system, it was impressive as one of the most sophisticated, comprehensive tools available to planners. Unfortunately, it will not be inexpensive. While pricing has not yet been set, the authors would not be surprised to see entry-level prices in the neighborhood of $20,000. This tool may be beyond the reach of emerging practices, but those planners transitioning from a broker/dealer to an independent RIA model would be well advised to check out the IDS platform.

Morningstar® Workstation Office Edition Portfolio Management

According to Morningstar, Inc., it is in the early stages of developing a portfolio management module for Workstation Office Edition. While no release date had been specified on the date this book was published, the authors' guess is that a first version should become available in mid-2005. Sources say that the initial portfolio module will be targeted primarily at planners who use core investment products (i.e., stocks, bonds, mutual funds), so it may not be a good choice for those who deal in derivatives or other esoteric instruments. For emerging practices, particularly those who use Morningstar® Workstation Office Edition, the combined product should offer good integration at a reasonable price.

OUTSOURCING

Not every planner has the expertise or the inclination to manage his clients' investments. If a planner can't add value by investing assets for his clients, he shouldn't do it; instead, he/she should find someone else who could.

Of course, a planner can hire one or more in-house investment experts, but if he or she is just starting out, or has a relatively small client base by choice, it may not be economically feasible to hire a full-time staff person. Consequently, outsourcing the investment function to an outside party may be a much more sensible approach.

Planners looking to outsource some or all of the investment management process have a wide variety of resources to choose from. Some providers offer unbundled services that allow planners to pick and choose what functions to outsource, while others offer a total "turn-key" package, which includes investment selection, account administration, reporting, business development, and relationship management tools. Providers include SEI Investments (www.seic.com) EnvestnetPMC (www.envestnetpmc.com), Morningstar Managed Portfolios (www.mp.morningstar.com), Lockwood Financial Services (www.lockwoodfinancial.com), and Russell (www.russell.com). Extensive information about the services the above mentioned firms offer is available on their websites.

The authors would like to highlight one firm that is new to the managed account business. They are unique for a couple of reasons. First, they started out primarily as a comprehensive financial planning firm. Second, their approach to managing client assets differs a bit from the norm.

CHOOSING A CUSTODIAN

Independent planners generally work with one or more firms that provide custodial services for their clients. The custodians that target independent RIAs provide a dedicated platform so that planners can access client accounts, perform block trades, download transactional and portfolio data into a reporting package, etc. The three custodians generally used by independent RIAs are Schwab, Fidelity, and TD Waterhouse. Unfortunately, there has been a growing reluctance on the part of the "big three" over the last few years to welcome emerging practices. All may welcome emerging practices on a case-by-case basis, but there could be strings, or minimum fees, attached. This has created somewhat of a dilemma for new entrants into the field.

Legend Financial Advisors, Inc.® (Legend®) is an SEC- registered investment advisory based in Pittsburgh, PA [(888) 236-5960]. As of July 31, 2004, they managed in excess of $200,000,000.

Legend® manages monies in two basic styles. They are as follows:

1. *Lower Volatility Portfolios –*

According to Lou Stanasolovich, CEO and President of Legend: "These portfolios are designed to provide long term equity-like returns but with bond-like risk. In other words, returns that range from 8% to 12% with standard deviations in the 3.5 to 7.5 range." By contrast, the S&P 500 has delivered a long-term return of approximately 10% with a standard deviation of 20. These portfolios are constructed with mutual funds that have a low correlation to each other, thereby creating a significantly smoother pattern of return than other investment strategies that deliver similar returns. The large majority of the funds that are utilized are either institutional funds or funds that are managed by boutique-type firms where the managers are the firm owners. Many of the funds utilized by Legend® are currently closed to planners and the general public, but Legend® has unique arrangements to provide access to these funds.

2. *Individual Stock Management –*

Legend® manages individual stock portfolios utilizing a quantitative approach to selecting stocks that is designed to minimize risk while maximizing return. Unlike many portfolio managers, Legend utilizes an all-cap approach to selecting stocks, equally-weighting them at the time of purchase. Stocks selected generally share a number of characteristics including: rising sales; good margins; return on equity exceeding 10%; a history of positive earnings surprises, and rising earnings estimates. At any point in time, there are generally 25 to 40 stocks in the portfolio.

Legend® provides their investment management through several custodians. In some cases, reporting is provided online by the custodian. In other cases, Legend® will provide reporting for an extra fee, in addition to their investment management service fee. Depending upon the investment management service desired, fees range from .35% to .50% exclusive of reporting costs.

The authors are currently aware of two custodians that seem more willing to accept business from emerging practices. They are AmeriTrade and Shareholder Service Group. AmeriTrade (www.ameritradeinstitutional.com) is an established firm that previously courted retail investors, so they are relatively new to the advisor service business. As a result, their infrastructure to service planners and their clients is not as well developed as the big three, but their pricing is competitive.

Shareholder Service Group (SSG) (www.shareholdersgroup.com) was launched in 2003 by Peter Mangan, who formerly managed custodial platforms for advisors at Jack White and TD Waterhouse. The firm's mission is to serve independent fee-based planners. The SSG platform offers integration with the Investigo portfolio and reporting system. It also offers integration with Laser App, an automated form filling application.

Established planners shifting to an independent RIA model have additional choices. They include Pershing (www.pershing), Raymond James (www.rjfsiad.com), and Bear Stearns (www.bearstearns.com).

CHAPTER ENDNOTES

1. Stephan Leimberg, Robert LeClair, Robert Doyle, and Thomas Robinson, *The Tools & Techniques of Investment Planning* (Cincinnati, OH: National Underwriter, 2004).

Chapter 38

DATA SOURCES, PRESENTATION SOFTWARE, AND PROFESSIONAL NEWS

In the interest of journalistic integrity and full disclosure, we must begin this chapter by pointing out the fact that both authors are somewhat conflicted with regard to the subject matter presented in this chapter. Currently, we both write regular columns for Morningstar Advisor (www.morningstaradvisor.com) an online publication owned by Morningstar, Inc. We also write on a somewhat regular basis for *Bloomberg Wealth Manager* (http://wealth.bloomberg.com/), and our last book, *Virtual-Office Tools for a High-Margin Practice*, was published by Bloomberg Press. In addition, both authors write for *Financial Advisor* magazine. In the past Joel Bruckenstein has also written for Horsesmouth (www.horsesmouth.com), and may do so again in the future.

Nevertheless, our experience with some of the vendors mentioned below, particularly Bloomberg and Morningstar, predates the beginning of our writing careers by many years. We believe both firms provide valuable resources to the financial planning community and that it would be a disservice to readers to exclude them from this chapter solely because they had the good taste and wisdom to engage our services from time to time.

DATA SOURCES

Morningstar

Morningstar is one of the most widely respected and recognized brand names in the independent advisory marketplace. Need proof? Try this – a 2003 study of independent advisors by Tiburon Strategic Advisors found that Morningstar, Inc. is, according to survey respondents, the most widely used financial planning software program among advisors. Morningstar's 61% utilization rate dwarfed its nearest competitor, Financial Profiles, which clocked in with a 25% utilization rate. Morningstar also garnered the highest satisfaction ratings in the category by a respectable margin. These statistics are particularly impressive in light of the fact that Morningstar did not sell a financial planning product when this survey was conducted! Such is the power of the Morningstar name among advisors.

In the same survey, Morningstar ranked number one in asset allocation software for both usage and satisfaction. Ultimately, though, it is data and research that have earned Morningstar the respect of the advisor community. In the Tiburon study, Morningstar dominated the utilization charts among independent reps with a 67% utilization rating. The next closest competitors were Yahoo (37%), Thomson/Weisenberger (29%), and Bloomberg (26%).

Products

Morningstar offers a wide range of print and digital products. The print products include: Morningstar Mutual Funds™ (the original print reports); Morningstar Funds® 500™ (an annual sourcebook of 500 "top" funds); and the Morningstar® FundInvestor™ newsletter (which is primarily targeted at retail investors). On the equity side, they offer Morningstar® Stocks 500™, the Morningstar® Stock Investor™ newsletter, and a book entitled *Five Rules for Successful Stock Investing*.

Morningstar Principia® software remains the company's flagship product for advisors. Modules are available for open-end mutual funds, closed-end mutual funds, stocks, variable annuities, variable life insurance, and separate accounts. The mutual funds module offers historical data, commentary, in depth analysis, screening functionality, and industry analysis. Most of the other modules are primarily quantitative, with little qualitative data.

Principia® allows advisors to build portfolios and analyze them at both the portfolio level and the individual holding level.

Morningstar.com is the firm's consumer website. It offers enough mutual fund information to satisfy the retail customer, but it is probably insufficient for the professional advisor. Morningstar.com offers a premium membership that costs $12.95 monthly or $115 annually. It offers more in depth information than the free site, but it still falls far short of what Principia® offers. However, those who only occasionally need to investigate an individual mutual fund may find it sufficient.

MorningstarAdvisor.com is a free website designed solely for professionals. Registration is required. The site contains news, data, and regular columns by experts in marketing, investments, retirement planning, practice management, and technology. Another premium service, 529Advisor.com, is available through the site and allows advisors to:

- Quantify the tax benefit of in-state plans;
- Determine which out-of-state plans are worth considering;
- Make accurate comparisons among plans;
- Evaluate the underlying funds that drive performance; and
- Calculate the likelihood that a particular plan will meet a client's needs.

Morningstar's newest, and most comprehensive, offering is Morningstar® Advisor Workstation™ Office Edition, an integrated web-based office platform for independent financial advisors. It includes capabilities for investment analysis, asset allocation and investment planning, portfolio construction, contact management, and client reporting.

The research area includes detailed information on more than 60,000 mutual funds, stocks, variable insurance products, exchange-traded funds, closed-end funds, and separate accounts. It also offers Morningstar proprietary analytics and analyst reports for more than 2,800 stocks and mutual funds. Office Edition can generate several reports, such as the Morningstar® Summary report, a high-level, one-page summary, and the Morningstar® Quicktake℠ report, which includes comprehensive historical and current investment data and analysis. Financial advisors can print reports or send them via e-mail as Adobe® Acrobat PDF attachments.

The new Office Edition includes a number of new analytical tools and client reports, such as "Similar Funds," "Fund versus Fund," and "Compare Funds." Office Edition also offers a "Value at Risk" graph, which helps financial advisors gauge a client's risk tolerance by illustrating the amount of money he or she could lose on a specific investment.

Through the reports area, Office Edition provides tracking and reporting features in one centralized place. Advisors can create three customizable Microsoft® Word documents: (1) The Investment Policy Statement; (2) the Investment Recommendations Report; and (3) the Consolidated Account Statement. For example, the Investment Policy Statement illustrates a client's goals and current financial situation and highlights the advisor's recommended investment plan and its expected results. The reports area also helps advisors monitor proposals, identify their clients' best- and worst-performing securities, and archive reports.

Within Office Edition, an advisor can organize contacts, set appointments, list and track tasks, and email research reports and proposals directly to their clients from the practice area. Advisors can import client information directly from Microsoft® Outlook®, ACT!™, and Goldmine®.

Advisors can export information directly to Microsoft® Excel, for greater flexibility.

Office Edition also offers expanded import functionality from StatementOne, an investment account data aggregator, and Advent Software®.

Advisor Intelligence

While Morningstar is clearly the leading source of comprehensive mutual fund data, Advisor Intelligence takes a different, but equally valuable approach. Rather than try to cover all mutual funds, Advisor Intelligence uses quantitative and qualitative methodologies in an attempt to distinguish some of the best active managers from each asset class and then present in depth coverage of them and their funds.

Advisor Intelligence is essentially a much-enhanced online version of the No Load Fund Analyst (http://www.nlfa.com/), a mutual fund newsletter (launched in 1989) that has consistently garnered favorable rankings for their model portfolios from Hulbert Financial Digest, a newsletter tracking service. In addition to providing in-depth coverage of a selected group of funds, Advisor Intelligence offers: model portfolios; asset class commentaries (along with advice on asset classes that should be underweighted and overweighted); manager interviews; due diligence reports; graphs; charts; and fund updates.

But there's more. Advisor Intelligence provides content that can be used by advisors in a number of ways. For example, they offer a quarterly summary that usually covers an asset class overview, a featured topic, and fund updates in a format that can be dropped into a newsletter template (which can be downloaded at their website). This content can then be edited by the advisor and used as an electronic newsletter or a printed one. Similar information is provided as a PowerPoint presentation for use in client meetings. Charts can be used in client communications and/or posted to the advisors website.

The client management section of the website contains additional tools (prospect letter, sample investment policy statement, client questionnaire, retirement planning questionnaire, client introductory letter, client welcome letter and a client data form). We believe that the materials contained in this section are uniformly well done and contribute to the overall value of the platform.

In summary, we think that Advisor Intelligence can serve one of two purposes. For those who lack investment expertise, the service can serve as a virtual outsourced solution. By employing one of the four active model portfolios, or one of the index models, advisors can offer their clients diversified portfolios of appropriate mutual funds that meet their clients risk profiles, at a reasonable price. And for those who take a more active role in the management of their client's assets, Advisor Intelligence can serve as a supplement to the work the advisor does on his or her own. In either case, it is a worthwhile investment.

Value Line

Value Line has long been synonymous with independent equity research and data. Like Morningstar, they now offer a wide array of print and data services. The *Value Line Investment Survey* continues to be one of the most widely used sources of independent equity research. The flagship print product covers roughly 1,700 equity issues. Every week, about 135 stocks in seven or eight industries are covered. All of the approximately 1,700 stocks and 94 industries are updated in a 13-week period. In addition to a wealth of quantitative data, the survey provides qualitative data such as industry analysis, company analysis, timeliness rankings, and forward-looking projections. The *Small and Mid-Cap Edition* covers approximately 1,800 additional, mostly small-capitalization, issues; this edition does not include analyst reports.

A lesser-known Value Line publication, the *Value Line Convertibles Survey*, is an excellent source of convertible bond information. The *Convertible Survey* ranks over 600 convertibles for potential risk and return. Approximately 80 warrants are also followed and evaluated.

Virtually all of the Value Line subscription products are now available electronically (www.valueline.com).

Bloomberg

The Bloomberg Professional® service integrates data, news, analytics, multimedia reports, and email onto a single platform. Roughly 250,000 financial professionals around the world use it. Bloomberg offers unparalleled depth of data, enabling access to more than 3,600,000 financial instruments.

While the Bloomberg service is a necessity for professional traders, its value to a financial planning firm is highly dependent upon the firm's investment process. Those firms that outsource some or all of the portfolio construction and security selection process most likely will not be good candidates for this service. However, those who regularly research equities, fixed income, and any other publicly traded instruments will find the Bloomberg Professional® Service an indispensable tool.

Ibbotson

Ibbotson Associates (www.ibotson.com) is a widely quoted source of historical market data. Their annual *Stocks, Bonds, Bills, and Inflation® Yearbook* contains a wealth of data on historical asset class returns, inflation, correlation coefficients and portfolio construction. Industry and company analysis, risk premia, and many other types of statistical data are available for both domestic and international markets.

BigCharts

If you are looking for a free service that provides charts of individual stocks, industry groups and indices, BigCharts (www.BigCharts.com) is a good place to start. In addition to charts, users can access other market data including news, analysts' comments, Securities and Exchange Commission (SEC) filings, and insider activity.

PRESENTATION SOFTWARE

Ibbotson Associates

Many readers are probably at least somewhat familiar with Ibbotson presentation materials. Ever see one of those charts that graph the growth of one dollar invested in four major asset classes (i.e., large-cap stocks, small-cap stocks, bonds and Treasury bills) from the end of 1925 to the present? Ibbotson probably produced it. In fact, it is their most popular graph.

Ibbotson sells two lines of presentation products: the print line and the PowerPoint line. The Ibbotson PowerPoint presentations are some of the best investment related materials in the business. They present important investment concepts backed by solid academic research and excellent graphics. Topics include: long-term investment performance; taxes and investment performance; economic downturns and recoveries; and the role of immediate annuities in retirement. The Asset Allocation Library, which is a collection of about 14 individual modules (plus some "bonus" slides), can be purchased as a package at a discounted price.

If you plan on growing your business by offering investment related seminars on a regular basis, you'll be hard pressed to find better quality material than those offered by Ibbotson.

Many of the most popular Ibbotson images are available as 8½" X 11" laminated prints. They are NASD reviewed, and they include an explanation of the graph and source information on the reverse side. A couple of charts are available as posters. There are also a brochure and a chart/pad, both of which can be handed out to clients. Ibbotson offers customization and personalization of printed materials, but with the exception of the brochures and chart/pads, the costs are probably beyond the means of a start-up firm.

Those who want an easy method of illustrating the value of a long term investment approach, as well as other investment concepts to clients will find Ibbotson materials an indispensable addition to their toolkit.

Kettley

Kettley offers a variety of products for financial planners, but to our mind, the most noteworthy is the Kettley Back Room Technician™, which contains a comprehensive library of financial planning concept illustrations. The library includes text, charts, and graphs covering a wide range of topics.

One thing that sets the Kettley Back Room Technician™ apart is its clean design and layman's language. It is very good at illustrating complex topics in language that clients can understand without over simplifying. The program has always been particularly strong at illustrating estate and wealth transfer concepts. A demonstration version of the software can be downloaded at the Kettley website (www.kettley.com)

Kettley also markets an Estate Planning Seminar kit, which includes PowerPoint slides, a how-to guide, talking points for each slide, and handouts.

Forefield

Forefield offers a number of presentation products that can be integrated into one's business. The two most relevant to this discussion are FMA Advisor™ and Forefield Seminars.

Forefield's flagship product, FMA Advisor™, is an online sales, research and client communication tool. A well-designed home page contains alerts, a watch/update list, and access to most of the platform's important features.

Advisors can prepare reports or presentations for their clients by selecting a topic, editing the list of suggested materials, and then printing them or saving them. All documents can be printed or downloaded in PDF or MS Word formats. By creating a folder for each client, all materials accessed or supplied to a client can be documented and saved for future reference.

Forefield seminars are collections of PowerPoint slides that include scripts, notes and client workbooks. Most of the currently available titles are basic in nature. They include estate basics, investment basics, annuity basics, and retirement planning.

Emerald

Emerald Publications (www.emeraldpublications.com) has long provided seminar materials to the financial service industry. The firm currently offers four comprehensive seminar packages. The Complete Financial Management Workshop offers a survey of the six core financial planning topics; Workplace Direct is designed specifically for those who target the employee workplace market. Your Enterprise is designed for the small business owner. And Taking Control is designed specifically for women. In addition, Emerald offers 20 shorter, focused seminars that cover a broad range of topics. Finally, the firm offers four special topic seminars which cover 529 Plans, taxes, 401(k) Plans, and a current events seminar. The latter is updated monthly and offers financial and economic data, trends, indicators and the like.

In addition, Emerald offers training on how to successfully use seminars to build a practice. They also offer direct mail services to support seminar campaigns.

Newkirk

Newkirk specializes in the financial service and healthcare industries. They produce a number of booklets that are appropriate for use as client education tools, mailings to clients and prospects, or premiums.

When a tax bill is passed that has implications for individuals and/or small businesses, Newkirk publishes a booklet, which can be imprinted with an advisory firm's name and address. They also produce an online summary of the booklet for posting to your website. In addition, they offer similar information in PowerPoint format for seminar use.

General guides for estate planning, year-end tax planning, retirement planning, and a number of other topics are available as booklets, web content, or PowerPoint slides too.

Over the years we have found Newkirk materials to be well written. They are not overly detailed, but they are informative and accurate. The information they supply is sufficient to satisfy the needs of most clients.

PROFESSIONAL NEWS

All of the print magazines that serve our profession maintain some sort of presence on the web. Here is a brief rundown.

Bloomberg Wealth Manager

While this is probably the best magazine in the business, its website is probably the worst. Some material from the current issue, along with some web-only content is usually available, but you cannot access back issues, and there is not much else to recommend it except for the fact that you can obtain continuing education (CE) credits by taking a short exam (one credit per issue).

Financial Advisor

Financial Advisor provides access to current and back issues, plus timely industry news. Advisors can sign up for a free semi-monthly electronic newsletter.

Financial Planning Magazine

With *Financial Planning* you can receive CE credits (upon successfully completing a quiz). However, the real draw here is the lively discussion boards, where the topics include business building, financial planning, industry buzz, marketing, and software.

Investment Advisor

This is another site offering industry news and CE credits, as well as access to back issues. Andy Gluck, one of the most widely read industry commentators, does his writing here.

OTHER USEFUL STUFF

Horsesmouth

Horsesmouth is a practice management and information portal, which seems to be geared more towards the B/D community than the RIA community, but there are numerous RIAs we know who use the service too. Each morning, subscribers to the service can receive "Daily Oats," an emailed briefing that includes news, as well as links to new content added to the site. Topics covered on a regular basis include business development, client management, marketing, prospecting, financial planning, and technology. Articles of interest can be filed electronically for later reference, so, if a user notices a few articles of interest, but can't read them at the moment, they can be filed for almost immediate access at a later date. The site can also be searched by numerous criteria, so the past articles and information serve as a knowledgebase of sorts over time. Horsesmouth regularly hosts discussion boards on timely topics, often with expert moderators. For further information visit (www.horsesmouth.com).

Inside Information

Inside Information is the brainchild of Bob Veres, the dean of financial planning journalists. He's opinionated, eclectic, honest, and the most knowledgeable financial planning journalist on the planet.

The Inside Information service includes the monthly *Inside Information* newsletter, which is packed with industry buzz, cutting edge ideas, and coverage of major financial planning conferences. Access to the Inside Information website (www.bobveres.com) is also included. In addition, members receive Media Reviews, a weekly round up of financial planning related articles published in the popular press and financial planning journals.

Virtual Office News

Virtual Office News (www.virtualofficenews.com) is the only publication devoted solely to the practice management and technology needs of financial service professionals. The service, which is owned and operated by your co-authors, Joel Bruckenstein and David Drucker, includes the monthly *Virtual Office Newsletter*, plus Price Watch, a periodic email alert that highlights technology bargains for advisors. In addition, members have access to the Virtual Office News website, which includes message boards and a list of recommended providers. On occasion, the service is able to negotiate attractive product or service discounts for members. A free sample issue can be downloaded at the Virtual Office News website.

Leimberg Information Services, Inc.

Leimberg Information Services, Inc. (LISI) (at http://leimbergservices.com) is Steve Leimberg's fast, frank, and informative e-mail newsletter/database providing almost daily coverage of cases, rulings, regulations, and legislation in the income, estate, gift, and generation-skipping areas. LISI also provides newsletters in the following categories: financial, estate, employee benefit and retirement, business, and charitable planning; and asset protection (with Eldercare soon to follow). One of the many things that sets this monthly service ($20 a month membership fee) apart is that LISI commentators are among the top authorities in the United States in their respective fields (e.g., Bob Wolf, father of the "total return unitrust" (TRU); Howard Zartisky, author of numerous highly respected texts on estate and business succession planning; and Jerry Kasner, an almost legendary lecturer and writer), and many other practitioner-scholars.

Another unique factor of LISI is the fact that you gain access not only to commentary on the case, ruling, or legislation, but you can view the actual text of the case, references to other cases, articles, and links to discussions of practitioners on various subjects. Bob LeClair, co-author of *Tools and Techniques of Investment Planning*, writes a weekly financial column.[1]

The easy-to-search database provides access to literally thousands of commentaries and cases on family limited partnerships (FLPs), business valuation, business continuation, and tax planning. LISI not only simultaneously searches its own database but also goes outside and searches selected other sites and even provides access to the Internal Revenue Code.

Tax Facts Online

At press time, development of the new *Tax Facts Online* product was underway with the debut scheduled in early 2005. The best-selling tax print references in the financial services industry are making the move to becoming a true online reference with enhanced functionality and expert-driven search capabilities. *Tax Facts Online* provides answers to financial advisors' questions on the income, gift, estate, and generation-skipping taxation of insurance, investments, employee benefits, business continuation, estate planning, education funding, and much more.

CHAPTER ENDNOTES

1. Stephan Leimberg, Robert LeClair, Robert Doyle, Jr., and Thomas Robinson, *The Tools & Techniques of Investment Planning* (Cincinnati, OH: The National Underwriter Company, 2004).

Figure 38.1

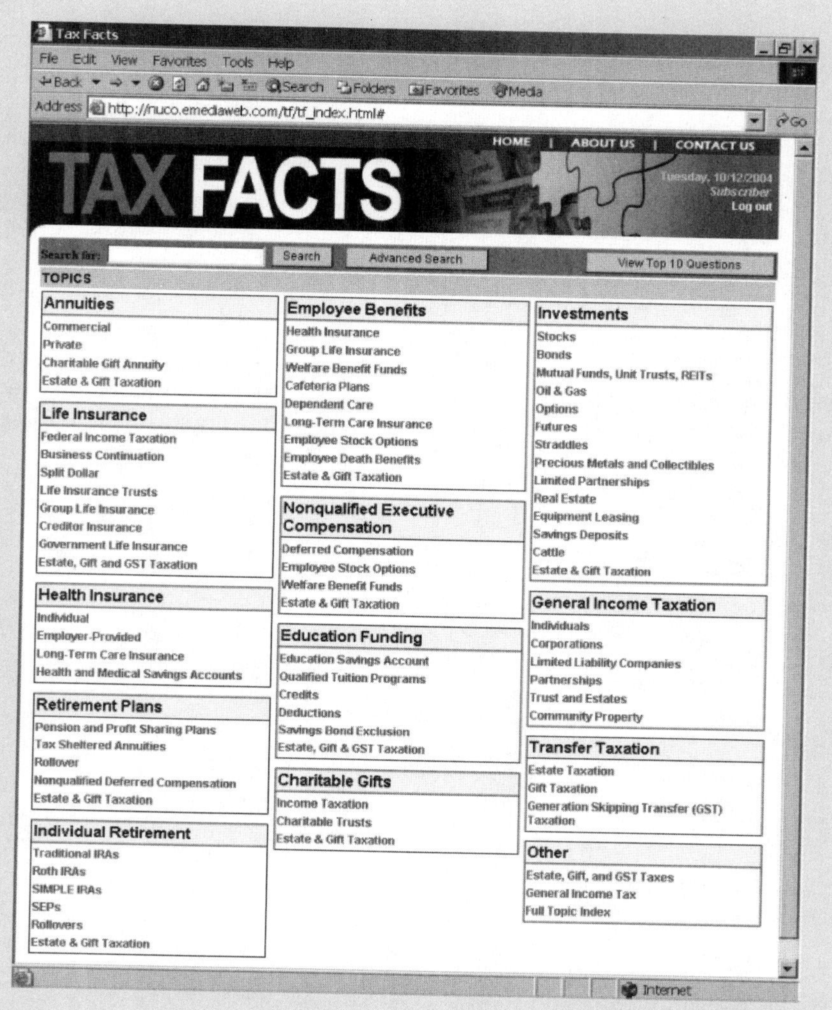
Tax Facts
File Edit View Favorites Tools Help
Back Search Folders Favorites Media
Address http://nuco.emediaweb.com/tf/tf_index.html#
Go
HOME | ABOUT US | CONTACT US
TAX FACTS
Tuesday, 10/12/2004
Subscriber
Log out
Search for:
Search
Advanced Search
View Top 10 Questions
TOPICS
Annuities
Commercial
Private
Charitable Gift Annuity
Estate & Gift Taxation
Life Insurance
Federal Income Taxation
Business Continuation
Split Dollar
Life Insurance Trusts
Group Life Insurance
Creditor Insurance
Government Life Insurance
Estate, Gift and GST Taxation
Health Insurance
Individual
Employer-Provided
Long-Term Care Insurance
Health and Medical Savings Accounts
Retirement Plans
Pension and Profit Sharing Plans
Tax Sheltered Annuities
Rollover
Nonqualified Deferred Compensation
Estate & Gift Taxation
Individual Retirement
Traditional IRAs
Roth IRAs
SIMPLE IRAs
SEPs
Rollovers
Estate & Gift Taxation
Employee Benefits
Health Insurance
Group Life Insurance
Welfare Benefit Funds
Cafeteria Plans
Dependent Care
Long-Term Care Insurance
Employee Stock Options
Employee Death Benefits
Estate & Gift Taxation
Nonqualified Executive Compensation
Deferred Compensation
Employee Stock Options
Welfare Benefit Funds
Estate & Gift Taxation
Education Funding
Education Savings Account
Qualified Tuition Programs
Credits
Deductions
Savings Bond Exclusion
Estate, Gift & GST Taxation
Charitable Gifts
Income Taxation
Charitable Trusts
Estate & Gift Taxation
Investments
Stocks
Bonds
Mutual Funds, Unit Trusts, REITs
Oil & Gas
Options
Futures
Straddles
Precious Metals and Collectibles
Limited Partnerships
Real Estate
Equipment Leasing
Savings Deposits
Cattle
Estate & Gift Taxation
General Income Taxation
Individuals
Corporations
Limited Liability Companies
Partnerships
Trust and Estates
Community Property
Transfer Taxation
Estate Taxation
Gift Taxation
Generation Skipping Transfer (GST) Taxation
Other
Estate, Gift, and GST Taxes
General Income Tax
Full Topic Index
Internet

Chapter 39

COLLABORATION TOOLS

Over the last few years, there has been a great deal of talk within the financial planning community about collaboration. But depending on the setting and the context, we may not always be talking about the same thing. For example, there could be collaboration between a number of financial planning firms to develop custom software in order to spread the cost over a larger revenue base. A financial planner and an estate planning attorney may collaborate to develop a client's estate plan. Collaboration can also mean a financial professional working with the end client over the Internet.

For the purpose of this chapter, we are defining "collaboration tool" as a technology that allows a financial professional to work with others "virtually" (i.e., a technology that allows one or more individuals to share information remotely).

You will probably recognize some of the products and services we discuss in this chapter because they have been mentioned elsewhere in this book, just not specifically in this context. You will also be introduced to new products and services that are being mentioned here for the first time.

We've held off discussing collaboration until the end of the book because it represents – to some extent – a new frontier in financial services, and it is a good example of how technology can lower costs, improve productivity, improve customer service, and improve the quality of lives all at the same time.

VIRTUAL OFFICES

As we've suggested throughout this book, there are two ways to build a 21st century financial planning practice. The first way is the traditional way, which involves hiring support staff and possibly experts in various related specialties (e.g., an estate planning attorney, an investment specialist, and a staff psychologist). The traditional method, by definition, entails accepting a great deal of additional overhead. If all of the experts have enough work to keep them busy full-time, and if you can charge your clients enough to cover the cost of their services, overhead, plus something additional (i.e., your profit), then all is well and good.

Unfortunately, the typical planning firm entering the market or attempting to expand today often cannot do this. Why? Well, first of all, when you start out, you will probably not have enough work to keep all of your staff fully engaged and profitable. Even as your business grows, some clients may not require all of the services you provide; hence, you will end up paying for more staff time (and related overhead) than you need.

The alternative is to adapt "virtual office" solutions to areas of your practice that do not justify a full-time employee. Two reasons one might choose virtual over traditional are:

1. There is not enough work to justify a full time staff member;

2. An independent contractor can perform the task more effectively; or

3. Both of the above.

If you decide to incorporate independent contractors (we refer to them as "Virtual Work Partners" or VWPs) into your practice, you will need an infrastructure to interact with them. If you spend considerable time out of the office, you will need the same type of infrastructure.

Many advisors choose to build their own set of virtual office tools by selecting different tools from different suppliers and cobbling them together into a useful infrastructure. We've already discussed some tools that can be used as part of such an infrastructure, and we will discuss some more later in this chapter. There are, however, a number of preconfigured packages of "virtual offices" that can be obtained that come "ready to go." Purchasing a "virtual office" is often analogous to renting a physical, turn-key office. You find a layout you like, pay your rent, pay for some utilities, and you are ready to go. Let's look at a few examples.

Groove Network

The Groove Network (www.groove.net) offers a number of plans that range from fairly basic to highly sophisticated. Their enterprise platform has been used by the United States government (Department of Homeland Security) and large corporations such as Boeing, Dell Computer, Microsoft, Pfizer, and Verizon. It is also widely used by medium and smaller sized businesses.

Groove integrates a number of virtual technologies, including email, instant messaging, file sharing, synchronization, calendaring, and project management into one unified platform. Groove enables a team of professionals to share documents that are always up to date. Files stored in a shared folder can be regularly synchronized so that all team members are always looking at an up to date document. A launch bar offers easy access to all platform features, and allows the user to see which team members are currently online. Off-line members can take work with them, then, when they go back online, all of the changes they have made will be shared with others.

Groove is highly customizable; non-technical staff can use the Groove templates to create customized forms. Programmers can create scripts, macros, and even applications that will work seamlessly within Groove.

Groove comes in a number of different configurations. As you move past the basic level, you get more customization, the ability to conduct virtual meetings, progress reporting, alerts, and other additional functions. For example, the Virtual Office Professional edition offers integration with Microsoft SharePoint Services.

If you are looking for a one-stop solution to your virtual office needs, Groove Network is definitely worth investigating.

Blue Tie, Inc.

BlueTie, Inc. (www.bluetie.com) specializes in providing cost effective communications and collaboration tools to small businesses. According to the firm's website: "BlueTie Business gives users all of the features and functionality of Outlook / Exchange for about half the price and with none of the downtime and administration issues associated with traditional client/server technology."

BlueTie's core business features include the following: email (which includes SecureSend, a patented email encryption and data transfer technology); a calendar; tasks; contacts; instant messaging; file sharing; and Palm synchronization. For those who prefer working within MS Outlook, BlueTie offers an application called Direct Connect, which allows users to synchronize calendars, contacts, tasks and email between BlueTie and Outlook.

For those who require a higher level of security, BlueTie offers BlueTieRx. This platform was originally designed to help the health care industry comply with the security and privacy provisions of HIPAA (The Health Insurance Portability and Accountability Act of 1996), but its security, contingency plans, auditing, and privacy controls appear to be well suited for financial planning firms as well.

BlueTie is not quite as customizable or as feature rich as Groove Network, but it is easy to use and reasonably priced.

Intranets.com

Intranets.com (www.intranets.com) is another service that allows users to set up collaborative spaces on the Internet. Features include: file sharing; group calendaring (it synchronizes with Palm and Outlook); a task manager; email; online databases; web conferencing (billed separately); opinion polls; and announcements.

If you decide to store a large volume of documents online, you may want to avail yourself of Intranets' upgrades, such as additional storage space, full text search capabilities, and SSL encryption. Customization service is also available.

4Team Online

4Team Online (online.4team.biz) allows Microsoft Office users to create a secure online space for sharing documents, schedules, calendars, and tasks. Currently, the feature set does not appear to be as extensive as those available from competitors, but it should be sufficient to meet the needs of some readers, and its prices are competitive.

VIRTUAL MEETING TOOLS

WebEx

WebEx is one of the best known names in web conferencing and video conferencing. As a collaboration tool, WebEx can be used to conduct meetings with Virtual Work Partners (VWPs). For example, if a new client engages your "virtual firm," you can collect all of the relevant data, and then present it to the specialists who will be involved in the case virtually. All meeting attendees will be able to see the information you are presenting, be it a PowerPoint presentation, documents, spreadsheets, etc., and share ideas in real time. Another WebEx technology allows you to share your computer screen with others so that you could, for example, work through a financial plan with a client while you are both connected virtually.

Microsoft Live Office

Microsoft Live Office can be used in a fashion similar to WebEx. Conference participants can be invited to view your desktop, or they can actually be given control of applications on your computer. You can capture a document, display it on the screen, and then annotate it as attendees watch and/or participate. PlaceWare for teams (a service of Live Office) can be used as a collaborative space for regular meetings with other professionals, or a regular meeting place for you and individual clients.

AdvisorSites Web Conferencing

AdvisorSites, the company specializing solely in the financial services community (see Chapter 27), also offers a web conferencing solution. While smaller and less well known than its larger competitors, the AdvisorSites Java based service is easy to use and affordably priced. An account entitles users to conduct an unlimited number of meetings per year. Pricing is dependent upon the maximum number of attendees per meeting. Advisors who host their websites through Advisorsites can private label their web conferencing site, and integrate it with the rest of their web presence.

For those who want to conduct a high volume of meetings with a limited group of participants per meeting, AdvisorSites Web Conferencing will almost certainly be the most cost effective solution.

GoToMyPC

While GoToMyPC was not designed primarily as a collaborative tool, it can be used for one-on-one collaboration. A number of advisors we know use GoToMyPC to collaborate by inviting a client or VWP to view or share control of their computer during an online meeting. GoToMyPC is a good solution for those who want remote access to their computer (which is the primary function of GoToMyPC) combined with the ability to conduct one-on-one virtual meetings.

GoToMeeting

GoToMeeting (www.gotomeeting.com) is a relatively new service from CITRIX Online, the parent company of GoToMyPC. With GoToMeeting, users set up an account which entitles them to conduct an unlimited number of meetings with up to 10 attendees per meeting. Meetings can be set up on the fly. They can include presentations, demonstrations, and document collaboration. This service looks to be particularly well suited to those who want to conduct regular virtual team meetings, and those who want to collaborate extensively online with a small group of clients (e.g., family members attending from different locations).

FINANCIAL PLANNING SOFTWARE

With modern financial planning software, and perhaps some additional software such as Adobe® Acrobat, reports from just about any financial planning program can be converted into a digital document, which can then be emailed to a client or posted to a shared space. However, a number of programs have additional collaboration or presentation capabilities built right into them. Let's look at a few examples.

MoneyGuidePro

As we went to press, MoneyGuidePro was probably our favorite online goal based financial planning program. Part of the reason we like MoneyGuidePro so much is its collaborative capabilities. MoneyGuidePro offers advisors a great deal of control over the collaborative process. For example, you can allow clients or prospective clients to perform their own on-line data entry, which can save time, reduce costs, and lend increased accuracy. At any time you can "lock" a plan, so that collaborators cannot change it, while at the same time creating an exact copy of the plan (with a single mouse click), which you continue to grant others access to. You can allow clients to create their own plans, or you can create a full plan, and then give client's limited access to a copy so that they can run additional "what-if" scenarios. If other advisors are involved in the financial planning process, you can grant them access to a plan (or a copy), so that everyone is up-to-date at all times. Most importantly, you can collaborate with any client, anywhere, at any time.

In a typical scenario, a client calls you up after reviewing a plan you've created and says: "Ms. Planner, this is a great plan that you've created for me, but I've been wondering what would happen should inflation exceed our expectations by 1% annually, over the course of the planning period?" Rather than work up a new planning document, mail (or email it) to the client, and schedule a meeting to talk about the results, wouldn't it be great to say: "Let's look at that scenario right now." With MoneyGuidePro, you can! In a matter of minutes, you and the client can both be online looking at the current plan at the same time. With a few keystrokes, you, the advisor, can illustrate what a 1% change in the inflation assumption would mean to this client's future. That's not the kind of service that clients have come to expect. That type of service far exceeds most client expectations! Good news for you; bad news for the competition!

MoneyGuidePro can send you alerts whenever a client accesses his or her plan. Perhaps this indicates that the client has an issue that you have yet to hear about, or perhaps they just are thinking about their plan. In either case, it might be appropriate to check in with the client (if they have not already contacted you) to make sure everything is okay.

MoneyGuidePro is an excellent client collaboration tool. We highly recommend that you try it out for free at www.moneyguidepro.com.

NaviPlan Offline / Online

In mid-2004, NaviPlan launched retail versions of both NaviPlan Standard and NaviPlan Extended version 9.0 in what they call an "offline" version. This totally redesigned architecture should set the stage for an ASP online version of NaviPlan before this book is released. Once the ASP is in place, the online version will, no doubt, provide many of the collaboration features offered by MoneyGuidePro. Since this new version's architecture enables online and off-line capabilities, advisors will be able to use the web-based platform as their primary workspace. The off-line functionality will enable advisors to "check out" a plan, work on it while offline, and then "check it back in," and thus update the previous online version to the latest version.

ONLINE FILE ACCESSIBILITY FOR CLIENTS

One Example: Mirra

A few years ago, a number of companies made the rounds at some of the regional and national financial planning conferences, offering to set up what they called "client lockboxes" or "client storage" on the web. This was nothing more than a hosted storage solution whereby advisors could set up a password protected folder online for each client, and post documents, reports, etc., which both the advisor and the client could access.

Today, hosted storage space sells for a fraction of what it used to. And servers have become so inexpensive (and in some cases easy to set up and maintain) that even the smallest firm can choose to create and maintain web folders for their clients (and Virtual Work Partners) in-house if they choose to do so.

The Mirra Personal Server offers just one entry-level example of how this might be done. With Mirra, a small advisory firm could create a folder for each client on a computer, upload the files to a Mirra Server, and then enable the clients to "share" the folder by going to the Mirra website, creating their own user name and password, and accessing the Mirra Server through the website.

Larger firms will probably want to gain more sophisticated capabilities by deploying a dedicated web server with sophisticated software. But the point is that a basic web storage capability that companies were charging hundreds if not thousands of dollars *per month* not long ago can now be purchased outright for less than $500. Now that's progress!

In summary, there are numerous inexpensive technologies at the disposal of planners today that can easily enable collaborative efforts with clients and or colleagues. The key to successfully implementing collaboration is to study the unique needs of your firm and find a reliable provider at a reasonable price. For those who intend to create a true "virtual firm" made up of experts across town or across the country, one of the integrated virtual office solutions is highly appropriate.

For those with more modest needs, a collaborative financial planning platform, combined with an online meeting tool and/or online storage space might be more appropriate. The good news is that many of the services listed in this chapter offer free trials, and they can often be rented for as short a period as a month so there is very little risk in taking them for a test spin. We think you will be happy that you did!

Appendix A

RECOMMENDED RESOURCES

Program	Web Site	Description
Financial Planning		
ExecPlan	http://www.sawhney.com/sawsys/execplan.htm	
ES Planner	http://www.esplanner.com/	
Fplan	www.fplan.com	Least expensive semi-comprehensive software
Integrate	www.integrate2000.com	
Interactive Advisory Software (IAS)	www.optima-tech.com	
MasterPlan Financial Software	www.masterplanner.com	
MoneyGuidePro	www.moneyguidepro.com	
Money Tree Software	www.moneytree.com	MoneyTree Silver
NaviPlan	www.naviplan.com	
Qplan	www.qplan.com	
WealthMaster	www.wealthtec.com	
Portfolio Administration:		
Advent	www.advent.com	
Captool	www.captools.com	
eWebPortfolio	www.ewebportfolio.com	
Interactive Advisory Software (IAS)	www.optima-tech.com	
Investigo	www.investigo.net	
PowerBroker	http://www.powerbrokertools.com/	
Schwab PortfolioCenter	http://www.schwabpt.com/products/portfoliocenter/	
Asset Allocation/Portfolio Analytics:		
AllocationMaster	www.allocationmaster.com	
Financial Engines	www.financialengines.com	
Ibbotson	www.ibbotson.com	
Morningstar	www.morningstaradvisor.com	Principia, WorkStation, Premium Service
Pertrac	www.pertrac2000.com	

RECOMMENDED RESOURCES (continued)

Contact Manager:

ACT!	www.act.com	
Goldmine	www.frontrange.com	
Junxure I	www.crmsoftwareinc.com	
Microsoft Outlook	www.microsoft.com	
Protracker	www.protracker.com	
ACT! Add-ons		
Act4Advisors	www.software4advisors.com/	
Brokers*ACT!	www.brokersact.com/	
CyberBroker	www.maxprosystems.com/	

Bookkeeping/Compliance:

The Consortium	www.liftburden.com/Product.htm	Forms, procedures, etc
Investment Advisor Software	www.FormADV.com	
Quickbooks	www.quickbooks.com	

Income Tax Planning/Research:

BNA	www.bna.com	
CCH Inc.	www.cch.com	
Internal Revenue Service	www.irs.gov	
Leimberg Information Services	http://www.leimbergservices.com/	
National Association of Tax Preparers	www.natptax.com	
Stockopter Stock Options Analyzer	www.stockopter.com	
Tax Facts	www.nationalunderwriter.com	

Retirement Planning Tools:

Barry Picker's Site	www.bpickercpa.com	
Brentmark Software	www.brentmark.com	
Ed Slott's IRA Page	www.irahelp.com	
Leimberg Information Services	http://www.leimbergservices.com/	
MRD Determinator	www.mrd-determinator.com	
Natalie Choate's Site	www.ataxplan.com	
Social Security Data	www.ssa.gov	

Estate Planning Tools:

Estate Planning Links	www.estateplanninglinks.com	
Five Wishes Form	www.agingwithdignity.org	
Number Cruncher	www.leimberg.com

RECOMMENDED RESOURCES (continued)		
Investment Research:		
Advisor Intelligence	www.advisorintelligence.com	
Bigcharts	www.bigcharts.com	
Morningstar	www.morningstar.com	
Value Line	www.valueline.com	
Insurance:		
Insweb Online	www.insweb.com	
National Assoc. of Ins. Commissioners	www.naic.org	
Quicken Insurance	www.insuremart.com	
Quotesmith Insurance Pricing	www.quotesmith.com	
Term Quote	www.termquote.com	
Weiss Rating	www.weissrating.com	
Education Funding:		
529 Plan Information and State Links	www.savingforcollege.com	
MorningstarAdvisor 529 Center	advisor.morningstar.com/departments/529	
Savings Bonds	www.usasavingsbonds.gov	
Document Imaging Software:		
Adobe	www.adobe.com	
Cabinet NG	http://www.cabinetng.com/	
CEO Image Systems Executive Assistant	www.ceoimage.com	
DocStar	www.docstar.com	
DocuXplorer	www.docuxplorer.com	
PaperPort	www.scansoft.com	
Scanning Hardware:		
Fujitsu ScanSnap*	www.ceoimage.com	* if paired with special CEO Package
Fujitsu 4120C	www.fujitsu.ca/products/imaging/colorduplex/fi4120c.html	Special discount available to VON subscribers
Canon DR-2080		For those who need a highly portable scanner
Xerox DocuMate 252	www.xeroxscanners.com	

RECOMMENDED RESOURCES (continued)		
Account Aggregation:		
ByAllAccounts CashEdge Yodlee	www.byallaccounts.com www.cashedge.com www.yodlee.com	
Transcription Software:		
IBM Via Voice Dragon Naturally Speaking	http://www-306.ibm.com/software/voice/viavoice/ www.scansoft.com/naturallyspeaking	
Website Design and Hosting		
AdvisorSites Advisorsquare	www.advisorsites.com www.advisorsquare.com	
Practice Management		
Inside Information MorningstarAdvisor Virtual Office News	www.bobveres.com www.morningstaradvisor.com www.virtualofficenews.com	Free Free sample issue to attendees
Consultants		
Joel Bruckenstein	www.joelbruckenstein.com	Technology consultant
David Drucker	www.daviddrucker.com	Practice management consultant
Trumpet Inc	www.trumpetinc.com	Systems, Goldmine
Favorite Miscellaneous Websites		
Behavioral Finance Research Library	http://www.undiscoveredmanagers.com/Behavioral%20Finance2.htm	
Crash Course in Wills and Trusts	www.mtpalermo.com	An introduction to basic estate planning.
Dalbar	www.dalbar.com	Reports, rankings, releases from this financial services research firm.
Dallas Federal Reserve Board	www.dallasfed.org	
Dimensional Fund Advisors	www.dfafunds.com	
Domania	www.domania.com	Offers tools designed to help homebuyers and sellers.
Elder Web	www.elderweb.com	Site devoted to long term care issues

RECOMMENDED RESOURCES (continued)		
Favorite Miscellaneous Websites (continued)		
FPTransitions	www.fptransitions.com	Information on buying, selling or merging a practice
Hussman Funds Research	http://www.hussmanfunds.com/researchInsight.html	
Investing Your Future	www.investing.rutgers.edu	This is an internet-delivered home study course designed and managed by Rutgers University.
My Stock Options	www.mystockoptions.com	
OptionWealth	www.optionwealth.com	Information on stock options
Pimco Funds	www.pimcofunds.com	Informative bond research
Smart Student's Guide to Financial Aid	www.finaid.com	Guide to financial aid
U.S. Trust Surveys	www.ustrust.com/ustrust/html/knowledge/	A section of the US Trust Website that includes all its surveys of the affluent.
Warren Buffet's Annual Letters	www.berkshirehathaway.com	Reports and essays from Warren Buffet and Charlie Munger
William Sharpe	http://www.stanford.edu/~wfsharpe/	
Organizations		
CFP-Board	www.cfp-board.org	
Financial Planning Association	www.fpanet.org	
NAPFA	www.napfa.org	
Magazines		
Association of Individual Investors	www.aaii.com	
Bloomberg WealthManager	www.wealth.bloomberg.com	Free
ConsumerReports	www.consumerreports.org	
Financial Advisor	www.financialadvisormagazine.com	Free
Financial Planning	www.Financial-Planning.com	Free
Investment Advisor	www.investmentadvisor.com	Free

RECOMMENDED RESOURCES (continued)

Practice Management Books

David J. Drucker and Joel P. Bruckenstein, *Virtual-Office Tools for a High-Margin Practice* (New York, NY: Bloomberg Press, 2002).

Harold Evensky, *Wealth Management: The Financial Advisor's Guide to Investing and Managing Your Client's Assets* (New York, NY: McGraw-Hill, 1996).

Sheryl Garrett, *Garrett's Guide to Financial Planning: How to Capture the Middle Market and Increase Your Profits* (Cincinnati, OH: The National Underwriter Company, 2002).

Roger Gibson, *Asset Allocation: Balancing Financial Risk* (New York, NY: McGraw-Hill, 2001).

Nancy Langdon Jones, *So You Want to be a Financial Planner* (Sunnyvale, CA: AdvisorPress, 2002).

Deena Katz on Practice Management (New York, NY: Bloomberg Press, 1999).

Deena Katz's Tools and Templates for Your Practice: For Financial Advisors, Planners, and Wealth Managers (New York, NY: Bloomberg Press, 2001).

Mary Rowland, *In Search of the Perfect Model: The Distinctive Business Strategies of Leading Financial Planners* (New York, NY: Bloomberg Press, 2003).

Bob Veres, *The Cutting Edge in Financial Services* (Cincinnati, OH: The National Underwriter Company, 2002).

Appendix B

CFP CODE OF ETHICS

CERTIFIED FINANCIAL PLANNER
BOARD OF STANDARDS, INC.

CODE OF ETHICS AND PROFESSIONAL RESPONSIBILITY

CFP | CERTIFIED FINANCIAL PLANNER™ | CFP®

The certification marks above are owned by Certified Financial Planner Board of Standards Inc. and are awarded to individuals who successfully complete CFP Board's initial and ongoing certification requirements.

Terminology in this Booklet

"Client" denotes a person, persons, or entity who engages a practitioner and for whom professional services are rendered. For purposes of this definition, a practitioner is engaged when an individual, based upon the relevant facts and circumstances, reasonably relies upon information or service provided by that practitioner. Where the services of the practitioner are provided to an entity (corporation, trust, partnership, estate, etc.), the client is the entity acting through its legally authorized representative.

"CFP Board designee" denotes current certificants, candidates for certification, and individuals that have any entitlement, direct or indirect, to the CFP certification marks.

"Commission" denotes the compensation received by an agent or broker when the same is calculated as a percentage on the amount of his or her sales or purchase transactions.

"Compensation" is any economic benefit a CFP Board designee or related party receives from performing his or her professional activities.

"Conflict(s) of interest" exists when a CFP Board designee's financial, business, property and/or personal interests, relationships or circumstances reasonably may impair his/her ability to offer objective advice, recommendations or services.

"Fee-only" denotes a method of compensation in which compensation is received solely from a client with neither the personal financial planning practitioner nor any related party receiving compensation which is contingent upon the purchase or sale of any financial product. A "related party" for this purpose shall mean an individual or entity from whom any direct or indirect economic benefit is derived by the personal financial planning practitioner as a result of implementing a recommendation made by the personal financial planning practitioner.

A **"financial planning engagement"** exists when a client, based on the relevant facts and circumstances, reasonably relies upon information or services provided by a CFP Board designee using the financial planning process.

"Personal financial planning" or **"financial planning"** denotes the process of determining whether and how an individual can meet life goals through the proper management of financial resources.

"Personal financial planning process" or **"financial planning process"** denotes the process which typically includes, but is not limited to, these six elements: establishing and defining the client-planner relationship, gathering client data including goals, analyzing and evaluating the client's financial status, developing and presenting financial planning recommendations and/or alternatives, implementing the financial planning recommendations and monitoring the financial planning recommendations.

"Personal financial planning subject areas" or **"financial planning subject areas"** denotes the basic subject fields covered in the financial planning process which typically include, but are not limited to, financial statement preparation and analysis (including cash flow analysis/planning and budgeting), investment planning (including portfolio design, i.e., asset allocation and portfolio management), income tax planning, education planning, risk management, retirement planning and estate planning.

"Personal financial planning professional" or **"financial planning professional"** denotes a person who is capable and qualified to offer objective, integrated and comprehensive financial advice to or for the benefit of individuals to help them achieve their financial objectives. A financial planning professional must have the ability to provide financial planning services to clients, using the financial planning process covering the basic financial planning subjects.

"Personal financial planning practitioner" or **"financial planning practitioner"** denotes a person who is capable and qualified to offer objective, integrated and comprehensive financial advice to or for the benefit of clients to help them achieve their financial objectives and who engages in financial planning using the financial planning process in working with clients.

Rev. 07/03

Code of Ethics and Professional Responsibility

Rev. 07/03

Rev. 07/03

PREAMBLE AND APPLICABILITY

The *Code of Ethics and Professional Responsibility* (*Code of Ethics*) has been adopted by Certified Financial Planner Board of Standards Inc. (CFP Board) to provide principles and rules to all persons whom it has recognized and certified to use the CFP®, CERTIFIED FINANCIAL PLANNER™ and CFP® certification marks (collectively "the marks"). CFP Board determines who is certified and thus authorized to use the marks. Implicit in the acceptance of this authorization is an obligation not only to comply with the mandates and requirements of all applicable laws and regulations but also to take responsibility to act in an ethical and professionally responsible manner in all professional services and activities.

For purposes of this *Code of Ethics*, a person recognized and certified by CFP Board to use the marks is called a CFP Board designee. This *Code of Ethics* applies to CFP Board designees actively involved in the practice of personal financial planning, in other areas of financial services, in industry, in related professions, in government, in education or in any other professional activity in which the marks are used in the performance of professional responsibilities. This *Code of Ethics* also applies to candidates for the CFP® certification who are registered as such with CFP Board. For purposes of this *Code of Ethics*, the term CFP Board designee shall be deemed to include current certificants, candidates and individuals who have been certified in the past and retain the right to reinstate their CFP certification without passing the current CFP® Certification Examination.

COMPOSITION AND SCOPE

The *Code of Ethics* consists of two parts: Part I – Principles and Part II – Rules. The Principles are statements expressing in general terms the ethical and professional ideals that CFP Board designees are expected to display in their professional activities. As such, the Principles are aspirational in character but are intended to provide a source of guidance for CFP Board designees. The comments following each Principle further explain the meaning of the Principle. The Rules in Part II provide practical guidelines derived from the tenets embodied in the Principles. As such, the Rules describe the standards of ethical and professionally responsible conduct expected of CFP Board designees in particular situations. This *Code of Ethics* does not undertake to define standards of professional conduct of CFP Board designees for purposes of civil liability.

Due to the nature of a CFP Board designee's particular field of endeavor, certain Rules may not be applicable to that CFP Board designee's activities. For example, a CFP Board designee who is engaged solely in the sale of securities as a registered representative is not subject to the written disclosure requirements of Rule 402 (applicable to CFP Board designees engaged in personal financial planning) although he or she may have disclosure responsibilities under Rule 401. A CFP Board designee is obligated to determine what responsibilities he or she has in each professional relationship including, for example, duties that arise in particular circumstances from a position of trust or confidence that a CFP Board designee may have. The CFP Board designee is obligated to meet those responsibilities.

The *Code of Ethics* is structured so that the presentation of the Rules parallels the presentation of the Principles. For example, the Rules which relate to Principle 1 – Integrity are numbered in the 100 to 199 series, while those Rules relating to Principle 2 – Objectivity are numbered in the 200 to 299 series.

COMPLIANCE

CFP Board requires adherence to this *Code of Ethics* by all CFP Board designees. Compliance with the *Code of Ethics*, individually and by the profession as a whole, depends on each CFP Board designee's knowledge of and voluntary compliance with the Principles and applicable Rules, on the influence of fellow professionals and public opinion, and on disciplinary proceedings, when necessary, involving CFP Board designees who fail to comply with the applicable provisions of the *Code of Ethics*.

Rev. 07/03

PART I – PRINCIPLES

These *Code of Ethics*' Principles express the profession's recognition of its responsibilities to the public, to clients, to colleagues and to employers. They apply to all CFP Board designees and provide guidance to them in the performance of their professional services.

Principle 1 – Integrity

A CFP Board designee shall offer and provide professional services with integrity.

As discussed in "Composition and Scope," CFP Board designees may be placed by clients in positions of trust and confidence. The ultimate source of such public trust is the CFP Board designee's personal integrity. In deciding what is right and just, a CFP Board designee should rely on his or her integrity as the appropriate touchstone. Integrity demands honesty and candor which must not be subordinated to personal gain and advantage. Within the characteristic of integrity, allowance can be made for innocent error and legitimate difference of opinion; but integrity cannot co-exist with deceit or subordination of one's principles. Integrity requires a CFP Board designee to observe not only the letter but also the spirit of this *Code of Ethics*.

Principle 2 – Objectivity

A CFP Board designee shall be objective in providing professional services to clients.

Objectivity requires intellectual honesty and impartiality. It is an essential quality for any professional. Regardless of the particular service rendered or the capacity in which a CFP Board designee functions, a CFP Board designee should protect the integrity of his or her work, maintain objectivity, and avoid subordination of his or her judgment that would be in violation of this *Code of Ethics*.

Principle 3 – Competence

A CFP Board designee shall provide services to clients competently and maintain the necessary knowledge and skill to continue to do so in those areas in which the CFP Board designee is engaged.

One is competent only when he or she has attained and maintained an adequate level of knowledge and skill, and applies that knowledge effectively in providing services to clients. Competence also includes the wisdom to recognize the limitations of that knowledge and when consultation or client referral is appropriate. A CFP Board designee, by virtue of having earned the CFP® certification, is deemed to be qualified to practice financial planning. However, in addition to assimilating the common body of knowledge required and acquiring the necessary experience for certification, a CFP Board designee shall make a continuing commitment to learning and professional improvement.

Principle 4 – Fairness

A CFP Board designee shall perform professional services in a manner that is fair and reasonable to clients, principals, partners and employers, and shall disclose conflict(s) of interest in providing such services.

Fairness requires impartiality, intellectual honesty and disclosure of conflict(s) of interest. It involves a subordination of one's own feelings, prejudices and desires so as to achieve a proper balance of conflicting interests. Fairness is treating others in the same fashion that you would want to be treated and is an essential trait of any professional.

Rev. 07/03

Principle 5 – Confidentiality

A CFP Board designee shall not disclose any confidential client information without the specific consent of the client unless in response to proper legal process, to defend against charges of wrongdoing by the CFP Board designee or in connection with a civil dispute between the CFP Board designee and client.

A client, by seeking the services of a CFP Board designee, may be interested in creating a relationship of personal trust and confidence with the CFP Board designee. This type of relationship can only be built upon the understanding that information supplied to the CFP Board designee will be confidential. In order to provide the contemplated services effectively and to protect the client's privacy, the CFP Board designee shall safeguard the confidentiality of such information.

Principle 6 – Professionalism

A CFP Board designee's conduct in all matters shall reflect credit upon the profession.

Because of the importance of the professional services rendered by CFP Board designees, there are attendant responsibilities to behave with dignity and courtesy to all those who use those services, fellow professionals, and those in related professions. A CFP Board designee also has an obligation to cooperate with fellow CFP Board designees to enhance and maintain the profession's public image and to work jointly with other CFP Board designees to improve the quality of services. It is only through the combined efforts of all CFP Board designees, in cooperation with other professionals, that this vision can be realized.

Principle 7 – Diligence

A CFP Board designee shall act diligently in providing professional services.

Diligence is the provision of services in a reasonably prompt and thorough manner. Diligence also includes proper planning for, and supervision of, the rendering of professional services.

Rev. 07/03

PART II – RULES

As stated in Part I – Principles, the Principles apply to all CFP Board designees. However, due to the nature of a CFP Board designee's particular field of endeavor, certain Rules may not be applicable to that CFP Board designee's activities. The universe of activities engaged in by a CFP Board designee is indeed diverse and a particular CFP Board designee may be performing all, some or none of the typical services provided by financial planning professionals. As a result, in considering the following Rules, a CFP Board designee must first recognize what specific services he or she is rendering and then determine whether or not a specific Rule is applicable to those services. To assist the CFP Board designee in making these determinations, the *Standards of Professional Conduct* includes a series of definitions of terminology (see page 2) used throughout the *Code of Ethics*. Based upon these definitions, a CFP Board designee should be able to determine which services he or she provides and, therefore, which Rules are applicable to those services.

Rules that Relate to the Principle of Integrity

Rule 101

A CFP Board designee shall not solicit clients through false or misleading communications or advertisements:

(a) *Misleading Advertising:* A CFP Board designee shall not make a false or misleading communication about the size, scope or areas of competence of the CFP Board designee's practice or of any organization with which the CFP Board designee is associated; and

(b) *Promotional Activities:* In promotional activities, a CFP Board designee shall not make materially false or misleading communications to the public or create unjustified expectations regarding matters relating to financial planning or the professional activities and competence of the CFP Board designee. The term "promotional activities" includes, but is not limited to, speeches, interviews, books and/or printed publications, seminars, radio and television shows, and video cassettes; and

(c) *Representation of Authority:* A CFP Board designee shall not give the impression that a CFP Board designee is representing the views of CFP Board or any other group unless the CFP Board designee has been authorized to do so. Personal opinions shall be clearly identified as such.

Rule 102

In the course of professional activities, a CFP Board designee shall not engage in conduct involving dishonesty, fraud, deceit or misrepresentation, or knowingly make a false or misleading statement to a client, employer, employee, professional colleague, governmental or other regulatory body or official, or any other person or entity.

Rule 103

A CFP Board designee has the following responsibilities regarding funds and/or other property of clients:

(a) In exercising custody of, or discretionary authority over, client funds or other property, a CFP Board designee shall act only in accordance with the authority set forth in the governing legal instrument (e.g., special power of attorney, trust, letters testamentary, etc.); and

(b) A CFP Board designee shall identify and keep complete records of all funds or other property of a client in the custody, or under the discretionary authority, of the CFP

Rev. 07/03

Board designee; and

(c) Upon receiving funds or other property of a client, a CFP Board designee shall promptly or as otherwise permitted by law or provided by agreement with the client, deliver to the client or third party any funds or other property which the client or third party is entitled to receive and, upon request by the client, render a full accounting regarding such funds or other property; and

(d) A CFP Board designee shall not commingle client funds or other property with a CFP Board designee's personal funds and/or other property or the funds and/or other property of a CFP Board designee's firm. Commingling one or more clients' funds or other property together is permitted, subject to compliance with applicable legal requirements and provided accurate records are maintained for each client's funds or other property; and

(e) A CFP Board designee who takes custody of all or any part of a client's assets for investment purposes, shall do so with the care required of a fiduciary.

Rules that Relate to the Principle of Objectivity

Rule 201

A CFP Board designee shall exercise reasonable and prudent professional judgment in providing professional services.

Rule 202

A financial planning practitioner shall act in the interest of the client.

Rules that Relate to the Principle of Competence

Rule 301

A CFP Board designee shall keep informed of developments in the field of financial planning and participate in continuing education throughout the CFP Board designee's professional career in order to improve professional competence in all areas in which the CFP Board designee is engaged. As a distinct part of this requirement, a CFP Board designee shall satisfy all minimum continuing education requirements established for CFP Board designees by CFP Board.

Rule 302

A CFP Board designee shall offer advice only in those areas in which the CFP Board designee has competence. In areas where the CFP Board designee is not professionally competent, the CFP Board designee shall seek the counsel of qualified individuals and/or refer clients to such parties.

Rules that Relate to the Principle of Fairness

Rule 401

In rendering professional services, a CFP Board designee shall disclose to the client:

(a) Material information relevant to the professional relationship, including, conflict(s) of interest, the CFP Board designee's business affiliation, address, telephone number, credentials, qualifications, licenses, compensation structure and any agency relationships, and the scope of the CFP Board designee's authority in that capacity; and

(b) The information required by all laws applicable to the relationship in a manner complying with such laws.

Rule 402

A CFP Board designee in a financial planning engagement shall make timely written disclosure of all material information relative to the professional relationship. In all circumstances and prior to the engagement, a CFP Board designee shall, in writing:

(a) Disclose conflict(s) of interest and sources of compensation; and
(b) Inform the client or prospective client of his/her right to ask at any time for information about the compensation of the CFP Board designee.

As a guideline, a CFP Board designee who provides a client or prospective client with the following written disclosures, using Form ADV, a CFP Board Disclosure Form or an equivalent document, will be considered to be in compliance with this Rule:

- The basic philosophy of the CFP Board designee (or firm) in working with clients. This includes the philosophy, theory and/or principles of financial planning which will be utilized by the CFP Board designee; and
- Résumés of principals and employees of a firm who are expected to provide financial planning services to the client and a description of those services. Such disclosures shall include educational background, professional/employment history, professional designations and licenses held; and
- A statement that in reasonable detail discloses (as applicable) conflict(s) of interest and source(s) of, and any contingencies or other aspects material to, the CFP Board designee's compensation; and
- A statement describing material agency or employment relationships a CFP Board designee (or firm) has with third parties and the nature of compensation resulting from such relationships; and
- A statement informing the client or prospective client of his/her right to ask at any time for information about the compensation of the CFP Board designee.

Rule 403

Upon request by a client or prospective client, the CFP Board designee in a financial planning engagement shall communicate in reasonable detail the requested compensation information related to the financial planning engagement, including compensation derived from implementation. The disclosure may express compensation as an approximate dollar amount or percentage or as a range of dollar amounts or percentages. The disclosure shall be made at a time and to the extent that the requested compensation information can be reasonably ascertained. Any estimates shall be clearly identified as such and based on reasonable assumptions. If a CFP Board designee becomes aware that a compensation disclosure provided pursuant to this rule has become significantly inaccurate, he/she shall provide the client with corrected information in a timely manner.

Rule 404

The disclosures required of a CFP Board designee in a financial planning engagement described under Rule 402 shall be offered at least annually for current clients, and provided if requested.

Rule 405

A CFP Board designee's compensation shall be fair and reasonable.

Rule 406

A CFP Board designee who is an employee shall perform professional services with dedication to the lawful objectives of the employer and in accordance with this *Code of Ethics.*

Rule 407

A CFP Board designee shall:

(a) Advise his/her employer of outside affiliations which reasonably may compromise service to an employer;
(b) Provide timely notice to his/her employer and clients about change of CFP® certification status; and
(c) Provide timely notice to clients, unless precluded by contractual obligations, about change of employment.

Rule 408

A CFP Board designee shall inform his/her employer, partners or co-owners of compensation or other benefit arrangements in connection with his or her services to clients, which are in addition to compensation from the employer, partners or co-owners for such services.

Rule 409

If a CFP Board designee enters into a personal business transaction with a client, separate from regular professional services provided to that client, the transaction shall be on terms which are fair and reasonable to the client and the CFP Board designee shall disclose, in writing, the risks of the transaction, conflict(s) of interest of the CFP Board designee, and other relevant information, if any, necessary to make the transaction fair to the client.

Rules that Relate to the Principle of Confidentiality

Rule 501

A CFP Board designee shall not reveal — or use for his or her own benefit — without the client's consent, any personally identifiable information relating to the client relationship or the affairs of the client, except and to the extent disclosure or use is reasonably necessary:

(a) To establish an advisory or brokerage account, to effect a transaction for the client, or as otherwise impliedly authorized in order to carry out the client engagement; or
(b) To comply with legal requirements or legal process; or
(c) To defend the CFP Board designee against charges of wrongdoing; or
(d) In connection with a civil dispute between the CFP Board designee and the client.

For purposes of this rule, the proscribed use of client information is improper whether or not it actually causes harm to the client.

Rule 502

A CFP Board designee shall maintain the same standards of confidentiality to employers as to clients.

Rev. 07/03

Rule 503

A CFP Board designee doing business as a partner or principal of a financial services firm owes the CFP Board designee's partners or co-owners a responsibility to act in good faith. This includes, but is not limited to, adherence to reasonable expectations of confidentiality both while in business together and thereafter.

Rules that Relate to the Principle of Professionalism

Rule 601

A CFP Board designee shall use the marks in compliance with the rules and regulations of CFP Board, as established and amended from time to time.

Rule 602

A CFP Board designee shall show respect for other financial planning professionals, and related occupational groups, by engaging in fair and honorable competitive practices. Collegiality among CFP Board designees shall not, however, impede enforcement of this *Code of Ethics*.

Rule 603

A CFP Board designee who has knowledge, which is not required to be kept confidential under this *Code of Ethics*, that another CFP Board designee has committed a violation of this *Code of Ethics* which raises substantial questions as to the designee's honesty, trustworthiness or fitness as a CFP Board designee in other respects, shall promptly inform CFP Board. This rule does not require disclosure of information or reporting based on knowledge gained as a consultant or expert witness in anticipation of, or related to, litigation or other dispute resolution mechanisms. For purposes of this rule, knowledge means no substantial doubt.

Rule 604

A CFP Board designee who has knowledge, which is not required under this *Code of Ethics* to be kept confidential, and which raises a substantial question of unprofessional, fraudulent or illegal conduct by a CFP Board designee or other financial professional, shall promptly inform the appropriate regulatory and/or professional disciplinary body. This rule does not require disclosure or reporting of information gained as a consultant or expert witness in anticipation of, or related to, litigation or other dispute resolution mechanisms. For purposes of this Rule, knowledge means no substantial doubt.

Rule 605

A CFP Board designee who has reason to suspect illegal conduct within the CFP Board designee's organization shall make timely disclosure of the available evidence to the CFP Board designee's immediate supervisor and/or partners or co-owners. If the CFP Board designee is convinced that illegal conduct exists within the CFP Board designee's organization, and that appropriate measures are not taken to remedy the situation, the CFP Board designee shall, where appropriate, alert the appropriate regulatory authorities, including CFP Board, in a timely manner.

Rule 606

In all professional activities a CFP Board designee shall perform services in accordance with:

(a) Applicable laws, rules and regulations of governmental agencies and other applicable authorities; and
(b) Applicable rules, regulations and other established policies of CFP Board.

Rule 607

A CFP Board designee shall not engage in any conduct which reflects adversely on his or her integrity or fitness as a CFP Board designee, upon the marks, or upon the profession.

Rule 608

The Investment Advisers Act of 1940 requires registration of investment advisers with the U.S. Securities and Exchange Commission and similar state statutes may require registration with state securities agencies. CFP Board designees shall disclose to clients their firms' status as registered investment advisers. Under present standards of acceptable business conduct, it is proper to use registered investment adviser if the CFP Board designee is registered individually. If the CFP Board designee is registered through his or her firm, then the CFP Board designee is not a registered investment adviser but a person associated with an investment adviser. The firm is the registered investment adviser. Moreover, RIA or R.I.A. following a CFP Board designee's name in advertising, letterhead stationery, and business cards may be misleading and is not permitted either by this *Code of Ethics* or by SEC regulations.

Rule 609

A CFP Board designee shall not practice any other profession or offer to provide such services unless the CFP Board designee is qualified to practice in those fields and is licensed as required by state law.

Rule 610

A CFP Board designee shall return the client's original records in a timely manner after their return has been requested by a client.

Rule 611

A CFP Board designee shall not bring or threaten to bring a disciplinary proceeding under this *Code of Ethics*, or report or threaten to report information to CFP Board pursuant to Rules 603 and/or 604, or make or threaten to make use of this *Code of Ethics* for no substantial purpose other than to harass, maliciously injure, embarrass and/or unfairly burden another CFP Board designee.

Rule 612

A CFP Board designee shall comply with all applicable renewal requirements established by CFP Board including, but not limited to, payment of the biennial CFP Board designee fee as well as signing and returning the Terms and Conditions of Certification in connection with the certification renewal process.

Rules that Relate to the Principle of Diligence

Rule 701

A CFP Board designee shall provide services diligently.

Rule 702

A financial planning practitioner shall enter into an engagement only after securing sufficient information to satisfy the CFP Board designee that:

(a) The relationship is warranted by the individual's needs and objectives; and
(b) The CFP Board designee has the ability to either provide requisite competent services or to involve other professionals who can provide such services.

Rule 703

A financial planning practitioner shall make and/or implement only recommendations which are suitable for the client.

Rule 704

Consistent with the nature and scope of the engagement, a CFP Board designee shall make a reasonable investigation regarding the financial products recommended to clients. Such an investigation may be made by the CFP Board designee or by others provided the CFP Board designee acts reasonably in relying upon such investigation.

Rule 705

A CFP Board designee shall properly supervise subordinates with regard to their delivery of financial planning services, and shall not accept or condone conduct in violation of this *Code of Ethics*.

ADVISORY OPINION 2001-1

Loans between CFP Board designees and their clients should be avoided in the client-planner relationship.

Background

The Board of Professional Review (the "BOPR") has generally viewed loans between CFP Board designees and their clients unfavorably and, in the majority of cases, to be a violation of the *Code of Ethics and Professional Responsibility* (*Code of Ethics*). Since the *Code of Ethics* does not have a rule that specifically prohibits such transactions, however, the BOPR has addressed the issue under various rules, depending upon the facts and circumstances of the case being examined.

Due to an increase in the number of disciplinary cases that involve the issue of loans between a CFP Board designee and his or her client, the BOPR is issuing this advisory opinion to clarify its position and to serve as a guide to both CFP Board designees and their clients.

Issue

Whether a loan between a CFP Board designee and his or her client(s) violates the *Code of Ethics*.

Analysis

Cases involving a loan between a CFP Board designee and a client involve an investigation of whether that CFP Board designee has violated the *Code of Ethics*. The BOPR has evaluated these cases under a number of rules, including, but not limited to, Rules 201, 202, 401, 402, 606, 607 and 703. To determine which, if any, rules have been violated, the BOPR considers:

- Whether the designee is a financial planning practitioner (as defined by the *Code of Ethics*).
- Whether the client is a family member or a financial institution. The degree to which the CFP Board designee is related to the client is relevant. (The rationale for considering the type of relationship is discussed later in this opinion.)
- Whether the terms and conditions of the loan are fair and reasonable to the client.

While any and/or all of the rules mentioned above, and others, may apply in a particular case, this advisory opinion focuses on two rules which are implicated in the majority of "loan" cases and are, therefore, most frequently cited by the BOPR: Rules 202 and 607.

Rule 202

Rule 202 of the *Code of Ethics* requires financial planning practitioners to act in the best interest of their clients. Accordingly, this rule applies to CFP Board designees who are acting as financial planning practitioners, defined in the *Code of Ethics* as:

"[A] person who is capable and qualified to offer objective, integrated and comprehensive financial advice to or for the benefit of clients to help them achieve their financial objectives and who engages in financial planning using the financial planning process in working with clients."

Borrowing from a Client

In cases involving a loan between a financial planning practitioner and a client, where the client is the lender and the practitioner is the borrower, the BOPR presumes that the practitioner is not acting in the best interest of the client.

Rev. 07/03

BOPR Recognizes Exceptions

There are two exceptions to this presumption:

(1) When the client is a family member; or
(2) When the client is a financial institution acting in its normal course of business activity.

The BOPR recognizes that borrowing and/or lending of funds between family members is a common, generally accepted, practice. Likewise, financial institutions are in the business of borrowing and lending funds and, as such, often provide loans to individuals, regardless of whether they are CFP Board designees. In both instances, loans between these groups can fall outside the scope of the planner-client relationship.

In either of the two situations described above, while the BOPR does not presume that the planner's borrowing of funds is a violation of Rule 202, it may still find that the transaction was not in the client's best interests if the financial planning practitioner is unable to establish that:

- The terms and conditions of the loan were clearly and objectively disclosed to the client, taking into consideration the client's level of sophistication;
- The terms and conditions of the transaction were fair and reasonable under the circumstances; and
- The client fully understood (a) the terms and conditions of the transaction and (b) the impact of the transaction on his/her financial situation.

Lending to a Client

In the more rare case where a financial planning practitioner lends funds to a client, the BOPR will presume that the practitioner is not acting in the best interest of the client, as a client who borrows funds from his or her planner is likely to be inhibited from ending the planner-client relationship, regardless of whether the client's financial planning needs are being met. Even if the financial planning practitioner can demonstrate that a particular loan to a client did not inhibit the client from ending the relationship, the transaction will still be presumed to be a violation of Rule 202 if (a) the loan was used as an enticement for the client to make a financial decision, including, but not limited to, purchasing a financial product, or (b) the loan had a below market interest rate and could be considered a form of rebate.

The exception to this presumption is when the client is a family member. Even if the client is a family member, however, the BOPR may still find that the transaction was not in the client's best interest if the financial planning practitioner is unable to establish that (a) the terms and conditions of the loan were clearly and objectively disclosed to the client, taking into consideration the client's level of sophistication, (b) the terms and conditions of the transaction were fair and reasonable under the circumstances, and (c) the client fully understood the terms and conditions of the transaction and the impact the transaction may have on his/her financial situation.

Rule 607

Rule 607 prohibits a CFP Board designee from engaging "in any conduct which reflects adversely on his or her integrity or fitness as a CFP Board designee, upon the marks, or upon the profession."

Rev. 07/03

As defined in the *Code of Ethics*, CFP Board designees include individuals who are currently certified, candidates for certification, and individuals who have any entitlement, either direct or indirect, to use the CFP certification marks. Accordingly, this rule has been interpreted to apply to all CFP Board designees regardless of whether they are practitioners, including candidates for certification, and individuals who have the right to renew their CFP® certification without re-taking CFP Board's CFP® Certification Examination.

Whether the Client is the Borrower or Lender

The BOPR interprets Rule 607 broadly, finding conduct which gives the "appearance of impropriety" to be a violation of the rule. Accordingly, the BOPR has taken the position that most loans between a CFP Board designee and a client give the appearance of impropriety and, therefore, reflect negatively on the integrity of the designee, the CFP marks and the financial planning profession.

BOPR Recognizes Exceptions

The same two exceptions discussed under Rule 202 (i.e., loans between a planner and a family member or loans between a planner and a financial institution) apply under Rule 607 when the planner is the borrower. In cases where the client is the borrower, only the family member exception applies. Even if one of the exceptions applies, the BOPR may still find that the transaction violates Rule 607 if the CFP Board designee fails to establish that:

- The terms and conditions of the loan were clearly and objectively disclosed to the client;
- The terms and conditions of the transaction were fair and reasonable under the circumstances; and
- The client fully understood (a) the terms and conditions of the transaction and (b) the impact of the transaction on his/her financial situation.

Summary

The BOPR urges all CFP Board designees to avoid the practice of borrowing from or lending to clients. This advisory opinion focuses on the two most frequently cited rules (Rules 202 and 607) in cases involving loans between CFP Board designees and their clients. CFP Board designees should remember, however, that the BOPR may find such transactions to be in violation of other rules in the *Code of Ethics*, as well.

Rev. 07/03

ADVISORY OPINION 2003-1

CFP Board designees must avoid possible misrepresentation when using the term "fee-only."

Background

The Board of Professional Review ("BOPR") views misrepresentation of compensation arrangements to be a violation of the *Code of Ethics and Professional Responsibility (Code of Ethics).* The *Code of Ethics* defines the term "fee-only" as denoting "a method of compensation in which compensation is received solely from a client with neither the personal financial planning practitioner nor any related party receiving compensation which is contingent upon the purchase or sale of any financial product." BOPR Advisory Opinions 97-1 and 97-2 allowed for a designee to use the term "fee-only" to describe the compensation received from a specific client, even if other methods of compensation were used with other clients, and to offer "fee-only" services to a client, even if the designee also received commissions from the same client or other clients for other services. In light of recent regulatory trends regarding the misrepresentation of methods of compensation, media focus on the issue, and the perceptions of the general public, the BOPR has redefined the appropriate use of the term "fee-only."

The purpose of this Advisory Opinion is to reduce confusion on the part of CFP Board designees, their clients, and the public, and to maintain consistency with other organizations' use of the term "fee-only." Thus, the Board of Governors withdrew Advisory Opinions 97-1 and 97-2 in January 2002 and the *Code of Ethics* definition can no longer be considered an accurate reflection of the BOPR's position on this issue.

Issue

When may a CFP Board designee use the term "fee-only" to describe the designee as an individual, the designee's practice or the designee's services?

Analysis

A fee arrangement exists when the CFP Board designee is compensated solely by the client, or another party operating exclusively on behalf of the client, for professional services provided. The BOPR has defined types of compensation arrangements. The following qualify as fees:

- *Hourly, fixed or flat fees;*
- *Percentage fees,* which are based on some aspect of the client's financial profile, such as assets under management or earned income; and
- *Performance-based fees,* which are tied to the profitability of the client's invested assets.

There are other compensation arrangements under which a CFP Board designee could be compensated for working with a client. In some of these arrangements, the designee may be paid by a third party for the recommending, referring or selling of a product and/or service. These arrangements, including, but not limited to the following, shall not be interpreted as fees under the *Code of Ethics:*

- *Commission,* generated from a product or service. In addition to traditional commissions, this includes, 12(b)1 fees, trailing commissions, surrender charges, and contingent deferred sales charges, even if used to reduce or offset other fees;

Rev. 07/03

- *Referral compensation,* providing compensation or other economic benefits to the CFP Board designee for recommending, introducing or referring a product or service provided by another person or entity, even if used to reduce or offset other fees.

Use of the Term "Fee-Only"

In order for a CFP Board designee to describe his or her compensation as "fee-only", all compensation from all clients must be derived solely from fees. Minimal exceptions may be allowed provided the compensation is inconsequential and independent of the purchase of any product or service. Likewise, when using terms including, but not limited to, "fee-only services" and "fee-only firm," the same requirements apply.

Potential Rule Violations

Cases involving misrepresentation of compensation arrangements or failure to disclose compensation arrangements warrant investigation of whether that CFP Board designee has violated the *Code of Ethics.* The rules implicated in this analysis include, but are not limited to, Rules 101(a) and (b), 102, 201, 202, 401, 402, 606, 607 and 702. The BOPR must consider whether the CFP Board designee is a financial planning practitioner (as defined by the *Code of Ethics*) in determining which, if any, rules have been violated. While any and/or all of the rules mentioned above may apply in a particular case, this advisory opinion focuses on three rules that would most often be implicated in a case involving misrepresentation of and/or failure to disclose compensation arrangements: Rules 101(a) and (b), 401 and 402.

Rule 401

Rule 401 of the *Code of Ethics* requires CFP Board designees to disclose to the client material information relative to the professional relationship, including compensation structure. The BOPR urges that disclosures under Rule 401 be clear, straightforward and unambiguous so as to be easily understood by all parties. In cases involving CFP Board designees who represent themselves as "fee-only" to a client but accept compensation not defined as fees by the BOPR from that relationship or other client relationships, the BOPR presumes that the CFP Board designee has failed to disclose material information relative to the professional relationship.

Rule 402

Rule 402 requires CFP Board designees in a financial planning engagement to make timely written disclosure of all material information relative to the professional relationship, in all circumstances and prior to the relationship, including sources of compensation. Adherence to the provisions of Rule 402 by CFP Board designees in financial planning engagements allows the public to make informed decisions about whether to use the professional services of the CFP Board designee. Rule 402(a) is violated when the CFP Board designee in a financial planning engagement, in the disclosure provided to the client, represents himself or herself as "fee-only" when, in fact, that designee accepts compensation not defined as fees by the BOPR in that relationship or other client relationships.

Rule 101(a) and (b)

Rule 101(a) and (b) prohibit CFP Board designees from soliciting clients through false or misleading advertisements and/or promotional activities. The use of the term "fee-only" must be used carefully and only when the CFP Board designee derives all compensation from all clients solely from fees. The BOPR presumes advertisements and/or promotional activities to be false or misleading when they contain the term "fee-only" and the CFP Board designee advertising or promoting his or her services accepts compensation not defined as fees from that client relationship or any other client relationships.

Summary

The public regards compensation structure as important information when choosing a financial planning professional. *The Code of Ethics* requires CFP Board designees to act with integrity and fairness toward the public in all activities. The appropriate use of the term "fee-only" in all public discourse provides a key opportunity for CFP Board designees to demonstrate professionalism by avoiding casual use of the term. The BOPR advises CFP Board designees to avoid using the term "fee-only" except when all compensation from all clients is derived solely from fees. CFP Board designees should also avoid the use of other terms designed to induce the public into a distorted belief that the designee receives "fee-only" compensation when in fact the designee receives commissions, referral compensation, or any other form of compensation not defined as fees by the BOPR.

SAMPLE DISCLOSURE FORMS

Following are two sample disclosure forms for use by CFP® certificants in complying with CFP Board's *Code of Ethics and Professional Responsibility (Code of Ethics)* disclosure requirements. The first form (Form FPE) may be used in financial planning engagements. The second form (Form OPS) is for use when providing other professional services.

These forms provide for certain disclosures to clients (or potential clients) as required by CFP Board's *Code of Ethics*, with corresponding Rules in the *Code of Ethics* referrenced in parantheses. The client acknowledgments at the end of each disclosure form are not required by CFP Board's *Code of Ethics*, but CFP certificants may wish to use them for their own purposes. Please note in Part II, section E of Form FPE, a CFP certificant shall not hold out as a fee-only financial planning practitioner if the CFP certificant receives commissions or other forms of economic benefit form related parties. (Refer also to Advisory Opinion 2003-1.) Also note that the disclosure of Part II, section B of Form OPS, is not required if the services contemplated by the client relationship have been completed. CFP certificants may use these forms, SEC Form ADV Part II, or a form of their own design or choosing as long as the required *Code of Ethics* disclosures are included in whatever form is used by the CFP certificant.

Compliance with the client disclosure requirements of the *Code of Ethics* is accomplished only when all material information relevant to the professional relationship (which includes everything required, pertinent and appropriate to the given client relationship) has been disclosed to the client or prospective client. Such disclosure should include, if material, (1) information about the financial condition of the CFP certificant and/or his or her firm which is reasonably likely to impair the ability of the CFP certificant to meet contractual commitments to the client and (2) any legal or disciplinary event relative to the CFP certificant that is material to a client's or potential client's evaluation of the CFP certificant's integrity or ability to meet contractual commitments to the client. Mere completion of a suggested disclosure form does not, in and of itself, constitute full compliance with the *Code of Ethics* disclosure requirements.

A blank form of each, in addition to a sample of how the forms might look when they are filled in, is included and may be copied for your use. The forms can also be downloaded as Word documents from CFP Board's Web site at www.CFP.net/certificants.

Rev. 07/03

SAMPLE CFP® CERTIFICANT DISCLOSURE FORM (FORM FPE)

For Use in Financial Planning Engagements

This disclosure form gives information about the CFP® certificant(s) and his/her/their business. This information has not been reviewed, approved or verified by CFP Board or by any governmental or self-regulatory authority. CFP Board does not warrant the specific qualifications of individuals certified to use its marks, nor does it warrant the correctness of advice or opinions provided.

PART I. GENERAL INFORMATION:
(Code reference - Rule 401)

A. Business affiliation:

B. Address:

C. Telephone number:

D. Information required by all laws applicable to the relationship (e.g., if the CFP certificant is a registered investment adviser, the disclosure document required by laws applicable to such registration):

PART II. MATERIAL INFORMATION RELEVANT TO THE PROFESSIONAL RELATIONSHIP
(Written disclosures required to be provided prior to the engagement)
(Code reference - Rule 402)

A. Basic philosophy of the CFP certificant (or firm) in working with clients:

B. Philosophy, theory and/or principles of financial planning which will be utilized:

C. Attached to this disclosure form, or summarized in the space provided below, are résumés of principals and employees of the CFP certificant's firm who are expected to provide financial planning services:

1. Educational background:

Rev. 07/03 Form FPE

2. Professional/employment history:

3. Professional certifications and licenses held:

D. Description of the financial planning services to be provided by the CFP® certificant:

E. Conflict(s) of interest and source(s) of compensation:

1. Conflict(s) of interest:

2. Source(s) of compensation:

3. Contingencies or other aspects material to the certificant's compensation:

F. Agency or employment relationships:

1. Material agency or employment relationships with third parties:

2. Compensation resulting from such agency or employment relationships:

G. Other material information relevant to the professional relationship:

Part III. ADDITIONAL NOTIFICATION

A. As a client or prospective client, you have the right to ask me, as a CFP® certificant, at any time for information about my compensation related to the services I provide you. I will communicate the requested information in reasonable detail as it relates to our financial planning engagement, including compensation derived from implementation. This disclosure of compensation:

1. May be expressed as an approximate dollar amount or percentage or as a range of dollar amounts or percentages;
2. Shall be made at a time and to the extent that the requested information can be reasonably ascertained;
3. Will be based on reasonable assumptions, with estimates clearly identified, and;
4. Will be updated in a timely manner if actual compensation significantly differs from any estimates.

(Code reference - Rules 402 and 403)

B. As a CFP certificant's personal financial planning client, you have the right to receive annually my current SEC Form ADV Part II or the current revision of the disclosure you received when our relationship began. (Code reference - Rule 404)

I hereby acknowledge receipt of this required disclosure.

______________________ /	__________	______________________ /	__________
Client's Signature	Date	Client's Signature	Date

Rev. 07/03 Form FPE

CFP® CERTIFICANT DISCLOSURE FORM (FORM FPE) – SAMPLE FILLED-IN FORM

For Use in Financial Planning Engagements

This disclosure form gives information about the CFP® certificant(s) and his/her/their business. This information has not been reviewed, approved or verified by CFP Board or by any governmental or self-regulatory authority. CFP Board does not warrant the specific qualifications of individuals certified to use its marks, nor does it warrant the correctness of advice or opinions provided.

PART I. GENERAL INFORMATION:
(Code reference - Rule 401)

A. Business affiliation:

B. Address:

C. Telephone number:

D. Information required by all laws applicable to the relationship (e.g., if the CFP certificant is a registered investment adviser, the disclosure document required by laws applicable to such registration):

PART II. MATERIAL INFORMATION RELEVANT TO THE PROFESSIONAL RELATIONSHIP
(Written disclosures required to be provided prior to the engagement)
(Code reference - Rule 402)

A. Basic philosophy of the CFP certificant (or firm) in working with clients:

Our approach to personal financial planning is to obtain from you significant financial and other information including your attitudes, goals and objectives; to analyze the information obtained in order to develop alternatives for your consideration; to educate you about the implications of selecting a particular alternative; to implement the alternative selected by you; and to periodically update the plan adopted. It is our goal to become your chief financial adviser and to coordinate the efforts of your other advisers in your best interests. We want you to be educated about your own financial affairs and to take an active role in managing them.

B. Philosophy, theory and/or principles of financial planning which will be utilized:

Our philosophy of financial planning is to gather adequate reliable information about a client's personal financial situation; to determine the client's goals and objectives, time horizon, and risk tolerance; to analyze all of the foregoing information in an objective manner and to develop recommendations for our clients based upon this thorough analysis and in the interest of rendering disinterested advice. In a personal financial planning engagement, we endeavor to consistently act in the interest of our client and to place his or her interest ahead of our own. Moreover, we believe that a client should be both informed and proactively involved in his or her personal financial affairs. Accordingly, we believe in holding frequent meetings with our clients to educate them about the financial planning process and their own financial situation.

Form FPE Rev. 07/03

C. Attached to this disclosure form, or summarized in the space provided below, are résumés of principals and employees of the CFP® certificant's firm who are expected to provide financial planning services:

1. Educational background:

John Doe:

Bachelor of Science degree in accounting from Hofstra University, 1971.
Master of Business Administration degree in Financial Services from Golden Gate University, 1975.

2. Professional/employment history:

John Doe:

Was employed as a stockbroker for DEF Brokerage for nearly ten years before becoming a partner in Comprehensive Financial Planning Services, Inc., in 1986 (see attached résumé).

3. Professional certifications and licenses held:

John Doe:

CERTIFIED FINANCIAL PLANNER™ practitioner
NASD Series 7 (General Securities) license - 1974
Life & Health insurance licenses - 1978, State of Arkansas

D. Description of the financial planning services to be provided by the CFP certificant:

Example 1:
This engagement is limited in scope to retirement planning only. Other types of personal financial planning services will not be performed by us, unless they directly affect your retirement plan, and you give us your express permission prior to performing such additional services.

Example 2:
You have expressed interest in asset management services. These services include:

- *Analysis of your current financial condition, goals and objectives, and development of a personal financial plan.*
- *Design of an investment portfolio appropriate to your individual circumstances, needs, goals, risk tolerance, investment experience and time horizon.*
- *Quarterly written reports on the status of your investment portfolio.*
- *Two meetings each year to review and update your objectives and financial status and provide an evaluation of your investment portfolio.*
- *Ongoing monitoring of your investment portfolio.*
- *Recommendations involving investment repositioning and current opportunities for new investments.*
- *Availability of our professional staff to answer questions.*

E. Conflict(s) of interest and source(s) of compensation:

1. Conflict(s) of interest:

Example 1:
John Doe represents Larry Peters, your business partner.

Example 2:
My broker/dealer permits me to sell only those securities products which it has approved.

2. Source(s) of compensation:

   Example 1: Fees from clients

   Example 2: Commissions from third parties

3. Contingencies or other aspects material to the certificant's compensation:

   I will not receive a commission unless you purchase the financial products recommended by me.

F. Agency or employment relationships:

1. Material agency or employment relationships with third parties:
   Life & Health Insurance Broker for DEF Insurance Company

2. Compensation resulting from such agency or employment relationships:
   50% commissions on first year life insurance premiums and 0.25% commission upon annual renewal.

G. Other material information relevant to the professional relationship:
John Doe is licensed only for the sale of mutual funds and variable annuities.

Part III. ADDITIONAL NOTIFICATION

A. As a client or prospective client, you have the right to ask me, as a CFP® certificant, at any time for information about my compensation related to the services I provide you. I will communicate the requested information in reasonable detail as it relates to our financial planning engagement, including compensation derived from implementation. This disclosure of compensation:

1. May be expressed as an approximate dollar amount or percentage or as a range of dollar amounts or percentages;
2. Shall be made at a time and to the extent that the requested information can be reasonably ascertained;
3. Will be based on reasonable assumptions, with estimates clearly identified, and;
4. Will be updated in a timely manner if actual compensation significantly differs from any estimates.

(Code reference - Rules 402 and 403)

B. As a CFP certificant's personal financial planning client, you have the right to receive annually my current SEC Form ADV Part II or the current revision of the disclosure you received when our relationship began. (Code reference - Rule 404)

I hereby acknowledge receipt of this required disclosure.

_______________________ /__________ _______________________ /__________

Client's Signature Date Client's Signature Date

Form FPE Rev. 07/03

SAMPLE CFP® CERTIFICANT DISCLOSURE FORM (FORM OPS)

For Use When Providing Other Professional Services

This disclosure form gives information about the CFP® certificant(s) and his/her/their business. This information has not been reviewed, approved or verified by CFP Board or by any governmental or self-regulatory authority. CFP Board does not warrant the specific qualifications of individuals certified to use its marks, nor does it warrant the correctness of advice or opinions provided.

PART I. MATERIAL INFORMATION RELEVANT TO THE PROFESSIONAL RELATIONSHIP

(Disclosures required to be provided at the time of entering into a client relationship)
(Code reference - Rule 401)

A. Material information relevant to the professional relationship:

B. Conflict(s) of interest:

C. Information required by all laws applicable to the relationship (e.g., if the CFP certificant is a registered investment adviser, the disclosure document required by laws applicable to such registration):

PART II. SUBSEQUENT DISCLOSURES

(Disclosures required to be provided subsequent to entering into a client relationship)

A. Changes in any of the following information since entering into a client relationship:
(Code reference - Rule 401)

1. Business affiliation:

2. Address:

3. Telephone number:

Rev. 07/03 Form OPS

4. Credentials:

5. Qualifications:

6. Licenses:

7. Compensation structure:

8. Agency relationships:

9. Scope of the CFP® certificant's authority in any agency relationship:

I hereby acknowledge receipt of this required disclosure.

_____________________ /__________ _____________________ /__________

Client's Signature Date Client's Signature Date

Form OPS Rev. 07/03

CFP® CERTIFICANT DISCLOSURE FORM (FORM OPS) – SAMPLE FILLED-IN FORM

For Use When Providing Other Professional Services

This disclosure form gives information about the CFP® certificant(s) and his/her/their business. This information has not been reviewed, approved or verified by CFP Board or by any governmental or self-regulatory authority. CFP Board does not warrant the specific qualifications of individuals certified to use its marks, nor does it warrant the correctness of advice or opinions provided.

PART I. MATERIAL INFORMATION RELEVANT TO THE PROFESSIONAL RELATIONSHIP

(Disclosures required to be provided at the time of entering into a client relationship)
(Code reference - Rule 401)

A. Material information relevant to the professional relationship:

I am a sales representative for ABC Securities and I am licensed to sell general securities through that firm. These products include mutual funds, stocks, bonds and other types of securities.

My compensation is based solely upon the sale of securities. Should you choose to purchase a product through us, I will receive a commission payable by a third party.

B. Conflict(s) of interest:

John Doe owns a partnership interest in ABC Securities.

C. Information required by all laws applicable to the relationship (e.g., if the CFP certificant is a registered investment adviser, the disclosure document required by laws applicable to such registration):

I am required by law to provide you with a copy of the most recent prospectus for any security that I recommend to you. I am required by law to provide you with a copy of the order confirmation for any securities transactions.

PART II. SUBSEQUENT DISCLOSURES

(Disclosures required to be provided subsequent to entering into a client relationship)

A. Changes in any of the following information since entering into a client relationship:
(Code reference - Rule 401)

1. Business affiliation:

2. Address:

3. Telephone number:

4. Credentials:

5. Qualifications:

Rev. 07/03 Form OPS

6. Licenses:

7. Compensation structure:

8. Agency relationships:

9. Scope of the CFP® certificant's authority in any agency relationship:

I hereby acknowledge receipt of this required disclosure.

____________________ / __________ ____________________ / __________

Client's Signature Date Client's Signature Date

Form OPS Rev. 07/03

CERTIFIED FINANCIAL PLANNER
BOARD OF STANDARDS, INC.

1670 Broadway, Suite 600, Denver, Colorado 80202-4809
P: 1-800-487-1497
F: 303-860-7388
E: mail@CFP-Board.org
W: www.CFP.net

CFP® | CERTIFIED FINANCIAL PLANNER™ | CFP®

INDEX

ABOUT THE AUTHORS

Joel P. Bruckenstein

Freelance magazine writer, book author, virtual office consultant and fee-only financial advisor, Joel P. Bruckenstein, CFP®, CMFC, CFS, is Senior Technology Editor at MorningstarAdvisor.com and Publisher of *Virtual Office News*. He frequently contributes articles to other financial planning publications including *Bloomberg Wealth Manager, Inside Information*, the *Journal of Financial Planning, NAPFA Advisor, Financial Advisor* and Horsesmouth.com. Mr. Bruckenstein's practice management and technology book co-authored by David Drucker, *Virtual-Office Tools for a High-Margin Practice: How Client-Centered Financial Advisors Can Cut Paperwork, Overhead, and Wasted Hours* (Bloomberg Press, 2002) has garnered universal praise from industry experts.

In addition to his writing duties, Mr. Bruckenstein is a practicing financial planner. He is the President of Global Financial Advisors, Inc., a fee-only financial planning and investment advisory firm located in Miramar, Florida. Mr. Bruckenstein is a Certified Financial Planner™ (CFP) licensee, Chartered Mutual Fund Counselor (CMFC), and Certified Fund Specialist (CFS). He is a former President of the Financial Planning Association (FPA) of the Greater Hudson Valley and former Chair of the FPA Government Relations Tax Subcommittee. He is a member in good standing of the National Association of Personal Financial Advisors (NAPFA), the premier organization of "fee-only" financial planners and the Financial Planning Association (FPA).

Bruckenstein' s expert opinions have appeared in the *Wall Street Journal, New York Times, Business Week, Baltimore Sun, Washington Post, Investment Advisor* magazine, *Investment News*, Gannett Newspapers, *New York Daily News, Kiplinger's Retirement Report, Journal of Financial Planning*, and other publications.

David J. Drucker

David J. Drucker, MBA, CFP®, is the co-author of *Virtual-Office Tools for a High-Margin Practice: How Client-Centered Financial Advisors Can Cut Paperwork, Overhead, and Wasted Hours* (Bloomberg Press, 2002), and editor of the monthly newsletter *Virtual Office News*. Drucker writes on practice management issues for other professional advisors as a contributor to *Bloomberg Wealth Manager, Financial Planning, Research* and *Financial Advisor* magazines, and as a monthly columnist for the MorningstarAdvisor.com website and the *NAPFA Advisor*. Drucker is a member of the American Society of Journalists and Authors, serving on its finance committee, and a member of the AICPA's Personal Financial Planning Section Editorial Advisory Board. He also serves on the Rydex Funds' Skip Viragh Award Advisory Board.

In addition to his writing, Drucker is a fee-only financial advisor who started his own advisory firm in the Washington, D.C. area in 1981 after working as a financial analyst in government and private industry for over ten years. Drucker still manages the financial affairs of a limited number of high-net worth clients as President of Sunset Financial Management, Inc., an Albuquerque, New Mexico state-registered advisory firm.

A principal in the firm of Practice Merger Consultants, Ltd. (www.practicemergers.com), Drucker helps other advisors prepare their practices for merger and/or acquisition, including helping them identify and negotiate with potential, well-matched merger/acquisition candidates, assisting them in structuring merger/acquisition contract terms, and showing them how to use strategic technology to improve the profitability of their merged entity.

Drucker is a member of the Financial Planning Association (FPA) and the National Association of Personal Financial Advisors (NAPFA), and has served in a variety of NAPFA regional board member and conference planning roles during his many years of membership. He was named by the readers of *Financial Planning* magazine to its 2003 list of "Movers, Shakers & Decision-Makers," and by *Worth* magazine as one of the "Best Financial Advisors" in the United States every year from the beginning of the *Worth* survey in 1994 through its 2001 listings, when Drucker cut back his financial planning activities. In May 1996, he was given the NAPFA Distinguished Service Award for his contributions to the fee-only financial planning community. He is the original author of INTEGRATE financial planning software used by him and other financial advisors nationwide, now developed and distributed by PlanWare, Inc.

Also a virtual office consultant, Drucker shows other financial advisors how to replace traditional, inefficient office systems with virtual office systems (outsourcing, paperless office technology, and other virtual tools) to improve profitability, and increase owner's compensation and leisure time.

Drucker's community service activities include his weekly volunteer work with the Animal Humane Association of New Mexico's (AHANM) Junior Humane program for children ages eight through 18, for which he received distinguished service awards in 2001 and 2002. In 2003, he was recognized by Helping Everyone Reach Out in Community Service (H.E.R.O.I.C.S.) for his volunteer efforts with AHANM. Drucker is also a volunteer worker with "Project Second Chance," a joint program of the Animal Humane Association and the New Mexico Youth Diagnostic and Development Center in which youth offenders are made responsible for the care of shelter dogs to promote the rehabilitation and growth of both species.

Edited by Stephan R. Leimberg

Stephan R. Leimberg is CEO of LISI, Leimberg Information Services, Inc., a provider of e-mail/internet news and commentary for professionals on recent cases, rulings, and legislation; CEO of Leimberg and LeClair, Inc., an estate and financial planning software company; and President of Leimberg Associates, Inc., a publishing and software company in Bryn Mawr, Pennsylvania.

Leimberg is the author of numerous books on estate, financial, and employee benefit and retirement planning and a nationally known speaker. Leimberg is the creator and principal author of the entire eight book *Tools and Techniques* series including *The Tools and Techniques of Estate Planning, The Tools and Techniques of Financial Planning, The Tools and Techniques of Employee Benefit and Retirement Planning, The Tools and Techniques of Life Insurance Planning, The Tools and Techniques of Charitable Planning, The Tools and Techniques of Income Tax Planning, The Tools and Techniques of Investment Planning,* and *The Tools and Techniques of Risk Management*. Leimberg is co-author, with noted attorney Howard Zaritsky, *Tax Planning with Life Insurance, The New, New Book of Trusts* with attorneys Charles K. Plotnick and Daniel Evans, and *How to Settle an Estate* with Charles K. Plotnick.

Leimberg is creator or co-creator of many software packages for the financial services professional including *NumberCruncher* (estate planning), *IRS Factors Calculator* (actuarial computations), *Financial Analyzer II, Estate Planning Quickview* (Estate Planning Flow Charts), *Toward a Zero Estate Tax* (PowerPoint Estate Planning Client Seminar), *Gifts That Give, Gifts That Give Back* (Powerpoint Client Charitable Planning Seminar), and Long-Term Care (Powerpoint Client Seminar).

A nationally known speaker, Professor Leimberg has addressed the Miami (Heckerling) Estate Planning Institute, the NYU Tax Institute, the Notre Dame Law School and Duke University Law School's Estate Planning Conference, The American Bar Association Planning Techniques for Large Estate and Sophisticated Planning Techniques courses of study, the National Association of Estate Planners and Councils, and the AICPA's National Estate Planning Forum. Leimberg has also spoken to the Federal Bureau of Investigation, and the National Aeronautics and Space Administration.

TOOLS & TECHNIQUES

Print • Online • CE Filed

ools & Techniques)nline Library

nleash the power of online earching with five of the top titles the **Tools & Techniques Series:**

- Estate Planning
- Employee Benefit & Retirement Planning
- Life Insurance Planning
- Financial Planning
- Charitable Planning

)nline #TTLIB $195.00

ne ***Tools & Techniques*** titles are ed for CE credit in most states. o to ww.nationalunderwriter.com/ce sign up for your CE exam today.

YMENT INFORMATION AND GUARANTEE

d shipping & handling charges to all orders as indicated. If ır order exceeds total amount listed in chart, or for overseas s, call 1-800-543-0874. Any order of 10 or more items or 50.00 and over will be billed for shipping by actual weight, s a handling fee. Any discounts do not apply to shipping handling. Unconditional 30-day guarantee. Product(s) naged in shipping will be replaced at no cost to you. ims must be made within 30 days from the invoice date. ce, information, and availability subject to change.

)RDER		TOTAL	S&H
)	to	$9.99	$3.00
0.00	to	$29.99	$5.00
0.00	to	$39.99	$6.00
0.00	to	$59.99	$7.00
0.00	to	$79.99	$9.00
0.00	to	$109.99	$10.00
10.00	to	$149.99	$12.00
50.00	to	$199.99	$13.00
00.00	to	$249.99	$15.50

SALES TAX (Additional)
Residents of CA, DC, FL, GA, IL, KY, NJ, NY, OH, PA, and WA must add sales tax.

Please send me the following : ***(please indicate quantity)***

The Tools & Techniques of Life Insurance Planning	______Book (#2700003) $74.95
The Tools & Techniques of Estate Planning	______Book (#2850013) $74.95
The Tools & Techniques of Practice Management	______Book (#2690000) $74.95
The Tools & Techniques of Investment Planning	______Book (#2730000) $74.95
The Tools & Techniques of Income Tax Planning	______Book (#2740000) $74.95
The Tools & Techniques of Employee Benefit and Retirement Planning	______Book (#2710008) $52.95
The Tools & Techniques of Financial Planning	______Book (#2770007) $74.95
The Tools & Techniques of Charitable Planning	______Book (#2500000) $52.95
The Tools & Techniques Online Library	______1 Year Subscription(TTLIB) $195.00

❐ Check enclosed* Charge My ❐ AMEX ❐ MC ❐ VISA (check one) ❐ Bill me

*Make check payable to The National Underwriter Company. Please include the appropriate shipping & handling and any applicable sales tax.

Card #______________________ CVV#**________ Exp. Date________
Signature______________________
Name______________________ Title______________________
Company______________________
Address______________________
City______________________ State__________ Zip+4__________
Business Phone (_______)______________________
E-mail______________________

**For Visa/MC, the three-digit CVV# is usually printed on the back of the card. For American Express, the four-digit CVV# is usually on the front of the card.

BB

The National Underwriter Company
A Unit of Highline Media LLC

Please send me the following : ***(please indicate quantity)***

The Tools & Techniques of Life Insurance Planning	______Book (#2700003) $74.95
The Tools & Techniques of Estate Planning	______Book (#2850013) $74.95
The Tools & Techniques of Practice Management	______Book (#2690000) $74.95
The Tools & Techniques of Investment Planning	______Book (#2730000) $74.95
The Tools & Techniques of Income Tax Planning	______Book (#2740000) $74.95
The Tools & Techniques of Employee Benefit and Retirement Planning	______Book (#2710008) $52.95
The Tools & Techniques of Financial Planning	______Book (#2770007) $74.95
The Tools & Techniques of Charitable Planning	______Book (#2500000) $52.95
The Tools & Techniques Online Library	______1 Year Subscription(TTLIB) $195.00

❐ Check enclosed* Charge My ❐ AMEX ❐ MC ❐ VISA (check one) ❐ Bill me

*Make check payable to The National Underwriter Company. Please include the appropriate shipping & handling and any applicable sales tax.

Card #______________________ CVV#**________ Exp. Date________
Signature______________________
Name______________________ Title______________________
Company______________________
Address______________________
City______________________ State__________ Zip+4__________
Business Phone (_______)______________________
E-mail______________________

**For Visa/MC, the three-digit CVV# is usually printed on the back of the card. For American Express, the four-digit CVV# is usually on the front of the card.

BB

The National Underwriter Company
A Unit of Highline Media LLC

Order the ***Tools & Techniques Series*** and other titles by The National Underwriter Company.

Save 5% Instantly when you order online at **www.NationalUnderwriterStore.com.** **Include code BB at checkout.**

The National Underwriter Company
A Unit of Highline Media LLC

PLACE
STAMP
HERE

ORDER DEPARTMENT
THE NATIONAL UNDERWRITER COMPANY
PO BOX 14448
CINCINNATI OH 45250-9786

PLACE
STAMP
HERE

ORDER DEPARTMENT
THE NATIONAL UNDERWRITER COMPANY
PO BOX 14448
CINCINNATI OH 45250-9786